Praise for *Guiding Teams to Excell*

"Through his work, John Krownapple has done an excellent job providing useful tools to support leaders of professional learning in their work. Using authentic vignettes that are transferrable to any educational context, Krownapple gives readers an opportunity to not only support educators in their path to cultural proficiency but encourages leaders to apply that framework as a mechanism to inform their own practice. This book is a must read for leaders focused on deepening their skill with equity work."

—Floyd Cobb II, Executive Director of Curriculum and Instruction
Cherry Creek School District
Greenwood Village, CO

"John's book is a unique contribution to both the literature on equity and skillful facilitation. It contains compelling theories and research along with thoughtful reflection prompts and well selected protocols that help readers deeply engage with the content. John makes clear connections between the knowledge and techniques of skillful facilitation and the psychological factors underlying the change process. This explicit treatment of the material helps readers not only understand the importance of thoughtful facilitation but also the reasons behind facilitative moves. This book is beautifully written—by combining narration with information, John crafts a very persuasive argument for culturally proficient facilitation. This book is a unique contribution to both the literature on equity and skillful facilitation."

—Dr. Jenni Donohoo, Provincial Literacy Lead
Ontario Ministry of Education
Toronto, Ontario

"In the book Guiding Teams to Excellence With Equity, *author John Krownapple takes culturally proficient learning and facilitating to a whole new level. The focus on mindfulness, listening, and questioning for creating spaces that move toward excellence with equity is vital in helping schools move from unhealthy, inauthentic engagement to healthy, vulnerable and authentic engagement. Since cultural proficiency is an inside-outside approach this book has a critical emphasis on facilitators doing their own work so they can move from their head to their heart just like they want participants to do. There is an old saying that all facilitators can be teachers but not all teachers can be facilitators. Krownapple provides the perfect combination of instruction, introspection and activities The book will not only help current facilitators go from 'good to great,' but also give hope, guidance, and support to those who have the potential to be facilitators and just don't know how. What a true gift to facilitators and those who will be impacted by the brilliance of this book."*

—Tracey DuEst, Diversity & Inclusion Consultant/Coach
Corwin, TriHealth, Xavier University
Cincinatti, OH

"As a school-based professional development specialist focusing on inclusion and equity, I found this book to be invaluable. Guiding Teams to Excellence With Equity *contains a wealth of information about professional learning and transformative change that is presented in a user-friendly manner. Combined with just the right amount of historical and legal information, this provides a clear explanation of "the why" behind our work. Krownapple steers clear of overloading the reader with educational jargon that can confuse those of us wanting to "get to the heart of the matter," and instead takes us on the Cultural Proficiency journey along with Jack—a character with whom we can all relate on some level."*

—James D. Goldsmith, Staff Development Teacher
Tacoma Park Middle School
Silver Spring, MD

"Guiding Teams to Excellence With Equity *is a rich resource for those of us who are attempting to facilitate deep and authentic work related to cultural competence, racial healing, and social justice. John Krownapple's voice is refreshingly personal, practical, and courageous.*"

—Gary R. Howard, Author, Speaker, Equity Consultant
Gary Howard's Deep Equity Process
Seattle, WA

"*John Krownapple uses dialogic episodes to clearly convey the journey of a Cultural Proficiency facilitator. Education leaders now have a resource that unpacks both the content and process needed to succeed in attaining the moral goal of educational excellence with equity.*"

—Michelle King, Associate Director of Communities
Learning Forward
Oxford, OH

"*When embarking on a new journey, having an expert guide to lead the way instills the traveler with the courage needed to successfully reach the goal set before them. John Krownapple is the expert guide for those starting to lead the cultural proficiency journey for the school, school system, or organization for which they serve.* Guiding Teams to Excellence With Equity *clearly outlines how to effectively navigate self and others through the personal work involved with self-discovery and a deeper appreciation of others. Each part of his guide explains the emotions of those asked to take part in cultural proficiency work, how to meaningfully explain what cultural proficiency is and is not, and how to facilitate cultural proficiency sessions.*

The fictional telling of Jack McManus' story is a story that the reader connects with; all they need to do is replace Jack's name with their own. Cultural proficiency is the understanding of one's story so that they can understand others' stories. In a meaningful way, John Krownapple illustrates the importance of sharing one's story by allowing us to see and feel Jack's journey.

Guiding Teams to Excellence With Equity *is a guide I wish was at my disposal when I first started as a cultural proficiency leader. But, like all good things, it came at just the right time; it will be used to help strengthen my ability to effectively facilitate professional learning for those just starting their journey. It is a guide I will share with new leaders as they begin their work with cultural proficiency.*"

—Eric Louèrs Phillips, Supervisor Accelerative Achievement & Equity, PreK–12
Frederick County Public Schools
Frederick, MD

"*The power of* Guiding Teams to Excellence With Equity *comes from the clear definitions offered for commonly used social justice and equity terms. Additional strength is the use of a continuing narrative using believable characters who struggle with the concepts making the book easy and enjoyable to read.*"

—Raymond Terrell, Interim Chair of Teacher Education
Miami University, Ohio
Oxford, OH

Guiding Teams to Excellence With Equity

Culturally Proficient Facilitation

John Krownapple

Foreword by Randall B. Lindsey

CORWIN
A SAGE Publishing Company

FOR INFORMATION:

Corwin

A SAGE Company

2455 Teller Road

Thousand Oaks, California 91320

www.corwin.com

SAGE Publications Ltd.

1 Oliver's Yard

55 City Road

London, EC1Y 1SP

United Kingdom

SAGE Publications India Pvt. Ltd.

B 1/I 1 Mohan Cooperative Industrial Area

Mathura Road, New Delhi 110 044

India

SAGE Publications Asia-Pacific Pte. Ltd.

3 Church Street

#10–04 Samsung Hub

Singapore 049483

Acquisitions Editor: Dan Alpert

Associate Editor: Kimberly Greenberg

Editorial Assistant: Katie Crilley

Production Editor: Veronica Stapleton Hooper

Copy Editor: Alison Hope

Typesetter: C&M Digitals (P) Ltd.

Proofreader: Ellen Brink

Indexer: Sheila Bodell

Cover Designer: Michael Dubowe

Marketing Manager: Charline Maher

Printed in the United States of America

Library of Congress Cataloging-in-Publication Data

Names: Krownapple, John, author.

Title: Guiding teams to excellence with equity : culturally proficient facilitation / John Krownapple; foreword by Randall B. Lindsey.

Description: Thousand Oaks, California : Corwin, 2016. | Includes bibliographical references and index.

Identifiers: LCCN 2016030579 | ISBN 9781483386980 (pbk. : alk. paper)

Subjects: LCSH: Culturally relevant pedagogy. | Educational leadership. | Teachers—Training of.

Classification: LCC LC1099 .K77 2016 | DDC 371.2/011—dc23
LC record available at https://lccn.loc.gov/2016030579

This book is printed on acid-free paper.

17 18 19 20 10 9 8 7 6 5 4 3 2

Contents

List of Illustrations

Foreword

Randall B. Lindsey

You hold in your hands an important book that represents the "next generation" of Cultural Proficiency work. John Krownapple is one of the new authors in what we have dubbed "the next generation." John may be a new author, but he is not new to the work of equity and access. For more than ten years he has been serving as the leader and as a facilitator of Cultural Proficiency in the Howard County Public School System (Maryland), a school system that is a leader and model for our nation in proactively addressing issues of equity and inclusion. John began his study of Cultural Proficiency under the tutelage of Brenda CampbellJones and Franklin CampbellJones, who are brave trailblazers, and he has grown to be their friend and colleague.

As someone in the second generation, John leads the way in communicating clearly the art of facilitating a deeply personal process that can help educational and other organizations move forward toward fully realized equity and inclusion. He has taken the theoretical and conceptual bases of Cultural Proficiency and grounded them in everyday practice. In this readable book, he shares with us the values and behaviors necessary to effectively facilitate our own learning as well as the professional learning of fellow educators. In doing this, John provides valuable and practical information about how to achieve the purpose of Cultural Proficiency: supporting educators' intentionality in addressing, narrowing, and closing access/opportunity and achievement/outcome gaps.

Facilitation represents the next generation of skills for leaders of professional learning. This is made obvious through the language in the chapter 10 facilitation rubric. Furthermore, when Learning Forward (an international association focused solely on increasing educator effectiveness through professional learning and school improvement) released its most recent set of standards in 2013, it shifted its language away from professional development to professional learning, thus helping us focus on the process of learning as opposed to episodic events of development. This book provides the support needed to develop the mind-set and skills necessary to guide the process of professional learning and growth in a culturally proficient manner. Since learning is a process, a skilled facilitator can make it easier. After all, the work of equity and inclusion is anything but easy. As history has proven, if it were easy we would already be there.

The work of Cultural Proficiency is multigenerational, and as such has its own history. The backstory for John's book, as with all Corwin books about Cultural Proficiency, began in 1980 at the Regional Assistance Desegregation Center, California State University, Los Angeles, where Raymond Terrell, Kikanza Nuri-Robins, and I came together to work.

Raymond was the dean of the School of Education and principal investigator for the Center, which provided technical assistance to school districts on matters related to race desegregation. Kikanza served full-time with the Center, and I served as project director of the Center and as chair of the Division of Administration, Counseling, and Foundations. The Center was funded by a federal grant to provide technical assistance to school districts in California, Arizona, and Nevada.

We quickly learned that schools and school districts needed professional development materials to support their efforts to provide equitable learning opportunities and outcomes to their diverse student populations. Our search for an approachable system of professional development to address issues arising out of desegregation led us to Terry Cross's 1989 monograph, *Toward a Culturally Competent System of Care* (Cross, Bazron, Dennis, & Isaacs, 1989). Adapting Cross's work from the field of mental health into language and examples of PK–12 education proved an easy task and led to the 1999 publication of *Cultural Proficiency: A Manual for School Leaders* (Lindsey, Nuri-Robins, & Terrell, 1999). Since then, many more Cultural Proficiency titles have been published involving more than two dozen authors. Additionally, numerous journal articles, news columns, and blogs have been written, disseminated, and utilized by educators around the world.

I hope this bit of history gives you some context to this book. Like Corwin's other Cultural Proficiency books, this is a free-standing volume. As with the other titles, it presents the tools of Cultural Proficiency in sufficient detail to fulfill your professional learning needs. If you are truly motivated to become a facilitator or to improve as a facilitator, this book will help you achieve that goal by awakening the facilitator that already is within you. It will lead you to becoming your best self—both as a person and as an educator.

As a writer and as a facilitator, John Krownapple enjoys employing popular culture references, especially cinema, to illustrate Cultural Proficiency concepts. If I could borrow from his technique for a moment, I'd say that if the original pioneers and theorists of Cultural Proficiency are *Star Trek: The Motion Picture*, John and his compatriots are *Star Trek: The Next Generation* who continue to lead us to new and better worlds.

One generation cultivates an environment for new growth, and the next generation grows in that environment. In my generation, much work was done to define Cultural Proficiency and apply it as a framework (concept and illustrations of practice); in John's generation, much work is yet to be done to clearly define, understand, and facilitate Cultural Proficiency as a journey (process) and to illustrate its progression (as John does so well in this book). One day in the future, members of this next generation will themselves pass the Cultural Proficiency baton to a new generation of leaders who will apply these principles to the world in which they live. They will not be leading in the same way as the generation that preceded them.

It bears repeating that Cultural Proficiency is a multigenerational work, with each generation building on the work of the previous generation. In that, it is the mirror image of systemic oppression and privilege, which is also the work of generations. Although our society and schools are not yet equitable and inclusive for all people and groups of people, they can be. We can do better. We will do better. By understanding and facilitating the process of transformation, we will rebirth ourselves. Go forth. Live long and prosper . . . and make the world more equitable.

Acknowledgments

During the past two years of writing this book, I've been incredibly grateful to the many people who've made my work with Cultural Proficiency possible. In no sense did I produce this book on my own. Any discovery or progress I've made was done by building on discoveries and progress of others. I have, indeed, stood on the shoulders of giants and I'd like to give a shout-out to as many of these greats as space allows.

My giants are heroes, mentors, role models, colleagues, friends, and family. The first hero I honor is Dr. Terry Cross for developing and publishing *Toward a Culturally Competent System of Care* in 1989. In this monograph, he provided brilliant and useful tools for addressing responses to diversity and differences in mental health care. This became the seminal text of the approach that would become known as Cultural Proficiency.

A decade later, a small group of equity leaders adapted Dr. Cross's tools for the field of education and published two important books: *Cultural Proficiency* (Lindsey, Nuri-Robins, & Terrell, 1999) and *Culturally Proficient Instruction* (Nuri-Robins, Lindsey, Lindsey, & Terrell, 2001). Randy Lindsey, Kikanza Nuri-Robins, Ray Terrell, and Delores Lindsey inspired me through their writing, and eventually they became more than distant heroes: they became mentors and role models. Throughout the time I've spent writing this book, Randy has freely shared his wisdom by providing ongoing feedback and guidance, sometimes at a moment's notice. Kikanza, Ray, and Delores have been supportive and responsive to every inquiry and request. Each is an incredible person, and I'm humbled and honored to call them friends.

In 2004 I met two of their colleagues. Brenda and Franklin CampbellJones became two of the most influential people in my life. They helped me see a different vision for myself—a new reality within which I would step up as a professional development leader for racial and social justice. Up to that point, I had not seen a white male in that role. Brenda changed that when she shared with me her doctoral dissertation (2002): "Against the Stream: White Men Who Act in Ways to Eradicate Racism and White Privilege/Entitlement in the United States of America." It was because of Brenda and Franklin's encouragement and support that I stepped out of my comfort zone of teaching, curriculum, and instruction and into a new world of facilitation, transformation, and Cultural Proficiency.

I am eternally grateful to Brenda and Franklin for seeing something in me that I did not see in myself at that time. They nurtured what they saw by extending loving support that fostered my growth as an equity leader and a facilitator of personal and organizational transformation. It is because of them that I am able to do this work. They were exceptional role models as facilitators, and they are the best mentors anyone could ask for. Beyond that, they are dear friends, and I consider them family.

Many of the concepts expressed in the pages of this book were things I've experienced, developed, explored, or discovered somehow in relation to lessons I've learned directly or indirectly through Brenda and Franklin. As a tribute to them, I've modeled two characters in their images within the fictional narrative in this book: Barbara and Frank. While fictitious and different from reality in numerous ways, the characters resemble Brenda and Franklin in my mind's eye and at times reflect conversations and experiences I've had with them.

To Brenda, Franklin, Randy, Kikanza, Ray, Delores, and all the other Cultural Proficiency authors and educational equity thought leaders: I offer a huge thank you for enriching my life and my work. In turn, I hope that this book adds value to your work of supporting schools and other organizations in their pursuit of equity, access, and inclusion. My sentiments are best captured by Lin-Manuel Miranda's words when he dedicated his groundbreaking hip-hop musical to the musical giants of the genre that inspired and influenced him: "This is my love letter to hip-hop" (Miranda, 2015a). "I really wanted the hip-hop community to embrace Hamilton because it's such a love letter to them," said Miranda in a *Vanity Fair* interview (Robinson, 2016). Similarly, I think of this book as one big love letter to the giants who have provided leadership for the approach that we call Cultural Proficiency.

Additionally, thank you to the many colleagues and friends with whom I've grown in this work over the years. There are many, and at the top of the list are Charlene Allen, Juliann Dibble, Shannon Keeny, Vivian Kelly, and Razia Kosi. Developing as a culturally proficient facilitator is a journey in and of itself, and we have traveled together on numerous legs of that journey.

Thank you to colleagues who gave me permission to craft fictitious episodes based on your real-life experiences. Although I've changed names, situations, and details, I have worked to preserve the integrity of critical moments that involve vulnerability, growth, and transformation.

To the many equity advocates and professionals who dedicated time to read various iterations of the manuscript and offered perspective and critical feedback, words hardly express the gratitude I hold for the generosity and integrity you offered this project. Those of you who offered feedback on early versions of the manuscript may hardly recognize this version. The two years of writing, revising, and rewriting has provided me with an invaluable growth experience that you helped to nurture. Thank you.

There are several other giants who influenced my thinking in meaningful ways. These people contributed to key themes and core concepts. First, I am indebted to the late Arthur M. Young, who developed a brilliant and fascinating theory of process. More recently, I am appreciative of Joan Schleicher of the Anodos Foundation, established in the memory of Arthur M. Young to carry on his work. Ms. Schleicher unexpectedly provided me perspective and enriched my understanding of process in ways that made a difference in this book. Last, I offer thanks to Lee Mun Wah who helped me begin to explore and understand the power of mindfulness as a facilitator.

I would be remiss if I did not recognize and thank Dan Alpert at Corwin. As my acquisitions editor, Dan guided me through the process of writing a book as a first-time author. As a tireless social justice advocate, Dan supported, encouraged, and pushed me when necessary. I am thankful to Dan as well as Kim Greenberg and Katie Crilley who supported me as an editorial team.

Finally, there's one person for whom a shout-out or acknowledgment is not enough. I want to recognize my mother, Una McManus, as the "great" she is to me. The best way to do so is to write directly to her. So, Mom, I hope you know what you've done for me—not only through the process of helping me write this book but also throughout my life. You've been with me every step of the way. You came to this country as a young woman from Ireland in difficult circumstances. But you put your two sons first, sacrificed, and found a way. You got your GED, completed college, and became a writer. Now, decades later, you helped mentor me with my first book. Your words made my phrases and paragraphs more enjoyable to read, and your feedback and suggestions made the concepts more accessible. I am so very thankful. You are my favorite collaborator and a gifted thinker and writer. You're my hero, mentor, role model, colleague, friend, and family. You're my guide to when to use semicolons. Working together on this project provided frequent opportunities to think together. The memory of sharing this process with you is one that I will always treasure. Above all others, yours are the shoulders I stand upon.

PUBLISHER'S ACKNOWLEDGMENTS

Corwin wishes to acknowledge the following peer reviewers for their editorial insight and guidance.

Joseph Dominguez
Principal
Santa Maria High School
Santa Maria, California

Suzanne Dotta
Director of Professional Learning
Rockwood School District
Eureka, Missouri

Michelle King
Associate Director of Communities
Learning Forward
Dallas, Texas

Angela Ward
Public School Administrator
Austin Independent School District
Austin, Texas

About the Author

John Krownapple specializes in facilitating professional learning and organizational development in support of schools pursuing excellence with equity. Since 2007 he has led the development and implementation of one of the first and most comprehensive Cultural Proficiency programs in the United States. John continues to administer this program for the Howard County Public School System (Maryland) in his role of coordinator for Cultural Proficiency. He has used the Cultural Proficiency approach with school system staff groups, system partners, community leaders, government officials, students, and families. As an educator for two decades, John has served as a district office administrator, professional development facilitator, curriculum specialist, and elementary teacher. He is also an adjunct professor at Johns Hopkins University and McDaniel College.

This book is dedicated to
Jillian, Josephine, and their entire generation, with hope that—when the time
arrives—they will become custodians of a world that is more virtuous,
peaceful, and just than ours is at this moment in time.

Introduction

IS THIS THE RIGHT BOOK FOR YOU?

Because you picked up and opened this book, you are probably interested in educational equity. There is certainly no shortage of titles addressing this topic, so is this the right book for you at this time? This book is for you if you fit one or more of these descriptors.

- Are you committed to making democracy possibly by ensuring its promise is kept for all our society's social groups, especially those who historically have been underserved and marginalized?
- Are you dedicated to eliminating disparities in educational outcomes that are predictable according to student demographic groups?
- Are you a champion of inclusion who understands the educational and societal benefits of tapping into the power of the diversity present in a classroom, organization, or community?
- Are you interested in understanding what must happen in order to transform schools, organizations, and communities so that they are places liberated from systemic oppression and its vestiges?
- Are you dedicated to equity and inclusion, yet new to the Cultural Proficiency approach?
- Are you experienced with the Cultural Proficiency approach and committed to your own learning, growth, and development as a highly effective leader of the work?
- Are you a school staff member, teacher, or administrator who wants your team, department, school, or community to become fully committed to inclusion and equity?
- Are you a content specialist (math, literacy, etc.) who works with adults and aspires to increase the effectiveness of your professional development services?
- Are you a leader of professional learning aspiring to develop as a group facilitator, to work more effectively across differences with adults, and/or to ensure you address inclusion and equity in all of your work?

This book is for you if you value humanity, fairness, inclusion, and the role our schools play within our diverse democracy. Everything else is secondary: job, positions, roles, experience with Cultural Proficiency, and so on. Most important is that you care about making a positive difference and so are willing to do the work to examine yourself and your professional practices in order to do a better job of supporting socially just schools.

WHY IS THIS BOOK NEEDED?

In 1999 Randall B. Lindsey, Kikanza Nuri-Robins, & Raymond D. Terrell wrote *Cultural Proficiency: A Manual for School Leaders*. In that book, they adapted the theories of Terry Cross (Cross, Bazron, Dennis, & Isaacs, 1989) from the field of mental health with the intent of supporting educational leaders seeking equity through systemic change. The authors' premise was that schools and school districts that integrated the Cultural Proficiency Framework with their core organizational values would reap significant positive outcomes for all students and their families, especially those historically underserved or marginalized. This was seminal work; the book detailed the Four Tools of Cultural Proficiency in the greatest depth of any resource in print.

Delores B. Lindsey joined the group for the subsequent project, *Culturally Proficient Instruction: A Guide for People Who Teach* (2001). This book expanded the audience by offering support to educators in the classroom. Applying Cultural Proficiency to classroom instruction was the first in what soon became a series of app books, all centered around the original manual. Each of the titles in the series has a distinct and focused application of the Tools of Cultural Proficiency. Each provides a lens through which educators can examine and improve a specific area of practice—counseling or coaching, for instance, or our response to English language learners, students in poverty, or LGBT (lesbian, gay, bisexual, and transgender) communities.

Although different from the set of apps, this book, too, is an application of Cultural Proficiency. As such, it applies the Cultural Proficiency Framework to professional learning—the art of group facilitation, to be precise. The book invites current or aspiring leaders of professional learning to reflect on their craft and critically examine what they do, why they do it, and how they can do it better, in a way that leads more directly to equitable and inclusive outcomes.

But this book is not an isolated application. Because of its unique focus on culturally proficient professional learning, this text can help schools and educators transform themselves and put into action the content and processes contained in all the other books. In this sense, this book can serve as a companion to *Cultural Proficiency: A Manual for School Leaders* (2009), and/or any of the other apps. The manual provides the framework (the concept) and professional development activities, and the apps provide illustrations of practice. This book details a process (journey) within which groups can use content from other sources (e.g., activities from the manual) to move from awareness to commitment to action.

In fact, this book can serve as a companion text for any book in any content area within our field of education. For instance, it would support a math or literacy coach in facilitating professional learning in a culturally proficient manner, regardless of what text (or lack thereof) they chose to use with a group. What exactly does it mean to facilitate professional learning in a culturally proficient manner? Chapter 10 paints a clear picture, but for now this brief explanation will have to suffice. First, this book helps facilitators of professional learning ensure effective cross-cultural interaction, inclusion, and equity for educators and adult learners. Second, it provides support for ensuring adult learners constructively consider issues that emerge from diversity in everything they do, thus leading to inclusive and equitable outcomes for students.

HOW IS THIS BOOK ORGANIZED?

The organization of this book supports your customized reading, learning, and utilitarian preferences and needs. The progression follows that of Simon Sinek's Golden Circle (2009): Why? How? What?

1. Part I focuses on Why: Assuming we value excellence with equity in education, why do we need Cultural Proficiency and culturally proficient facilitators?

2. Part II focuses on How: How can we use Cultural Proficiency as content (framework) and process (journey) to actualize excellence with equity in education?

3. Part III focuses on What: What do facilitators do in order to work with groups in a culturally proficient manner?

These three parts can be helpful for future reference. Need help articulating the purposiveness of Cultural Proficiency? Refer to part I. Are you facilitating a group's journey and need a facilitator map? Refer to part II. Looking for on-the-ground techniques as you develop as a culturally proficient facilitator of professional learning? Flip to part III.

Regardless of your needs for future reference material, your initial read of this book should be from start to finish. By doing so, you will experience the content as it builds. Additionally, you will experience a fictional story arc that spans all three parts. The story narrative is from the point of view of Jack McManus, a math curriculum specialist who starts his Cultural Proficiency journey as a disgruntled seminar participant but who eventually becomes a highly skilled facilitator for inclusion and equity. Jack is a white male, relatively youthful and tall (six foot). Although much of Jack's character and experiences are drawn from my own (including his outward appearance and several seminar scenarios that I've experienced), Jack is not me. He's not completely anyone. Jack's character, thoughts, and actions are a composite—a mosaic—of me, of facilitators and colleagues, of people I've observed in workshops, and of seminar participants with whom I've interacted as their group's facilitator.

WHY INCLUDE A FICTIONALIZED NARRATIVE THROUGHOUT?

The presence of an ongoing narrative throughout this book may seem—at first—unconventional for this genre. However, after closer analysis, it makes complete sense. Storytelling and personal narratives are powerful methods of teaching and learning. They possess the unique power of adding nuanced and subjective perspectives to generally accepted ideas, and therefore have the power to challenge the status quo. When at their best, the stories shared are born from first-hand experiences—from the perspective of the storyteller. That power fuels the journey to excellence with equity. Telling, listening to, and trusting each other's stories and lived experiences is central to the process. Thus, the presence of a story within this nonfiction book is symbolic and reflective of the heart of this work: the work of social justice.

As a reader and as an advocate for inclusion and equity, you might agree with the power of storytelling but wonder why the author would choose to fictionalize the story instead of keep the facts and details exactly as they happened in real life. Here is my rationale. The fictionalized story of Jack McManus has several benefits over a pure memoir of John Krownapple. First, it adds an element of interest and novelty to a genre that can become saturated with theory. To that end, using techniques of fiction offers greater freedom as a writer—more flexibility to shape Jack's experiences to complement concepts, theories, and research for andragogical purposes in a way that a memoir could not. Finally, tools of fiction provide a structure for enjoying and feeling satisfied with the read. This is why Jack's story has a full arc that spans from the start of chapter 1 to the end of chapter 16.

Still, I draw Jack's experience and general progression from that of my own. As such, his perspective is also that of a white man in the United States. That is important. As a reader and advocate for inclusion and equity, you might also wonder why the author would choose to tell a story that centers around diversity and social justice from this perspective. First, it is the perspective with which I am familiar—since I am white and male—and to which I can lend an authentic voice. In this context, writing a story from the point of view of a character with a race/ethnicity other than white seems inauthentic.

Also, making the fictional Jack white and male is symbolic and representative of the power dynamic implicit with Cultural Proficiency. Since (as colleague and friend Brenda CampbellJones reminds us) white landowning men of economic means were the only group that never had to be amended into the United States Constitution, that is the group that has long served as the unstated norm that visibly represents a legacy of power and privilege within our society. Jack's symbolic role challenges the reader to recognize and use their own power and privilege for purposes of social justice. For instance, in schools, administrators and teachers are custodians of the power conferred on them through their positions, regardless of their race or gender. Cultural Proficiency provides pragmatic support for what we can do with that power to redress unfair policies and practices that marginalize and disenfranchise groups of people. By relating to Jack's internal process, the reader receives support for facilitating their own growth into a culturally proficient facilitator.

WHY THE "INCORRECT" USE OF PRONOUNS?

The book frequently employs the word *they* as a singular pronoun. This is purposeful and done with a purpose. In this form, the pronoun provides a gender-neutral alternative to using *he* or *she* or even *he or she.* This choice of language is a reflection of my recent growth in understanding gender fluidity and challenging assumptions of gender as binary.

On first glance sentences using the singular form of *they* may cause you as the reader to pause. Sentences may sound grammatically incorrect. That's because this usage is, indeed, grammatically incorrect when using traditional rules. However, while writing this book it became apparent to me that the evolution of our consciousness has outpaced the evolution of our rules of language. Making this decision to use more-inclusive language was a reminder that the work of Cultural Proficiency is ethical in nature. It is a small reminder that following the letter of the law is not the same as doing what is right and socially just.

The choice between convention and using a gender-neutral pronoun is an example of predictable dilemmas we encounter on the Cultural Proficiency journey. Another example is illustrated in the chapter 14 vignette. In that scene, the characters experience a moment of awareness when presented with the notion that use of the term *cultural blindness* as a negative descriptor is ableist. In that moment, the dilemma presents itself: stick with convention and tradition or engage and adapt by aligning behavior with values of inclusion and equity. Although the vignette is fictionalized, it is based on my own experience and describes the dilemma my colleagues and I have faced with the use of this language.

In offering these examples, my intention is to highlight the inevitable conflict each of us will experience at one time or another when engaging in this work. Working through both of these dilemmas was predicated on my awareness of the language usage being an issue of exclusion, inequity, or cultural incapacity in the first place. In both situations, there was a time when I was completely unaware of this. And that time was not so very long ago. By no stretch of the imagination do I claim to have arrived. Because Cultural Proficiency is a journey, I anticipate the opportunity to work through many more dilemmas and contradictions in my future!

HOW CAN YOU USE THIS BOOK?

The formatting of this book encourages periodic reflection by providing questions and space for you to respond in writing. It also encourages group learning. Every chapter contains at least one dialogic activity. These activities serve at least two purposes. First, they support small or large groups within which individuals are studying this book and learning together. The activities use protocols that structure dialogue in ways that promote increased understanding. Second, they provide examples of facilitative techniques that—if new to you—can enhance your repertoire as you develop into a culturally proficient facilitator. To further support your development, chapter 10 contains a facilitation rubric. The rubric serves as a reflective as well as a goal-setting tool. Additionally, part III contains vignettes that accompany the rubric and illustrate a plethora of "What would you do?" situations from the perspective of an aspiring culturally proficient facilitator. The situations in each of the vignettes center on one of the five Essential Elements of Cultural Competence. Finally, chapter 16 provides an opportunity for you to craft your own professional learning plan to guide your next steps as a culturally proficient facilitator.

Part I

Why—An Effective Approach to Excellence With Equity

Why do we need Cultural Proficiency? *Why* do we need culturally proficient leaders of professional learning? Those are two separate questions with two separate answers. However, both answers begin with the recognition of purposiveness in Cultural Proficiency: its goal of excellence with equity in education.

This goal can't be limited to equity-focused professional development specialists. It's much too important. Excellence with equity is the ultimate goal for all responsible educators, including those of us who take on leadership roles supporting the professional learning of our colleagues, as well as those of us in curriculum planning, special education, administration, math, reading, science, performing arts, and every other nook and cranny in the field of education.

If we want excellence with equity, we need to be excellence with equity. We need to "be the change we want to see in the world," to paraphrase words attributed to Gandhi. If we want the goal of excellence with equity in education, all of us in education need to be culturally proficient educators.

That's why we need Cultural Proficiency, and that's why we need culturally proficient leaders of professional learning. We need ten thousand culturally proficient teachers who will teach ten thousand more.

The goal of excellence with equity is easily defined: every student benefits from a culture of high expectations—and not just those students lucky enough to attend schools in advantaged communities, and not just those students fortunate enough to benefit from the self-fulfilling prophecies of placements in "high" tracks in segregated and homogeneous classrooms.

It means every student has the specific supports they need for equal access and opportunity. It means every student feels a sense of belonging, benefits from tapping into the power of diversity, and develops the aspirations and skills to form authentic relationships across differences. Providing our students excellence with equity is clearly the moral duty of schools in our diverse democracy.

Our schools play a vital role and have grave responsibilities in supporting the development of a diverse society that keeps the promise of democracy for all its citizens. These responsibilities include providing environments, curricula, and instruction that ensure high expectations, inclusion, cultural competence, and equity for every student.

Fulling the responsibilities nested within the commitment to excellence with equity is critical in a culture whose legacy of systemic oppression is made visible through artifacts such as predictable and disproportionate educational outcomes according to race, family income level, language, and disability. To neglect these responsibilities is to collude with forces of social dominance that corrode and decay our democracy. This is true whether we are leading classrooms full of youths or professional development workshops full of adults.

Since our goal is excellence with equity, we must find a means (in other words, a process) to reach that goal. To be effective, the process must be predictable and grounded in proven theory. It must produce the desired effects. It must be capable of being replicated and sustained.

That process is Cultural Proficiency.

Part I of this book explores the *why* behind our need for Cultural Proficiency and culturally proficient leaders of professional learning. To that end, Part I balances and illustrates informational text with narrative episodes involving a fictional character named Jack McManus. Although Jack is fictive, his experiences, perspectives, and transformations are not. They are drawn from the lives of many individuals involved with Cultural Proficiency, including me.

Jack is an educator who has an awakening and emerges from his initial complacency and reluctance, and becomes an ally for social justice and a culturally proficient facilitator of professional learning. Our story begins before that emergence, when he served as the math curriculum specialist for Stocklin County Public Schools.

He loved his work, the students, and being an educator. He'd started his career teaching two years in elementary school. He then taught middle-school math for eight years, before moving into administration in the district office five years before our story begins. Although he misses the classroom, he finds real fulfillment through helping math teachers build classroom community and engage diverse learners in mathematics.

Then, one quiet Monday morning, Jack was blindsided by an "invitation" that led him into the world of Cultural Proficiency as a reluctant seminar participant. Let's follow Jack as he embarks on this unexpected journey through an unwanted invitation. To his surprise, this journey changed his life—both his professional and his personal life—for the better. It can do the same for you and me.

1 Why This? Why Now? Why Me?

Words like "freedom," "justice" and "democracy" are not common concepts; on the contrary, they are rare. People are not born knowing what these are. It takes enormous, and above all, individual effort to arrive at the respect for other people that these words imply.

—James Baldwin
(The Price of the Ticket, *1985*)

The spirit of democracy is not a mechanical thing to be adjusted by abolition of forms. It requires change of heart.

—Mahatma Gandhi

Justice is what love sounds like when it speaks in public.

—Michael Eric Dyson
(I May Not Get There with You, *2001*)

Until the great mass of people shall be filled with the sense of responsibility for each other's welfare, social justice can never be attained.

—Helen Keller
(Out of the Dark, *1920*)

We cannot teach people anything; we can only help them discover it themselves.

—Galileo Galilei

I have made myself what I am.

—Shawnee Chief Tecumseh (Address to
General William Henry Harrison, *1810*)

We have to confront ourselves. Do we like what we see in the mirror? And, according to our light, according to our understanding, according to our courage, we will have to say yea or nay — and rise!

—Maya Angelou (Mother Jones, *1995*)

GETTING CENTERED

You have most likely chosen this book because you want to help yourself and others work in a way that fosters diversity and inclusion, high expectations, cultural competence, and/or equity. In short, you want to do your best to guide the Cultural Proficiency journey for yourself and others. Take a few moments to write your response to this question: Why do you do this work (or aspire to do this work)?

_____

_____

_____

_____

EPISODE ONE: AN INVITATION THAT DIDN'T SEEM SO INVITING TO JACK

Jack's heart sank as he read the e-mail from the director of his department. It was an invitation—a summons, really—to attend a Cultural Proficiency seminar. For a full five days! The term _Cultural Proficiency_ was new, Jack observed, but surely this seminar was just another cultural diversity training effort? With his heavy workload and the fact that he had already completed several diversity presentations, surely he didn't need another one?

What had begun as a promising Monday was quickly going south. Jack had dropped off his two daughters at school, rushed to his office, and arrived ten minutes early. With those ten precious minutes, he'd hoped to get a jump-start on his week. He was behind on three deadlines and had two observations of math teachers that afternoon. His main project of overhauling the district's math curriculum was more demanding than he'd anticipated: his calendar was jammed for months with meetings, workshop presentations, and observations and consultations with math teachers.

This invitation to a five-day seminar seriously disrupted his plans. The seminar was in three weeks, and his director had instructed him to clear his calendar for those five days. With so many pressing tasks and deadlines, how would he make up that time? What's more, Jack had never experienced those types of presentations to be particularly helpful. The topic may have been diversity, but people—perhaps including himself—had always been reluctant to discuss anything of substance having to do with the subject. He didn't need a repeat of these tedious sessions. But apparently Lillie Cohen, the director of his department and his immediate supervisor, thought differently.

He read the e-mail again.

Dear Jack: You are invited to participate in a leadership cohort that will explore Cultural Proficiency through a five-day seminar facilitated by two international consultants, Drs. Barbara Campbell and Frank Westman. Over the past few months, they have served as facilitators of a similar process for the superintendent, senior leadership, the board of education, local government officials, and community leaders. As a result, Stocklin County Public Schools leadership has recommended and approved formation of this leadership cohort, tasked with supporting the start of a widespread focus on facilitating Cultural Proficiency for Stocklin staff. You would be an important asset to this group and overall process. If you accept, please clear your calendar for the first week of next month. Thank you for your commitment to every student in Stocklin County.

Sincerely,
Lillie Cohen
Director of Curriculum and Instruction
Stocklin County Public Schools

"Cultural Proficiency . . . what the . . ." Jack's grip tightened around his coffee mug. Surely Lillie had made a mistake? He was already culturally sensitive! What was Cultural Proficiency anyway? Some sort of "sensitivity training" for staff who didn't have any common sense when it came to dealing with people who didn't look like them? Or who'd broken the "rules" of political correctness? Or didn't know the rules to begin with? There were people around with bigoted backgrounds or tendencies, but Jack, as the product of a multiracial high school and a liberal city, knew the score.

"Can't I just take a test that proves I'm not a racist?" Jack muttered. "I don't have time for this!" Dark clouds seemed to gather over his head. Moments ago, getting caught up on work seemed within his grasp. Now he felt that possibility slip-sliding away. Snatched away, rather, by this lesser priority.

Jack's jargon detector went into high alert. What was up with the term *facilitate*? It seemed like the latest edu-speak buzzword. Perhaps the district leaders were rebranding diversity presenters as *facilitators* to make these tiresome workshops seem more interactive. Lillie's phrase that these international facilitators had facilitated "a similar process" had Jack scratching his head. Since when was a seminar a *process?* Was this more jazzed-up jargon?

Even the name of the workshop was annoying. Cultural Proficiency. He'd first heard the term a few months ago, and its use was on the rise. Without questioning anyone or putting much thought into it, Jack figured it was the most recent trendy term for diversity or maybe multicultural education.

Like many of his colleagues, Jack had only cursory knowledge of district leadership's recent involvement with Cultural Proficiency consultants. He knew they'd been meeting in response to numerous issues—some downright troubling issues—that had emerged as the result of the growing diversity of the student population in Stocklin County. The leadership had stated that their goals were to improve the school system. Jack knew what some of these issues were:

- Stocklin staff members were struggling to have productive conversations in response to disaggregated data. Results were mixed. District-wide student data had clearly exposed disproportionate student outcomes according to race and ethnicity as well as between and among other student groups. But it was almost as if some staff members would rather not engage in the equity conversation at all than to risk saying the wrong thing or using the wrong term with the result of possibly being labeled as prejudiced by what some staff referred to as "the political correctness police."

- Public response to the recent school redistricting process had become racialized and politicized. The community seemed divided. At least one hate group had emerged, writing threatening letters to district-level administrators and to an African American school principal. The messages were to keep "those" kids out of "our" community.
- To date, Stocklin County School System had experienced two decades of population growth, doubling in size from approximately twenty thousand to forty thousand students. Student demographics according to race shifted from

  - 76% to 47% White,
  - 10% to 16.5% Black/African American,
  - 8% to 16% Asian,
  - 3.5% to 12% Hispanic,
  - 0.5% to 0.5% Native American, and
  - 2% to 8% Two or More Races.

- Families in the district now spoke more than twice as many languages as they had one decade prior: fifty-three different languages, representing seventy different nations. Most spoke English, Spanish, or Korean.
- At the start of the school year, the headline in the local newspaper read, "Stocklin: Now a Majority Minority County." This headline spurred polarizing conversations. A local blogger wrote about how the increasing diversity was "ruining this once-great community." Meanwhile, a national magazine had identified Stocklin as the country's second-best community in which to live, citing its high-performing schools, quality community amenities, and ethnic diversity.
- The school superintendent had identified global and cultural competence as "21st-century skills" for every student to become college, career, and community ready. One of the first priorities was to increase world language curricular offerings and expand these offerings into the elementary schools. Another priority was ensuring excellence (inclusion, high expectations, and cultural and global competence) with equity in curriculum, instruction, classroom and school environments, and district policies.

Jack knew these facts, figures, and priorities. He was an educator committed to his profession, to his community, and to his students—especially underserved students on the margins. Thus, he was sympathetic and supportive of the district's stretching itself to improve service for the increasingly diverse population. But he struggled to understand why he, Jack McManus, personally needed training in Cultural Proficiency, especially for five days. Wasn't that preaching to the choir? He was already on their side!

During Jack's five years as the district's math curriculum specialist, his goal had been to make math accessible to all students. Wasn't that culturally proficient? In fact, he was in the middle of an overhaul of math curriculum and instruction that was being well received by teachers, praised by leaders (including the head of the local NAACP), and recognized by several national organizations. These new instructional units applied sound theory and research to engage diverse learners. They leveraged group work employed numerous learning modalities, and even integrated the arts. This approach gave students a voice. Jack believed that he was already serving the diverse students of

Stocklin County by doing what he did best. If he could just finish this overhaul of math curriculum and instruction and get all teachers sufficiently trained, he would be able to rescue students on the margins.

Jack couldn't shake the idea of an actual test for antiracism: a formal test that would identify staff in need of diversity training. "If only the department had a test, they'd see that I don't need this," he ruminated. "I'm white but have an antiracism resume. I went to a diverse high school with a multiracial group of friends. My college electives dealt with diversity and sociology. I was in the first wave of education majors required to take the multicultural education teacher preparation course. I'm focused on closing the achievement gap through curriculum and instruction."

Tough luck. This so-called invitation may have been worded politely, as if he had the freedom to refuse—but he didn't have a choice. Not really. Not if he valued his career. Not if he wanted to avoid being labeled as someone inclined toward insubordination. He didn't want to end up like his social studies counterpart whose career—rumor had it—had been stalled indefinitely because she spoke out against a superintendent's initiatives years ago.

Still, Jack thought, Lillie Cohen was an educator he respected. Her commitment to social justice was a trait he admired and emulated. In addition, she was highly competent. Jack had never seen her display poor judgment. So perhaps . . . perhaps she knew more than he did. Perhaps he should be a little more open to this facilitation process she obviously believed in.

Still . . . five full days! He was losing control of his overcrowded calendar. He was being yanked away—for a huge chunk of time—from his work to attend this event. Ironically, this would delay his completion of the curriculum and the corresponding teacher training that would actually benefit students being oppressed.

Trying not to clench his teeth, Jack cancelled his appointments. Never had there been such an uninviting invitation as Lillie Cohen's invitation to Cultural Proficiency. Jack leaned back in his chair. Through the window, he could see the tired, gray January snow falling. He felt tired at having to meet all these demands. He looked at the ceiling. The panel with the water stain still hadn't been replaced. His cubicle—small to begin with— now seemed tiny and cramped.

Jack felt irritated and blamed Lillie. Yet he admired her. It was a good thing she hadn't wandered into his cubicle at that moment, he thought. He might have uttered a curt word or two!

He sat and fumed: "Why this? Why now? Why me?"

Reflection

What is familiar to you about Jack's experience thus far? What is unfamiliar? How would you describe Jack's energy state (his emotional state in response to the e-mail message)? What words reflect his state? What is relatable to your experiences?

_____

_____

_____

_____

Why do you think Jack's supervisor is inviting him to this Cultural Proficiency seminar?

_____

_____

_____

_____

WHY CULTURAL PROFICIENCY?

In our episode about Jack, he was genuinely puzzled about Cultural Proficiency. He assumed it was a new name for diversity and sensitivity trainings. Just more of the same. At this point, Jack had not put forth the effort to check his assumptions. He was, at worst, complying with the invitation out of fear of being perceived badly. At best, he was grudgingly acquiescing to his supervisor's judgment.

Let's look at assumptions behind Jack's belief that this seminar was more of the same. Cultural Proficiency is not the same old ideas dressed up in new jargon. It is not a seminar, although people can engage with Cultural Proficiency in seminar form. For a start, Cultural Proficiency is a unique idea with a specific framework. It's more than theory—it is also a process. As a process, Cultural Proficiency is a metaphorical journey of change. This journey—when undertaken with goodwill and assisted by skilled facilitation—leads to the realization of our better selves and to schools that serve all students well. In short, Cultural Proficiency can help us achieve the moral purpose of schools in a diverse diverse democratic society—to ensure _excellence with equity_ in education (Blankstein & Noguera, 2015; Ferguson, 2007, 2015; Howard, 2015a; Lindsey, Kearney, Estrada, Terrell, & Lindsey, 2015; U.S. Department of Education, 2013).

Achieving _excellence_ alone may not be enough. For, as equity and social justice educator Gary Howard (2015b) reminds us, (1) excellence without inclusion is segregation and (2) excellence without equity is nothing more than elitism. In a democracy, excellence without equity is an oxymoron. Conversely, equity alone is not enough, because without excellence, equity could equate to mediocrity. Considering these caveats, what does _excellence with equity_ look like? From a Cultural Proficiency standpoint, it is a way of being within which educators advocate for and ensure that every student receives the benefits of these assets:

- _High expectations:_ Access to a high-quality education, based on (1) a belief that every student will meet and exceed rigorous standards, and (2) a fundamental assumption that every educator will educate students to the highest of standards.
- _Inclusion:_ (1) A strong sense of belonging, and (2) the educational benefits of a diverse environment and curriculum.
- _Cultural competence:_ An ability to interact effectively with individuals across cultures and dimensions of difference.
- _Equity:_ The specific supports that a student needs in order to access a high-quality education, as opposed to the same supports everyone else receives.

The Cultural Proficiency journey proceeds through several identifiable Phases. These Phases move from the Awareness Phase to the Commitment Phase, and from the Commitment Phase to the Action Phase. Awareness begins with inward exploration into the uncharted terrain of our inner world of unconscious assumptions and cultural conditioning. This Phase involves acknowledging, identifying, confronting and—when necessary—removing and replacing assumptions that act as barriers to equity and equality. When allowed to remain unexamined and unchallenged, these assumptions support and maintain the existing structural systems of oppression and privilege. Working through this stage can be uncomfortable (and this is where facilitator support is particularly helpful), but it will be well worth it for educators to stick with the process.

The Awareness Phase helps develop a greater understanding of one's self and one's organization, in addition to greater insight into the larger social, political, and cultural context. It helps educators (and other leaders) understand the dynamics of power that manifest in entitlement and as institutionalized privilege and oppression. As the process continues, growing awareness takes shape in the form of commitment, which powers the journeyers (educators engaged in Cultural Proficiency) through the Phase of intentional moral action. This type of action involves aligning or improving policies, procedures, and practices to reflect our awareness and commitment. It's the process of *inside-out* change.

In addition to manifesting as a journey (the process), Cultural Proficiency is a framework (the content) that provides guidance and pragmatism for realizing excellence with equity in education. The Cultural Proficiency Framework (the content) contains four components that are called the Tools of Cultural Proficiency (Cross, 1989; Lindsey, Nuri-Robins, & Terrell, 2009).

1. *The Barriers:* Values, beliefs, behaviors, and systems that inform a worldview that prevents/restricts individuals and organizations from working, educating, and interacting effectively and harmoniously across cultures.

2. *The Guiding Principles:* Values and beliefs that inform a worldview that enables individuals and organizations to work, educate, and interact effectively and harmoniously across cultures.

3. *The Continuum:* Language for describing degrees of effectiveness of policies, practices, values, and behaviors in working, educating, and interacting across cultures.

4. *The Essential Elements:* Behavioral standards for measuring and planning for effective work, education, and interaction across cultures.

In its most essential form, Cultural Proficiency is a comprehensive approach to shaping a healthy environment—an organization's climate and culture. Lindsey et al. (2009, p. 4) define Cultural Proficiency as "a model for shifting the culture of the school or district; it is a model for individual transformation and organizational change. Cultural Proficiency is a mind-set, a worldview, a way of being assumed by a person or an organization for effectively describing, responding to, and planning for issues that arise in diverse environments. For some, Cultural Proficiency is a paradigm shift from viewing cultural differences as problematic to learning how to interact effectively with other cultures."

How is Cultural Proficiency different from other approaches to inclusion and equity? Why is it not old ideas dressed up in new jargon? First, it is not an off-the-shelf program: it is customizable to address the particular issues of individual educators, schools, offices, and communities. But the most significant differentiating aspect is that Cultural Proficiency is anchored in the belief that people must start by gaining clarity around *their own* individual and organizational assumptions, values, beliefs, and responses to dimensions of difference (Lindsey et al., 2015) including but not limited to race, ethnicity, social class, language, nationality, faith, ability, age, gender, and sexual orientation. This means making the time and putting forth the effort to work on one's self. It's why Cultural Proficiency is called an *inside-out* approach to achieving excellence with equity in education.

WHY CHOOSE EQUITY?

External approaches to excellence with equity have not gotten us far enough. Take our nation's aspiration for equity in education as an example. The evidence is in (and has been in for quite some time) that we have fallen short of providing every student exactly what they need to succeed academically: we do not distribute opportunity equitably (U.S. Department of Education, 2012, 2013). This shouldn't be news, and our current situation continues to call for urgent action. At the same time, the United States has certainly not remained apathetic or idle in response to its long-standing educational inequality.

Over the past sixty years, the United States has mandated equity in education through a series of judicial and legislative actions such as *Brown v. Topeka Board of Education* (1954), *Elementary and Secondary Education Act* (1965; ESEA), *Title IX* (1972), and *No Child Left Behind Act* (2002; NCLB) (see table 1.1). On December 10, 2015, President Barack H. Obama expanded those efforts by signing into law the *Every Student Succeeds Act* (ESSA).

Table 1.1   Analysis of Three Acts Addressing Social Inequality

Legislation	*Civil Rights Act* (1964)	*No Child Left Behind Act* (2002; NCLB)	*Every Student Succeeds Act* (2015; ESSA)
Spirit of the Law (moral goals)	Liberate U.S. citizens from systemic oppression (present since European colonization of North America) and discrimination based on race, color, religion, sex, or national origin. Guarantee equality for every U.S. citizen regardless of race (Kennedy, 1963). Bring justice and hope to all U.S. citizens and bring peace to the country (Johnson, 1964).	Liberate students from failing schools by reauthorizing the *Elementary and Secondary Education Act* (ESEA; 1965) to correct a system in which students from some demographic groups were more likely to succeed and other students were more likely to be left behind (White House, 2002). Increase student performance and reduce race- and class-based disproportionality in student outcomes between student demographic groups.	Liberate students from failing schools by reauthorizing the *Elementary and Secondary Education Act* (ESEA; 1965) to ensure teachers, schools, and states have what they need to meet the goals established in 2002 with the NCLB: provide every child with an excellent teacher and high-quality education (White House, 2015).

Legislation	Civil Rights Act (1964)	No Child Left Behind Act (2002; NCLB)	Every Student Succeeds Act (2015; ESSA)
Letter of the Law (technical goals)	• Prohibit discrimination in public places. • Desegregate schools and other public facilities. • Make employment discrimination illegal.	• Disaggregate data to prevent schools from effectively hiding achievement gaps among student groups. • Establish state standards, test students annually, track progress, and ensure every student demographic group reaches proficiency in reading and math by 2013–2014.	• Uphold protections for underserved students. • Maintain accountability expectations for low-performing schools. • Expand access to high-quality preschool. • Require every school to teach every student to high standards.
Status toward achieving the Spirit of Law (results)	Fifty years later, social inequality according to race still exists (Light, 2014), as evidenced by disparities between groups in • Median household income, • Average family wealth, • Percentage of demographic groups in poverty, • Unemployment rates, • Incarceration rates, • Housing, and • Education.	Fourteen years after Congress passed NCLB, achievement gaps between student demographic groups still remain. There is no consensus that NCLB's test-driven accountability system has led to increased growth in student performance or narrowed achievement gaps (National Education Association [NEA], 2015).	To be determined.

On that day President Obama stated, "With this bill, we reaffirm that fundamentally American ideal—that every child, regardless of race, income, background, the zip code where they live, deserves the chance to make of their lives what they will" (U.S. Department of Education, 2015). The ESSA contains many equity-related provisions including (for the first time) the requirement that schools prepare *all students* to succeed beyond PK–12 by meeting college- and career-readiness standards.

Mandates like these are laudatory in a society attempting to realize democracy by ensuring social justice through liberating itself from a tradition of perpetuating social and educational inequality. However, as with previous efforts, a tension remains between the spirit (intent) and the letter (literal interpretation) of the law because—by its very nature—a *behavioral response* from educators to a *legislative mandate* can take us only so far, and that's not far enough.

Legislative mandates for equity in education and society have not succeeded in attaining the moral goal (the spirit of the law) set out in these judicial and legislative actions: that of liberating our students from systemic oppression. Despite the fact that legislative mandates have reached several technical goals (the letter of the law) and have caused some positive educational and social changes, they have fallen far short of delivering equitable student outcomes and of transforming the system into a system free from institutionalized inequity (figure 1.1).

Figure 1.1   Equity for Equal Access and Opportunity

EQUALITY	**EQUITY**	**LIBERATION**
Equal Treatment: Assumption that same supports result in equal access	**Equitable Treatment:** Assumption that different interventions/supports create equal access	**Removal of Systemic Barriers:** Assumption that interventions/supports are not needed for access in a fair and just system, free from systemic inequity

Adapted with permission from Center for Story-Based Strategy & Interaction Institute for Social Change | Artist: Angus Maguire. www.storybasedstrategy.org; http://interactioninstitute.org/; http://madewithangus.com/

WHY CHOOSE INCLUSION?

In spite of its well-intentioned goals, the standards-based educational reform movement that culminated with NCLB (2002) and led to ESSA (2015) may have actually worked *against* our nation's youths receiving the benefits of diverse and inclusive schools and classrooms. The movement started under President Ronald W. Reagan with the publication of *A Nation at Risk* in 1983 (National Commission on Excellence in Education, 1983). It formed national goals and content standards under President George Herbert W. Bush in 1989 and enacted a standards-based vision under President William J. Clinton in 1994. It was then—in the 1990s—when K–12 policy context shifted in ways that accepted and emphasized separate but equal (equally accountable) schools and classrooms—what some have referred to as *neo-Plessyism,* drawing from a landmark U.S. Supreme Court ruling that upheld segregation as constitutional (table 1.2).

Before the 1990s, K–12 schools in the United States had a growing focus on multicultural education and curriculum development with an intention of teaching and learning within diverse environments. Emerging research was substantiating the value of social outcomes, group work, and pedagogy that emphasized relating across differences and—overall—ongoing and intentional engagement with diversity so that students might receive maximum educational benefits.

However, during the 1990s the K–12 educational policy context shifted away from this diversity and inclusion focus and toward a focus on equity and outputs. The mantra became educating all students to high standards and closing achievement gaps in any

Table 1.2 Timeline of Higher Education and K–12 Educational Research, Policy, and Legal Strategy on Issues of Racial/Ethnic Diversity

Prior to 1955	Early Affirmative Action/Desegregation Litigation *Sweatt v. Painter (Higher Ed)* *McLaurin v. Oklahoma State Regents for Higher Education (Higher Ed)* *Brown v. Board of Education (K–12)* Across all of these cases, researchers and lawyers pressed for an emphasis on: 1. Tangible Factors: equal access for all students to buildings, resources, and faculty 2. Intangible Factors: Status, prestige and the reputation of the institutions; association with other students (future alum); and changing the "hearts and minds" of all students
Late 1950s to Early 1970s	Implementation and Ongoing Litigation Focus of K–12 and higher education on student assignments/admissions, racial balance, and outcomes (test scores, graduation rates, etc.) Greater focus on things that could be counted (Tangible Factors); Less focus on Intangible Factors, including sociocultural issues on campuses and in classrooms
Late 1970s to 1990s	Post-Milliken and Post-Bakke Access/Admissions issues (Tangible Factors) became more complicated Focus on Intangible Factors (hearts and minds), including campus hostility related to race; campus climate and inter-racial understanding; curriculum and pedagogical issues, including ethnic studies, sociocultural issues within classes and detracking movement that addressed the social construction of ability

Mid 1990s to Today	K–12 Policy and Context Works Against Promoting the Education Benefits of Diversity Fragmented school districts and interdistrict segregation Accountability over diversity: Neo-Plessyism School desegregation litigation wanes and remains focused on 14th Amendment issues Most educational research on sociocultural issues in K–12 pedagogy not connected to desegregation/diversity	Higher Education Focus on Education Benefits of Diversity Growing body of research to support evolving litigation on affirmative action and 1st Amendment rights of universities; higher education leaders champion the arguments re: preparing students for global economy and society

Source: The Century Foundation. (2016). *How Racially Diverse Schools and Classrooms Can Benefit All Students*. Used with permission.

environment, including environments racially and socioeconomically diverse or isolated. Educational equity became about teaching every student well in *any* neighborhood, school, or classroom. There was no need to focus on integration and inclusion as long as the focus was on equal outputs.

While the nation narrowed its attention to the use of standardized test scores to measure progress, our public schools seemed to become less concerned about actively developing diverse and inclusive—or even integrated—schools and classrooms to influence positive educational outcomes for all. What resulted from this era of heavy-handed accountability and standardized testing is a "public education system that is simultaneously becoming increasingly diverse in terms of its student population and increasingly segregated and unequal" (Wells, Fox, & Cordova-Cobo, 2016, p. 6). In 2016 U.S. schools were more racially and socioeconomically segregated than they had been for decades (U.S. Government Accountability Office, 2016).

Figure 1.2 Four Types of Diverse Environments

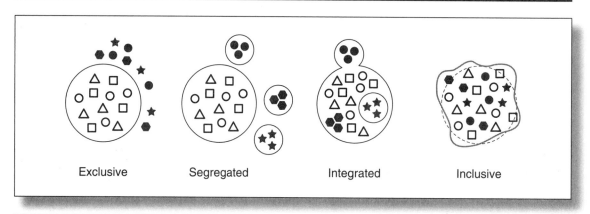

Exclusive   Segregated   Integrated   Inclusive

Source: Theodor Heuss Kolleg, *Diversity Dynamics: Activating the Potential of Diversity in Trainings*. Retrieved from: http://www.theodor-heuss-kolleg.de

Meanwhile, as our K–12 trajectory was becoming clear in the 1990s, higher education in the United States moved in the other direction (table 1.2). Leaders of the nation's colleges and universities worked to establish policies (such as race-conscious admissions) to help shape campuses that are often more diverse than the college students' prior PK–12 schools. But proximity does not ensure connectivity, nor does it guarantee that students receive any of the other benefits of diversity. Campuses also have to be inclusive (figure 1.2).

Certainly our institutions of higher education have much work to do around inclusion, as evidenced by the 2015 surge of college student activism calling for such (Barnhardt & Reyes, 2016; Wong, 2015). Nevertheless, the commitment of higher education to diversity and inclusion has been strengthened over the past two decades as the result of its own research that revealed the numerous educational benefits of diversity and inclusion for *all* students. These benefits are not restricted to minority students, which is a common misperception (Bowman, 2010; Crisp & Turner, 2011; Engberg, 2007; Gurin, Dey, Hurtado, & Gurin, 2002; Haas, 1999; Ruggs & Hebl, 2012). Benefits of diversity and inclusion include

- Boosted self-efficacy;
- Greater social and emotional well-being;
- Enhanced learning outcomes;
- Increased intercultural and cross-racial knowledge, understanding, and empathy;
- Better preparation for employment in the global economy; and
- Increased democratic outcomes.

In its report, *How Racially Diverse Schools and Classrooms Can Benefit All Students*, The Century Foundation—a progressive public policy think tank that seeks to foster opportunity, reduce inequality, and promote security at home and abroad—concluded that the lack of maximizing educational benefits through diversity and inclusion as a defining theme within PK–12 schools and classrooms is troubling (Wells, Fox, & Cordova-Cobo, 2016, p. 20). The foundation urges stakeholders to pay more attention to this issue and use it to envision a PK–12 system that develops the empathy, understanding, and cross-cultural skills requisite of a healthy and increasingly diverse democratic society.

WHY INSIDE-OUT?

These facts show that achieving moral goals of inclusion and equity requires more than a *behavioral response* from educators to a *legislative mandate*. It requires a *moral response* from educators to a *mandate of the heart*. For example, we must work toward equitable student outcomes because we believe it's right and morally just to do so, not because we'll get punished if we don't. We must create diverse and inclusive schools because we value humanity and the well-being of students, even in the absence of an external mandate forcing us to do so. Inclusion and equity are each a moral summons.

When it comes to morality, policy and legislation in and of themselves are limited. In the best of all possible worlds (Voltaire, 2000), we would do what is morally right without the pressure of the law; but in the world we live in, legal constraints and demands can function to push us toward better behavior. Still, if we do what's right simply because of the fear attached to not following the law, that's a problem. Fear of sanction or punishment is a negative motivation that results in minimal compliance, at best. Once minimal compliance is met and the fear is removed, motivation ceases (Deming, 2000).

We will surely continue to allow exclusive or segregated—or at best integrated (figure 1.2)—schools and classrooms unless we educators *value* the *why* behind inclusion. We'll continue to fall short of our equity aspirations (figure 1.1) unless we stop reacting mindlessly to the technical aspects of equity mandates. Instead, we need to choose to move their spirit forward (Lindsey, 2011). Mandates clearly serve to protect us from our worst selves, but they do not bring about our better selves. And to fulfill the promise of democracy through our schools, we need to work on becoming our better selves, and becoming our better selves is a personal journey.

THE JOURNEY TO BECOMING OUR BETTER SELVES

Cultural Proficiency is a journey from *who we currently are* to *who we want to be*. It's a continuing, never-ending journey, because becoming one's better self requires ongoing work. Furthermore, this journey is an inside-out process of change that begins with changing one's self. The absence of an inside-out process may be the reason it takes so long for the moral outcomes of legislative changes to appear. To help us understand the benefits of focusing on the personal and internal process of change, let's turn to the work of William Bridges (2009), a world-famous expert in the human aspects of change.

Bridges (2009) posits that most organizational change efforts fail or linger indefinitely because we as leaders do not attend to the transitions people must go through as a result of change. The key point here is that *change* is different from *transition*. Change is external; it can and does happen overnight (for instance, NCLB or ESSA can be a bill one day and the law the next). However, transition is internal. It does not happen overnight. It can be largely hidden because it takes place in the hearts and minds of people.

For instance, NCLB resulted in changes (letter of the law) of practice and policy such as disaggregating student data according to demographic groups. Its moral goal (spirit of the law) required a transition *from* a system that sees itself as responsible for sorting and selecting the winners from the losers (the "best and the brightest" from the "worst and the dimmest") and *to* a system that sees itself as responsible for educating *all* students to high standards, leaving no student behind. Without managing this transition, educators, schools, and school systems end up wandering around in the psychological wilderness, which is the limbo between the old sense of identity and the new (Bridges, 2009, p. 8). This space is the wasteland where organizations (people) may keep the letter of the law but are not committed to its spirit, essence, or intent. Wandering in the wilderness is not simply squandering time: when it comes to educating our nation's youths, this metaphoric wandering is an immoral and inane waste of an entire generation's brainpower, potential, and vitality that contributes to the decay of our democracy.

Table 1.3 Cultural Proficiency: Developing a Healthy Mind-set

FROM UNHEALTHY MIND-SET Operating from an us/them hierarchy focused on fixing *them*.	TO HEALTHY MIND-SET Working in community focused on transforming *our* practices.
• Blame • Holding schools accountable • Fixing students • Underachieving students • Giving students a voice by empowering them • Closing the achievement gap • Atomistic view of excellence and inclusion—separate entities • Exclusive schools and classrooms • Atomistic view of excellence and equity—separate entities • High expectations for some • Equity and excellence in opposition—only one at a time can exist • Letter of the law • Actions based on meritocracy myth • Achievement gap • Remediation • Atomistic view of developing caring relationships and delivering instruction—separate entities • Essentialized notions of diversity: dichotomous categories • Believing multicultural education benefits only minority students	• Shared responsibility • Supporting professional responsibility • Becoming better self • Underserved students • Amplifying student voices by creating conditions for enabling agency and self-empowerment • Ensuring excellence with equity[1] • Holistic view of excellence and inclusion—excellence without inclusion is segregation • Inclusive schools and classrooms • Holistic view of excellence and equity—excellence without equity is elitism • High expectations for all • Equity and excellence in concert—equity without excellence results in mediocrity • Spirit of the law • Systems that perpetuate social equality • Educational debt[2] • Reconciliation • Holistic view of culturally sustaining pedagogy through developing caring teacher–student relationships • Holistic notions of diversity: intersectionality and dimensions of difference • Believing Cultural Proficiency benefits students, teachers, and society

Notes:

1. Ronald Ferguson (2015) of Harvard University's Achievement Gap Initiative recommends educators and policymakers focus more on "excellence with equity" and less on "closing the achievement gap."

2. Gloria Ladson-Billings (2006) offers the concept of "educational debt" as a responsible alternative to the "racial achievement gap," a phrase that she posits supports deficit thinking.

But we have the power to stop wandering. It's our choice. The direct route to educational excellence with equity is Cultural Proficiency; this is a journey that starts with self and results in profound school change. The crucial and defining element that makes Cultural Proficiency work where many other approaches have failed or produced mediocre results is that Cultural Proficiency provides solid theoretical and pragmatic support for the all-important transition period. We cannot move from the oppression of systemic exclusion and inequity in education to the democracy of culturally proficient schools without an internal transition that involves developing clarity about our new identity and what it is that we truly value and believe. The Cultural Proficiency journey provides us with guideposts and other tools to help us navigate that transitional period in a direct and efficient manner.

Even with Cultural Proficiency, we cannot expect to arrive overnight or in the blink of an eye. This journey is not like jumping into the *Millennium Falcon* with Han Solo yelling, "Punch it!" and Chewbacca thrusting our vehicle into light speed. Not hardly. Cultural Proficiency involves reflection and dialogue, which take time. It requires us to slow down to build momentum to go fast (CampbellJones, 2013). It must be noted, however, that slowing down does not mean inaction. That is a false dichotomy that rightly arouses suspicion, especially among individuals whose identity includes groups historically served poorly by our society's painstakingly slow historic progression toward socially just outcomes—a movement that started with the Emancipation Proclamation (January 1, 1863) and more recently inched forward with the Every Student Succeeds Act (2015). Simply put, delaying action any longer is not acceptable. Thus, in the context of Cultural Proficiency, slowing down to build momentum to go fast means progressing carefully and acting deliberately in an informed, strategic, and efficient manner. We build speed as we go.

By engaging in this process, we allow ourselves to be born as proactive leaders. We consciously develop a commitment to a healthy mind-set of teaching and learning in a diverse democratic society. (table 1.3). We choose to change our minds and give birth to new thinking—as individuals and as a whole generation of educators—to let go the old traditions of inequality and to embrace new ways of seeing, engaging with, and responding to diversity.

This new and healthy response is possible. As Dewitt Jones (1996) says, "We will see it when we believe it." We can do it if we value the principles of democracy, if we believe that inclusion and equity in education are moral mandates of our hearts, and if we act with the will to educate all children (Hilliard, 1991; Lindsey, Roberts, & CampbellJones, 2013). We can do this with sustainability *if* we embark on a journey that begins with examining our values, beliefs, and actions with the intent of becoming our better selves. In doing so, we can—as the phrase attributed to Mahatma Gandhi suggests—"be the change we wish to see in the world."

WHY FACILITATION?

The Cultural Proficiency journey (the process) is challenging. Thus, those on the journey benefit from learning and leading with a knowledgeable and skilled facilitator. To facilitate means to guide, ease, or make a process possible. Thus, facilitation is implicitly linked to process, which is a series of steps toward a goal. As such, facilitators of Cultural Proficiency guide groups and make their journeys easier.

Table 1.4 Group Facilitation Misconceptions

Misconception	Reality
1. Facilitator is synonymous with trainer or presenter.	Quite the opposite. Trainers and presenters set objectives and share information with a group. Facilitators use tools and techniques to draw out information from a group as it progresses in a process toward accomplishing its own objective.
2. Facilitation is a buzzword for interactive presenting.	Facilitation means structuring interaction for participants within a group to make the group's work easier than if they did not have a facilitator. Facilitation is not a buzzword for simply using questions, small groups, or constructivist learning approaches within trainings or presentations.
3. Facilitating is easier than presenting.	Facilitating a group requires deep knowledge, skills, and abilities. It does not come easily, especially for those trained in teaching, who often have to unlearn professional practice and develop new assumptions.
4. Facilitation methods are magic.	A group that has a highly skilled facilitator must still work hard to accomplish its objectives. A facilitator doesn't pull gimmicks and tricks that will solve the group's problems for it. However, to the untrained eye, skillful facilitation might look like magic. Not so. It is a discipline with principles, tools, skills, and techniques that can be learned.

Source: Adapted from The Institute of Cultural Affairs. *Caution: Misconceptions about Facilitation.* http://www.icab.be/top/top_3.html

As Jack intimated in this chapter's episode, many misconceptions exist about group facilitation (table 1.4). In actuality, facilitation is a discipline of its own, quite different from presenting, training, and teaching. According to Hunter (2007, p. 19), "Facilitation enables a group of people to achieve their own purpose in their own agreed way." Furthermore, Sibbet (2002, p. iv) defines facilitation as "the art of leading people through processes toward agreed-upon objectives in a manner that encourages participation, ownership, and creativity from all involved."

Facilitation is more art than science. As an art, facilitation is a body of expertise that includes principles, skills, and practices. It is concerned with helping individuals within groups to have the opportunity to fully participate in setting goals and achieving those goals. In general, facilitation ultimately makes it easier for groups of people to adapt in order to fulfill work and life goals (Sibbet, 2002).

What, then, are the duties and responsibilities of educators who assume the facilitator's role of guiding groups on their Cultural Proficiency journey? Essentially, the function of culturally proficient facilitators is to serve groups interested in ensuring excellence with equity in education. Facilitators lead by example, guiding people step by step through transformative processes into our better selves where we can create a new and better reality, one within which all educators effectively educate all children. A culturally proficient facilitator's knowledge base includes the following:

- A nuanced understanding of the *why*—why schools in a democratic and diverse society need Cultural Proficiency and why Cultural Proficiency must be facilitated and not simply presented (part I of this book).
- An in-depth and experiential grasp of the *how*—how to use the Cultural Proficiency Framework (content) on the Cultural Proficiency Journey (the process) in pursuit of excellence with equity in education (part II of this book).
- Knowledge, skills, and abilities with the *what*—what culturally proficient facilitators value, believe, and do in professional practice (part III of this book).

Reflection

What ideas are resonating with you in regard to the need for the inside-out process of Cultural Proficiency to achieve excellence with equity in education? Why?

transcend current reality

_____

_____

_____

What ideas do you wish to explore in regard to the need for facilitators?

_____

_____

_____

_____

Please revisit table 1.3. What ideas are resonating with you? Why?

shifting mindset

looking outward

_____

_____

DIALOGIC ACTIVITY

1. Respond to or review your responses to the three reflection questions.

2. Use first turn/last turn protocol (table 1.5) to explore perspectives and discover individual and shared meaning.

Table 1.5 First Turn/Last Turn Protocol

Step	Procedure
1.	Form a group of four to eight people. Ensure each person has three index cards.
2.	Silently and individually respond or review your responses to reflection questions.
3.	On each of the three index cards, write the idea from the text that is resonating with you. (One index card per reflection question.) On the back of the index card, write *why* that idea is resonating with you.
4.	Start: The designated person in the group starts by reading (without commentary) their idea related to the question.
5.	Listen: The starter listens as each person in the group comments on the idea.
6.	Share: The starter reads (without commentary) the back of the index card: why the idea is resonating with them. The round ends.
7.	Repeat steps 4–7 for as many rounds as it takes to exhaust the index cards. Each person will have at least one turn being the starter.
8.	After rounds are finished, open a general discussion in response to the text and ideas that were shared but not explored in depth.
Tips:	• Strictly follow protocol for steps 4–6. No cross talk. • Resist the urge to comment immediately after sharing your idea. • If someone shares the same idea someone else had written on their index card, that person can simply read the "why" when it's their turn to comment. • During step 8, pay attention to sharing airtime, seeking to understand, and posing dialogic questions such as why, when/where, and who questions. • As a variation, cut step 3.

Source: Adapted from Robert Garmston and Bruce Wellman (2009), *The Adaptive School,* p. 212.

2 Assumptions About the Work

Seek first to understand and then to be understood.

—Stephen R. Covey
(The 7 Habits of Highly Effective People, *1989*)

When women and men understand that working to eradicate patriarchal domination is a struggle rooted in the longing to make a world where everyone can live fully and freely, then we know our work to be a gesture of love.

—bell hooks
(Talking Back: Talking Feminist, Thinking Black, *1989*)

In order to love purely, we must surrender our old ways of thinking.

—Marianne Williamson (A Return to Love, *1992*)

We really are 15 countries, and it's remarkable that each of us thinks we represent the real America. The Midwesterner in Kansas, the black American in Durham—both are certain they are the real American.

—Maya Angelou
(Washington Post Magazine, *1978*)

Thoughts have power; thoughts are energy. And you can make your world or break it by your own thinking.

—Susan L. Taylor (quoted in Angelou, 1978)

The universe is energy, energy that responds to our expectations.

—James Redfield (The Celestine Prophecy, *1993*)

The most important decision we can make is whether this is a friendly or hostile universe. From that one decision all others spring.

—Albert Einstein

GETTING CENTERED

Review these quotations about energy, expectations, beliefs, perspective, and power. Take a few moments to think about diversity trainings or other diversity-focused professional development events in which you have participated. Did you seek them out on your own, were you invited, or were they mandated? Going into the event(s), what expectations did you hold? How would you describe your energy? The space below invites you to record your thoughts.

_____

_____

_____

_____

Perhaps you've always jumped at the opportunity to attend events focused on diversity and equity and/or inclusion. But let's be honest: Jack is not alone in his grumpy reluctance to drop everything, write sub plans, and cancel meetings to attend such an event. We certainly have colleagues who've experienced Jack's resistance. Some of us may have been in Jack's shoes ourselves at one time or another. We may believe we're doing just fine with diversity. After all, we're not bigots who need this stuff. Or perhaps we've experienced marginalization and believe the meetings are better suited for colleagues from dominant groups. Either way, we believe it's for them.

We already do our jobs well. We see the "isms" (racism, sexism, heterosexism, anti-Semitism, etc.) as indicators of bad behaviors or even of bad people. Or perhaps we see these mind-sets as markers of people who have yet to see the light. Nevertheless, we can't imagine that we ourselves could be active participants in maintaining systemic oppression. Perhaps we're not even aware of such systems. Or we might assume that members of oppressed groups do not and cannot participate in keeping systems of oppression in place. The bottom line is we don't believe this meeting, workshop, or seminar is for us.

Furthermore, some of us may suspect that diversity, culture, or difference are just code words for the word *race*. And in our work, we tell ourselves, it's not all about race anymore. Sure there are still some racists out there, but, for the most part, we figure that issue was pretty much resolved during the civil rights era. If there's still a problem, it must be with other people, not us. Some of us who identify as white may believe it's those other white people who need to evolve. Some of us who identify as persons of color may think that it's really white people who need to attend Cultural Proficiency seminars. Regardless, again, it's for them.

But such self-assurances can be treacherous. They prevent us from discovering what we don't yet know, no matter how we self-identify. And as Jack soon discovered, there was much he didn't know. Nor did he know what he didn't know. It wasn't a matter of simply having good intentions; good intentions aren't enough. Let's join Jack again as he begins to walk a new and at times rocky road.

Reflection

What are your reactions to any of these thoughts? "Good intentions aren't enough." "We believe it's for them." "We can't imagine that we ourselves could be active participants in maintaining systemic oppression." "Jack is not alone in his grumpy reluctance." Other?

_____

_____

_____

_____

EPISODE TWO: JACK'S EXPECTATIONS, INTERRUPTED

Two days later, Jack arrived in the parking lot of the downtown hotel where the conference room had been rented for the five-day seminar. He had arrived early. He sat in his car waiting for a colleague to come along so he didn't have to walk in alone. After all, what if he were first to arrive? Would that give the presenters the opportunity to size him up, catch him off guard, and get him to talk about racism—a field riddled with land mines—right away? He didn't want to risk it. He didn't even want to be here.

Above all, he wanted to avoid the possibility of being stereotyped, targeted, and used as an example, as white males sometimes were in these situations. Or at least that's what he expected based on what he'd heard from white male colleagues who'd worked at the district office longer than he had. Jack wasn't taking any risks. He figured it was prudent to limit direct contact with the facilitators and to arrive with someone else. If that someone happened to be a racial minority, even better.

So, when Julie Cho's car pulled up, Jack grabbed his laptop and unfolded his six-foot frame from his dark green sedan. He called out to Julie, the language arts specialist, and then walked with her toward the hotel entrance, exchanging the usual family updates as they entered the building. The seminar room was the first to the right.

Standing outside the room was Fatima Akram, the other language arts specialist. She wanted a word with Julie regarding an early-morning parental concern about curriculum. The two women stepped to the side, leaving Jack standing alone in the doorway. He scanned the room. It was exactly how he'd imagined: The furniture was arranged like every other workshop or seminar over the past fifteen years of his career. Six circular tables filled the room, each with six chairs. About half the tables were filled, and a few people were talking quietly. Like every other diversity session, the presenters were African American. They were standing up front, near the data projector, talking with Lillie Cohen.

Jack figured these facilitators must be the consultants with whom the board had been working: Barbara Campbell and Frank Westman. Probably in their mid-fifties, both were trim and tall. Frank's look was that of a scholarly professor: brown tweed jacket with black dress slacks, plaid tie with standard white dress shirt. Bespectacled for function, not fashion. Put a textbook in one hand, and the whole ensemble could have outfitted Harrison Ford as Dr. Henry "Indiana" Jones (before he left the classroom on his adventures, of course). Barbara had a university president look: well-tailored navy blue dress suit and sensible but stylish high heels. Her hair was pulled back, giving the impression that she wasn't hiding from anything. There was no missing the authority in her demeanor.

Jack was aware that both consultants had doctorates and worked for universities. From his experience, that meant they were full of data and current research but probably out of touch with the day-to-day realities of working in the trenches of a school system.

Still determined to avoid contact, Jack scanned the room for a safe seat. On the far side at the back, he spotted an empty place at Tom Joy's table. Jack smiled. Tom was an old friend from Jack's first year of teaching. Tom has been his principal. As the youngest teacher, Jack was at a disadvantage to being taken seriously. But Tom had been totally supportive of the young (and then baby-faced) teacher. Now Tom was the district's coordinator of fine arts, and he'd collaborated with Jack in developing the new math curriculum.

Julie and Fatima were still deep in conversation, and Jack realized that his original plan to walk in with Julie wasn't an option. He ducked his head and hurried toward Tom. He kept his gaze averted as he maneuvered past the consultants. He felt like a kid trying to tiptoe past a room in which his parents were located.

Then, to his horror, Jack's peripheral vision saw a navy-blue blur approaching at a rapid pace. Busted. Jack considered changing direction or pretending not to see. But he had no talent for subterfuge. It wasn't who he was. In any event, to ignore the facilitator would be rude. She was just doing her job. Jack stopped and lifted his gaze to meet Barbara's broad smile. She was a stately woman with a polished look. Her right hand was extended in a proffered handshake. Jack took her hand, noticed the strength of her handshake, and was surprised when her other hand briefly touched his left elbow. The gesture communicated warmth and sincerity. It certainly didn't feel like intimidation or power-over, the dynamics he'd expected from the facilitators.

If she knew he'd been trying to sneak past, she didn't show it. Jack felt a little ashamed. Her voice was low, throaty, and confident.

Barbara: Hi, my name is Barbara. What's yours?

Jack: Jack McManus. I'm the math specialist here.

Barbara: Oh! I've heard about you. I used to be a curriculum specialist, too. It's hard work. And, from what I've heard, you've done great things with the math curriculum. It's impressive. Thank you for what you do for each and every student here in Stocklin.

Jack: Thank you. I'm surprised you've heard about my work.

Barbara: Gathering information about our participants is important to Frank and me. We spent about two days preparing to facilitate Cultural Proficiency for your group today. Half of that time we spent learning about each of you.

Jack: Wow. I've presented to teachers for years, and I've never done that. I spend all of my prep time putting together my agenda and creating my slides.

Barbara: Well, today is all about you, so we felt we had to prepare as best as we knew how. We're going to get started in a minute, Jack. Sit wherever is comfortable. I'm truly glad to meet you, and I realize that you had to clear five days on your calendar. Thank you, sincerely, for being here today.

Jack nodded to Barbara and headed toward Tom. Tom looked up from his laptop with a strained smile that Jack interpreted as "I don't want to be here either," and returned to typing at a furious rate. As Jack sat down and pulled out his laptop to take notes, he noticed that he felt ill at ease. Definitely surprised, a bit confused, and maybe even suspicious. Why had Barbara and Frank gathered so much information about him and the other participants? What exactly did they know about him? Personal stuff? That he was divorced with two children and lived in the suburbs? Why did they need that information? What did Barbara mean when she said this workshop was all about the participants? She had said, "Today is all about you."

Jack took a deep breath and told himself to chill out. He was being unreasonable and suspicious. He didn't like feeling that way. He hoped that the facilitators' need to research participants would become clear in time. Nevertheless, it had been a pleasant surprise when Barbara complimented his work and achievements. Already this workshop—or at least the facilitators—was shaping up to be different from what he'd expected. In his mind (based on his and others' experiences) diversity presenters were often standoffish, some had an attitude of superiority, and a few seemed to be angry or downright militant. Certainly none had been as friendly or personable as Barbara. It might have been easier if she had been standoffish. Now Jack wasn't sure what to expect.

Still, Jack figured the workshop itself would unfold along certain lines. He couldn't imagine how it could differ from other diversity workshops. He was prepared to "sit and get"—in other words, to sit quietly and receive lectures, to listen and take notes. The facilitators would probably show slides of data the participants were already familiar with. Disproportionate achievement according to race and ethnicity. They'd opine that teachers treated students who were black and Hispanic—especially male black and Hispanic students—unfairly. They'd tug on heartstrings and lecture about what needed to be done differently. Participants would feel guilty, uncomfortable, and perhaps irritated. Jack groaned, looked at his watch, and visualized the unfinished projects on his desk. He admitted the truth to himself: he was dreading this.

He stole a surreptitious glance at his colleagues. Most were checking their phones or laptops; a few were chatting; the science curriculum supervisor was rocking back on his chair, arms folded, staring off into space. Tom was still typing. Jack wondered how many, like himself, did not want to be here. People seemed unusually quiet, and the atmosphere felt subdued. Did he perceive a lack of enthusiasm? Did they also think that they didn't need this particular workshop? Or was Jack projecting his own feelings?

These were colleagues Jack respected, people who cared about students. Why else were they in education? They were all district leaders, for crying out loud. Plus this group itself was visibly diverse. "I guess I'm a member of the choir again," thought Jack, his frustration gnawing at him. "And these consultants are about to preach to us. We do good work. But it's never good enough."

Above all, Jack expected guilt to be used as workshop strategy. As he sat there and thought about all of this, he felt his heart rate increase, and he could feel his frustration heading toward anger. He should be working on his curriculum overhaul. That's what could actually change outcomes for minority students. He could name many staff members who should be here instead of him. People who "just didn't get it." But those weren't the people in the room. If Jack wasn't so annoyed, he might have felt bad for the facilitators.

Reflection

What is familiar to you about Jack's experience thus far? What is unfamiliar?

_____

_____

_____

_____

Review the episode and describe Jack's energy. Besides positive or negative, what labels could you use to describe them? What were the indicators of such energy?

_____

_____

_____

_____

Review the episode and describe Jack's expectations of the seminar. How might Jack's expectations shape his experience during this seminar? What can facilitators do to support a positive experience?

_____

_____

_____

_____

THE POWER OF EXPECTATIONS

Like Jack in our episode, when participants arrive at seminars they have expectations about what will happen. These expectations are largely shaped by their past experiences. Sometimes they are shaped by what participants have heard about similar seminars from other people or from the media. If left uninterrupted by new and different experiences, these expectations can become self-fulfilling prophecies.

Jack entered the seminar with the expectation (among others) that he wasn't going to benefit from the experience. He believed that he wasn't one of the Stocklin staff members who needed this type of seminar—or, rather, who needed what he assumed this seminar was going to be. If Jack could surface and challenge the assumptions behind his belief, he could choose to change his assumptions and—in doing so—change his mind. In fact, supporting this kind of reflection is a primary responsibility of Cultural Proficiency facilitators. They help groups of people go beneath the surface of behaviors, recognize and study their assumptions, and change their minds as necessary.

This approach is supported by the work of organizational development thought leaders (Argyris, 1990; Schein, 2010; Senge, 1999), who have long asserted that sustainable change happens beneath the surface, in the realm of our morality and ethics and minds. Actions flow from expectations; behaviors are born from beliefs. Assuming this to be true leads to the conclusion that meaningful change in practice and policy within our organizations starts with changing the values, assumptions, and beliefs within our minds.

To change the traditions that have marginalized and underserved certain groups for generations requires transforming our culture. Shaping our culture—including the cultures within our institutions and schools—requires changing our minds. Changing our minds requires surfacing (or discovering and bringing to the conscious level of our thinking), examining, and changing unhealthy values, assumptions, and beliefs. Facilitators of Cultural Proficiency make the transformation process easier by using mental models such as the *Ladder of Inference* (Argyris, 1990) to help groups stay focused on the aspects that guide their actions: their values and beliefs.

Chris Argyris, Harvard Business School professor emeritus, developed the *Ladder of Inference* during his work on the subject of individual and organizational learning. The ladder became a hypothetical model for better understanding how individuals act within organizations. It illustrates how values inform behaviors, showing how abstractions within our belief systems progress toward concrete and observable actions.

A later version of this ladder (Senge, 1994) included a reflexive loop to illustrate how our beliefs influence how we experience the world around us. First, we select data from our environments based on our beliefs, and then these data form the basis of our experience. In other words, what we perceive and experience reflects our thoughts, and our thoughts reflect our values and our beliefs about what is true. Thus it is through our beliefs that we construct the reality that we experience as our reality. Indeed, it is difficult to overestimate the power of our beliefs when it comes to forming and informing our actions and behaviors. Once we understand this cause-and-effect link, it becomes obvious that we need to question our thoughts before we can change our minds and our cultures.

CampbellJones, CampbellJones, and Lindsey (2010) utilized the *Ladder of Inference* in a template for analyzing situations of professional practice in order to see "how observable action is a composite of subjective processes" (p. 43). The template helps us examine cognitive processes that happen in the blink of an eye. Figure 2.1 uses this template to illustrate the subjective processes beneath the surface of Jack's resistance to authentic engagement with the seminar.

According to the scenario depicted by figure 2.1, Jack's beliefs (about his not needing to attend this seminar) influence the data he selects. Specifically, he pays close attention to the other participants. Moving up the ladder, he interprets the selected data by adding meaning based on his values: "This is a diverse group of good and respected colleagues." Climbing to Rung 4, Jack's subjective processes continue by relating the assigned meaning to his assumptions (assumptions are things we implicitly accept as truth). In this case, Jack assumes that Cultural Proficiency is for people who don't yet "get it" and need to be

Figure 2.1 Jack's Reality

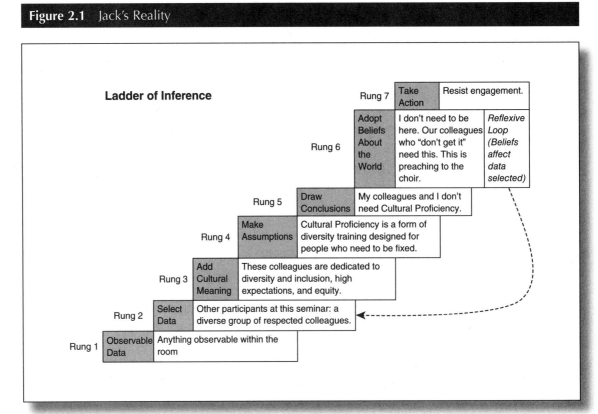

Source: Adapted from CampbellJones, CampbellJones, and Lindsey (2010), p. 42.

"fixed," which allows him to easily draw the conclusion (Rung 5) "My colleagues and I don't need Cultural Proficiency." Conclusions such as this reinforce his existing beliefs relative to his current context (Rung 6). This strengthens the reflexive loop and also gives rise to Jack's observable actions: resisting authentic engagement with the seminar.

In *Other People's Children*, Lisa Delpit (1996, pp. 46–47) writes, "We do not really see through our eyes or hear through our ears, but through our beliefs." Think about that a moment: we see (or perceive) through our beliefs. Therefore, if Jack's belief system were different from that in figure 2.1, he would construct a different reality. Figure 2.2 considers this by altering Jack's belief system at the assumptive level (Rung 4). A different assumption gives rise to different conclusions, beliefs, and actions. The result—the reality experienced by Jack—is dramatically different, more personally positive, and more open to transformational change and growth than Jack's original reality. In this new reality, Jack is still in the choir, but he realizes and appreciates that choirs need to practice (CampbellJones, 2014).

The critical point of difference between these two realities takes place at the assumptive level (Rung 4)—two different assumptions (hypotheses) about the nature of Cultural Proficiency. In this second reality, Jack assumes that Cultural Proficiency supports leaders in realizing their values of inclusion and equity. That assumption informs his conclusions about the nature of his (and his colleagues') relationship to Cultural Proficiency, reinforces his beliefs, and leads to his authentic engagement.

Not only do the expectations of participants inform their actions and influence the data they select, but their expectations also manifest as energy. As their expectations show

Figure 2.2 Jack's Alternative Reality

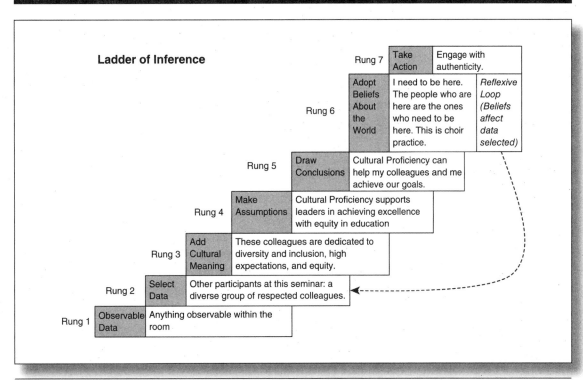

Source: Adapted from CampbellJones, CampbellJones, and Lindsey (2010), p. 42.

up as behaviors, participants give off positive or negative energy ("vibes") that influence the energy of those around them. Recognizing various energy states of participants and groups is an important role of facilitators so they can help to shift the energy to positive states supportive of Cultural Proficiency.

ENERGY STATES

As illustrated in Episodes One and Two, Jack entered the seminar with a particular energy state, driving force, or motivation. The behaviors and thinking of individuals (participants) and cultures (groups) are driven by such energy states. Energy is either positive or negative. Some energy states are unhealthy and fuel divisive, combative, oppressive, and hurtful behaviors. Other energy states are healthy and fuel unifying, conciliatory, humane, and healing behaviors. Whether positive or negative, energy states also vary in their degrees of intensity or strength. Table 2.1 lists energy states in order of least intense (top) to most intense (bottom) (Zohar & Marshall, 2004).

Effective facilitators need to understand, gauge, and manage energy (Garmston & Wellman, 2009; Hunter, 2007; Sibbet, 2002). The energy of a group includes its ebbs and flows, degrees of excitement or inspiration, emotions of participants, and the manners in which participants work and move. These dynamics manifest as group and individual behavior. For example, two participants engaged in dialogue are driven by (at least) the positive energy state of exploration. A participant who blames others for their feelings may be driven by the negative energy state of anger.

Table 2.1 Energy States

FROM UNHEALTHY Negative Motivations	TO HEALTHY Positive Motivations
• Self-assertion (−1) • Anger (−2) • Craving (−3) • Fear (−4) • Anguish (−5) • Apathy (−6) • Guilt and shame (−7) • Depersonalization (−8)	• Exploration (+1) • Cooperation (+2) • Power within (+3) • Mastery (+4) • Generativity (+5) • Higher service (+6) • World soul (+7) • Enlightenment (+8)

Source: Adapted from Danah Zohar and Ian Marshall. (2004). *Spiritual Capital: Wealth We Can Live By.* San Francisco, CA: Berrett-Koehler Publishers, Inc.

Predictably, conversations about equity, diversity and inclusion, and social justice within Cultural Proficiency events will elicit strong emotions that influence a group's energy states. To overcome the Barriers to Cultural Proficiency, these conversations must inevitably focus on topics of privilege, entitlement, and oppression. These topics often generate strong negative energy that shows up in the form of emotional reactions ranging from anger to guilt (Lindsey et al., 2013, p. 39). Facilitators help individuals and groups observe, process, and understand these emotional reactions as they learn to recognize the effects of systemic privilege and oppression. A skilled facilitator can then help a group choose to shift from unhealthy to healthy energy states. After this positive shift, exploration and cooperation drive the group to learn how to work more effectively with students, families, and colleagues across varying dimensions of difference.

Overall, the Cultural Proficiency journey is fueled by positive energy. Thus, culturally proficient facilitators manage dynamics in ways that help individuals and groups choose to operate from higher energy sources. But first, these facilitators must be able to assess a group's culture and gauge its energy.

In the case of Jack's seminar, Barbara and Frank were likely attending to energy of the group from the moment the first participant arrived. As a skilled facilitator, Barbara surely acted with intentionality, attempting to influence Jack's energy in positive ways. Her body language, spoken words, physical proximity and touch, and awareness of her own energy state all mattered.

Part III of this book further explores what culturally proficient facilitators do to assess, manage, and adapt to various states of energy. Their goal is always to help groups shift and normalize positive energy states, solidifying the motivations that (1) empower cycles of improvement, and (2) fuel collective-efficacy ("we can do this") for Cultural Proficiency. According to Zohar & Marshall (2004, p. 126): "The dynamic of lasting shift is from motivational shift to behavioral shift to cultural shift." Positive shifts do happen, and when it comes to facilitation of Cultural Proficiency, these shifts don't happen by accident.

Reflection

Pause and review the ideas presented in this chapter. In the space below, please record

- Three ideas that reinforce your beliefs,
- Two ideas new to you or that challenge your beliefs, and
- One question the ideas in this chapter provoke.

_____

_____

_____

_____

DIALOGIC ACTIVITY

1. Focus on the one question recorded in the Reflection.

2. Use round-robin responding protocol (table 2.2) to explore perspectives and discover individual and shared meaning.

Table 2.2 Round-Robin Responding Protocol

Step	Procedure
1.	Form small groups of four to eight people.
2.	Introduce the activity. Focus on the opportunity to practice the skill of listening to the perspectives of others.
3.	Each group selects a participant to start.
4.	The participant shares their question with their group without explanation or their own answer. The small group allows approximately thirty seconds of silence.
5.	One at a time (round-robin style), other participants respond to the question in a minute or less. The group allows a short period of silence in between each response.
6.	The participant who posed the question thanks the group for providing thoughts in response to their question.
7.	Repeat steps 4 to 6 for as many rounds as there are people in the group. Each person will have a turn to be the starter.
8.	After completing all rounds (time permitting), the small group can open up a discussion about ideas members found interesting.
Tips:	Strictly follow protocol for steps 4–6. Do not allow cross talk.

3 An Environment of Authentic Engagement

The authentic self is the soul made visible.

> —*Sarah Ban Breathnach* (Simple Abundance, 2008)

Authenticity is a collection of choices. . . . It's about the choice to show up and be real. The choice to be honest. The choice to let our true selves be seen.

> —*Brené Brown* (The Gifts of Imperfection, 2010)

I am invisible, understand, simply because people refuse to see me.

> —*Ralph Ellison* (Invisible Man, 1952)

This country is never safe for people of color. Its schools are not safe; its streets are not safe; its places of employment are not safe; its health care system is not safe.

> —*Tim Wise* (No Such Place as Safe, 2004)

We propose revising our language, shifting away from the concept of safety and empha-sizing the importance of bravery to help students better understand—and rise to—the challenges of dialogue on diversity and social justice issues.

> —*Brian Arao and Kristi Clemens* ("From Safe Spaces to Brave Spaces," 2013)

Courage does not mean to be unafraid. Even the bravest have fears. Courage means to do what we think is right in spite of our being afraid.

> —*Arthur Hoffnung* (For the Love of Torah, 1970)

For me, forgiveness and compassion are always linked: how do we hold people account-able for wrongdoing and yet at the same time remain in touch with their humanity enough to believe in their capacity to be transformed?

> —*bell hooks* (McLeod, 1998)

GETTING CENTERED

Review these quotes and consider the need for authentic engagement within the Cultural Proficiency journey. Consider your own identity and your intersecting dimensions of difference (race, gender, sexual orientation, etc.). For you, what are the issues related to showing up and being real in conversations related to various types of systemic privilege and oppression?

_____

_____

_____

_____

EPISODE THREE: IT'S JACK'S CHOICE, AND IT'S OUR CHOICE

Our Jack is a conscientious, punctual kind of guy, so he appreciated that the seminar started on time. Lillie Cohen, Jack's director, took the podium at the head of the room to introduce the facilitators.

Lillie: Good morning. Thank you for prioritizing this meeting. It's my pleasure to introduce our two consultants, Barbara Campbell and Frank Westman. Barbara actually lives here in Stocklin County, and Frank lives a few hours away. They are both amazing. I got to know them over the course of five days, when they facilitated a group of administrators that included me, the superintendent, and even county government leaders. The experience was not what I'd expected. It was truly transformative. It was a process that got us to a better place. It was unlike any professional development I've experienced. Today we will begin a journey together. With that, I give you Barbara and Frank.

Frank: Welcome! We're honored to serve as your facilitators. Cultural Proficiency is a broad topic, and it is all about you. It's a process of inside-out change. It's a journey. We're going to start by inviting you to reflect on your expectations for the day through an exercise we call "My Journey" (CampbellJones & Associates, 2005). Its purpose is two-fold. First, it will help you get centered. Second, it will help us assess and respond to you as a group and ease your journey.

Barbara: So, please turn to your first handout, where you'll find three questions. (1) What have you been thinking and feeling in anticipation of today? (2) What do you want to accomplish? And (3) How hard are you willing to work? Using the scale of 1 (not hard) through 6 (very hard), explain why you chose that number. Take the next few minutes to write down your thoughts.

Jack scanned the handout. As he read, he paused, holding his pen mid-air. These questions felt a little . . . intrusive. He'd never encountered questions asking for this level of reflection and self-disclosure at the beginning of a workshop. Nor had he ever done anything similar as a presenter. How honest should he be? What would his colleagues and supervisor think of him if he disclosed his frustration at having to clear his calendar for a five-day workshop that he believed that he didn't need?

He started to scribble a not-so-honest response. It felt phony—inauthentic—yet safe. His hand tightened around his pen. He felt caught between a rock and a hard place. Should he play along and endure five days of phoniness? Or should he put himself out there and risk hurting his career by not being sufficiently politically correct?

After struggling a few moments, Jack raised his hand and made eye contact with Barbara. He stood up and approached her. "Would you mind talking to me outside?" he asked, his voice low. She smiled and looked over at Frank, who gave her an approving nod. Jack and Barbara exited the room into the hallway.

Jack: I'm struggling with this activity.

Barbara: What you are struggling with specifically, Jack?

Jack: Well, my supervisor is Lillie, who's in the room. I'm concerned about sharing my true feelings openly with her here. I suspect that I'm not the only one who's feeling conflicted and worried about this type of disclosure. There are other participants whose supervisors are present.

Barbara: Yes, we know you report to Lillie. We're also aware of the power dynamics in the room. Tell me about your struggle.

Jack: It's your questions. Do you really expect us to be honest?

Barbara: I'm sensing there's an opinion behind that question.

Jack: Um, yes . . . people aren't going to expose themselves with their bosses or subordinates present. Certainly not on this topic. There's not enough trust.

Barbara: What about you, Jack? Do you believe that people are not truthful when in a supervisory/subordinate relationship?

Jack: I've always had open and honest relationships. I trust Lillie and her leadership. So no, that's not what I believe.

Barbara: Then what beliefs are making you uncomfortable right now?

Jack: It's the context of this seminar that's difficult. I think some people in the room don't want to be here. In fact, I'm not sure I want to be here. But if we write our true feelings about how we feel about being here, our answers might be judged as lack of professional commitment. Worse, someone could be perceived as insubordinate or even intolerant of diversity. It feels like a double bind with no good solution.

Barbara: I heard you say, "It's the context of this workshop that's difficult." When you say "context," you mean . . .

Barbara paused just long enough for Jack to feel uncomfortable. He sensed she was going to remain silent until after he spoke.

Jack: I mean in the context of a diversity workshop. Talking about equity. Cultural Proficiency. You know, things like racism.

Barbara: I appreciate your honesty. Let me ask you this: You said that you don't think others in the room want to be here. Do you value being here, Jack?

Jack paused. He broke eye contact and looked down at the plush, patterned hotel carpet. The directness of Barbara's question took him by surprise. This was getting a little deep and personal. Should he give her the answer he figured she wanted? That would be compromising himself. No, he'd come clean with her. He met her gaze squarely.

Jack: I value cultural diversity, Barbara . . . but . . . well . . .

Barbara: Jack, I noticed you're pausing before answering that question.

Again, Barbara was calm, still, and seemed comfortable with silence. She maintained eye contact. Her kind, keen gaze told Jack that he was not being judged. He didn't feel he was expected to give approved answers; she was asking for honesty.

Jack: Well, the truth is I didn't seek out this opportunity. My director invited me, and . . . it's not that I don't want . . . well . . . it's just that I have so much work to do back at the office. It's not that I don't value Cultural Proficiency . . .

Barbara: What conclusions have you drawn about Cultural Proficiency, Jack?

Jack: You know, that it's diversity training. Learning about cultural groups and how to teach them. That type of thing.

Barbara: What led you that conclusion?

Jack: I've been to a several diversity training workshops. In each, the presenter focused on closing the achievement gap and teaching specific cultural groups. Sometimes it was as focused as strategies for specific genders within specific racial groups.

Barbara: I see. What if I told you Cultural Proficiency was something different? That it works with diversity and equity, but also a whole lot more. What if I told you this approach was something you haven't encountered before?

Jack: You've got my attention, for sure. I'm curious. But I have deadlines coming up with my math curriculum overhaul. The work is actually about engaging diverse learners. I'm not sure how I'm going to make up the time I'm missing this week. Sorry to be blunt, but I can't help wondering if this is going to be a waste of my time. Especially since it's five whole days.

Barbara: You design good math curriculum, and you're unsure of how you're going to make up this time. Is it that you value your work on math curriculum more than your work here?

Jack: I wasn't thinking about being here as my work. Honestly, I see this workshop as taking me away from my work.

Jack noticed that Barbara seemed unruffled by his remarks, even though they could be interpreted as criticism of the value of her seminar, or at least of its value for him. In fact, she seemed peaceful and anything but upset. Jack wondered how he would react if their roles were reversed.

Barbara: Let me ask you a couple of question that might help. First, what assumptions do you have beneath your conclusions about Cultural Proficiency? About this seminar? Second, how do you feel about being chosen to be here? Actually, Jack, you don't have to answer those questions right now. Really, it's not me who needs the answers. I think you'll find that the answers—when they come to you—will help you on your own personal journey.

Jack: Okay, I'll think about my assumptions.

Barbara: I'm inviting you to write them and share them as part of the current exercise. We'd better get back inside because Frank and I need to facilitate the group. But first there's something I want you to know: the choice is always yours, Jack. Cultural Proficiency is a journey that requires authentic engagement. As for answering the "My Journey" exercise questions honestly, only you can decide how honest and vulnerable you're willing to be during our time together. I assure you that the more you dare to engage—to be "all in"—the more you, as well as the entire group, will take away from this experience. If you engage with authenticity, I assure you this workshop will be worth your time. I appreciate your honesty and vulnerability with me right now. It's a gift. I thank you. And I see you.

Barbara's eyes sparkled. Her hand brushed Jack's shoulder as she turned back into the room. Jack felt reassured. For a few moments, he stood alone in the hallway. Did he dare write his true feelings in those answers? After all, the superintendent wanted this event—the same superintendent who'd picked Jack for his current position. Would it be smart to play the "company man" and act happy to be here? If he played that charade, how could he speak honestly about his reluctance? How could he act happy to risk his professional reputation by talking openly about race, gender, class, and culture—and who knew what else—for five days in a room filled with district leaders, including his boss? Might as well be happy to have the opportunity to walk through a minefield.

Jack noticed his surprisingly strong resistance to this idea of vulnerability. He'd always seen vulnerability as weakness. It could be treacherous, he believed, especially for leaders. Especially for relatively young male leaders like himself. Being the youngest staff member, Jack often felt the need to counter perceptions of his assumed inexperience. He'd heard snide comments, seen contemptuous looks. Even as a new elementary school teacher, he'd tried to downplay his youthful appearance by wearing glasses (that he needed only for night driving). Now as a school district leader, he was required to deliver what was expected: expertise, maturity, decisiveness, and, above all, competence—not vulnerability.

Jack believed that vulnerability in leadership undermined perception of competence. Vulnerability made a leader look indecisive, and, in the worst case, overly emotional, even whiney. Exposing his true thoughts and feelings at work was not something Jack did, especially in the current volatile politically correct climate. One misstep, one wrong word, one misperceived action could cost a career. He'd heard about these situations.

If that happened, what good would vulnerability do him then? Vulnerability seemed another buzzword, and a duplicitous one. District leaders were mentioning it, colleagues were reading books about it, and TV talk show hosts advocated it. Jack's response had been to keep his head down until the buzz blew over.

Despite these misgivings, Jack sensed this seminar was going to be different from his expectations and experiences. Barbara was not what he expected. So far, she hadn't used guilt or shame. She was intuitive, calm, authentic. Her attitude seemed to be one of gratitude. Overall, she was tremendously positive and seemed to have genuine sensitivity to his feelings and experiences. Never had a presenter shown such concern, and never before had he been invited to freely choose the extent of his engagement. That invitation was refreshingly honest and without coercion. It conveyed trust and faith. And yet, and yet . . . to fully engage with vulnerability seemed like such a huge and foolhardy risk.

Reflection

What is familiar to you about Jack's experience in this episode? What is unfamiliar?

_____

_____

_____

_____

How does your identity relate to vulnerability in the context of conversations about systemic racism, sexism, ethnocentrism, heterosexism, and so on? What does being vulnerable require from you? What do you need from others? What do you need from the overall environment?

_____

_____

_____

_____

THE VULNERABILITY DILEMMA

Although Jack had not reached this insight, many educators immediately recognize that Cultural Proficiency is exactly what they've needed to help them change the system from within. It's a comprehensive approach to bringing about meaningful change. It provides tools, and it provides process. Additionally, it's humane, responsible, and sustainable because it starts with awareness and understanding of self. For those of us (and those who came before us) who work tirelessly to make inclusive democracy possible through our schools, Cultural Proficiency is what we've been looking for. We can't wait to get started. However, not all our colleagues share this enthusiasm or perspective, at least not yet. So far, Jack illustrates this for us.

In this chapter's episode, Jack recognized his resistance to vulnerability. He perceived it as uncertainty, risk, and emotional exposure (Brown, 2012b). This resistance posed a dilemma for him. On the one hand was the choice for vulnerability; this would open up areas of potential growth, but it would also open up the possibility of negative emotions and energy, discomfort, and pain. On the other hand was the choice to wear metaphoric armor for emotional, psychological, and professional protection; wearing this armor would effectively close off the possibility of new experiences, human connection, learning, and growth, though.

This dilemma is common when embarking on the Cultural Proficiency journey. Even experienced journeyers need to continually choose vulnerability as the depths of exploration expand and the contexts of conversations change. This is especially the case for those in positions of influence. Thus, effective facilitators must first resolve this dilemma for themselves before they can provide guidance for other journeyers. Having resolved their own dilemma, skilled facilitators extend vulnerability through authentic engagement with the group.

We can profitably ask: What exactly is vulnerability? Our culture generally views it negatively, as evidenced by scanning common definitions. Dictionaries define vulnerability as being capable or susceptible to being wounded or hurt; being open to attack, criticism, or temptations; or being open to assault. With this kind of perception, no wonder we avoid vulnerability.

But there is another, positive way to look at it. Brené Brown (2012a) defines vulnerability as daring to show up and let ourselves be seen. She describes vulnerability as engaging authentically; as being "all in" (p. 2), and as "the core, the heart, the center of meaningful human experiences" (p. 12). Understood in these ways, vulnerability is the heart and soul of Cultural Proficiency.

Choosing to be vulnerable is what Brown (2012a) calls "daring greatly"—being simultaneously brave and afraid. We may feel fear, but we don't let fear control us. As Nelson Mandela (1995, p. 622) put it, "I learned that courage was not the absence of fear but the triumph over it." In facing our fear and deciding to journey through it, we choose to recognize that some things are more important than fear. For us, these more important things include the possibility of excellence with equity, reconciliation, and becoming our better selves.

The Cultural Proficiency journey invites each one of us to show up, starting with admitting to ourselves that we don't know what we don't know. Vulnerability is laying aside our need to be right, along with any self-deception that we already know everything worth knowing. Vulnerability means we are willing to see things in different and possibly new ways. In this sense, vulnerability could be defined as being open to what was previously unknown or hidden to us. It's radical self-honesty. As the Greek philosopher Socrates said, "The only true wisdom is in knowing you know nothing." We begin our search for wisdom with admitting our ignorance. In this way, we can define vulnerability as wisdom, or at least as the beginning of wisdom.

A facilitator helps participants choose vulnerability. To effectively do so with all participants, facilitators develop a perspective of vulnerability that includes sociopolitical dimensions. Without such, individualistic or culturally reductionistic views of vulnerability could result in disengagement and disillusionment among some participants—particularly those of us who regularly navigate the dominant culture from its margins. Therefore, facilitators work to understand how culture, power, and social context affect the willingness to choose vulnerability.

VULNERABILITY AND SOCIAL CONTEXT

The risks involved with choosing vulnerability differ from participant to participant based on their social contexts (Landreman, 2013). Because identity is a unique composite of various dimensions of difference—demographic categories and group memberships—participants' willingness to become vulnerable while exploring issues of identity, power, oppression, and privilege may vary depending on "which identities hold the most salience for a given participant at a given time" (Arao & Clemens, 2013, p. 139).

For instance, Jack's various dimensions of difference (Generation X'er, able-bodied, U.S. citizen, male, heterosexual, white, etc.) invite him to perceive different degrees of risk in regard to different topics: ageism, ableism, xenophobia, sexism, heterosexism, racism, and so on. As a member of a historically advantaged racial group, he might be more reticent in a conversation about racism than one about ageism. Regardless, different perceived risks and fears may influence the degree to which he or any other participant would be willing to be vulnerable.

For those of us from historically privileged/entitled groups and currently well-served by the system, Brené Brown's (2012a, 2012b) explanations of vulnerability may ring true without question or sideways glance. Choosing to show up and be seen; be brave and scared at the same time; and embrace uncertainty, risk, and emotional exposure might capture exactly what we recognize we need to do differently in order to engage with authenticity in cross-cultural dialogue on the journey.

However, those of us from historically oppressed groups and/or currently marginalized by the system may experience different and/or additional dimensions of vulnerability. Our daily lives might require navigation through the dominant culture in ways that already demand consistent and predictable risk-taking, acceptance of uncertainty, and simultaneously brave and scary action. Furthermore, like Ralph Ellison's *Invisible Man* (1952), at times we may think that we don't even have the option to show up and be seen because the dominant culture simply refuses to see us. Instead it opts to perceive a projection of its own stereotypes about our identity groups—especially groups with externally visible markers such as race, gender, physical ableness, socio-personal aesthetics (i.e., physical attractiveness), or even age. Thus when it comes to choosing vulnerability within historically unsupportive environments, those of us from historically oppressed or marginalized groups experience risks and sources of fear in ways that are different from the ways those of us with identities supported by the dominant culture experience them.

Yet Cultural Proficiency invites every participant to choose vulnerability. That means embracing risk, regardless of how risk manifests for each of us. In doing so, we are choosing to face and move through the sources of fear specific to our own social context.

Diversity and social justice educators Brian Arao and Kristi Clemens (2013) provide examples of various barriers to vulnerability. They posit that participants from historically privileged and entitled groups experience the following sources of fear and other negative energy states that can block vulnerability:

- Facing evidence of the existence of their unearned privilege and how they have benefitted from oppressive acts and systems.
- Reflecting on how and to what degree they have colluded with or participated in oppressive acts.

- Hearing stories of pain and struggle from historically disadvantaged social identity group members.
- Fielding direct challenges to their worldview from peers.

On the other hand, participants from historically oppressed and marginalized groups may be reluctant to choose vulnerability because of the likelihood of the following:

- Heightened pain, discomfort, and resentment resulting from sharing and listening to direct experiences with oppression (Arao & Clemens, 2013).
- Defensive moves of colleagues from entitled and privileged groups who dismiss or minimize their experiences of oppression, who condemn them as hypersensitive or unduly aggressive when expressing pain they experience as a result of oppression, or who disengage entirely due to an inability (e.g., white fragility) or unwillingness to tolerate even a minimal amount of discomfort (DiAngelo, 2011; Sparks, 2002).
- Being expected to assume the role of educator for unaware dominant group members, a role that can elicit anger, sadness, and fear of repercussions (Arao & Clemens, 2013).
- Historical lack of safety when not assimilating into the dominant culture, when criticizing the dominant system, or when naming their oppression and its perpetrators, especially if they are impassioned while doing so (Leonardo & Porter, 2010).

Each group (the privileged and the oppressed) faces different risks when choosing vulnerability. What is the essential difference? The answer can be expressed in two words: guilt and anger (Lindsey et al., 2013 p. 45). For those of us from historically oppressed groups, choosing vulnerability when presented with situations our past experience has deemed predictably painful, unsafe, disingenuous, or generally disappointing is a decision that risks generating negative energy that can feed into a sense of anger, agitation, or anguish. For those of us from historically entitled groups, the choice for vulnerability risks generating negative energy that can feed into a sense of guilt, helplessness, or shame.

It's clear that fears and risks differ significantly based on each participant's identity and the saliency of particular dimensions of difference. It's also clear that all participants experience the common dilemma of whether to choose vulnerability or protective armor. Facilitators help participants navigate this dilemma by strategically and skillfully shaping supportive learning environments.

THE NEED FOR BRAVE SPACE

Traditionally, facilitators of diversity and social justice conversations have used the term *safe space* to describe learning environments that enable participants to engage with authenticity. Essential to this notion is the facilitator's responsibility to foster an environment where everyone is able to fully participate without fear of attack, ridicule, or denial of experience (Holley & Steiner, 2005). Use of the term *safe space* intends to reassure fearful or anxious participant that they will, in fact, have a comfortable experience. However, promoting safety as the defining element of the learning environment may work against the type of engagement requisite for Cultural Proficiency.

Arao and Clemens (2013) argue convincingly for an alternative term: *brave space.* They build on healthy safe-space tenets such as establishing ground rules so that participants agree to expectations for engaging with one another. However, the concept of brave space challenges the notion that safety is necessary or always possible in conversations about diversity, inclusion, equity, and social justice. Instead of promoting an illusion of a risk-free environment that is absent of fear, brave space acknowledges the unavoidable risk, struggle, and discomfort (antitheses of safety) that accompany authentic engagement.

It should be noted that the words *safe* and *brave* are not mutually exclusive. We're not trading safety for violence. As Arao and Clemens write, "Violence of any kind—physical, emotional, and psychological—is antithetical to the aims of social justice work" (2013, p. 139). In that sense, the word *brave* does not mean treacherous. It means that it's necessary to liberate the character of the discussion from safe and guarded politeness into something more real.

Arao and Clemens (2013) drew inspiration from the concept of courageous conversations about race (Singleton & Linton, 2006; Sparks, 2002) to counter the unrealistic expectation of safety by recommending that facilitators instead emphasize the need for courage and risk-taking. By shifting the focus to courage instead of comfort, facilitators help participants rise to the challenge of Cultural Proficiency. They help groups better position themselves to journey toward their goals: becoming their better selves and achieving excellence with equity.

Reflection

The past three sections contained statements about vulnerability, social context, and brave space that may have resonated intensely with you. Some of the information may have rung true. Other information may conflict with your lived experience or worldview. The space below invites you to record your reactions to these three sections of text.

_____

_____

_____

_____

Review the bulleted lists of barriers to vulnerability in the section "Vulnerability and Social Context." Which are most poignant for you? From your perspective and lived experience, what barriers are missing from the lists?

_____

_____

_____

_____

REMOVING ARMOR THROUGH WORTHINESS

Given the perceived challenges of vulnerability, facilitators of Cultural Proficiency can expect some participants—regardless of race or ethnicity (or other dimensions of difference)—to show up wearing metaphorical armor. The motivations for putting on armor might differ from person to person, but it always serves the same purpose: emotional protection. Vulnerability is about removing the armor. As an aside, *armor* is a particularly applicable metaphor here. Armor is something worn into battle. But Cultural Proficiency is not a war. You can't achieve real peace through violence. All that is achieved through war is subjugation. That is why Cultural Proficiency is the quintessential peace effort.

Brown (2012a) employs the war metaphor by using the term *shield* to describe three forms of emotional defense (table 3.1). These are the self-imposed barriers to vulnerability that we must identify and name, Brown posits, in the process of removing our armor and choosing vulnerability (i.e., peace).

According to Brown (2012a), the key to putting down these defensive shields and taking off our armor is worthiness—a strong sense of love and belonging. That's what enables us to choose vulnerability. So how do we get some of this worthiness? Truth is, we don't get it through accomplishments or good deeds. We won't get it if we lose weight, land that job or promotion, fix our marriages, or interrupt acts of oppression. Actually, we won't ever get it . . . because we already have it. In reality, there is nothing to defend against because each of us is already whole and worthy in ourselves. We can't get worthiness from external sources, but we can recognize, realize, and cultivate our own inner worthiness. We do so by practicing courage, connection, and compassion (table 3.2).

Table 3.1 Shields as Barriers to Vulnerability

Shield	Potential Manifestations for Participants
Foreboding Joy: Imagining dreadful outcomes	I have better things to do. This is going to be a waste of time, divisive, and inflammatory. This will depress me. I'm going to feel agitated or angry. I'm going to feel guilty, helpless, or generally bad about myself. If I don't assimilate into the dominant culture, my career won't advance.
Perfectionism: Believing worth is based on approval gained for type and quality of actions	I don't know what to say and how to say it. I'm going to make a mistake. People are looking for me to misstep and not use the most up-to-date language. If I mess up, I'll be perceived poorly. I must portray an image that I have arrived at the destination. I'm going to be judged. Assimilation is the only way.
Numbing: Embracing anything that deadens the pain of discomfort and shame	Discussing commonalities and avoiding differences. Talking about dimensions of difference other than race. Switching the subject. Deflecting. Blaming the oppressed for causing discomfort. Resigning oneself to the status quo. Disengaging. Caretaking the privileged: Reassuring someone confronting their own privilege that they are not a bad person just because they've received unearned benefits from entitlement.

Source: Adapted from Brené Brown's "10 Guideposts for Wholehearted Living" within *The Gifts of Imperfection*.

Table 3.2 Creating a Transformative Learning Environment

FROM UNHEALTHY ENGAGEMENT Protective Armor and Inauthentic Engagement	TO HEALTHY ENGAGEMENT Vulnerability and Authentic Engagement

• Anger and guilt
• "Safe space"
  ○ Learning through comfort
  ○ Illusion of safety
  ○ Polite discussion
  ○ Guarded conversations
 	
• Sense of inadequacy
  ○ Cowardice
  ○ Relationship gap
  ○ Resentment
 	
• Dysfunctional behavior
  ○ Discount, deflect, resist, and retreat
  ○ Resist change
  ○ Accept oppression and subordination
  ○ Be unaware of entitlement and privilege or inactivity in response to awareness
	• Confidence
	• Brave space
	  ○ Learning through disequilibrium
	  ○ Reality of risk
	  ○ Courageous conversation
	  ○ Genuine dialogue
	
	• Sense of worthiness
	  ○ Courage
	  ○ Connection
	  ○ Compassion
	
	• Functional behavior
	  ○ Affirm, receive, accept, and advance
	  ○ Reflect on practices willingly
	  ○ Accept self-determination
	  ○ Accept personal responsibility

COCREATING A TRANSFORMATIVE ENVIRONMENT

The recipe for an environment that supports transformation and healing contains three essential and interrelated ingredients: worthiness, vulnerability, and authentic engagement. Facilitators play a critical role in helping group participants cocreate this context. Sure, it's important to design and implement activities that foster participant vulnerability and authentic engagement. More importantly, though, effective facilitators serve as role models by demonstrating vulnerability and authentic engagement themselves. As Malcolm X once said (Howard, 2015a, p. xv), "You can't lead where you won't go." Applied to Cultural Proficiency, this means that a facilitator's job is to lead a group to a place where everyone lays down their armor and chooses peace and authentic engagement.

Facilitators provide such leadership by engaging in their work with a strong sense of their own worthiness. Brown (2012a) refers to those of us who do so as the *wholehearted;* she provides ten guideposts for wholehearted engagement. These guideposts can serve as principles for facilitators to demonstrate worthiness, vulnerability, and authentic engagement. Through this modeling, these wholehearted facilitators influence group members to do likewise. Table 3.3 provides journal prompts to prepare for wholehearted facilitation by reflecting on and envisioning these principles.

Choosing to facilitate groups from a place of worthiness by demonstrating vulnerability and authentic engagement goes a long way to helping groups create the context for transformation through Cultural Proficiency. It enables participants to first be vulnerable in their inner conversations—the inner self-talk that we all have with ourselves.

Table 3.3 Wholehearted Facilitation: Worthiness, Vulnerability, and Authentic Engagement

Cultivate	Let Go of	Facilitator journal prompts and reflection questions
Authenticity	What People Think	• If participants really knew me, beyond my professional persona and assumptions about my perceived identity groups, they would know _____. • If I knew participants would extend love and not judgment toward me, my family, or my loved ones, I'd tell these stories about my lived experience: _____. • If I lived by the principle that what other people think of me is none of my business, then _____.
Self-Compassion	Perfectionism	• I make sure participants know that I am still on my journey toward _____. • I forgive myself for _____. • If I viewed feedback and suggestions as gifts, I would _____. • If I gave my energy to myself instead of to others' opinions of me, I would _____. • If I wasn't afraid to make mistakes or fail, I would _____.
Resilient Spirit	Numbing and Powerlessness	• For me, being comfortable with discomfort feels/looks/sounds like _____. • Today, things I can do to work against oppressive systems are _____. • I believe it is unjust to delay acting on my commitment to end oppression because _____.
Gratitude and Joy	Scarcity and Fear of the Dark	• When facilitating, I feel most alive when I am _____. • When facilitating, I don't worry about what skills or abilities I lack, such as _____. • During my life transition of _____, I am grateful for my time in the darkness: _____. • Ordinary moments of true connection with participants that bring me joy are _____. • I am grateful to be able to do this work because _____.
Intuition and Trusting Faith	Need for Certainty	• I help groups find their own answers by _____. • If I followed my gut and didn't look for assurances from others I would _____. • When taking action based on the vibes I pick up, I believe that things will work out because I assume _____.
Creativity	Comparison	• My unique qualities shine through my facilitative practices in these ways: _____. • I avoid the trap of conforming to and competing with my colleagues by _____. • When I'm facilitating at my best, I see it as art, in these ways: _____.
Play and Rest	Exhaustion as a Status Symbol and Productivity as Self-Worth	• I love facilitating because it aligns with my skill set of _____. • I remind myself that a packed schedule and past accomplishments are not sources of pride or brag-worthy status symbols in these ways: _____. • If I made sure that I got the sleep, rest, and rejuvenation I need with this work I would _____.
Calm and Stillness	Anxiety as a Lifestyle	• If, when facilitating, I set aside all distractions such as e-mails, texts, etc., I could _____. • I practice mindfulness while facilitating by _____. • If I were to set aside quiet time reserved solely for reflection I could _____.
Meaningful Work	Self-Doubt and What I'm "Supposed To" Do	• What I find most meaningful and inspiring in this work is _____. • My gifts that I need to share with the groups that I facilitate are _____. • If I were to show up to my work as my true self and let go of the facade I wear to make the dominant culture more comfortable for me, _____.
Laughter, Song, Dance	Being Cool and Always in Control	• In my role as a facilitator, I dance like nobody's watching by _____. • If I were laugh with participants, I would _____. • If I were to lead using music and motion, I would _____. • While facilitating, I use the arts as a medium to _____. • I create emotional and spiritual connections through laughter, song, and dance by _____.

Source: Adapted from Brené Brown's "10 Guideposts for Wholehearted Living" within *The Gifts of Imperfection*.

Through that inner dialogue, they can choose to be honest with themselves: to admit and embrace imperfection, to be willing to be wrong or incomplete in their understanding and perception, and to celebrate the fact that we can all grow in cross-cultural effectiveness and that we can grow together. Without inner vulnerability, there is no change. Without inner vulnerability, there is no responsibility or self-determination. There is only more of the same.

As facilitators, if we neglect the choice to see vulnerability and humility as strengths that we choose for ourselves, we put others at risk. Instead of helping groups embark on the Cultural Proficiency journey, we may unwittingly invite them on a trip leading to culturally *improficiency*. This term captures the essence of skilled incompetence (Argyris, 1990), a nonvulnerable dance that may pay lip service to Cultural Proficiency but actually keeps the status quo firmly in place.

SKILLED INCOMPETENCE: AVOIDING VULNERABILITY

The term *skilled incompetence* has an interesting history. In his study of how routine behaviors can wreak havoc within organizations, business theorist Chris Argyris coined the term *skilled incompetence*. He used it to describe how people—leaders in particular—within an organization become good at behaving in a specific way (skill) that ends up producing the results they may not want or intend to bring about (incompetence). In the context of Cultural Proficiency, people develop skill with avoiding vulnerability in conversations. Instead of removing their protective armor and defensive shields, they become skilled at wearing and polishing them.

Skilled incompetence prevents us from engaging in the process that would transform our schools in ways supportive of a healthy democracy. Thus, because of skilled incompetence, too many schools remain plagued by unhealthy issues emerging from diversity: increasingly segregated and unequal classrooms and schools, gaps in access and expectations among student demographic groups, and predictable disproportionality in student outcomes according to those same groups (U.S. Department of Education, 2012; Wells, Fox, & Cordova-Coba, 2016).

THE PARADOX OF INAUTHENTIC ENGAGEMENT

As facilitators, if we avoid vulnerability we promote some degree of inauthentic engagement. The term *inauthentic engagement* reflects a relational dynamic based on an absence of vulnerability that takes place between a person and another person, a group of people, or a task. Inauthentic engagement prevents us from being our most open and honest selves as we interact with each other, our tasks, and ourselves. It hinders meaningful connections and closes the door to transformation.

During their hallway conversation in Episode Three, Barbara promised Jack that the seminar experience would be well worth his time if he engaged with authenticity. Thus,

Barbara challenged Jack to engage in multiple ways, each with honesty and vulnerability: with himself, the group, the exercise, and the unknown.

In her gentle challenge, Barbara displays the wisdom of a culturally proficient facilitator. Facilitators must, above all, promote authentic engagement. To do otherwise is a waste of everyone's time. Furthermore, inauthenticity compromises the health and well-being of the individuals, the group, and the larger organization.

When environments encourage behavior that alienates people from themselves (inauthenticity), the results are toxic (Gino, Kouchaki, & Galinsky, 2015). Through inauthentic behavior, people violate the principle of being true to themselves. Psychological distress ensues. Metaphorically, we put ourselves into a box and close the lid. We hide behind professional masks. We play politics at work. We do or say what we think we're supposed to in order to protect ourselves, advance our careers, get what we want, or simply avoid causing what we perceive may be a problem. The results are disastrous. We don't do our best work. Eventually, we burn out, check out, or leave. Or perhaps worse, we soldier on incompetently. Inauthenticity is commonplace in relational environments: schools, seminars, workplaces, and even friendships and marriages.

Individual inauthenticity is certainly unhealthy. When entire groups are infected with the dynamic of inauthenticity, the results extend beyond individual ill-being (i.e., the opposite of well-being) and into organizational malaise, inefficiency, and general dysfunction. When individuals within a group cannot be vulnerable and authentic with each other, positive outcomes are undermined. In fact, these groups end up taking action in direct contradiction to their stated purpose. They create a paradox: they defeat the goal they set out to accomplish.

Take Jack's vulnerability dilemma, for instance. He is part of a leadership group assembled to become (and help their school district become) more culturally proficient. If Jack chooses to keep private his negative feelings about attending, he would engage with inauthenticity. He would "go along to get along," wearing his protective armor, behind which he would secretly believe the event was wasting his time. His inauthenticity would be motivated by his fear of being perceived badly. This lack of being true to himself would cause him conflict, stress, and perhaps anxiety. This malaise would strengthen his barrier (or shield) to authentic engagement with the group and with Cultural Proficiency.

Now imagine that every group member had similar feelings and took similar actions. They would fail to engage authentically with each other, themselves, and the task. Essentially, the group would be a bunch of individuals pretending to engage but privately yearning to be elsewhere doing other things. Frustration and anger (even if not expressed) would grow beneath the surface over the five days. By the end, participants would feel so relieved to be out of their misery that they would head out the door and never want to look back.

The group members would be no more culturally proficient than when they started. Most likely, they would have developed sufficient resentment to become less committed to this sort of work. As a result, the entire school district would suffer—most of all the students already on the margins—and any future efforts at Cultural Proficiency would be more challenging. The sad irony is that these educators who are dedicated (in theory, at least) to educational equity and inclusion would have worked against the very effort that could have transformed the system to that end. Through inauthenticity, the group would have defeated its own goal.

Management expert Jerry B. Harvey describes this cycle of inauthenticity through a cautionary anecdote (1974, p. 63). The following is a widespread and commonly told version of Harvey's *The Abilene Paradox.*

On a hot afternoon visiting in Coleman, Texas, the family is comfortably playing dominoes on a porch, until the father-in-law suggests that they take a trip to Abilene [53 miles north] for dinner. The wife says, "Sounds like a great idea." The husband, despite having reservations because the drive is long and hot, thinks that his preferences must be out-of-step with the group and says, "Sounds good to me. I just hope your mother wants to go." The mother-in-law then says, "Of course I want to go. I haven't been to Abilene in a long time."

The drive is hot, dusty, and long. When they arrive at the cafeteria, the food is as bad as the drive. They arrive back home four hours later, exhausted.

One of them dishonestly says, "It was a great trip, wasn't it?" The mother-in-law says that, actually, she would rather have stayed home, but went along since the other three were so enthusiastic. The husband says, "I wasn't delighted to be doing what we were doing. I only went to satisfy the rest of you." The wife says, "I just went along to keep you happy. I would have had to be crazy to want to go out in the heat like that." The father-in-law then says that he only suggested it because he thought the others might be bored.

The group sits back, perplexed that they together decided to take a trip which none of them wanted. They each would have preferred to sit comfortably, but did not admit to it when they still had time to enjoy the afternoon.

Source: Wikipedia. *Abilene paradox.* Retrieved from https://en.wikipedia.org/wiki/Abilene_paradox

As facilitators, we can learn much from this story about the dismal effects of inauthenticity. It points us to the necessity of impressing on participants the need to "skip the trip to Abilene" (skip inauthentic engagement) and instead embark with authentic engagement on the Cultural Proficiency journey. There is no way around or shortcut to authentic engagement. In fact, authentic engagement itself is the way to becoming our better selves.

Reflection

Take a moment to review the chapter and consider the ideas presented about vulnerability and authentic engagement. What resonated with you? Why?

Within organizations, to what degrees have you experienced authentic engagement as the norm? How might your organization look different if each person engaged with each other with authenticity? How might society look different?

_____

_____

_____

_____

How does vulnerability look from your vantage point, considering your identity and dimensions of difference? Who might you need to be in order to help groups remove barriers to authentic engagement, to "skip the trip to Abilene," and embark on the Cultural Proficiency journey?

_____

_____

_____

_____

DIALOGIC ACTIVITY

1. Individually write and/or review reflections from this chapter.

2. Use the helping trios protocol (table 3.4) to share reflections, listen to different perspectives, increase understanding, and generate common meaning in response to this chapter.

Table 3.4 Helping Trios Protocol

Step	Procedure
1.	Participants form triads. Letter off A–B–C.
2.	Person A selects, shares, and talks about his/her reflections without interruption. B and C listen. (Use a designated time period such as four minutes.)
3.	B and C ask clarifying questions and A responds. (Use half the time period you used in step 2.)
4.	A, B, and C dialogue about A's reflections. (Use same time period as in step 2.)
5.	Repeat steps 2 to 4 for B and then repeat again for C.
Tips:	• Display the time parameters for steps 2–4 on chart paper. Consider projecting an online stopwatch if there are numerous trios.

Source: Adapted from CampbellJones, CampbellJones, and Lindsey. (2010), p. 47.

4 A Process of Transformation

Without a sense of identity, there is no need for struggle.

—*Paulo Freire* (The Politics of Education, *1985*)

Perhaps one of the most difficult things for a facilitator to do is to allow someone to struggle. To rescue people from the struggle immediately shuts off an opportunity for them to learn and grow. Supporting and encouraging them through the struggle is much more rewarding for everyone involved.

—*Trevor Bentley* (Facilitation, *2000*)

Nothing ever goes away until it has taught us what we need to know.

—*Pema Chödrön* (When Things Fall Apart, *2005*)

Maybe you have to know the darkness before you can appreciate the light.

—*Madeleine L'Engle* (A Ring of Endless Light, *1980*)

To bring about structural change, lasting change, awareness is not enough.

—*Barack Obama* (2016)

Ojibwe prophecies speak of a time during the seventh fire when our people will have the choice between two paths. The first path is well-worn and scorched. The second path is new and green. It is our choice as communities and individuals.

—*Winona LaDuke*
(Launching a Green Economy for Brown People, *2008*)

If you are neutral on situations of injustice, you have chosen the side of the oppressor.

—*Desmond Tutu* (quoted in Brown, 1984)

GETTING CENTERED

Review these quotations. What resonates with you? Why? In your personal life, have you experienced a transformative process that involved going through a struggle or a time of darkness? In what ways do you see Cultural Proficiency as something more comprehensive than simply changing behaviors or trying new techniques (such as new teaching strategies)?

_____

_____

_____

_____

THE FUEL OF TRANSFORMATION: OUR WILLINGNESS TO BE DISTURBED

Vulnerability and authentic engagement precede transformation. They are essential to the process of transformation that is Cultural Proficiency. In *Turning to One Another*, Margaret Wheatley (2008, p. 42) writes, "As we work to restore hope to the future, we need to include a new and strange ally—our willingness to be disturbed." In other words, the essence of transformation is our willingness to be open to seeing things differently; and, it is important to note, what we see may initially disturb us.

To see things differently, we need to stop clinging to our original individual points-of-view. Albert Einstein was talking about this concept when he said, "We can't solve problems by using the same kind of thinking we used when we created them." That is why we can progress on our Cultural Proficiency journey only when we admit that our individual perspectives fail to provide us with the full picture. We don't have all the answers. That's vulnerability: letting go of our certainty; expecting and accepting that we will not understand (at first) but will grow into understanding as we move along. Our beliefs will be disturbed. Perhaps we can even learn to welcome these disturbances.

This is why we assemble in seminars, workshops, meetings, discussion groups, and such: to disturb each other. Not in a mean-spirited way, of course, but in a way that interrupts our usual patterns of thinking. When we allow ourselves to be vulnerable, we are able to authentically engage in relationship with each other, as well as to engage in relationship with uncertainty. We learn to listen carefully to one another instead of advocating for our own positions. We listen for differences, surprises, and disturbances in ideas and perspectives instead of clinging to what we think we know. These disturbances help us see our own beliefs more clearly and, subsequently, help us surface the assumptions and values behind our beliefs. Once visible, we (as individuals and as organizations) have the opportunity to consciously choose these assumptions and values again or to jettison them and develop new ones more in line with our goals (Wheatley, 2001).

When we choose to surrender our beliefs and accept new positive truths about others, we are choosing to transform into our better selves. Transformation is more than abstract change: it's a thorough and dramatic change in form—a metamorphosis. After all, you could theoretically change a caterpillar into a butterfly by gluing wings onto it. But the caterpillar will transform into a butterfly only after it goes through its own process of shedding, dissolving, and reforming itself into a different creature. During the middle of its process, the caterpillar literally dissolves its own tissue, digesting itself into a soupy mess—a metaphoric broth filled with chunky bits of organs and clusters of cells. Brené Brown (2015, p. 28) describes this middle stage of any transformational process in her book *Rising Strong*: "The middle is messy, but it's also where the magic happens." Although well worth it, a transformative process is a tough (and somewhat yucky) process; it's certainly not nice and neat.

Likewise, personal and organizational transformation is tough, messy, and time-consuming. Unlike Clark Kent changing into Superman, the caterpillar doesn't open a door, step into a chrysalis, quickly change its clothes, and then emerge a butterfly. Although we can quickly change surface-level behaviors (add a diversity activity, adopt new words, hang up a multicultural bulletin board, try new instructional strategies), we aren't transformed until we progress through our own journeys of interrupting old patterns of thinking, shedding unhelpful expectations and beliefs, dissolving unhealthy assumptions into a yucky mess, and forming a new identity (way of seeing ourselves) by choosing to change our hearts (attitudes) and minds (core values and beliefs).

Essentially, transformation into our better selves is why we gather in community on our Cultural Proficiency journey. With guidance from an effective facilitator, we assist each other in our process of transformation. Through authentic engagement, we help one another change our hearts and minds. That is real, sustainable change. Once we could only crawl; now we can fly. Like the butterfly, we can't go back to what we were before.

Reflection

What are your reactions to any of these thoughts? "A transformative process is a tough (and somewhat yucky) process; it's certainly not nice and neat." "We can quickly change surface-level behaviors, but we aren't transformed until we progress through our own journeys." "Transformation into our better selves is why we gather in community." Other?

_____

_____

_____

_____

EPISODE FOUR: SEEING WITH JACK'S NEW EYES

Jack's seminar was drawing to an end. The powerful and positive transforming experience of the past five days had wildly exceeded anything he could have imagined. He glanced at his smartphone and could hardly believe that only ninety minutes remained. Barbara's voice interrupted his thoughts.

Barbara: In twenty minutes, we'll gather in a circle at the back of the room where we'll share reflections about the past five days. But first you'll have time to write your reflections. We invite you to write about your journey during this seminar. You have blank space for this in your handouts. Feel free to move outside this room, if you like. I'll ring the chime when it's time to return.

Jack left the room and found an unoccupied couch in the hallway. He flipped to the blank pages at the back of his handouts. His thoughts raced. How to get started? He wanted to write about his journey—the process he was beginning to understand. He also wanted to write about the ways he had changed. He decided the best way to start journaling was to just start writing.

It's hard to believe that I didn't want to be here. I had expected to be lectured about different cultures, achievement gap data, and what we needed to do differently. To my surprise, I ended up learning about myself—more than I could have imagined. More than I even knew about myself a week ago. I'm now different. I feel different. And I now see myself and my role within the school district much differently.

Somewhere over the course of these five days, I started to question my motivation and the effectiveness of my efforts to serve each of our students well. I've realized that despite my best intentions, some of the ways in which I've been working with curriculum and with fellow educators were most likely perpetuating the very same system of oppression from which I've been trying to rescue our underserved students. I know for sure that from now on I'll be working in a different manner, in a way informed by Cultural Proficiency.

I realized that I've been thinking about my work as rescuing underserved students from the margins. If I'd been asked, I would have said that I was doing it for them. They're the victims of oppressive systems and they deserve justice. I've been thinking of myself as someone who can empower them—a hero of sorts. After all, I've always believed that helping others is the right thing to do. All of this has fed into a sense of pride I've had for myself and my work.

But now I wonder how much my actions have been fueled by subconscious guilt related to privilege. I've been aware of my privilege for a long time, but now I realize that I've tried to distance myself from it. I think I've even worked to become an exception from the system in the eyes of others. (Perhaps a "good" heterosexual, right-handed, cisgender, white male?) I've focused my work (and my frustrations) on "other" people with power and privilege—the classroom teachers who need to change and other educators (especially white educators) who "don't get it."

Relatedly, I also wonder if I've become dependent on praise and acceptance from students, families, professional organizations, and groups such as the NAACP (who recently praised my math curriculum work). These accolades have been fueling me. But I don't want that to be the source of my motivation. I want to be my best self, and that means my motivation has to be sustainable and come from within.

The good news is that I feel like these five days have helped me become clearly in tune with my passion for justice, and it's sustainable. I want to do my work as an educator for "us"—me, you, and our collective future. In fact, there is no "them." I want to work in community, with (not just for) students, families, marginalized and historically under-served groups. . . . And with others who are well-served by the dominant culture (instead of trying to separate myself from "them").

I now realize that all of us—the well-served and the badly served—are harmed by systems of oppression and privilege, and we all need to liberate ourselves from these systems. Racism harms me as a white person, although not in the same or comparable ways that it harms a black person. Similarly, sexism harms me as a man. In fact, all of the "isms" keep all of us from connecting with our full humanity, achieving our full potential, experiencing love through authentic relationships, and liberating ourselves spiritually.

I also realize that I can't actually empower anyone other than myself. I can, however, use my power to create space where people can empower themselves. I'm going to start with the space I create for the math teachers whom I serve. I know that I haven't been as effective as I could be in working with them.

Reflection

This is a good place to pause and notice how you are reacting to the ideas woven into Jack's reflections about how his identity is changing. What ideas stick out for you? How are you reacting on an emotional level? On an intellectual level?

_____

_____

_____

_____

Jack stopped writing for a moment. He gazed up and imagined how his math workshops could look differently if he led with participants instead of for them. But he didn't want to run out of writing time without getting all his thoughts and reflections about these five days down on paper. He continued writing.

Reflecting on the ways I've changed is helping me understand what Lillie Cohen meant when she invited me to participate and embark on this "journey" through a "facilitated process." This seminar—this facilitated journey—was something quite different from a presentation or a training. And to think that I dismissed these terms as the latest jargon buzzwords when Lillie used them in her e-mail originally inviting me to this seminar. Ouch. Well, we live and learn. Facilitation, process, journey, transformation—they are exactly the right words. There's no way a presenter could have presented to me my own journey. I had to go through my own process of transformation: discovering things about my self, understanding who I want to be, committing to becoming different, and coming out on the other side transformed. I see that now.

I've even thought critically about that loaded term that's thrown around so much: politi-cally correct. *I've used it myself and a few of my colleagues at the office like to joke about* the "politically correct police." People who feel negatively about diversity work—even some politicians—use it as if it were an infringement or a straightjacket. It seems like it's always used pejoratively. But it does have a positive meaning. What does that term represent if not to be socially motivated? To be motivated by concern for the greater good of the whole? To recognize the us factor and to want to see that reflected in the use of language?

And I understand more about the term facilitate and the role of a facilitator. As facilitators, Barbara and Frank helped me . . . helped all of us on our journey. They're process-helpers. That role is definitely different from my usual role of presenter in the classroom or my workshops. In the future, I'd love to learn more about what they do and how they do it. For now, though, I want to reflect on my process of transformation. It would help to start at the beginning.

The first day of the seminar shook me up. I felt disoriented. Instead of talking about students, we were talking about ourselves—in great depth. Much more than the usual quick ice-breaker at the start of a workshop. After a few hours, it really confused me. However, I now see that much of the first day helped us, as a group, turn our attention inward and develop trust. We needed to reflect on our lived experience, our beliefs, and our values.

During that same time, we were learning and practicing communication skills for listening, inquiry, and dialogue. This was also different for me. I expected to get information from the presenters about teaching students . . . not to practice processes that would improve my communication skills and relationships. That's when the pieces started falling into place for me. I started to understand Lillie's description of "a process led by our facilitators." They were outfitting us with tools for our journey by having us engage in these exercises. They were helping us make it easier to have open, honest, and remarkably real conversations about diversity, inclusion, equity, and social justice. They were guiding us as we started to travel together on our Cultural Proficiency journey. The more we practiced dialogue and explored our own stories about diversity, the more trust I felt in the room. We were able to dig deeper with every conversation.

One of the remarkable things the facilitators did was help us create working agreements with the goal of creating brave space. I hadn't heard the term brave space before, but the concept made sense. We had to work together in a way that helped us each courageously confront ourselves and engage with each other around topics that are often taboo—race, class, privilege, sexual orientation, etc. We couldn't let fear, guilt, or anger stop us. So we made agreements.

Several working agreements I found particularly helpful were to speak and listen with an open mind, expect to be disturbed, and agree that what we share here stays here. We revisited all of our agreements every day in order to affirm them and assess how we were doing with them. On Day 3 we even amended "what we share here stays here" by tacking on "but we take our insights with us." After the second day, I think we all knew that this experience was changing us in meaningful ways and we wanted to make sure that we would also make meaningful changes within our practices after the seminar was over.

At one point, we must have seemed reluctant to speak honestly in a discussion that involved the topic of sexual orientation. Barbara had us raise our hands and feel our backs *to remind us that we had a backbone (CampbellJones & Associates, 2005). We had a great laugh! As we discussed this simple exercise of connecting with our spines, the point became clear. We do, indeed, already possess all the power that we need. We already have backbones. Courage isn't the absence of fear: it's experiencing fear and moving ahead anyway. Barbara and Frank helped us get in touch with that power.*

Reflection

In what ways does Jack's reflections affirm your beliefs about high-quality professional learning as a means to the ethical goal of excellence with equity in education? What do you question?

_____

_____

_____

_____

On Day 2, I had what I can only describe as a courageous conversation with Tom Joy, my former principal from my elementary-school teaching days. We were paired up to discuss our reactions to a video that focused on race and identity. During that conversation, Tom had shared some of his experiences as an African American man working in Stocklin County for twenty years. Then he simply asked me, "So what's it like for you to work here as a young white man?" I paused at his question. After a few seconds, I spoke with 100 percent honesty. "I don't know. I don't think I've ever really thought it out."

That's when it hit me. It's because of my white privilege that I hadn't thought about it long enough to have a thought-out response. I'd never felt any need to do so. That was a new level of insight for me regarding ways in which the dominant culture serves me well (and didn't serve Tom well). There were things I didn't need to even think about. I realized that I can't distance myself from privilege, but that's exactly what I've been unconsciously trying to do.

Tom asked some great questions that helped me process my experiences as a "young white man." We talked about my experiences as well as others' experiences with me. We explored how people who self-identify other than white may experience me—especially people with whom I don't have an authentic relationship. It became clear that the first things people notice about me are that I'm white and male. They don't see the real me; they see their own projections of assumptions associated with whiteness and maleness.

No matter how nuanced or atypical my life has been, people who don't know me see me as white and male. Period. They don't see that I moved here from another country, started out in poverty, lived in a housing project, and was raised by a mother who was single and on welfare for several years. They'll see a simpler story: White. Male. Advantaged. They'll subconsciously attach all the cultural meanings and privileges they associate with whiteness and maleness to me, associations such as all-American boy, suburbs with a white picket fence, etc. Basically, they'll assume the best—not the worst—of the American narrative based on my external and immutable characteristics.

The conversation with Tom also helped me better understand some of my other dimensions of difference and my own experiences with systemic disadvantage. Specifically, we discussed my experience as a lone male elementary-school teacher on an otherwise all-female staff (except Tom, who was the principal). In that context, my age and gender worked against me in a number of ways. Tom helped me deepen my understanding of the dynamics behind the suspicion I sometimes felt from students' parents, my discomfort at social gatherings planned by the all-female social committee, and the sideways glances I'd sometimes get when I'd tell noneducators that I was an elementary-school teacher. In that context, I was not well served by the dominant culture. No wonder I felt such a huge relief when I made the jump to middle school.

Furthermore, being the only male teacher in an elementary school wasn't my only problem. At age twenty-one, I was the youngest staff member and I looked even younger than my years. This seemed to undermine my credibility with my older colleagues. I remember a few hurtful comments and snide looks. Around that time, I'd started wearing glasses for night driving. After a few friends told me the glasses made me look more mature and professional, I started wearing them to work—all the time. Doing that damaged my eyesight and now I actually need to wear glasses. All because of my efforts to appease the dominant culture.

Although the intensity of this example doesn't compare to that of racism, sexism, or heterosexism, it does help me continue to develop sensitivity to and respect for other people's feelings and experiences with systemic oppression. Especially those with the highest stakes: succeeding in school, gaining employment with decent wages, having access to health care. It makes me wonder about the ways people change themselves to fit in with the dominant culture and its normative values. Makes me think about the physical damage—not to mention the emotional, psychological, and spiritual damage— that follows those efforts. Seems to me the farther out you are on the margins, the more you have to change aspects of yourself in order to cash in on the dominant culture's benefits. That is . . . unless we focus on changing the dominant culture. Aha. There it is—the insight.

All of this is helping me gain clarity around what I can do with my own socialization, privilege, and power. I know I can't distance myself from privilege. I can, however, illuminate it and take responsibility for doing what I can to change society's patterns of injustice. In that way, I can use my power to dismantle the systems that confer the unearned privilege in the first place.

I can start by working in a more culturally proficient way with the math teacher workshops I lead. I know that I can do more to encourage authentic, critical conversations and reflection about these issues. I've spent years teaching teachers what they should do. But I'd never thought about facilitating an ongoing conversation about why we have become who we are and what we must do to become who we want to be. The Cultural Proficiency Framework will help. It gives me, my fellow math educators, and their schools the tools for how to use our privilege and power for equity and equality.

Reflection

How are you reacting to the ideas woven into Jack's reflections at this point? Through your lived experience, what ideas can you relate to? What ideas can't you relate to?

_____

_____

_____

_____

The conversation with Tom was only one of many challenging, worthwhile, and enlightening conversations we had as a group. These conversations weren't always easy for us. I know they weren't for me. Sharing my personal experiences with colleagues, reflecting on my own complicity and privilege, and listening to painful stories of others' oppression and mistreatment wasn't fun. It wasn't as if we were sitting around the campfire singing Kumbaya and roasting marshmallows. At various times, I felt uncomfortable, nervous, even scared.

It was during those times of discomfort that Barbara and Frank amazed me most. Several times, our emotions flowed freely. There were tears. Once, a close friend's anger surfaced. Whenever emotions ruled our group, the facilitators worked their magic. They seemed to be okay with the silence that followed outbursts. After the silence, they always asked just the right question to open us up as individuals and to bring us together as a group. And they did everything with such positive energy and spirit.

I can best describe this part of the process as the darkness. It wasn't dark just because of sadness involved with oppression: it was dark because it was the unknown. In truth, each of us was "in the dark" in various ways long before this seminar. However, by courageously choosing to explore, share, and listen to what was outside of our lived experience, we were choosing to sit in the darkness. Although often uncomfortable and scary, it was well worth it. In the end, the experience led me to insights I never could have imagined when I first walked into the seminar. It also led us to commitment as a group working for equity.

As we continued to explore the unknown and discover insights, something clicked for me. It clicked for all of us, I think, as if we had coalesced around a group commitment: to do whatever we can as district leaders to shape a culture of excellence with equity. Because culture represents the predominant values and beliefs, we need to work together as educators to surface and examine our own values and beliefs. That requires us to question our tradition of how we educate students. We—as a system—need to do more of what we've been doing here over the past five days. If we make this type of critical approach our norm, then we can interrupt the traditions of inequity and exclusion and create a new tradition of excellence with equity.

I wouldn't trade the conversations and insights I've gained for the world. I can only describe them as emerging from the darkness and stepping into the light.

Barbara's chime rang and Frank's voice called everyone to the back of the room. Jack stood up and moved in that direction. He could hardly wait to hear what reflections the others would share about their experiences.

Reflection

How are you reacting to the metaphors of sitting in the darkness and emerging into the light? What's coming up for you?

_____

_____

_____

_____

A PROCESS OF TRANSFORMATION

In his written reflection, Jack describes his process of inner growth and consciousness development. Throughout the ages, this growth process has been described through various metaphors and analogies. Russian mystic and philosopher George Gurdjieff compared inner transformation to a butterfly's metamorphosis. Islamic scholar and Persian poet Rumi talked about it in evolutionary terms, such as growth from animal nature to human, human nature to angel, and angelic nature to a state that we cannot yet imagine. Sufi mystics, such as Rumi, likened the seeker's inner process to the journey of a traveler on the path. Advaita Vedanta—school of Hindu nondualistic philosophy—illustrated refinement of human consciousness by employing changes in states of matter, such as ice to water to steam.

Perhaps the use of light as metaphor for consciousness (and Consciousness) is used more than any other. The Jewish mystical Kabbalah posits the existence of a spark of the divine in every human being. In Christianity, Jesus described both himself and his disciples as the light of the world. Buddhism refers to a divine light within every person.

A common analogy for inner growth and consciousness development is the process of enlightenment—the dawning of the light. The word _enlightenment_ implies a journey: an emergence from a previous state of darkness and subsequent movement into the light. Here, darkness is the unknown (unconsciousness). In this analogy, darkness is not bad; it just is. Swiss psychologist Carl Gustav Jung (1967, p. 23) described the role of darkness in the process of enlightenment when he wrote, "The beginning, where everything is still one, and which therefore appears as the highest goal, lies at the bottom of the sea, in the darkness of the unconscious." In other words, darkness gives birth to light.

In his reflection, Jack used darkness and light to describe the progress of his own Cultural Proficiency journey. Without using the terms, he described the _inside-out_ and _emergent process_ that includes three essential Phases. Table 4.1 provides information— including a metaphoric representation related to enlightenment—about each of these three Phases. In the course of describing Cultural Proficiency as a journey, part II of this book provides more detail about these three Phases. The remainder of this chapter

Table 4.1 Enlightenment as a Metaphoric Journey: Three Phases		
Phase of Process	**Aspect of Enlightenment Metaphor**	**Stages and Details**
Awareness (Inside)	*Sitting in the darkness*	Looking within. Exercising vulnerability. Developing group trust. Surfacing and sharing stories, beliefs, and assumptions. Exploring the unknown. Using the Cultural Proficiency Framework to increase awareness.
Commitment	*Emerging from the darkness*	Discovering meaning. Developing new perspectives. Committing to Cultural Proficiency as a way of being. Dedicating attention and energy to actions that support excellence with equity.
Action (Out)	*Moving toward the light*	Using the Cultural Proficiency Framework to plan for improving practices and policies. Implementing intentional moral action. Implementing strategic planning. Harvesting results. Influencing the system.

focuses on sitting in the darkness as an uncomfortable yet necessary stage in the process of transformation, enlightenment, and stepping into the light. Sitting in the darkness is the inside portion of the inside-out process; the inside-out process is the stage during which we develop the awareness that leads us to commitment.

SITTING IN THE DARKNESS

Jack described the metaphor of sitting in the darkness when he wrote about feeling uncomfortable, nervous, and even scared at times, and when he recounted exploring what had been previously unknown to him. This is the dark period of the journey—akin to the mystical dark night of the soul—that is a requisite phase of the transformation process.

Consider the caterpillar inside its chrysalis or the seed buried underground. Both sit in the dark. Similarly, the Cultural Proficiency journey invites us to voluntarily step into the darkness. This darkness is what we do not (yet) know, what is beyond our lived experiences. It involves listening to others' stories, especially when doing so is discomforting. It also involves trusting the experiences of those who seem different from us. They may appear to be different, but because of our common humanity they are not separate from us. We are always meeting ourselves. There is no "other"; there is only "us."

Darkness is also a metaphor for what we find uncomfortable or even painful. When we sit in the darkness listening to each other, we share, explore, and discover our participation in traditions that maintain and propagate systems of privilege and oppression like institutionalized racism, heterosexism, classism, ableism, xenophobia, and so on. Through doing this, we begin to recognize and remove our self-imposed barriers to cultural competence and proficiency. This phase of the journey requires us not only to sit in the darkness, but also to remove the barriers to the light.

Sitting in the darkness is the Awareness Phase—a delicate period in the Cultural Proficiency process. Guiding it requires substantial skill of facilitators, who must be prepared to intervene on multiple levels. Sharing stories of oppression and privilege can trigger negative energy states such as fear, which can cause the brain to downshift into the reptilian brain—the limbic system—that controls the fight-or-flight response. Without effective facilitator intervention at this point, negative motives can consume a group: conversations can shift from dialogue to debate, and participants can shift from excited and engaged to cynical and disillusioned. The group's energy can devolve into a fight or flight where participants resort to intellectual debate (fight) in order to escape (flight) vulnerability. Due to our society's painful history of inequality, injustice, and social dominance, it's all too easy to try to distance ourselves by projecting anger, guilt, blame, and shame (which are manifestations of fight in this situation) instead of engaging with authenticity.

This is when we need to remember—or be reminded of—our courage, and then to extend that courage into courageous conversations (Singleton & Linton, 2006). Courage is not the absence of fear; it is acting despite feeling afraid. This lesson was learned by the Cowardly Lion (*The Wizard of Oz;* Baum, 1910), who believed his fear made him cowardly. The shame and guilt he felt as a result blocked his recognition of his innate courage. Like him, we are not cowardly because we feel fear. Each of us has the innate courage to make the transformational journey through the wilderness of inherited (and often culturally destructive, incapacitating, and/or reductionistic) beliefs and assumptions. Through that transformation we can return home, like Dorothy did in the *Wizard of Oz* (Baum, 1910)— back to our natural and best state—into a place of community where we safeguard freedom and equality for everyone.

When we sit in the darkness, it's helpful to recognize and acknowledge the presence of the fear that sits with us. Without fear, there would be no need for courage. In her poem "What to Do in the Darkness," Marilyn Chandler McEntyre (2004) offers words to support us in claiming our power through courage, responsibility, and self-determination while sitting in the darkness.

Go slowly

Consent to it

But don't wallow in it

Know it as a place of germination

And growth

Remember the light

Take an outstretched hand if you find one

Exercise unused senses

Find the path by walking it

Practice trust

Watch for dawn

McEntyre (2004) invites us to have patience and trust the process. On our Cultural Proficiency journey, sitting in the darkness is a temporary but necessary experience. It fosters awareness, leads to commitment, and fuels the intentional moral action necessary to overcome the painful, divisive, and oppressive legacies of our shared history and to create new traditions that secure the promise of democracy for everyone. Before the light of dawn, there is always the darkness of the night.

The need for darkness is obvious in our analogy of the butterfly's metamorphosis. The caterpillar created a dark space for itself. To someone lacking knowledge of the transformational process, it might seem that the caterpillar created its own coffin. For once in that dark space, it quite literally digests parts of itself by releasing enzymes that break down its tissues, turning them to mush. To the untrained eye the dark space could be seen as nothing more than a sack of a liquidated caterpillar.

But to someone who understands this biological process of transformation, it's merely a period in the organism's process of changing into a completely different form. For within that sack of mush are essential embryonic cells (just as within each of us is our essential humanity). These sets of embryonic cells are called *imaginal disks*; they grow rapidly into the wings, legs, antennae, and organs of the butterfly that will soon emerge from its dark space into the light of the world. If that butterfly could talk, it surely would not describe its time in the darkness as a fun time. It would probably describe it as a time of intense discomfort, to put it mildly. However, it would also recognize its time in the darkness as an absolutely necessary part of an amazing and life-changing process. In fact, there is a proverb that says "Just when the caterpillar thought the world was over, it became a butterfly."

Cultural Proficiency can be a life-changing process for the better. That's why those of us on the journey continuously choose—courageously so—to sit in the darkness for a while. In that dark space, we can get in touch with our essential humanity and rebuild ourselves into butterflies. Adopting this perspective helps us see sitting in the darkness as a necessary period of growth in the process of becoming our better selves. Messy? Probably. Miraculous? Absolutely.

EMERGENCE AND NECESSITY OF STRUGGLE

All Phases of the Cultural Proficiency process involve struggle, particularly the phase of emerging from the darkness. The struggle is a necessary part of a group's journey, and it's important for facilitators to enable constructive struggle and not perpetuate codependency. Thus, they resist well-meaning urges to jump in to help, do participants' or groups' thinking for them, and thus short-circuit the process. After all, Cultural Proficiency is a process, not a problem to be fixed. The importance of a facilitator possessing the ability to observe the struggle is captured in an unknown-authored, widely available, and often-adapted anecdote about a butterfly emerging from the darkness.

A man found a butterfly chrysalis. (A butterfly makes a chrysalis; a moth makes a cocoon.) One day a small opening appeared in the chrysalis. The man sat and watched the butterfly for several hours as it struggled to squeeze its body through the tiny hole. Then it stopped as if it couldn't go any further. So the man decided to help the butterfly.

He took a pair of scissors and snipped off the remaining bits of cocoon. The butterfly emerged easily, but . . . it had a swollen body and shriveled wings. The man continued to watch it, expecting that any minute the wings would enlarge and expand enough to support the body.

Neither happened. In fact, the butterfly spent the rest of its life crawling around on the ground. It was never able to fly. Here is what the man in his kindness and haste didn't understand: the butterfly can fly only because it has to struggle to come out of the chrysalis. The pushing forces enzymes from the body to the wing tips, strengthening the wing muscles and reducing body weight. Without outside interference, the process starts with struggle and ends with the butterfly flying after it emerges from the chrysalis.

Culturally proficient facilitators understand that a group's struggle is what makes the group and the individuals within the group strong. In Cultural Proficiency, emerging from the darkness involves removing barriers to the light. The group must remove its own barriers; doing so is not the work of the facilitators. Therefore, skilled facilitators resist impulses to control information or group activity (as they would if they were wearing the hat of presenter or trainer). Control that leads to codependency won't help the group build its capacity to fly. It may instead ensure the group's fate is similar to that of the stunted butterfly that was destined to crawl around on its belly until its earth-bound demise.

TRANSFORMATIVE LEARNING

Jack's reflections also illustrate transformative learning. Mezirow (2000) describes transformative learning as growth that involves changing the frames of reference that we use to make sense of our lives. Our frame of reference—or our worldview—operates like a pair of eyeglasses that filter our reality; the lens structures the way that we interpret our own identity and the meaning of our experiences. Our worldview (that is selective by its very nature) is what guides our actions and provides the rationale for those actions. When we engage in transformative learning, we consciously and intentionally choose the lens through which we see. We make this choice in accordance with our highest values. The result is the development of a different worldview of self and others. It's like wearing a new pair of magical eyeglasses that change the way we experience everything around us. It's a new way of seeing and a new way of being.

To illustrate how transformational learning differs from other types of personal and organizational learning, Lindsey et al. (2013) describe three types of learning: single-loop, double-loop, and triple-loop. Figure 4.1 displays the relationship between these three types of learning, each applicable to individual or organizations.

Single-loop learning represents efforts in learning how to change behavior. For instance, this pattern of learning is reflected in a school that receives training on implementation of a new instructional strategy. The focus is on improving behavior to improve effectiveness of results. The individual (or organization) learning the new behavior does not question the theory, thinking, and assumptions behind the new actions.

Double-loop learning extends the single-loop pattern into two dimensions. Here the focus is on questioning and changing the assumptions and theory behind the behavior. For instance, this pattern is reflected in a school that focuses on understanding premises behind cooperative approaches to learning and implications for diversity and inclusion. What emerges from double-loop learning is an entirely new way of thinking and, subsequently, doing things.

Triple-loop learning adds a third level—the level requisite to Cultural Proficiency— where individuals learn how to learn about who they are and what they are about (identity).

Figure 4.1 Triple-Loop Learning

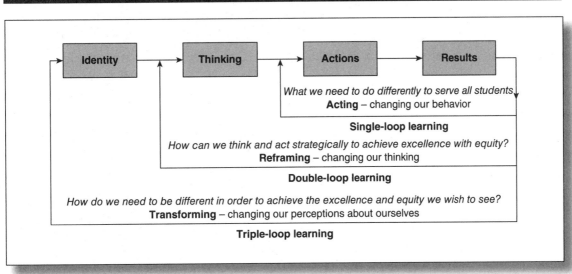

Sources: Double-loop learning adapted from Chris Argyris. (1990). *Overcoming Organizational Defenses: Facilitating Organizational Learning*. Needham, MA: Allyn & Bacon. Triple-loop learning adapted from Robert Hargrove. (1999). *Masterful Coaching*.

This involves learning and then using communication techniques such as effective questioning and skillful listening. Through engaging in this form of learning, we can gain breakthrough insights about our own beliefs and perceptions and those of others. Hargrove (2008) describes the triple-loop as transformational learning because it allows individuals and organizations to transform their ways of being and to become capable of fundamentally different and sustainable assumptions and patterns of behavior.

Reflection

From this chapter about the process of transformation, what resonated with you? Why? What ideas are you struggling with? Why?

_____

_____

_____

_____

In what ways are you connecting with the ideas about sitting in the darkness? Personally? Professionally?

_____

_____

_____

_____

How might your lived experiences with transformation help you effectively serve groups as a facilitator of Cultural Proficiency?

_____

_____

_____

_____

DIALOGIC ACTIVITY

1. Individually write and/or review responses to the three prior reflection questions.

2. Use three-step interview protocol (table 4.2) to share reflections, listen to different perspectives, illuminate thinking, and increase understanding in response to this chapter.

Table 4.2 Three-Step Interview Protocol

Step	Procedure
1.	Participants form pairs. Note that this is an interview protocol allowing each speaker time (uninterrupted) to speak. Determine who will interview first and who will speak first.
2.	Interviewer poses reflection questions, one at a time, during the first interview.
3.	Interview proceeds for a designated amount of time (e.g., nine minutes, or about three minutes per question).
4.	After the designated time, participants switch roles in order to conduct the second interview for the same designated amount of time.
5.	After the second interview, pairs square to form quartets. Participants introduce their partner and share highlights from their partner's responses.
Tip:	Before squaring, allow time for partners to discuss what they have permission to share about each other's responses.

Source: Adapted from Laura Lipton and Bruce Wellman. (2011a). _Groups at Work: Strategies and Structures for Professional Learning_. Page 52.

5 Emergent Change

Does the flap of a butterfly's wings in Brazil set off a tornado in Texas?

—Edward Lorenz
(The Essence of Chaos, *1993*)

I felt a great disturbance in the Force.

—Obi-Wan Kenobi (Kurtz & Lucas, 1977)

And systems don't change easily. Systems try to maintain themselves, and seek equilibrium. To change a system, you need to shake it up, disrupt the equilibrium.

—Starhawk ("Toward an Activist Spirituality," 2005)

When we are in the midst of chaos, let go of the need to control it.

—Leo Babauta ("The Illusion of Control," 2011)

All great changes are preceded by chaos.

—Deepak Chopra (Spiritual Solutions, 2012)

Real change comes from having enough comfort to be really honest and say something very uncomfortable.

—Michelle Obama
(quoted in Powell & Kantor, 2008)

I believe we can change the world if we start listening to one another again. Simple, honest, human conversation.

—Margaret J. Wheatley
(Turning to One Another, 2008)

GETTING CENTERED

Review these quotations. Which of them resonates with you? Why? How have you experienced the difference between influence and authority? How do you react to these two very different terms: *planned change* and *emergent change*?

_____

_____

_____

_____

EPISODE FIVE: CHANGING THE WAY JACK LOOKS AT CHANGE

Three months had passed since Jack attended his first Cultural Proficiency seminar. Only three months—ninety days—yet that seminar and himself before the seminar seemed to Jack to be long ago and a world away. In that former world, Jack now saw that although he had thought of himself as culturally sensitive and as someone who valued equity, he had unwittingly been part of upholding the status quo, the built-in system of inequity in education. Good intentions alone had not been enough. Although his heart had been in the right place, he had lacked the tools for change that Cultural Proficiency had so recently given him.

Now he saw that inclusion and equity weren't a surface treatment. It wasn't simply a matter of applying his professional talents to restructuring the county's math curriculum so that teachers could attend to students' diverse learning styles and modes of processing information. As important as that work was, it wasn't sufficient by itself. It was, Jack thought, a bit like rearranging the deckchairs on the *Titanic* as the ship headed toward the fatal iceberg. A more comprehensive, structural remedy was needed. The ship needed to be steered in a different direction. The entire system needed a course correction to get its trajectory headed toward making inclusive democracy possible and preparing every student for the twenty-first century.

It began with him, as Jack had learned from the inside-out process, and with changing his own mind. But the process led to changing the structure that educators had been taking for granted for hundreds of years. That legacy was designed to categorize, sort, and select the best and the brightest from the less worthy and problematic. Winners and losers. It was the built-in system of upholding its own (supposed) superiority and dominion at the cost of minimizing, alienating, and ignoring groups to the degrees that they varied from dominant culture values. Thus huge swaths of student potential were being wasted. How was that moral, or in the country's best interest? In its current form, the educational system was not helping all students—nor was it helping all educators—become their better selves.

With this greater clarity, Jack could no longer passively accept the status quo that said, "This is just how things are. This is the real world. Get used to it." The structure itself (not just parts within the structure, such as his math curriculum) needed to be called into question. Jack now saw his role in the world differently, particularly his role in the world of education. He was unwilling to wait any longer for things to right themselves in some slow trickle of social ebbs and flows meandering toward equality. Now he saw lack of justice as plain injustice; no longer was he willing to look away when it came to injustice in himself and in the system he worked for.

He was finally getting it. He might have arrived late to the party, but he felt welcomed and glad to be there. Through the seminar, he'd found his mission. This mission had always been there, apparently, but he hadn't seen it clearly because he lacked the tools. Those tools were the theory and language of Cultural Proficiency; the life-changing process of Cultural Proficiency; and the support of colleagues who were also committed to this visionary journey.

Where this vision would lead him to personally, he wasn't sure yet. He just knew he was on a path bigger than himself. In addition to finishing up his math curriculum overhaul, his immediate task was to apply what he had learned through Cultural Proficiency to helping the county's math teachers make progress toward a new vision for diversity and inclusion, high expectations, and equity for all students.

Practices and policies needed to change. Jack saw that plainly. Too much student potential was still being stymied and wasted. Too few Hispanic, black, and female students took advanced math classes and STEM career trajectories, for example. Too many students—regardless of cultural identities—were expressing that they barely knew their classmates due to the huge amount of time they spent on test prep, individual drills, and content cramming. Too many students and educators were experiencing stress, anxiety, and even depression. Jack believed urgently that business could no longer continue as usual. He wanted his math teachers to believe this, too.

He realized that Lillie Cohen, his supervisor and long-time role model, had always been motivated by this urgency. She'd always walked the talk, and for years she'd been trying various diversity trainings for Stocklin County educators. Jack hadn't realized the enormity of the task she'd been tackling: steering the *Titanic* away from danger and into safe waters. In other words, working to change the system and the culture. He hadn't gotten it. But now he did. Obviously Barbara and Frank's Cultural Proficiency approach was Lillie's latest attempt, and it had worked for Jack and his fellow seminar participants. Now he wanted to be on board with this mission of systemic course correction.

To that end, he'd changed the way he worked with the math teachers. During his biweekly professional development workshops, Jack was more proactive and confident about bringing diversity, inclusion, and equity to the forefront of every discussion. He tried to talk less, listen more, and create a space where math teachers could have conversations that were truly meaningful. He hoped that these workshops would provide the teachers with an experiential model for having meaningful conversations in the classroom.

In these workshops, Jack was taking risks, experimenting with new techniques, and trying to tap into the expertise of the teachers. He wanted to strike a balance between delivering his usual content and letting participants discuss issues. He'd even sent Barbara and Frank an e-mail asking advice about a culturally proficient way to have data conversations. Barbara responded promptly and guided him to an impressive process for data-informed dialogue to help participants surface, explore, and challenge their assumptions about data. She'd thanked Jack for his proactive leadership, given him her cell phone number, and assured him to not hesitate to reach out for other types of support.

While using the data-informed dialogue process, Jack glimpsed what it might look like to work with the math teachers in a completely different way. Working with a dialogue process was a new experience for him. It felt good, like a healthy shift in practice. It didn't feel like he was presenting to his teachers. Instead, it felt like he was learning with his colleagues. It reminded him of his experience in the Cultural Proficiency seminar. However, although his new process felt like an improvement, it was still fundamentally different from what Barbara and Frank had done.

For a start, in his workshops Jack was still in the driver's seat. He was planning the changes that he believed were best for students, and he was passing on this information to his teachers. He'd even stated that he expected all math teachers to use the data-driven dialogue process from now on. He would be checking on them. Being so directive felt very unlike Barbara and Frank's approach. They hadn't instructed the seminar participants to use any particular technique (unless a specific request had been made for one), and yet their method had achieved a commitment to excellence with equity that Jack's method hadn't.

Although the math teachers were giving positive feedback about his newly styled workshops, they weren't expressing the type of commitment Jack knew was needed. According to the teachers, the workshops were becoming an oasis, a place of rejuvenation that supported their well-being. They were learning much about math instruction and were enjoying professional conversations.

While this was all well and good, Jack wasn't making the impact that he knew was possible and necessary. The teachers weren't seeing themselves differently. They certainly weren't saying that these workshops were life-changing. They were not becoming social justice allies. When Jack asked them to share what they were doing differently, he wasn't hearing much more than slight variations to the status quo. More furniture rearrangements on the *Titanic*. He yearned for them to catch the vision and urgency that Cultural Proficiency had given him.

For that, he needed help. He wanted to replicate what he had experienced during the five-day seminar. So after a workshop one Thursday afternoon, he decided to follow up on Barbara's offer of support, and he reached out to her for advice.

Reflection

What is familiar to you about Jack's experience so far in this episode? What is unfamiliar? What details resonate with you about the way Jack perceives the transformation of his identity into a social justice ally?

_____

_____

_____

_____

Closely examine the language used to describe Jack's thinking about the way in which he works with Stocklin County math teachers. Describe the degrees of alignment (or misalignment) between his emerging identity and the way he thinks about working with teachers.

_____

_____

_____

_____

Jack punched in Barbara's cell phone number. She answered her phone right away.

Barbara: Good afternoon. Barbara Campbell here.

Jack: Hi, Barbara. It's Jack McManus from Stocklin County School System.

Barbara: Jack! Great to hear from you. I thought you'd call. What can I do for you?

Jack smiled. He decided he'd get right to the heart of things.

Jack: So, how did you and Frank do it? How did you make us change?

Barbara: We didn't make you change, Jack. You chose that.

Jack: Well then, I need to know your magic tricks. Your secret. I've been adapting the way I work with my math teachers, but I'm not having the impact that you had on us. I'm not changing my teachers like you changed us. They're not catching the vision to become social justice allies.

Barbara: Jack, I'm just about to make some coffee. I'm going for a run later, but I have some free time right now if you'd like to stop by to discuss this. Plus, it'd be nice to see you.

Jack: Well, sure. I just finished a workshop and my schedule is clear.

Barbara: Great! I'll text you my condo address. It's only a few miles from the district office.

Jack: Sounds good. I'll head right over. Thank you, Barbara.

As soon as he received her text, Jack got into his car, started his navigation app, and drove toward Barbara's condominium. He was looking forward to this. He hoped to get the answers he needed. It was a bright spring day, and the trees glimmered soft green with new leaves. As he parked in front of Barbara's condo, Jack admired the crocuses in Barbara's small yard with their vivid splashes of colors: purple, lilac-blue, orange, and white.

Before he could knock, Barbara's door swung open. There she stood, smiling pure sunshine. She wore a bright blue track suit. She hugged him, then ushered him into the living room. Light poured through the floor-to-ceiling windows, giving the room an ethereal glow. Barbara asked Jack to make himself comfortable on the burgundy leather couch. On the glass coffee table sat a silver coffee service, ready to go, with a plate of strawberries.

Barbara: I remembered that you're a coffee lover, too. Can I pour you a cup? You take it black with no sugar and no cream, right?

Jack: Wow, I can hardly believe you remembered. Yes. Thank you.

She poured coffee into delicate bone-china cups, passed one to Jack, and settled herself into a matching leather armchair. Her memory amazed Jack. During the seminar, she would bring up little things that had happened or had been said hours or even days before. This would always help the group make connections, develop deeper insights, and move forward. Perhaps it was one of her secret facilitator tricks.

Barbara: It's good to see you. So, you said you've been working differently.

Jack: Yes. I've been bringing diversity, inclusion, and equity to the forefront of all my professional development workshops for math teachers.

Barbara: Is this new? In the seminar, I remember you expressing it as a core value.

Jack: I've always been supportive of social justice and equality. However, in Stocklin our diversity-related workshops have been a mixed bag. Some have been helpful, while others seemed patronizing. None has inspired me as powerfully as yours did.

Barbara: What was different about your experience with me and Frank that resulted in these changes in your workshops?

Jack: Your seminar helped me see myself differently. The Cultural Proficiency values were there—inside me—but you helped me remove the barriers to seeing them. Also, I realized that since I'd never seen a white male leading this kind of work, specifically when dealing with race, I'd never seen myself as a leader in equity work. That is, until one specific moment when Frank mentioned that he sometimes facilitates with his friend Ron. He later mentioned that Ron was white. That made me pause. I realized that I'd immediately assumed Ron was black, and didn't change my mind until Frank said otherwise. That insight totally interrupted my pattern of thinking. I saw that I'd had beliefs about what type of person can lead these conversations, and that those beliefs were based on assumptions. And, most important of all, that I could choose to change my beliefs. Honestly, Frank's mentioning Ron was a huge influence in my seeing myself differently.

Barbara: That's a great anecdote, Jack. You could use it someday in a workshop or seminar you're facilitating. It would model vulnerability. Now back to why you're here. To recap: You developed clarity about your identity during our seminar, and since then you've been changing the way you serve Stocklin's math teachers?

Jack: Yes, if by serving you mean leading professional development for my math teachers. When you say *serve*, are you referencing the servant leader model?

Barbara: Absolutely. As you know, servant leadership focuses on the growth and well-being of the people and the community. It's different from leadership that focuses on accumulating and exercising power from the top down. Servant leaders share power and help others develop by putting others' needs and agendas first.

Jack
That describes you and Frank. That describes who I want to be. That even relates to why I'm here today. I need to know more about what you did during our seminar. Specifically, what did you do to make us change?

Barbara:
To understand what we did, we'll have to discuss who we are as facilitators—particularly our beliefs about change. But first, tell me more about what you've been doing differently.

Jack:
Basically, I've been making more space for discussion during my presentations. I even used that data-informed dialogue process you told me about, and it was terrific. But it bothers me that I'm not impacting change like you did. Whatever you did, you did it flawlessly. It was like a work of art.

Barbara:
Flawlessly—not hardly. As facilitators, Frank and I constantly reflect on what we could have done better. Facilitation is similar to Cultural Proficiency in that you never really arrive. You're always in a state of becoming an expert facilitator.

Jack:
Even so, you're clearly an expert on making people change.

Barbara:
Do you believe that we made you change?

Jack:
Not in the sense of using force, coercion, manipulation, or even direction. You never forced us to do anything. You never told us what we should believe or do. You treated us like professionals—as equals—with warmth and respect. It felt like you truly cared for us.

Barbara:
We did. We do. Caring is the only way to facilitate a group. You must love and honor them. On top of that, you must choose to love and honor them where they're at. Love brings out the best in both parties, and that was our goal: to help the group bring out its best self. And, as far as not making you change, you're correct. Neither Frank nor I believe that it's possible to make people change.

Jack:
Then what do you believe about change?

Barbara:
I believe that every person—and every group—is always free to choose whether or not to change. It's impossible to coerce anyone. Remember the old adage: "A man convinced against his will is of the same opinion still"? That's because a man—or a person, rather—possesses free will. Since a group is simply people organizing or people who are organizing, the same principle applies. A group has to decide for itself both when and how it will change. That's because a group—like a person—is a living system, not a machine that can be programmed. Ultimately the Stocklin County School System has the freedom to choose whether it wants to be a culturally proficient organization. No facilitator could ever force or coerce it to do so.

Jack: Then what do you do to impact groups and cause such profound change?

Barbara: We don't try to impact groups. We don't even use that word. That's power-over language of dominion and control. Instead, we influence. That's power-with language. You see, people are always changing. That's a given. The question isn't, "How can we get people to change?" The question is, "How can we best influence a group within which people are always in the process of changing?" Frank and I influence in a number of ways, and we draw from a number of mental models for change. One model that is always part of our backdrop is Chaos Theory.

Jack: Chaos Theory. . . . I've heard about the butterfly effect. Doesn't that have something to do with Chaos Theory?

Barbara: That's right! It's about influence. The theory is that even the flutter of a butterfly's wings can make enough wind to disturb a weather system in ways that can eventually lead to huge changes, such as a hurricane on the other side of the world. Systems may look chaotic or random, but there are always underlying conditions and patterns. For facilitators, it's helpful to recognize that little things matter. Little things can influence a group in ways that result in big changes over time. Meg Wheatley [2006] writes about this in her book *Leadership and the New Science*.

Jack: I remember that book from an organizational development course I once took. I remember discussing the butterfly effect. But to be honest, most of the book didn't make much sense to me. Seemed too abstract. I still have it, though.

Barbara: Good! Have another look. It'll make much more sense given your seminar experience. It will help you understand why Frank and I approach this work with an emergent approach to change instead of a planned approach.

Jack: I've never thought about emergent change, Chaos Theory, the butterfly effect, or any of the ideas in that book when running my workshops.

Barbara: Why would you? In your workshops, you've been a presenter, and a good one from what I've heard. Presenters don't need to think the way facilitators think. The job of a presenter is to do just that: to present. You give information and you teach. You impact. Facilitators work differently. They influence. In order to influence as a facilitator, you need some key ideas and mental models. Give me a few minutes, and I'll make a list of several books that may help you think about change.

Barbara stood up and hurried into the kitchen. Jack heard her opening and shutting drawers searching for a pen and paper. He thought about the words she'd used that particularly resonated with him: influence, free will, change. He helped himself to a couple of strawberries and finished his coffee. Sooner than he expected, Barbara returned, handing him a list of books written on a piece of paper.

Barbara: Here you are. You can borrow my copies if you don't have these at your office.

Jack: Thank you. Hey, our conversation reminded me of one of my favorite movies—*Inception* [Thomas & Nolan, 2010]. Have you seen it? Leonardo DiCaprio and his team enter different levels of people's dreams in order to access their subconscious minds. The word *inception* meant planting a simple thought so far in the recesses of the subconscious that the person, when conscious, would believe they'd come up with an original idea and had the free will to choose to act on that idea. However, creativity and free will were illusions once inception had taken place.

Barbara: No, I don't care much for science fiction. I prefer Westerns. But I've heard Frank mention that movie. He's seen it, plus about every other science fiction movie ever made. You'll have to discuss it with him when he's next in town.

Jack: You've known each other a long time, huh?

Barbara: Yes. Going on twenty years. We cofacilitated groups for more than a decade when we both lived in Oregon. That reminds me—as you continue to lead math workshops in a more culturally proficient manner, you should start thinking about a cofacilitative partner. Like any relationship, you'll need to put time and effort into its development. You'll find that a healthy partnership is the best way to do this work. That's been our experience. Frank and I have developed our partnership to a point where even traveling for hours is well worth the effort.

Jack: I'll start thinking. Working in partnership will surely stretch my skill set.

Barbara: Great. Oh, and in case you're worrying, Frank and I did not do inception! Nor did we use any other mind control or brainwashing techniques. We merely influenced, using mental models that represent science, nature, and the evolution of consciousness. Take another look at Chaos Theory in Meg Wheatley's book. Skim through it. See what jumps out. Also look at the change models in the other books. Let me know if you want to discuss any of them. This type of work is critical to the health of our educational system and our nation. It's not easy work, and it's easy to become fatigued. So know you're not alone in it. As I said before, don't hesitate to reach out.

Before leaving Barbara's condominium, Jack scanned the list of books she had given him.

Change

Leadership and the New Science—Wheatley (1999, 2006)

Managing Transitions—Bridges (2009)

The Dance of Change—Senge (1999)

Overcoming Organizational Defenses—Argyris (1990)

He sensed that he was beginning to get the answers he was looking for.

Reflection

Within this episode, what ideas reinforce beliefs you hold? What ideas are new and worth remembering? What information are you struggling with? Why?

_____

_____

_____

_____

What does the term *emergent change* mean to you? How does it differ from your experience with change initiatives you have experienced within a school, school system, or other organization?

_____

_____

_____

_____

TWO WAYS TO APPROACH CHANGE

When it comes to the ways people approach organizational change, there are two predominant categories: planned change and emergent change (Burnes, 2004). Planned change generally represents an approach that views change as structured sets of steps, assuming movement from one state to another in a sequential and often linear manner. The following quote represents a belief aligned with this approach. "I get the information, I give it to you, you implement it, results improve." This approach relies on assumptions that an organization's environment is known and variables within it can be controlled.

Emergent change generally represents a perspective that change is fluid, pervasive, continuous, and naturally occurring within an organization. This approach relies on assumptions that change is all around us and we need to be responsive and adaptive. The following quote represents a belief aligned with this approach. "Who would benefit from talking with whom about how they see the world in order to create disturbances that interrupt normal patterns of thinking and influence behavior in a manner consistent with our change initiative?"

Numerous metaphors can represent planned change, but the simplest of them all is Gareth Morgan's (2006) machine metaphor. The idea of an organization as a machine is reinforced by words and phrases such as *roll-out, top-down, bottom-up, centralized,* and *decentralized.* Use of the machine metaphor is helpful for some organizational change efforts, particularly those with certainty and without ambiguity. For example, implementing an information technology (IT) system update would respond well to a planned change approach (Smith, King, Sidhu, & Skelsey, 2015).

However other change efforts require a different metaphor: the metaphor of an organization as a living organism. These change efforts are less concerned with swift

Table 5.1 Approaches to Changing an Organization's Culture and Capabilities	
FROM **UNHEALTHY APPROACH** **Planned change for them**	**TO** **HEALTHY APPROACH** **Emergent change for us**
• Impact • Imposition • Swift and sudden • Short period of turbulence • Behavior and quick results • Machine • Mandate and force • Power-over • Simple and inflexible • Control • Dependence • Maternal and/or paternal power • Give to • Subordinates • More/different in same paradigm • Empowerment of others	• Influence • Request • Developmental and deliberate • Extended period of patience • Identity and sustainable capabilities • Living system • Invite and volunteer • Power-with • Complex and adaptive • Chaos • Freedom • Community power • Create with • Colleagues • Challenge of the old paradigm, support of the new • Shaping conditions that enable agency and self-empowerment

change for quick results and are more concerned with building an organization's capacity, transforming its identity, and supporting its sustainability. Cultural Proficiency is one such an effort. And as such, effective facilitators take an emergent approach as opposed to a planned approach to change (table 5.1).

EMERGENT CHANGE IN CHAOS

In the previous episode, Jack asked Barbara how the facilitators "made" his seminar group change. Like other people who have experienced the transformative power of Cultural Proficiency through the help of a skilled facilitator, Jack wondered if the experience had been "magic." He'd never before experienced such a profound transformation; in addition, during the entire process the facilitation seemed effortless and seamless. Of course Jack didn't mean literal magic, but he was mystified at the remarkable shift he'd witnessed in himself and his colleagues. It seemed well beyond the ordinary.

Implicit in his comments and questions to Barbara were Jack's own beliefs and assumptions about change. One of his assumptions was that it is possible to make someone change. This assumption is often echoed within organizations through statements such as "I don't understand why they're not doing what they're supposed to be doing. After all, I gave them all the information they need." Or this statement: "We already rolled it out. They got the training during the staff meeting. They should be doing it." The beliefs and assumptions behind these types of statements are that an authority can make change happen by transferring information to a person or a group of persons and then change happens automatically. This belief is perfectly appropriate . . . when dealing with machines.

With a machine, we flip a switch or turn a key and change happens automatically: the power comes on. It's a linear cause-and-effect situation. But people are not machines; groups (of people) are not machines; organizations (full of groups of people organizing around a central purpose) are not machines. People are alive, and vitality is the essence of organizations. Mechanistic assumptions appropriate for effecting change in machines and setting them in motion simply do not apply to the profound dynamics of change in humans and organizations. This is not the paradigm out of which Cultural Proficiency operates.

Instead, Cultural Proficiency is a humanistic model that deals with people as persons and meets each person where they are at on the journey. Cultural Proficiency exists in a worldview where organizations and groups (that Cultural Proficiency views as groups of persons rather than as a human monolith) are viewed as living, nonlinear systems that self-organize without a directive leader attempting to control their behavior.

THE ILLUSION OF CONTROL

In fact, leadership efforts to control people and change are doomed to fail. To reference popular culture again, this is the message mathematician Dr. Ian Malcom attempted to convey in an early scene in the movie *Jurassic Park* (Kennedy Molen, & Spielberg, 1993). In the scene, park owner John Hammond (Richard Attenborough) was giving Ian Malcom (Jeff Goldblum) a sneak-peek tour of his modern-day theme park located on a tropical island that he had populated with cloned dinosaurs. Although amazed, Malcom said that it was unwise to have dinosaurs revived from extinction, and he warned that the park was a disaster waiting to happen. Hammond countered this warning, saying that visitors would be safe when visiting the park because he had taken every precaution to control the dinosaurs, including containing their reproductive capacities. Malcom, an expert in Chaos Theory, did not agree that Hammond could control nature in this manner. "Life finds a way," he asserted.

Living systems do indeed find a way. Vitality wants to happen and will happen. Change emerges from systems adapting to their conditions. The study of the behavior of complex systems is the focus of Chaos Theory, which is a discipline within the field of mathematics. Chaos Theory has taught us that what may appear as chaos, unpredictability, or a lack of control in organizations (i.e., systems) has an underlying order that we can understand and influence by attending to the essential conditions that support the system's ability to access its own innate intelligence and then change as needed.

Organizational behavior expert Margaret Wheatley (2001, 2006, 2008) draws from Chaos Theory—as well as from quantum physics and molecular biology—to apply its lessons to the discipline of leadership and organizational change. She writes that life seeks patterns, freedom, and interdependence, and finds it through the formation of systems. As a complex system self-organizes, there is the appearance of a mess, or chaos. Within the mess, systems are actually forming around shared interests. These shared interests are the strange attractors of Chaos Theory that possess a magnetic property that pulls the system into visible shape. In an organization the behavior of people is influenced by and circles around these strange attractors that are—in the case of an organization or group—its core values and beliefs. The core values and beliefs (along with their history and purpose) are the center of the organization's identity.

INFLUENCING EMERGENT CHANGE

Life organizes around the way it sees or perceives itself—around its identity (Wheatley, 2007). As a group of people self-organize around the way their group perceives its purpose (identity), structures, patterns, and processes appear. In other words, change emerges. These outcomes are unpredictable—not susceptible to prediction or to being foreseen—from the components that created them (Zimmerman, 2010). Thus, we could call emergent change in organizations cocreation: the fashioning of a new reality by the system and for the system that arises from flowing with the energy present within the system rather than from outside control. The consciousness of the system forms, reforms, and transforms itself by drawing on its own intrinsic elements (e.g., beliefs, values) for survival and growth (Arena, 2009). It's a circular, self-referential process. We observe ourselves because we are aware of our existence; we are aware of our existence because we observe ourselves.

Whoa! Let's pause for a moment. Facilitators need not spend too much time contemplating this mind-bending paradox—unless they have a particular affinity for quantum physics and the new sciences, of course. We can save that type of contemplation for philosophers, *Star Trek* fans, and perhaps saints and sages. But leaders of professional learning can still make good use of Chaos Theory when taking on the role of facilitator. We need only spend time acknowledging the legitimacy of these three dynamics.

1. The process of self-reference *does* happen as a self-organizing system changes itself: Groups and individuals will always refer back to their histories, experiences, and values and beliefs when processing information. They will refer to their inner world when processing new information from their outer world.

2. Emergence in and of itself is neither positive or negative: it just is (Dickens, 2012, p. 50). As people within groups interact and self-organize, structures, patterns, and processes form, reform, and transform. Although complex, emergent change simply happens. All of these concepts are shifting and dynamic; everything constantly changes. From individuals within the groups to the patterns of behavior that emerge from their interactions, these concepts are analogous to "clouds emerging from the physics and chemistry of water vapor" (Waldrop, 1992, p. 184) and the conditions with which the vapor interacts. The changing and moving clouds are neither good nor bad. They just are.

3. Self-organizing systems possess three essential domains. These domains—identity, information, and relationships—are the areas to which facilitators attend in order to influence emergent change. Wheatley and Kellner-Rogers (1996) describe these three domains as operating "in a dynamic cycle within which the three elements are so intertwined it becomes difficult to distinguish among them." Table 5.2 extracts these domains from the dynamic of emergent change and relates the functionality of each to organizations.

Table 5.2 Emergent Change: Three Domains of Self-Organizing Systems

Domain	System Function	In organizations, this condition is about _____.
Identity	Make sense of itself (the consciousness)	Who we think we are includes our • Vision and mission, • Values and beliefs, • Interpretations of our group's history, • Present decisions and activities, and • Sense of our group's future.
Information	Form itself (the medium)	Applying values by assigning meaning (value) to data (in-forms) to create the information that • Flows through the organization, • Changes the people in the organization, • Is the difference that makes a difference, and • Creates the conditions for the emergence of effective responses to the environment.
Relationships	Access information and influence identity (the pathways)	The ways of accessing intelligence include • People accessing other people, • People accessing the intelligence of the whole organization, • Impromptu and unplanned connections that give rise to new venture undertakings, and • Trust and appreciation.

The dialogue within Episode Five contains an illustration of the dynamic of these three entangled domains. Jack explained to Barbara how, as a white male, he never saw himself (identity) taking the lead role in diversity and social justice efforts. But through interactions with Frank (relationship) he learned about Ron, a friend of Frank's who is white and who is also a facilitator of Cultural Proficiency.

This new information created a disturbance and informed Jack's vision of himself as a possible facilitator of Cultural Proficiency, or at least as a presenter who can take on a leadership role and directly address issues involving diversity, inclusion, and equity. This change in identity/vision that emerged from the dynamic interplay among information, relationships, and identity then governed the changes in Jack's behavior (how he presented his workshops). When he had allowed his belief system to be disturbed—like tossing a rock into a pond—by the information about Ron, Jack chose to cocreate his own future in a way that was different from the one he would have had if he had been closed to this new information.

For facilitators, Chaos Theory is a powerful mental model for influencing change in groups aspiring to excellence with equity. Although the path of self-organization cannot be foreseen—because it is emergent change (change that is coming into being)—facilitators can utilize the three domains by embedding them within the intentions behind their actions (what strategies they use, what interventions they make, how they craft an agenda, etc.). The domains can serve as a backdrop for facilitators in making decisions that will best help the group progress on its Cultural Proficiency Journey (table 5.3). Use of this backdrop, though, is contingent on the facilitators' core value of freedom and their belief and trust in the innate intelligence and talents of the group to learn what it needs to learn, decide what it needs to decide, and act how it will choose to act.

Domain	Examples of reflective questions to inform facilitator decisions
Identity	• How does this group see its purpose relative to Cultural Proficiency? • Is the group expressing a healthy or unhealthy worldview? • How do individuals within this group see themselves? • What values and beliefs govern this group's actions? • To what extent are their practices and policies aligned with excellence with equity? • How does this group interpret its history? Does it acknowledge systems of oppression and privilege? Does it recognize the vestiges of historical systems of oppression and privilege? • To what extent does the group value continuous improvement for excellence with equity? To what extent does the group value democratic schools?
Information	• What is the nature of the diversity present within the group? • What types of expertise exists in the room and where does it reside? • What life experiences do individuals in this group have with systems of oppression and privilege? • What emotions are surfacing and why? • Who is talking? Who is not? Who needs to talk? • What culturally proficient practices exist within the experiences of participants in the room?
Relationships	• Who is talking with whom? • Who needs to talk with whom? • Does the group possess the type of information that it needs to access and process, or would it benefit from external information such as a reading, video, or guest speaker? • What is the nature of the discourse (e.g., dialogue, polite conversation, skilled discussion, debate) between participants?

Table 5.3 Chaos Theory: Backdrop for Facilitators

Reflection

In what ways are you relating the information in this chapter to your experiences regarding management of change within organizations? Management of diversity-related initiatives? What are you feeling in response to the ideas in this chapter?

_____

_____

_____

_____

Please revisit table 5.1. What is resonating with you? What thoughts does it provoke? What information are you struggling with? Why?

_____

_____

_____

_____

In what ways can you use the ideas from this chapter to improve your practice?

_____

_____

_____

_____

DIALOGIC ACTIVITY

1. Individually write and/or review responses to the three prior reflection questions.

2. Use the World Café protocol (table 5.4) to explore perspectives, discover individual and shared meaning, and deepen understanding in response to this chapter.

3. Secure materials for the activity: butcher paper or chart paper (placed like a tablecloth) on each table, markers or crayons at each table, and a timer projected on a screen.

4. For this activity, use the World Café with these questions for each round.
   a) Round 1: Getting centered/quotes question, start of chapter
   b) Round 2: Reflection question 1, end of chapter
   c) Round 3: Reflection question 2, end of chapter
   d) Round 4: Reflection question 3, end of chapter

Table 5.4 World Café Protocol

Step	Procedure
1.	Form groups of three to five individuals. Each group sits at a different table. This discussion protocol has rounds.
2.	Facilitator starts the round by displaying a question/prompt and provides silent time (e.g., two minutes) for individual drawing or writing on the table's butcher paper.
3.	For a designated time, participants share ideas in response to the question/prompt for the round.
4.	After the designated time, the group chooses a historian. The historian stays at the table. Everyone else disperses to different tables for the next round. That round, each table will have combination of participants different from the previous round.
5.	For a designated time (e.g., two minutes) each historian summarizes the discussion that took place at that table for the new combination of participants present.
6.	Repeat steps 2 to 6 until the final round. For the final round, participants will gather in their original (Round 1) table.
Tip:	• Near the end of each completed round—before participants disperse to new tables—consider choosing a new historian so that the historians also receive the benefit of changing tables. • Visit www.theworldcafe.com for tips and principles for the World Café method.

Source: Adapted from The Creative Commons Attribution (2016). _The World Cafe._ Retrieved from www.theworldcafe.com

6 Internal Capacity for the Work

And since justice is what love looks like in public, you can't talk about loving folk and not fighting for justice.

—Cornell West (Interview, 2009)

Genuine love is rarely an emotional space where needs are instantly gratified. To know love we have to invest time and commitment. . . . Many people want love to function like a drug, giving them an immediate and sustained high. They want to do nothing, just passively receive the good feeling.

—bell hooks (All About Love, 2001)

In our work in whole-system change, my colleagues and I have shown time and again that if you give people skills (invest in capacity building), most of them will become more accountable.

—Michael Fullan (The Principal, 2014)

Each generation will reap what the former generation has sown.

Chinese Proverb

We may have all come on different ships, but we're in the same boat now.

—Martin Luther King Jr.

Yes, we can!

—Barack Obama (presidential campaign slogan, 2008)

¡Si, se puede!

—Delores Huerta and Cesar Chavez (United Farm Workers motto, 1972)

GETTING CENTERED

Review the quotes on the previous page and consider the need for strategically investing resources in building an organization's capacity for Cultural Proficiency. What resonates with you? Why?

_____

_____

_____

_____

EPISODE SIX: AN INVITATION THAT SEEMED MUCH MORE INVITING TO JACK

Jack's smiled as he read the e-mail from the director of his department, Lillie Cohen. She was inviting him to have a conversation about Cultural Proficiency with her and Barbara Campbell. What began as a promising Monday morning was only getting better. He was ahead on all deadlines and was planning to invest some time proactively checking in with several of the school-based math colleagues whom he served. Now, in addition, he was going to be able to talk with Lillie and Barbara about what had become his passion, Cultural Proficiency.

He read the e-mail again.

Dear Jack: Good morning. If you are available today at 11:30, please join me in my office for a conversation with Barbara Campbell. Barbara and I have had an ongoing discussion about the future of Cultural Proficiency in our school district. I'd like to invite you into our conversation, starting with our meeting today. Please let me know if that works for you.

Lillie Cohen
Director of Curriculum and Instruction
Stocklin County Public Schools

"I'd like to invite you into our conversation . . . ." Jack smiled again. He felt honored. Just a couple of weeks ago, he was at Barbara's condo having an enlightening professional conversation about change. The ideas Barbara shared had helped him continue to grow in the way he served his colleagues, the district's math teachers. He hoped Lillie's invitation would lead to more conversations that would challenge and stretch him. He shot back an acceptance e-mail and then, for the time being, turned his attention to supporting his colleagues in the schools.

Later that morning at the district office building, Jack took the elevator to Lillie's floor and strolled to the side of the building where her new office was located. It was no surprise that he'd rarely seen Lillie over these past three months. Most days, Jack was out of the office, either in schools or conducting workshops at the district's professional learning center across town. Lillie's door was cracked open. Jack peeked in. She and

Barbara were sitting and chatting at the round table in front of her desk. A third chair awaited his arrival. He interrupted their conversation with a light knock. In unison, they looked up and smiled. Lillie motioned for Jack to come in. "Hello, Jack! Great to see you." said Barbara.

The three of them spent a good five minutes catching up—mainly about Jack's daughters' activities—before Lillie turned the conversation to professional matters. To Jack's surprise, she offered him an invitation so aligned with what he wanted that it seemed he had almost willed it into existence.

Lillie: Jack, as you know I'm committed to the Cultural Proficiency approach to help our school system change for the better. It's not just another initiative or a flavor-of-the-month. Cultural Proficiency is going to be our way of being, the way we do business. Barbara and Frank have helped us get off to a great start, but we have much work to do.

Jack: I get it. I've been wanting to talk with you with you for weeks. I feel like I finally understand what you've been working toward all these years.

Lillie: Thanks, Jack. I'm nearing the final season of my career, and I'm filled with hope about where we're headed. Over the years, I've been searching for something that works. Something with the "stickiness factor." To be frank, it's been a struggle. Some days and years I've felt pretty beaten down. As you probably know, Cultural Proficiency is not our first attempt—not hardly—to get traction toward inclusion and equity. But I've found Cultural Proficiency to be quite different. What's your opinion?

Jack: I love it! As someone who's experienced other diversity-related efforts, I agree that Cultural Proficiency is different. Yes, it gives fresh tools and a process that works, but it's also different because of the facilitation. Actually, it's different because of our facilitators. Barbara and Frank are incredible. And Lillie, I want to thank you for keeping on keeping on during the tough times when so few of us were getting it. You've brought us this far.

His eyes moved from Lillie to Barbara.

Jack: Barbara, you've been such a help to me, even after the seminar.

Barbara: Thank you, Jack. You said, "It's also different because of the facilitation." Say more about what you mean by that.

Jack: I was blown away! I'd never experienced anything like your facilitation process. I thought I was pretty good at leading professional development workshops. Until I met you and Frank, that is. Your approach fascinates me.

Barbara: Both Frank and I think highly of you, too.

Lillie: Jack, I've seen an aptitude for this work in you ever since you were with your middle-school students in the classroom. Barbara has told me about how proactive you've been with reaching out for support. I've also been hearing great things about your recent math workshops. You're not waiting for directions—you're already acting on your beliefs. With great results.

Jack: Thank you, both of you. I'm not facilitating Cultural Proficiency, but I'm definitely trying to work in a more culturally proficient manner.

Lillie: That's the type of movement we need in every corner of our district. Jack, we're committed to Cultural Proficiency, and we need make it sustainable. To that end, we need to grow internal consultants. You see, one of the first things Barbara and Frank told the superintendent's executive team was that we need to think strategically for our future and not become dependent on external consultants. They said their goal was to help us build our own capacity and to work themselves out of a job.

Barbara: Yes. Stocklin County needs champions of Cultural Proficiency—what we're calling internal consultants—who can do from the inside what we do from the outside.

Lillie: So, our next step is to identify our emerging champions and help them grow into facilitators. We want to start by investing in someone who shows potential and displays initiative. Jack, you definitely have both qualities. So tell me, can you see yourself doing what Barbara and Frank do? Facilitating?

Jack looked at Barbara. By her grin, he could tell that she already knew his answer. He looked back at Lillie. She was smiling also.

Jack: Wow, I'm humbled and honored. Yes, I would love to facilitate like that. I'd have a great deal to learn, though. By no means do I feel prepared to lead others' journeys by myself.

Lillie: That's okay. You'll have all the support you need to develop as a facilitator. We'll start slow. And to be clear, I'm not offering you a position, not yet. You'd still operate as math curriculum specialist, but you'd be taking on the role of a Cultural Proficiency facilitator. We'll figure out the details along the way.

Jack: I definitely feel capable, and I'm excited and motivated. Barbara, you and Frank did an excellent job of helping our group develop a "we can do it" attitude—and the Tools of Cultural Proficiency definitely help build facility. But I don't know if I can work your kind of facilitator magic. I'm no Barbara or Frank.

Barbara: Of course not: You're Jack! Part of why you display such potential is that you've consistently showed up as yourself, with vulnerability. Also, I've heard you refer to our facilitation as "magic" a few times now. Although it may seem like magic, it's not. It's an art of highly developed, well-researched skills based on paradigms with solid theories, tools, and techniques. All of which can be learned and mastered. All of which we know you can learn and master. It may seem like magic because it works so well and because it's so different from the way you're used to working as a presenter and teacher. In fact, facilitation is a completely different paradigm with rules quite different from those you follow when presenting.

Jack: Barbara, you continue to help me learn and grown. You're like a mentor to me.

Lillie: Well, that's actually what I was hoping to talk about. Let's make that mentoring relationship official. In your new role, Jack, you'll have increased access to Barbara as your mentor. We have a three-year plan. During that time, we want to grow our in-house facilitators. You, Jack, will be our first facilitator protégé. In turn, down the line, you'll become a mentor to others. Sound good?

Jack: Yes. Thank you, Lillie. Thank you for believing in me and thank you for this opportunity.

Lillie: And I thank you, too. Your willingness to move this work forward means everything to me. In a moment, I have to head out for an appointment with the superintendent. Before I leave, I have big news, and I'm happy that I can share it with you first. Later this afternoon, the superintendent will announce that—as of tomorrow—I'll be serving as the Stocklin County deputy superintendent.

Jack and Barbara shared congratulatory wishes. They both expressed confidence that Stocklin County's students and staff would benefit from Lillie's increased level of influence.

Lille: In my new position, Cultural Proficiency is still my top priority. It's the approach that will help us transform our system for the better. And whoever succeeds me as the next director of curriculum will need to be someone with a high commitment to inclusion and equity. Now, if you'll excuse me, I need to get to my meeting. Feel free to stay here in my office for as long as you want.

Reflection

What types of reactions are you having to the conversation involving Lillie, Barbara, and Jack? How do you see yourself and your work in this scene?

_____

_____

_____

_____

This scene represents Stocklin County Public School System crossing the next threshold in the process of making Cultural Proficiency its way of being. What is familiar to you about this approach to creating a sustainable change initiative? What is unfamiliar?

_____

_____

_____

_____

PLANNING FOR SUSTAINABILITY

Stocklin County Public Schools brought in Barbara and Frank as external consultants to help the district become a culturally proficient organization. But that was just the first phase of a larger plan. Helping any organization (district, school, department, etc.) move its Cultural Proficiency efforts beyond a pilot to a program, or beyond a workshop to a way of being involves collaborative planning for long-term sustainability. Minimally, external consultants such as Barbara and Frank must work with organizational leaders to establish broad goals that deal with the following:

- Increasing the organization's leadership capacity: broad-based skillful involvement in the work of leading Cultural Proficiency.
- Developing the organization's capabilities to facilitate Cultural Proficiency.

The big-picture responsibility of external Cultural Proficiency consultants is to facilitate (make easier) the organization's journey (process) to becoming culturally proficient. Or, in other words, those consultants make it easier for an organization to become a learning

Table 6.1 Four Cultural Proficiency Leadership Roles

Role	Distinctions
Consultant	• Possesses expertise of Cultural Proficiency and facilitation. • Advocates for Cultural Proficiency Framework and/or journey. • Informs regarding processes and protocols. • Specializes in transformational learning designs. • Advises for managing transitions and leading profound change. • Advocates for particular choices or actions.
Presenter	• Teaches Cultural Proficiency Framework and Tools; Cultural Proficiency journey stages; and facilitation knowledge, skills, and attitudes. • Can adopt different stances: expert, colleague, novice, or friend. • Uses numerous strategies: simulations, lectures, cooperative learning, etc. • Offers effective presentations: clear instructional outcomes, standards for success, and assessment techniques.
Facilitator	• Makes Cultural Proficiency journey (the process) easier. • Conducts learning events (e.g., seminars) where the purpose is embarking and progressing on the Cultural Proficiency journey. • Directs processes and choreographs energy. • Focuses on one content and one process at a time. • Does not act as a content expert or a person with authority over the group.
Coach	• Helps individuals or groups take action toward a goal while simultaneously helping develop expertise in planning, reflecting, problem solving, and decision making. • Takes on a nonjudgmental stance. • Uses open-ended questions, pausing, paraphrasing, and probing. • Focuses on individual's/group members' perceptions, thinking, and decision-making processes to mediate resources for self-directedness.

Source: Adapted from Robert J. Garmston and Bruce M. Wellman. (2009). *The Adaptive School: A Sourcebook for Developing Collaborative Groups.* Norwood, MA: Christopher-Gordon Publishers.

organization with the internal capacity to effectively and relentlessly pursue excellence with equity. To that end, external consultants must take on roles other than facilitator as they work with the organization. They must also be consultants, presenters, and coaches. They must help future (internal) Cultural Proficiency facilitators like Jack recognize these different roles and learn when and how to shift between them. Table 6.1 provides an overview of the four leadership roles, based on descriptions provided by Garmston and Wellman (2009).

When an external consultant or, as with Barbara and Frank, a consultant team signs on with an organization to help that organization grow in Cultural Proficiency, the consultants proceed according to a predictable pattern. This is the consultant-to-coach pattern, and the endpoint is high organizational capacity. The endpoint is when the consultants work themselves out of a job. They enter the relationship with the organization as consultants, but they exit as coaches (Costa & Garmston, 2016). Along the way, most of their work is done in the role of facilitator.

The consultants focus on building the organization's leadership capacities and capabilities so that the organization becomes capable of leading its own Cultural Proficiency and can, in time, do without their services. The goal is to help an organization develop sustainability as well as self-directed learning and leading. To that end, leaders of Cultural Proficiency treat the consultant-to-coach pattern as a fractal; that is, they repeat the pattern in all interactions at every level and in every corner of the organization. That would include all professional learning experiences ranging from seminars to everyday conversations. Every interaction is a capacity-building opportunity. The result of this type of fractal pattern is a new way of being for the organization (Wheatley, 2006).

COLLECTIVE SELF-EFFICACY: YES, WE CAN!

In order to help the organization build its internal capacity, consultants focus on increasing the self-efficacy of individuals as well as the collective-efficacy of the organization with regard to Cultural Proficiency. Self-efficacy is an individual's beliefs in their own capabilities (Bandura, 1997). It's the "Yes, I can!" mentality. Collective-efficacy is basically the group equivalent of self-efficacy except that it is more than the sum total of the self-efficacy of persons within the group. In collective-efficacy, the whole is greater than the sum of its parts.

Collective-efficacy is the group's beliefs about its own capabilities and capacity (Mischel & Northcraft, 1997), and it is reflected in a group's response to questions such as, "Do we believe that we have what it takes to stand on our own as a culturally proficient organization?" and "Do we believe that we have what it takes to eliminate the opportunity and expectation gaps related to our student groups?" Collective-efficacy answers "Yes, we can!" When a group believes they can guide their own Cultural Proficiency, they have high collective-efficacy; they can make Cultural Proficiency sustainable in their organization and thus outgrow their reliance on outside help. Involvement with external consultants then becomes a luxury instead of a necessity.

High levels of collective-efficacy and self-efficacy bring remarkable results to an organization. Research also consistently relates collective-efficacy to improved student achievement. Schools that possess high collective-efficacy believe that they have the knowledge, skills, and will to meet their goals and overcome obstacles, so they end up doing just that (Garmston & Wellman, 2009). In his ground-breaking and ongoing study of meta analyses, John Hattie (2009, 2011) argues that a student's self-efficacy/self-expectations is one of the most powerful—if not the absolutely most powerful—influences on student achievement.

Furthermore, when Hattie (2015) factored in an impressive meta-analysis (Eels, 2011) focused on the relationship between collective teacher efficacy and student achievement, he interpreted collective self-efficacy (the amount of high self-efficacy in a group/school) to have the larger effect size—a whopping 1.57—than any other educational influence studied to date. That effect size is over four times the size (0.40) of an influence Hattie equates with and quantifies as one year of growth for one year in the classroom. Greater bang for the buck would be hard to imagine.

With such undeniably profound results, it's logical that external Cultural Proficiency consultants should focus first and foremost on self- and collective-efficacy. When collective-efficacy with Cultural Proficiency is low, the organization needs a consultant. When it's high, the organization benefits more from a coach. The same rule applies with seminar groups and at the individual level.

To help Stocklin County Public Schools move forward, its external consultants must help Jack (and any other future Cultural Proficiency facilitators) learn to become an internal consultant, operating from within the organization where he can reiterate this pattern (the growth pattern of consultant-to-coach) for groups and schools throughout the district. To be successful in that effort, Barbara and Frank have to help Jack build his own self-efficacy concerning his facilitation of Cultural Proficiency.

Reflection

Consider this declaration about how people work to help organizations build internal capacity: They enter the relationship with the organization as consultants, but they exit as coaches (Costa & Garmston, 2016). Respond with a paraphrase, question, idea, or personal connection.

_____

_____

_____

_____

Consider the concepts behind self- and collective-efficacy. What experiences have you had that involved someone helping you believe that you could do something? Describe that experience. To what extent have you prioritized developing self- and collective-efficacy in others within your work? What can you do to make developing them priority?

_____

_____

_____

_____

EPISODE SEVEN: HOW JACK AND BARBARA SEE JACK

Jack and Barbara stayed in Lillie's office to discuss the new role he was taking on—that of Cultural Proficiency facilitator.

Barbara: How are you feeling about this opportunity?

Jack: Excited! It's amazing for me to think back to how all of this started. I didn't even want to be a seminar participant, and now I'm going to help lead the seminars. Back then I didn't think I needed to be there. I thought my way of responding to differences and diversity was ahead of the curve. I didn't see how I was imprisoned by my own thinking.

Barbara: Say more about being imprisoned by your own thinking.

Jack: I didn't know what I didn't know. At the time, I felt self-actualized because I saw myself as someone working on behalf of "them," our underserved student groups: black, Hispanic, poor, and even female students when it came to math. My curriculum work was my intervention for them. I saw myself as some sort of hero, actually. I never considered leading with our students, and I didn't realize my own internalized attitudes and behaviors that ultimately perpetuate systems of oppression and privilege. For instance, I didn't see how focusing on helping "them" was reinforcing my own dominance. I think many educators are in the same boat. The vast majority of us aren't malicious. We just don't know we're in a boat—trapped in a boat, really.

Barbara: You're speaking to the essence of our work and its systemic nature. Yes, we're all in a boat. In the same boat, actually. Those of us served well by the dominant culture may not even see the system or the culture—we can't see the boat. Unaware of our dominance, we see ourselves as free as birds and as the standard for what is normative.

Jack: Right. In that mind-set, we don't realize that we are just as bound and enclosed as those that we perceive as "other," as different and in need of our help. But in reality, "we" are just as enclosed by our rules, values, and beliefs as everyone else. We're just unaware of it. Unaware of our need to change. Unaware of our need for self-actualization through our collective liberation. "We" are just as subjugated as "them." In fact, there really is no "them." There is only "us."

Barbara: Your boat is a terrific metaphor. It reminds me of a solid information processing strategy we use with groups—Synectics (Prince, 1968). Let's play with it for a minute. So, if our current dominant culture is like a boat because we are all floating around out there in it, then what is Cultural Proficiency?

Jack: It's like a course correction because it wakes us up to the fact that we're all in a boat and we're also horribly off course. We could be adrift or even about to hit an iceberg. Cultural Proficiency helps us get back on course.

Barbara: Can we really say "get back" on course, though? This boat was never headed toward a land of liberty, equality, and justice for all. From the beginning of this country as we know it, those values were reserved for a select group of people.

Jack:	True. So, instead of getting back on course, Cultural Proficiency helps us create a brand new course toward a land of an inclusive democracy's promise—liberty and justice for all. And all means all.
Barbara:	I love the imagery. We make a great team, Jack. I'm looking forward to working together as cofacilitators in our Cultural Proficiency workshops and leading these types of conversations with participants.
Jack:	Me, too. It wasn't long ago that I was telling you about how I was changing the way I see myself. How I'd always been committed to social justice, but that I'd never seen myself leading conversations about oppression and privilege until Frank's mention of his friend and cofacilitator who was white and male.
Barbara:	You mentioned your being white and male. Why?
Jack:	I've been reflecting on it, about the unearned privilege that comes along with those categories. Before Cultural Proficiency, the concept of privilege wasn't new to me. What changed—with the help of your facilitation of the process—was my response to my unearned privilege.
Barbara:	How did you shift your perception and response?
Jack:	I realized that I had attached negativity to it: guilt and possibly—at a deeper level—a fear of unworthiness. But that changed. More accurately, I chose to change the way I see it. Now I think of unearned privilege as a tool or an opportunity. I can use my privilege to help dismantle systems of oppression and privilege. My privilege happens to involve whiteness and maleness, as well as other dimensions. But just like power in general, it's really what you do with it. Does this make sense?
Barbara:	Absolutely. From my perspective, you're becoming a social justice ally.
Jack:	Sounds good, but what exactly do you mean by that term?
Barbara:	An ally is someone who recognizes the unearned privilege they receive from systemic oppression and who then uses their power to change those systems. For example, I became a social justice ally working to end heterosexism—prejudice against homosexuals based on the assumption that heterosexuality is the norm—when I realized the unearned benefits conferred on me because I'm heterosexual.
Jack:	Able-bodied people who work against ableism. Men who work to end sexism.
Barbara:	You got it. You're recognizing how you benefit from various patterns of societal injustice, and you see yourself as someone who wants to work against those systems. To help all of us recognize our power and then use it to end traditions and conditions that marginalize and disempower students.
Jack:	Got it. So, does that mean I've arrived? Am I culturally proficient now? Ha!
Barbara:	What it means, in all seriousness, is that (1) you're on the journey and (2) you're recognizing the Barriers to Cultural Proficiency within your lived experience. You're overcoming those internal barriers by choosing differently. You're now

seeing yourself as someone who wants to consciously work to end the systemic "isms" and cocreate new and healthier systems. Now, we need to work on your seeing yourself as a facilitator, too.

Reflection

This scene implies the importance of embarking on the personal journey before trying to facilitate a journey for others. What experiences do you bring to this discussion?

_____

_____

_____

_____

Jack brings his personal lens to this work. He discusses two important dimensions to his cultural identity: gender and race. What lens do you bring to this work? In what ways do you recognize the importance of acknowledging and exploring your dimensions of difference?

_____

_____

_____

_____

INVESTING IN CHAMPIONS

The dialogue within the previous scene provides additional context for understanding why Lillie (in consultation with Barbara) decided to invest in Jack as a future internal consultant, a person working inside the district who can take on various roles to help the district continue to move toward excellence and equity. They recognized Jack as an emerging champion—someone taking action and assuming leadership based on his commitment to Cultural Proficiency. They committed to nurture his development by providing him the support he will need to grow into a facilitator of the work. By investing in Jack, Lillie supported his professional learning while simultaneously advancing the organization's evolution.

Identifying emerging champions for any change effort and then supporting their growth is essential to building internal capacity for that change effort (Fullan, 2014; Grantmakers for Effective Organizations, 2004). Champions of Cultural Proficiency are people who vigilantly work to ensure that growth toward excellence with equity is always a priority within the organization. They represent a metaphoric conscience of an organization, whispering in its ear reminders to apply the lens of Cultural Proficiency to any decision-making process. While external consultants may initially play this role, they also help the organization recognize the importance of growing internal champions to succeed them. Thus, external consultants provide guidance through the process of growing internal consultants by helping the organization consciously invest time and resources into the development of the right people.

These right people are the champions, people who—before learning how to facilitate the journey for others—display a strong commitment to the work and an emerging understanding of who they are (identity) relative to Cultural Proficiency. They have clarity around aspects such as their purpose, motivation, understanding of power, and relationship to systems of oppression and privilege.

ASPIRING ALLY IDENTITY DEVELOPMENT

Barbara described Jack's growth process as one of becoming a social justice ally. The perspective of an ally is foundational to the effectiveness of a facilitator of Cultural Proficiency. Anne Bishop provides this helpful definition of an ally on her website www.becominganally.ca:

> Allies are people who recognize the unearned privilege they receive from society's patterns of injustice and take responsibility for changing these patterns. Allies include men who work to end sexism, white people who work to end racism, heterosexual people who work to end heterosexism, able-bodied people who work to end ableism, and so on. Part of becoming an ally is also recognizing one's own experience of oppression. For example, a white woman can learn from her experience of sexism and apply it in becoming an ally to people of colour, or a person who grew up in poverty can learn from that experience how to respect others' feelings of helplessness because of a disability.

Although foundational, the perspective of an ally does not guarantee culturally proficient actions. The efforts of allies are not always effective toward achieving their goals. Keith E. Edwards (2006) used this foundational assumption to create the Aspiring Social Justice Ally Identity Development conceptual model. In it, Edwards establishes the nonlinear and aspirational nature of aspiring ally development, and focuses on different foundational motivations of the model's three different statuses (table 6.2). Edwards's use of the term *status*—an individual's relative standing—recognizes the limits of the term *stage*, primarily because an individual can simultaneously be in more than one stage. Overall, Edwards created the model to support the development of people aspiring to act as social justice allies.

As such, this model provides culturally proficient facilitators with an excellent tool for self-reflection. These facilitators, like any aspiring social justice ally, may act from any of the three statuses at any particular time, due to constantly changing personal and environmental factors. Because of this, Edwards (2006, p. 53) posits, "The *Ally for Social Justice* status is an aspirational identity one must continuously work towards."

This model also provides a framework that can assist consultants and organizational leaders (such as Barbara and Lillie) with their efforts to identify emerging Cultural Proficiency champions and support their development into internal consultants.

Table 6.2 Aspiring Ally Identity Development

	Aspiring Ally for Self-Interest	Aspiring Ally for Altruism	Ally for Social Justice
Motivation	Selfish—for the people I know and care about	Other—I do this for *them*	Combined Selfishness—I do this for *us*
Ally to_____	Ally to a person	Ally to a target group	Ally to an issue
Relationship w/Members of Oppressed Groups	Working *over* members of the target group	Working *for* members of the target group	Working *with* members of the target group
Victims of Oppression	Individuals with personal connection are or could be victims—my daughter, my sister, my friend	They are victims	All of us are victims—although victimized in different ways and unequally
Focus of Problem	Individuals—overt perpetrators	Others from the agent group	System
View of Justice	Incidents of hate are exceptions to the system of justice	We need justice for them	We need justice for all
Spiritual or Moral Foundation	I may simply be following doctrine or seeking spiritual self-preservation	I believe helping others is the right thing to do	I seek to connect and liberate us all on spiritual and moral grounds
Power	I'm powerful—protective	I empower them—they need my help	Empower us all
Source of Ongoing Motivation	Motivator (my daughter, my sister, my friend) must be present	• Dependent on acceptance/praise from the other • Easily derailed by critique by other • Often leads to burnout	Sustainable passion—for them, for me, for us, for the future
Mistakes	I don't make mistakes—I'm a good person, and perpetrators are just bad people	Has difficulty admitting mistakes to self or other—struggles with critique or exploring own issues—highly defensive when confronted with own behavior.	Seeks critiques as gifts and admits mistakes as part of doing the work and a step towards one's own liberation—has accepted own *isms* and seeks help in uncovering them
Relationship to the System	Not interested in the system—just stopping the bad people	Aims to be an exception from the system, yet ultimately perpetuates the system	Seeks to escape, impede, amend, redefine, and destroy the system
Focus of the work	Perpetrators	Other members of the dominant group	My people—doesn't separate self from other agents
Privilege	Doesn't see privilege—wants to maintain status quo	Feels guilty about privilege and tries to distance self from privilege	Sees illumination of privilege as liberating and consciously uses unearned privilege against itself

Source: Keith E. Edwards. (2006). "Aspiring Social Justice Ally Identity Development: A Conceptual Model." *NASPA Journal 43*(4): 39–60. Used with permission.

The Aspiring Social Justice Ally Identity Development model can help leaders like Barbara and Lillie better understand how emerging champions are seeing themselves as allies. With that understanding, they can plan and provide appropriate next steps to help emerging champions develop as social justice allies, culturally proficient facilitators, and—ultimately—internal Cultural Proficiency consultants. For instance, Lillie and Barbara identified Jack as an aspiring ally for social justice and decided his next step should be to become a facilitator. This is the type of wise decision-making present in organizations that build internal capacity for Cultural Proficiency.

Reflection

What resonates with you about the Aspiring Ally Identity Development model? In what ways do you see yourself and your experiences within the model? In what ways do you see colleagues within the model? How can the model help you on your journey?

_____

_____

_____

_____

In what ways has this chapter helped you develop insight regarding wise decision-making present in organizations that build internal capacity for Cultural Proficiency?

_____

_____

_____

_____

DIALOGIC ACTIVITY

1. Review the chapter and highlight passages that contain ideas significant to the reader.

2. Use save the last word for me protocol (table 6.3) to explore perspectives, clarify and deepen thinking, and develop shared meaning in response to the chapter.

Table 6.3 Save the Last Word for Me Protocol	
Step	**Procedure**
1.	Participants form groups of four to five individuals. Each group sits at a separate table and chooses a timekeeper. This discussion protocol has rounds.
2.	Group members silently review the highlighted portions of the reading.

Step	Procedure
3.	To start the round, a designated participant shares what they consider to be the most significant passage by reading it aloud. This person does not add any commentary (i.e., they do not share why it was significant to them).
4.	Group members pause to consider the passage before talking.
5.	In turn, the other group members comment (one minute or less each) on the passage.
6.	The original participant then shares their commentary (three minutes or less) in response to the passage, sharing why it was significant to them and building on what was shared, as appropriate.
7.	Repeat steps 3 to 6 until all group members have initiated a round.
8.	Open the conversation to a larger dialogue, inquiring about ideas shared during the rounds.
Tip:	• Variation: Repeat steps 3 to 6 for the entire time. Group members have multiple opportunities to initiate a round.

Source: Adapted from National School Reform Faculty. Protocol originally developed by Patricia Averette. Retrieved from http://www.nsrfharmony.org/system/files/protocols/save_last_word_0.pdf

7 Paradigm Shift From Presenter to Facilitator

When you change the way you look at things, the things you look at change.

—Wayne Dyer (Change Your Thoughts—
Change Your Life, *2007)*

Becoming a facilitative leader means changing how you think in order to change the consequences you help create.

—Roger Schwarz
(The Skilled Facilitator, *2002)*

It's not about "what can I accomplish?" but "what do I want to accomplish?" Paradigm shift.

—Brené Brown (Presentation, 2012c)

When a paradigm shifts, everyone goes back to zero . . . past success means nothing.

—Joel Barker (The Future Edge, 1992)

Just because some people can do something with little or no training, it doesn't mean that others can't do it (and sometimes do it even better) with training.

—Carol Dweck (Mind-set, 2006)

It's not about perfect—it's about effort. Bring that effort every single day. That's where transformation happens. That's how change occurs.

—Jillian Michaels
(quoted in Ambandos & Michaels, 2012)

The effects of mere experience differ greatly from those of deliberate practice, where individuals concentrate on actively trying to go beyond their current abilities.

—K. Anders Ericsson, R.Th. Krampe, & C. Tesch-Romer,
(The Role of Deliberate Practice in the Acquisition
of Expert Performance, *1993)*

GETTING CENTERED

These quotations relate to the topic of learning to work successfully within a new paradigm. Please read them sequentially, from first to last. What resonates with you? Why?

_____

_____

_____

_____

EPISODE EIGHT:
MENTORING THROUGH JACK'S BIG SHIFT

Jack met with Barbara—his new mentor—once a week, either by phone or in person, to discuss his progress, ask questions, and get feedback. He also started apprenticing as a facilitator with Barbara and Frank by cofacilitating with them during their seminars for the school district. These seminars took place at the district's professional learning center across town from Jack's office.

When he started cofacilitating with Barbara and Frank, Jack felt awkward. He thought of himself as a hybrid of two metaphors: a third wheel that had been thrown into the deep end of the pool. He sometimes cofacilitated with Barbara, sometimes with Frank. In either configuration, the third person took the role of observer and gave feedback to the other two after the seminar. To Jack, his being asked to give feedback at this stage was a puzzle to him. Surely he didn't know enough to provide helpful feedback. Nevertheless, Barbara and Frank always solicited feedback from him through questions. Soon Jack found himself asking similar questions of them in order to get the type of feedback he needed. He kept a small notebook handy and jotted down questions and comments to discuss with them during lunch or at the day's end.

More often than not he felt like a failure at facilitation. He often hesitated and second guessed himself. His presenter and classroom skills weren't cutting it in this environment. Now he understood Barbara's statement about facilitation following different rules. Sometimes he simply did not know how to respond. At times he froze like a deer in the headlights when participants expressed strong emotions. Once—midway through the first day of a seminar—an angry woman jumped up and yelled, "I don't need to be here! You're not going to make me feel guilty for being white!" Jack was at a loss. He took a mental and physical step back. Frank, attuned to Jack's discomfort, moved out of observer role to cofacilitate with Barbara for the next few hours while Jack watched and learned.

Jack wasn't always reminiscent of a deer in the headlights, though. At times he presented information. Presenting felt natural, but presenting was exactly why he felt unsuccessful as a facilitator. He was giving information rather than facilitating change. To act as a facilitator at all Jack had to consciously and methodically work against his long-standing habits. He had to first think and then act, instead of acting without thinking first. It was like learning to ride a bicycle, only harder.

Actually, the experience was like already being a skilled bike rider and then having to learn to ride a totally different type of bike with a different set of rules: turn the handlebars left, and the wheel goes to right; turn the handlebars right, and the wheel goes to the left. With every turn, Jack had to outthink his instinct and muscle memory. Almost everything he had learned about bikes or presenting to groups was now useless; he had to unlearn all his familiar patterns.

Having to think before every action was mentally tiring. Jack also found it stressful to be frequently confronted with seminar situations that he didn't yet know how to handle. At those times, he almost regretted setting out on the facilitation path. It wasn't fun feeling incompetent, and he often wished there were a manual or book to guide him, but there wasn't. He and Barbara and Frank were, in effect, writing the book as they pioneered this path. When Jack was under stress, he found it difficult to think clearly, and he automatically fell back into his habitual pattern, which was to present information. There was no denying or ignoring these occurrences. Barbara made sure that Jack was aware of his actions—every single time—whenever he'd revert to his presenter habits.

If facilitation was a dance, Barbara would point out when Jack was doing the Hokey Pokey (by himself) to a tune that called for the East Coast Swing with a partner. Jack often thought, "Why in the world am I doing this to myself?" He wasn't used to failure. He found it ironic that he used he used to teach his middle-school students that learning to fail was essential to success. Back then, he'd made this his classroom motto and hung a huge poster of basketball hero Michael Jordan saying, "To learn to succeed, you must first learn to fail." Perhaps it was time for Jack to live this motto himself, he thought. Still, he desperately wanted to avoid spending too much time learning to fail. He wanted to succeed, so he looked to Barbara and Frank for more and more feedback. Through their feedback, Jack realized that he, in fact, was doing very well . . . at learning how to fail.

Barbara was highly skilled at providing Jack with direct feedback. She didn't beat around the bush, and she owned that. "Jack, right now I'm not your coach: I'm your consultant and I have some expertise to pass on to you." A recurring theme was that stress was causing Jack to fall back on what his nervous system knew and understood best—presenting. Barbara's remedy was that he needed to step back, breathe through the crown of his head, and with his breath, push all the energy out through his feet. Relax, stay grounded, don't try to do too much too soon, and trust his cofacilitator. Her feedback included the following:

- You're telling them things again. When you tell them, you keep them from discovering things for themselves. And you're using up all the airtime. Give explanations only when the group requests it. Notice when you feel the need to "give" them information. Let go of that need. Pause, step back, breathe. Ask a question, let your cofacilitator intervene, or invite in other voices. Remember what Maya Angelou said: "People won't remember what you said or did; they will remember how you made them feel." As facilitators, we help everyone to feel included.
- When Lisette was sharing what it's like for her as a black woman working in the school system, I noticed your body language. You looked nervous and perhaps scared. If guiding conversations about race rattles you, try to reframe. Forget that we've learned this subject is taboo. Instead, focus on the facts. Get curious about what Lisette is sharing. Invite the group to reflect back her words to her without

attaching any interpretation or commentary. Invite Lisette to notice what's happening with her internally as she shares her experience and when she hears her words mirrored back. A question such as, "What's it like for you to speak about your experience as a black woman in the school system?" would refocus the group's energy on process. Then people can talk about who they need to be in order to do what they have to do.

- Jack, you said, "I'm going to give you five minutes for this." That's power-over language. You're taking a presenter stance again. Try saying, "You'll have five minutes for this." Or even better, "You'll have as much time as you need. I'll check in with you in about five minutes." Remember, our actions and language need to support the concept that this event is all about them. This is their work. We're just helping them do what they must do. We're not directing and controlling them, so we need to shed the type of language that suggests we have the power and we'll give them some when we deem it necessary.

- You opened that discussion with, "What did you learn?" That's not a bad question, but it jumped right to "the head." It focused on content rather than process. Later, when you shared content that you had learned, you were actually inserting yourself as if you were a participant. Remember, your role is facilitator. You're not a content expert. It may help if you practice opening group discussions with questions that keep you focused on process: "What was that process like for you? What stood out?" or invitational statements like, "Let's discuss what you just experienced." Those types of openers also promote mindfulness of the process in the participants.

Jack knew that although Barbara's feedback was pointed, terrifically consistent, and sometimes blunt, it was always constructive. She was always on his side. He trusted her implicitly, and he wasn't disappointed. Every time she'd deconstruct something, she would build him back up with advice, encouragement, and good cheer.

Frank handled feedback differently, yet he was equally effective in supporting Jack's growth and in bolstering his confidence. Frank maintained a coaching role, which provided a nice balance to Barbara's consulting stance. He asked reflective questions during downtime and even answered Jack's questions with questions, which often helped Jack find his own best answers. Frank's feedback often sounded like this:

- Hmm, that's a good question. So you're wondering what you should have done to close that discussion instead of telling the group what they just learned? Let me ask you this: What other options did you have?

- So, what did it feel like when Gina started crying as she was telling her story? What did you notice about yourself? How can you stay centered so you can focus on guiding the group's energy and not get swept away into it? What do you need from me as your cofacilitator in situations like that?

- Yes, during the group discussion, I agree that you focused in on one person's comments a little too quickly. What could you have done to open the discussion back up? Or, what could you have done—before having them converge on that person's comments—to keep the group in a divergent state of exploring possibilities?

As Jack gained experience, he fell short less often. He also had glimpses of success that fed his spirit and propelled him forward. These were moments where he was gliding, dancing with the group and his facilitator partner—and he was actually grooving with the music! More precisely, in these moments he felt as if he had finally mastered one more dance step—albeit still a beginner's step. He'd get a whiff and a taste of success, and Barbara would swoop in to remind him to slow down and savor the moment. She'd ask him to describe what just happened, and then she'd shower him with positive feedback that inspired him to believe that he could dance on stage someday—maybe even dance professionally—as long as he chose to keep logging his hours on the dance floor and relentlessly pursuing feedback.

Whenever Jack mastered a step, he knew he'd have trouble varying from it for a while and that doing the same step throughout the entire song would feel constraining and would probably expose his inexperience. But sticking with the structure of that one step felt safe, so that's what he did. Over a period of weeks and many seminars, he practiced dancing the step to familiar songs, and he'd learn minor variations along the way. Eventually, he learned how to improvise and do a different step. As long as he kept the beat, he could express himself in different ways, and things worked out fine. Barbara complimented any and all of his attempts to improvise, even when he felt awkward or foolish. She'd say things like, "You're engaging and adapting, and that's what this work is all about."

Processing Barbara's and Frank's feedback on top of actually facilitating the group left Jack exhausted at the end of each seminar day. He was stretching, and it was obvious that he had limits to how much he could stretch in any one session. Sometimes he'd pass out in his favorite chair right after getting home on a seminar day. He needed a full night's sleep after those days. He also started to notice that with each session—each seminar experience—he was able to stretch a little more. There was no doubt he was adapting and growing, and he was starting to truly believe that he would be able to do this work well.

Reflection

What is familiar to you about Jack's experience in this episode? What is unfamiliar? What do you find intriguing? What do you find useful?

_____

_____

_____

_____

GROWING INTO A NEW PARADIGM

In Episode Seven, we see Jack aspiring to shift his behavior from that of a presenter to that of a facilitator. Along the way, we witness him experiencing several of the challenges associated with growth and behavioral change. The challenges he experienced are consistent with the Barriers to Cultural Proficiency, which this book explores in part II.

The principles illustrated in Episode Eight are as follows:

- **Growing into a culturally proficient facilitator involves shifting paradigms.** Paradigms are frameworks with governing principles: basic assumptions, ways of thinking, and methodologies. The shift from diversity presenter/trainer to Cultural Proficiency facilitator involves at least two paradigm shifts: (1) training on diversity (outside-in) versus Cultural Proficiency (inside-out), and (2) presentation versus facilitation. Diversity trainer/presenter behavior and Cultural Proficiency facilitator involve two completely different sets of governing principles.

- **When a paradigm shifts, it is normal for us to experience resistance to change.** As change expert and futurist Joel Barker (1992) puts it, "When a paradigm shifts, everyone goes back to zero. Your past success means nothing" (p. 140). In other words, even the world's best presenter has no advantage for performing well within the facilitation paradigm. In fact, people and groups who excel in one paradigm may be disadvantaged in the new paradigm because of long-standing habits. In addition—and this is a paradox—we experience resistance to change even when we actively want that change. This resistance is part of human nature.

- **Executing behaviors and skills within a new paradigm requires conscious attention and slow, deliberate, and intentional action.** Established habits (automatic execution of highly practiced and well-learned skills) are encoded within the part of our brain that handles our procedural memory—the part of our long-term memory responsible for knowing how to do things without deliberation. However, developing new habits involves the higher-functioning part of our brain (neocortex) that handles our working memory—the part of short-term memory responsible for conscious processing. Because we are learning how to grow from presenting into the new paradigm of facilitating, we are not going to be able to act with automaticity. We are going to have to both think and act. On our journeys, the Cultural Proficiency Framework serves to guide our conscious attention, deliberate processing, and intentional moral action. You could call it a type of mind-set training (performed and practiced by the participants, not by any outside force).

- **Experiencing stress, anxiety, and exhaustion will cause us to revert to well-established patterns of behavior.** When we encounter external stimuli that trigger strong emotions, our brains downshift to our reptilian brain—the place that controls our fight-or-flight response. This part of our brain (brainstem in partnership with the limbic system) responds with the well-practiced skills and behaviors encoded within our procedural memory. As a survival mechanism, when under stress or in danger, the reptilian brain dominates the neocortex, preventing us from thoughtful deliberation. When learning to be a culturally proficient facilitator, external stimuli may trigger an internal emotional response that brings about old patterns of behavior, even though we may "know" better. We may feel internal conflict as a result. These emotional responses may show up in forms such as aggression and the need to have power over the group, a participant, or the cofacilitator; anger or annoyance; anxiety and a craving to perform well; or fear of conflict, failure, or some other perceived threat.

- **Mastering performance within a new paradigm involves deliberate practice, quality feedback, and reinforced improvement of practice.** Through his research on the role of deliberate practice in behavioral change that leads to extraordinary focus, Anders Ericsson (Ericsson, Krampe, & Tesch-Rober, 1993) argued that it takes ten thousand hours of deliberate practice for someone to rise to world-class performance in any field. Malcolm Gladwell popularized that number through his book *Outliers* (2008), and Macklemore and Ryan Lewis extended the prolificacy of its use in mainstream popular and hip-hop culture through their song "Ten Thousand Hours" on their Grammy Award–winning album *The Heist* (2012). Regardless of Ericsson's emphasis on establishing a specific quantity of time to achieve mastery, those of us aspiring to be culturally proficient facilitators can glean a couple of valuable lessons from his research. The first is that we must hold a growth mind-set (Dweck, 2006). In other words, we need to believe that we can all grow into being skilled facilitators; our performance isn't contingent on innate intelligence or talent. Experience is the key factor in developing expertise; high levels of competency requires high amounts of time and intentional practice. Furthermore, we can extend the implications of Ericsson's work by factoring in feedback. After all, without the corrective effect of feedback it certainly is possible to practice something for years and be no better at it than when we started. Thus, culturally proficient facilitators seek feedback from everyone: colleagues, participants, and mentors. Quality feedback reinforces improvement within practice. As practice improves, performance improves and mentors shift more often to coaching roles.

Reflection

Consider these five principles of behavioral change in new paradigms. Which principle(s) speak to your experiences? How do they do so? Which principle(s) do you question? Why?

_____

_____

_____

_____

In what ways can these principles help you work as a facilitator of Cultural Proficiency? How can they help you help others who may be struggling to leave behind unhealthy traditions and work differently within a new paradigm in order to serve students better?

_____

_____

_____

_____

EPISODE NINE: JACK REVERTS UNDER PRESSURE

Meanwhile in the district office, the term *Cultural Proficiency* was a hot topic. The term was now used regularly. News had spread about capacity building efforts to grow internal facilitators. Jack had been apprenticing for two months, and Julie Cho, Tom Joy, and Fatima Akram were about to start with Brenda's mentorship.

Jack was the first internal consultant for Cultural Proficiency to receive a support request from within the district. It came from Bill Black, the director of school administrators. His e-mail was flagged as "urgent."

Dear Jack: I've heard that you're our in-house person to contact for help with Cultural Proficiency. Are you able to run a two-hour session during our next principals' meeting? It's one week from today. I apologize for the short notice. We've adjusted the agenda because we've received an official complaint from our administrator's union. Several principals feel that the district does not support them in successfully leading data conversations in response to disaggregated student data, which involves addressing race, among other demographic categories. Personally, I was glad to hear this because I think it presents an opportunity for us to get into diversity and equity work with a more positive motivation than if the decision to hold such a session came from "above." So, during next week's meeting, principals can choose one of two breakout sessions. I'm hoping that you'll run a session focused on Cultural Proficiency and data conversations. Please let me know if this is possible. If yes, please send me a rough outline of your session ASAP. Again, sorry about the quick turnaround. Regardless this is a great opportunity, and I don't want to miss it. Thank you!

Sincerely,
Bill Black
Director of School Administrators
Stocklin County Public Schools

Jack immediately thought about the data-informed dialogue protocol he had learned about through Barbara and Frank. The protocol ensured equal participant voice and promoted an understanding of people's own viewpoints, beliefs, and assumptions. It would be perfect. Jack accepted Bill's request and immediately created a new document and began typing his plan.

Within an hour, Jack sent Bill a plan for a session titled "Culturally Proficient Data Conversations." It included this outcome: "Participants will learn and practice a protocol for data-driven dialogue in order to provide effective leadership of disaggregated data conversations." Additionally, he included an outline for the session.

Jack sat back in his chair, folded his arms, and grinned. He felt good, confident, successful. It was a familiar feeling, similar to the rush he felt when he conducted his mathematics workshops. After so much trudging through learning how to cofacilitate with Barbara and Frank, this successful feeling felt particularly welcome. He was back—but now he was Jack 2.0. This time, he was dealing with a completely different audience and a purpose above and beyond the boundaries of his usual math discipline.

It felt great to have planned it by himself. How satisfying. Perhaps his growth as a facilitator was ahead of schedule. Perhaps learning to fail as Barbara's protégé had paid off. He couldn't wait to share this with her. Good thing they had a two-hour, face-to-face meeting in his cubicle the next day. He printed the documents connected to this project to share with her.

The following morning, Barbara arrived right on time, as usual. She held two cups of coffee, and her laptop strap was slung over her left shoulder. Jack took the coffees and placed them on the round table that somehow fit in the corner of his cramped—better yet, cozy—cubicle. They sat down, and Jack got right to business by handing her the documents.

Jack: I have something exciting to share. Take a look at these.

Barbara: Great! What are all these papers?

Jack: I'm doing my first solo Cultural Proficiency session, and it's with the district's principals. I printed the e-mail exchange—the invitation and my response. I also printed my plan for the session. The pages are in order. Go ahead and read them. I'd like to use some of our time today to discuss this, if you're game.

Barbara: Of course.

She looked through the papers and began reading. Jack reviewed a copy that he had made for himself. When finished, Barbara looked at Jack, paused, and flashed a quick smile.

Jack: Isn't this exciting?

Barbara: What excites you most about it all?

Jack: First, district leaders are starting to request support for Cultural Proficiency and are using me as a resource. Second, I responded with confidence. I was able to put together a plan pretty quickly. I mean, all of this is great, right?

Barbara: I agree. It's great that leaders in the district are seeking and finding support inside the district. That's certainly our goal. And, at the same time, we need to slow down and take a closer look at this situation. Let's discuss your response.

Jack picked up her vibes, and they weren't what he had expected. Her energy made him pause. Suddenly, he didn't feel so masterful and confident in his plan. Had he overlooked something?

Barbara: I have a few questions. Then we'll explore your options. I think this is a good opportunity for me to coach you and then for us to collaborate to finalize your plan. What do you think?

Jack: Okay . . . yes.

Barbara: Great. First, let's talk about your intent. What are you trying to accomplish?

Jack: Exactly what Bill requested. Help participants learn about Cultural Proficiency and data conversations. This is reflected in my outcome and agenda.

Barbara: I notice you said "my outcome and agenda." To what extent did you engage the group in developing your outcome and agenda?

Jack: What do you mean? They asked me to do that. That's why Bill contacted me.

Barbara: He contacted you for support. It's part of your job as an internal consultant to figure out what type of support is best for his group. Did you talk to any of the principals to learn about their group? Did you interview a few of them or work with them to develop an outcome that they could own? Did you at least ask Bill for feedback on the outcome and agenda?

Jack: Well . . . no.

Barbara: My first question is a basic and foundational question: Is your intent to facilitate the group or to present to the group?

Reflection

At this point, consider reviewing the episode with this purpose: notice details of Jack's behavior that indicated his intentionality. What did his actions express as far as operating as a presenter or facilitator? The space below invites you to record your observations and interpretations.

_____

_____

_____

_____

Jack: My intention is to facilitate. It's Cultural Proficiency so I'm definitely facilitating.

Barbara: Do you believe that it's impossible to present Cultural Proficiency?

Jack: Well . . . I don't believe that. I mean, you've helped me recognize that I slip into presenting all the time. So, yes, presenting Cultural Proficiency is surely possible. It can be presented like any other content, but simply presenting Cultural Proficiency is—in the end—ineffective, I believe. Like we've discussed: we can't present a journey that a group will take. The group must make its own journey. Our role is to guide and make the journey easier. The best way is to facilitate, not to present.

Barbara: Right. Yet, to me, this plan looks like your intent is to present. Specifically, it looks like you want to teach the principals the data-driven dialogue protocol.

Jack paused for a second. He had a light-bulb moment and then noticed that he suddenly felt disheartened. He spoke slowly.

Jack:	Oh . . . yes. . . . I suppose you're right. I didn't even realize it. Now I feel a little foolish.
Barbara:	Don't. It's neither good nor bad. This isn't the time for judgment or condemnation.

Jack had heard these words from Barbara (and Frank) many times. But hearing them again right then helped him relax, take a breath, and let go of his self-judgment.

Barbara:	What's important is your clarity: what you're doing and why you're doing it. It helps you to be transparent about your role and relationship with your group. Presenting to them would be completely appropriate if your goal is to teach them this protocol. Do you know if that's their goal?
Jack:	Yes, it is. Well, actually, I'm not quite sure. Bill wasn't that specific. Ugh. I feel like I just fell back into my default presenter mode. I can hardly believe it. I even fell back into presentation while I was planning and preparing. Wow. But I don't want to present to this group. I don't think that would be best.
Barbara:	Why might presenting be the less-than-best option?
Jack:	Now that I think about it, it might send the wrong message. I can see the danger. If I go in there and give them a protocol, they may think that's what Cultural Proficiency is all about. I can hear it now: "Yeah, I had that Cultural Proficiency training already. Jack McManus came in and did it for us." My presentation might misrepresent the journey as one of simply receiving information rather than engaging in the process. Ugh. I'm not sure what to do at this point.
Barbara:	At this point, how can I best help you? I can be your consultant and give you advice, be your collaborator and work with you, or be your coach and help you find the answers on your own. Which works best for you?
Jack:	Collaborator. I want to work through this with you.
Barbara:	The first thing we need to do is talk with Bill and gain clarity about his request. We'll need to learn all we can about the group. That's the first step of the planning protocol we will use. When preparing to facilitate groups, the rule of thumb is to dedicate three times the length of the session to planning and preparation—in this case six hours.
Jack:	What? Six hours! For a two-hour session? I knew you and Frank did thorough preparation work, but I'd no idea you dedicated that much time.
Barbara:	Yes, it's the responsive and responsible way to serve a group. We haven't brought you in on the comprehensive preparation work yet. We will soon. But let's get back to our planning session for the principals. We'll spend the first two hours of our six hours of planning and prep just learning about the participants and assessing the culture of the group. I know this is not what you're used to doing, but I assure you that it's well worth the investment. Frank and I actually spent several days learning about your seminar group when we were preparing for your five-day event.
Jack:	Wow. Yes, I remember you telling me things that you had learned about me before we ever met. It caught me off guard and made me a little suspicious.

Barbara: Actually, Jack, I believe the suspicion was already in you. I'd shared some information with you, and then you selected the data and the interpretation of that data that reinforced your existing beliefs. I just shared facts; you gave those facts the meaning you wanted. Your suspicion of our preparation was really a projection onto Frank and myself of the ill-at-ease feelings that you already had about experiences you perceived as similar to that seminar. As you know, this happens all the time. With you, I knew what was happening. And I didn't take it personally.

Jack: This is good to remember right now, as we're planning for the principals. They're going to bring with them their assumptions and beliefs related to Cultural Proficiency. We need to learn much more about them if we're going to meet them where they are.

Barbara: Exactly. We'll do just that as we develop the group's outcomes over the second two hours. We're going to be specific and thorough. Precise and relevant outcomes will make the rest of our planning easy.

Jack: Then the last two hours for everything else?

Barbara: Yes. The last two hours for everything else: the content, protocols for how they'll interact, and—finally—the agenda.

Jack: That's completely different from how I'm used to working with presentations. The agenda is usually the first thing I do. If our first task is learning about the group, we could still get a lot done during the time we have left together today. How should we get started?

Barbara: I have the planning protocol, template, and questions saved on my laptop. I'll e-mail you the files right now, and we can get to work. If you do end up wearing the facilitator hat with this group, you shouldn't work alone if you can help it.

Jack: I didn't even think of working with a partner. Fell back into old patterns again. Having a cofacilitator would help. With Cultural Proficiency, there's too much group behavior and interaction to observe for one person to handle well.

Barbara: It's also easy to get swept away by the group's energy—even in subtle ways—especially when things get emotional or heavily opinionated. If you get swept away, your cofacilitator needs to stay centered and be there for the group.

Jack: Okay. I'll text Fatima and Julie to see if either of them is available.

Barbara: Great idea. Remember to include your partner in the remainder of your planning so she will also have ownership of the event. Don't do what Frank and I have done thus far, neglecting to bring you in on the planning.

Jack: Will do. Hey . . . wait a moment. Are you saying you made a mistake? That you should have brought me into the seminar planning process before this? I didn't think you or Frank made mistakes!

Barbara: Ha! Told you. What can I say? We're all in a state of becoming.

For the remainder of their two-hour mentoring meeting, Jack and Barbara began the planning process for the principals' meeting. This process helped Jack better understand the difference between approaching this work as a presenter and approaching it as a facilitator. He felt that he'd just made a giant step forward.

Reflection

From this dialogue, what is resonating with you? Why? What rings true? What do you question? What do you want more information about?

_____

_____

_____

_____

A PARADIGM SHIFT INTO CULTURALLY PROFICIENT FACILITATION

Jack's tendency to fall back into old patterns of behavior is not unique to Jack. It's something each of us can expect as we learn to facilitate groups' Cultural Proficiency, especially if our training and experience has been in teaching. That is because facilitating is not the same as teaching. Teaching is presenting. Facilitating is guiding a group as it moves toward its goals. Thus, in the educational world, facilitating Cultural Proficiency is guiding a group through a journey that leads to transformation for excellence with equity in education. Table 7.1 provides language for each of these two paradigms in order to describe movement away from training people about diversity (or any other subject) and toward facilitating a group's Cultural Proficiency journey.

Table 7.1 Facilitation for Cultural Proficiency

FROM TRAINING FROM A DIVISIVE PAST Informed by Barriers to Cultural Proficiency	TO FACILITATING FROM AN EMERGING FUTURE Informed by Guiding Principles of Cultural Proficiency
Tolerance for Diversity: **The focus is on them.**	**Transformation for Excellence with Equity:** **The focus is on our practice.**
The trainer/presenter . . .	The facilitator . . .
Assumes the stance of content expert and presents information and strategies about how to work with cultural groups.	Models authentic engagement in learning about the participants' own individual and organizational culture and what is necessary to facilitate the Cultural Proficiency journey.

(Continued)

Table 7.1 (Continued)

FROM **TRAINING FROM A DIVISIVE PAST** Informed by Barriers to Cultural Proficiency **Tolerance for Diversity:** **The focus is on them.**	TO **FACILITATING FROM AN EMERGING FUTURE** Informed by Guiding Principles of Cultural Proficiency **Transformation for Excellence with Equity:** **The focus is on our practice.**
Purges, demeans, or discounts differences (voices other than the trainer's own, different perspectives, diverse strategies, and cultural differences) when presenting about diversity.	Values differences: inclusive environments and learning, participant voice, diverse perspectives, and a variety of facilitation strategies. The facilitator helps a group focus on understanding personal and organizational response to differences, the need for redressing inequity, and the benefits of inclusion.
Establishes authority; sets the agenda, presents the content; and avoids inquiry, conflict, and divergent thinking. Uses episodic or isolated events and activities.	Models vulnerability, engenders trust, and engages with authenticity to foster brave space. Builds collective efficacy for inquiry, dialogue, conflict resolution, creative problem solving, and moving through stages of the journey.
Responds to requests for diversity trainings with standard presentations that adhere to the agenda set by the trainer.	Customizes learning experiences and intervenes with moves, strategies, and energy that help the group progress on its journey.
Implements train-the-trainer trainings, maintaining control and/or group dependency on the trainer or the trainer's trainings and materials.	Builds organizational leadership capacity and capabilities to facilitate Cultural Proficiency. Facilitator incorporates policies, procedures, and practices that ensure culturally proficient professional and organizational development.

Deliberate practice and quality feedback over time will establish new habits within the paradigm described in the right-hand column of table 7.1. The importance of developing these habits is well expressed within the walls of the U.S. Navy Fighter Weapons School (aka Top Gun): "Under pressure you don't rise to the occasion, you sink to the level of your training. That's why we train so hard" (Anonymous U.S. Navy Seal). Yet this only partially describes the challenge Jack experienced in this chapter's episodes.

Early in this chapter, Jack used the metaphor of a different type of bike with a different set of rules to describe the challenge of his paradigmatic shift: his challenge of unlearning old habits and replacing them with new habits that had completely different governing principles. It might surprise you to learn that this bicycle—called the Backwards Brain Bicycle—actually exists. It's the perfect metaphor for the shift away from the left to the right column on table 7.1.

Engineer Destin Sandlin of the YouTube channel "Smarter Every Day" tells the story about how one of his engineering friends, Barney, designed this backwards bike as a challenge and a joke. Barney flip-flopped the steering mechanism on a regular bike so that the wheel turned the opposite way the handlebars turned (which is reverse to the way a bicycle normally works). Barney then challenged Destin to ride the bike.

Destin took the challenge. He thought—in fact, took for granted—that he could master riding this new backwards bike within minutes. Since he was an engineer, he had a solid grasp of the structural changes made and how those changes would affect the bike's steering. Destin had been riding bikes since boyhood, so it was a deeply ingrained skill. He jumped on the modified bike, pumped the pedals, and promptly fell off. To his amazement, he discovered that he needed eight months—yes, eight months of daily practice—to overcome his brain's established patterns of bike-riding. He fell off the modified bike many times during those eight months, but then one moment, the new skill clicked in his brain and, wobbly at first, he gained mastery of his new skills within his new paradigm.

From this experiment, Destin's conclusion was that knowledge is not the same as understanding. Certainly he had knowledge of how to ride a bike. He also had knowledge of the engineering behind the modified backwards bike. However, he didn't develop understanding until he embraced the risk of living within the new paradigm, powering through the darkness and difficulty, and practicing, practicing, practicing. Eventually, his understanding evolved into a completely different way of thinking and doing—a different way of being.

Like Destin Sandlin with his Backwards Brain Bicycle, we need knowledge and we also need deliberate practice, practice, practice so that our understanding will evolve and support us as effective facilitators of Cultural Proficiency. That's because deeply held assumptions that drive behavior get coded in our muscle memory; our bodies remember simple hypotheses (assumptions) such as if a steering mechanism turns left, the vehicle turns left. It gets programmed or coded into our muscles—with the result that it just feels right—particularly in the case of a largely automatic activity such as riding a bike or driving a car.

Even if we're consciously aware of a change in the governing rules (as Destin was when he first got on the modified bike), that doesn't mean our bodies and brains understand the new rules yet. It takes significant and intentional work to produce real and lasting change in behaviors because change takes place at the assumptive level. Similarly, profound change in schools and other organizations requires changing the shared assumptions that generations of educators have internalized and codified into educational practices and policies. (This codification into practices and policies is analogous to Destin's muscle memory of riding a regular bike.)

Part II of this book helps us develop knowledge of the manner in which culturally proficient facilitators work by providing necessary information about Cultural Proficiency as a framework and as a process. Then, part III presents illustrative information about what culturally proficient facilitators actually do. All this information provides the foundation and guidance that informs our deliberate practice, practice, practice.

Reflection

Describe your response to the Backwards Brain Bicycle anecdote. How is it analogous to your work? In what ways might it represent the challenges and opportunities involved with Cultural Proficiency? With the work of becoming a culturally proficient facilitator?

_____

_____

_____

_____

DIALOGIC ACTIVITY

1. Review the chapter and highlight passages that contain ideas of significance.

2. Use the four levels of text protocol (table 7.2) to explore perspectives, deepen understanding in response to the text, and explore implications for participants' work.

Table 7.2 Four Levels of Text Protocol

Step	Procedure
1.	Participants form groups of three to five individuals, sit in a circle, and choose a timekeeper. This discussion protocol has rounds.
2.	Group members silently review the highlighted portions of the reading.
3.	A designated participant starts a round by sharing (five minutes): • Level 1: Read selected passage aloud. • Level 2: Share a personal connection to the passage (emotional response or past experience and the accompanying emotional response). • Level 3: Share thoughts about the passage (interpretations). • Level 4: Share implications for their work (decisions or specific actions).
4.	Other group members respond to what was shared (two minutes).
5.	Repeat steps 3 to 4 until all participants have had an opportunity to share a selected passage.
6.	After all rounds, groups discuss implications for work that have been shared.
7.	Debrief the process.
Tip:	• Provide time for participants to write about the four levels before step 3. • Stick to time limits. • During rounds, if another participant has already shared a selected passage from the text, the person sharing should choose another passage. • Variation for step 6: Small groups share out implications for work.

Source: Adapted from Southern Maine Partnership. Originally developed by Camilla Greene: *Rule of 3 Protocol,* November, 2003. Retrieved from: http://www.schoolreforminitiative.org/doc/3_levels_text.pdf

PART II

How—Cultural Proficiency

If a picture is worth a thousand words, so is an allegory. Let's take an allegorical overview of Cultural Proficiency as a vehicular journey. Change is a journey. We have our destination: excellence with equity in education. We have our map: Cultural Proficiency theory (including this book). Cultural Proficiency is process; in our allegory, process is the driving. Cultural Proficiency is also content; content provides the theoretical framework that is the car (imagine a little red car, if you like). This car (the framework) is made up of numerous parts (the tools) that remain idle and stationary unless they are ignited and powered through human action.

The ignition is our free will. The engine is dialogue lubricated with authentic engagement. The fuel is vulnerability. The car takes us from where we are to where we want to be. Or in other words, we work together to cocreate culturally competent and proficient practices in our schools. We're in it for the distance. At some points, we get snarled in traffic and slow to a crawl. At other times, we burn rubber. But as we rack up the miles together, we'll discover ourselves to be on the best, most meaningful road trip of our lives.

Facilitators make the trip easier. They lead by example, drawing from their expertise. They possess deep understanding of the content or framework (the car), both applied (how to drive it) and theoretical (how all of its inner workings and features operate). They have experiential understanding of the process. They know the journey and they help groups navigate the terrain. In other words, effective facilitators know how to plan and guide groups through the various stages of their journey. They maximize efficiency, enjoyment, and fulfillment. They also know what to do if there is a breakdown.

Part II of this book provides information you can use to build a strong foundation for facilitating Cultural Proficiency. Part I focused on the why:

- Assuming we value excellence with equity in education, why do we need Cultural Proficiency and culturally proficient facilitators?

Part II will focus on the how:

- How can we use Cultural Proficiency as content (framework) and process (journey) to actualize excellence with equity in education?

Chapter 8 explains the Cultural Proficiency Framework and provides us with the opportunity to explore each of its four tools. Chapter 9 offers a Cultural Proficiency process map that facilitators can use to help guide their groups along their journey.

8 The Cultural Proficiency Framework (The Content)

It is important for an agency to internally assess its level of cultural competence.

—Terry L. Cross (Cultural Issues and Responses, *1989*)

So must we see the need for nonviolent gadflies to create the kind of tension in society that will help men rise from the dark depths of prejudice and racism to the majestic heights of understanding and brotherhood.

—Martin Luther King Jr.
("Letter from Birmingham Jail," 1963)

Technology is nothing. What's important is that you have a faith in people, that they're basically good and smart, and if you give them tools, they'll do wonderful things with them.

—Steve Jobs (quoted in Goodell, 1994)

Never let your fears prevent you from doing what you know is right. Not that you shouldn't be afraid. Fear is normal. But to be inhibited from doing what you know is right is dangerous.

—Aung San Suu Kyi (quoted in Victor, 1998)

GETTING CENTERED

You may be new to the Cultural Proficiency Framework. You may have had prior exposure to it. Or you may be experienced using it to improve behavior, practices, and policies. If you have had experience, how have you used the framework and what are your hopes for using it more comprehensively? If you are new to the framework, how do you hope it will help you?

_____

_____

_____

_____

CULTURAL PROFICIENCY AS CONTENT

Cultural Proficiency outfits us with the appropriate set of tools for our journey. Terry L. Cross and colleagues (1989) initially conceptualized the Tools of Cultural Proficiency within the field of social work and mental health and included them in their study Toward a Culturally Competent System of Care. About ten years later, a group of thought leaders introduced the tools to the field of education. Randall B. Lindsey, Kikanza Nuri-Robins, Raymond D. Terrell, and Delores B. Lindsey (Lindsey, Nuri-Robins, & Terrell, 1999; Nuri-Robins, Lindsey, Lindsey, & Terrell, 2001) began applying Cross's work with the intent of providing educators with a framework to shape schools that work for all students. Table 8.1 displays each of the Four Tools of Cultural Proficiency and describes the specific ways each Tool functions and provides us utilitarian support on our Cultural Proficiency Journey.

Table 8.1 Four Tools of Cultural Proficiency

On our Cultural Proficiency journey, this Tool_____	Helps us to_____
Barriers to Cultural Proficiency	Identify and describe what gets in the way of our progress by showing us the impediments to Cultural Proficiency that are nested within behaviors, beliefs, and values. We must remove, dismantle, or overcome the barriers in order to develop a healthy worldview and effective behaviors, practices, and policies within culturally diverse democracy.
Guiding Principles of Cultural Proficiency	Have a compass to direct our progress by providing us a moral philosophical framework. We use the Principles to identify and describe the core values and beliefs that inform a healthy worldview supportive of effective behaviors, practices, and policies within culturally diverse democracy.
Cultural Proficiency Continuum	Navigate our environment by supplying descriptive language for our values, behaviors, practices, and policies. We use the continuum to identify and describe six distinct ways of perceiving and responding to diversity. These span a range from unhealthy (undesirable and ineffective) to healthy (desirable and effective).
Essential Elements of Cultural Competence	Move forward and conduct course corrections as necessary by offering standards. We use the essential elements as benchmarks for developing, implementing, and improving, and for measuring the effectiveness of behaviors, practices, and policies.

Source: Adapted with permission from Lindsey, Nuri-Robins, and Terrell (2009).

This chapter explains each of the four tools by offering definitions, illustrations, and tables and figures. It will conclude with an opportunity to explore how the four tools relate to each other and work together to form a framework. For a facilitator, working to understand the details and nuances of the Cultural Proficiency Framework is analogous to taking the time to understand how to operate a vehicle and read a map before undertaking the responsibility of facilitating a group into its own discovery of vehicle, map, and journey.

THE BARRIERS

The Barriers to Cultural Proficiency operate together to form a barrier or shield that blocks our progress toward excellence with equity in education. Table 8.2 extracts, names, and defines the four common barriers. Although we can place these concepts into four neat columns within an orderly table for the andragogical (the adult version of pedagogical) purposes of this book, these concepts function in a more complicated and interrelated manner. When manifesting themselves as beliefs, behaviors, practices, and policies, they exist in an entangled state and as such form the Barriers to Cultural Proficiency.

The first barrier, unawareness of the need to adapt, lies within our individual and collective belief systems. It is difficult if not impossible to see a problem until one believes that the problem exists. Thus, overcoming the unawareness of the need to adapt means seeing and interpreting things differently. Facilitators help individuals and groups surface and reconsider assumptions about things they may believe to be certainties. A group does this by processing new information (i.e., disturbances to its system). Facilitators use mental models such as the Ladder of Inference (Argyris, 1990) and Chaos Theory (Wheatley, 2001, 2006, 2008) to help groups overcome this barrier.

The second barrier, resistance to change, manifests in many ways. Although it shows up in behaviors, it is rooted in both our belief systems and our nervous systems. People may believe change is a threat to their way of seeing the world and to the comfortable

Table 8.2 Barriers to Cultural Proficiency

Barrier	Definition
Unawareness of the need to adapt	Not recognizing the need to make personal and organizational changes to better serve people within your organization
Resistance to change	Opposing or struggling with modifications or transformations that alter the status quo in the organization
Systems of privilege and oppression	Institutionalized practices and policies that produce inequities by awarding unearned benefits (privilege) and undeserved penalties (oppression)
A sense of entitlement	Belief that one's achievements and benefits are deserved because they were fairly earned and awarded

Source: Adapted with permission from Lindsey, Nuri-Robins, and Terrell (2009).

space they have created within the existing system. They may end up dragging their feet with, rebelling against, or sabotaging change efforts such as Cultural Proficiency. This can be classified as psychological and social resistance to change; however, it is also biologically based neurological resistance.

Neurological resistance is when we resist change because the well-established patterns of behavior familiar to our brains feel comfortable and normative. For example, when it comes to the issue of ensuring the education of every student regardless of demographics, we may declare with conviction that change is most certainly necessary. However, resistance to change shows up when—despite our good intentions—we slip or fall back into the old practices and policies because they are what we are used to. They feel normal.

Change requires more than good intentions. Changing involves the discomfort of abandoning familiar patterns. It then requires addressing the change with deliberate practice and focused intention until the change becomes the new normal and we become comfortable with it. Resistance to change is natural and predictable, and we need to deal with this resistance in practical and pragmatic ways. Resistance is only a barrier when it is not addressed in a helpful manner. Facilitators draw from change models to help groups overcome their resistance.

Third, systems of privilege and oppression exist throughout most organizations in the forms of institutionalized racism, sexism, heterosexism, ageism, ableism, and so on. These systems can be supported and sustained without the permission or even the knowledge of the people whom they benefit. These systems deny groups of people rights and benefits (oppression and marginalization) while awarding those same rights and benefits to others (privilege or entitlements), "often in unacknowledged and unrecognized ways" (Terrell & Lindsey, 2009, p. 27). Phrased differently, people perpetuate systems of oppression and privilege because they continue to confer unearned benefits to entire groups of people. These unfair systems remain a barrier if they are not acknowledged, countered, overcome, and/or dismantled. To those ends, facilitators help groups experience and recognize systems of oppression and privilege through the awareness stages of the journey (chapter 9). Later, they assist groups in implementing intentional and redressive moral action to counter these systems.

Finally, a sense of entitlement arises from unawareness and "indifference to benefits that accrue solely by one's membership in a gender, race, or other cultural group" (CampbellJones et al. 2010, p. 101). This barrier emerges when we are not willing to consider whether or not our achievements were influenced by systems of oppression and privilege. Without awareness and reflection, we may attribute what we have accrued solely to individual competence, character, or hard work; in other words, we discount the presence and influence of the system in favor of the personal.

Just to be clear: Cultural Proficiency is not against individual merit. It's all for merit and achievement within a system that provides a level playing field for all participants. It's unfair and unjust "merit" that's the problem. Facilitators help groups overcome this barrier by first helping them develop awareness of the systems at work. Then, facilitators promote reflection and dialogue about whether or not what we have—individually and organizationally—was earned or awarded in a fair and just manner.

Culturally proficient facilitators possess the capability to help individuals and groups experience, acknowledge, describe, and personalize the Barriers to Cultural Proficiency.

To be effective, facilitators must be able to do this and be able do it well. It is the discovery and ownership of the barriers that propels a group through the awareness stages of its journey and solidifies the group's commitment to culturally proficient action.

Reflection

What resonated with you from this section on the barriers?

_____

_____

_____

_____

What are some examples of the barriers within your school or organization?

_____

_____

_____

_____

DIALOGIC ACTIVITY

1. Individually write and/or review the reflections from this section.

2. Use idea-to-example mixer protocol (table 8.3) to tap into the information present within the group by helping participants share reflections, generate additional examples, listen to different perspectives, and increase understanding of the barriers.

3. Prepare for the activity by placing a sheet of chart paper in four different areas of the room (wall or table). On each sheet, write one of the four barriers.

Table 8.3   Idea-to-Example Mixer Protocol

Step	Procedure
1.	Facilitator places chart paper in a different area of the room (wall or table) according to the different topics.
2.	Group divides into four smaller groups—one group per chart paper/barrier. Each group gets one marker and gathers in its designated chart paper/barrier area.
3.	Round 1: For (established time), record examples for this topic within your organization.

(Continued)

Table 8.3 (Continued)

Step	Procedure
4.	Person with the marker stays. Everyone else in each group attempts to evenly disperse to different charts/barriers.
5.	Round 2: For (established time), person with marker first reviews what was recorded during previous round then continues to record examples of that topic.
6.	Repeat steps 4 to 5 twice more (four rounds total).
7.	After Round 4, each group identifies (designated number) examples group members believe best illustrate that topic within the school, school system, or other organization.
8.	Facilitator guides a dialogue (small and/or whole group) in response to the process of generating, discussing, and sharing examples of the topics.
Tip:	• Before moving on to the next round, each group selects a different person to stay at the chart paper so it isn't always the same person.

THE GUIDING PRINCIPLES

Whereas the barriers are obstacles that get in our way or slow down our journey, the Guiding Principles of Cultural Proficiency help us to stay on course in the direction that leads to excellence with equity in education. The guiding principles provide a "moral philosophical framework" (Terrell & Lindsey, 2009, p. 23) that prevents us from wandering too far off into unproductive or even hazardous wildernesses by engaging in unproductive conversations or buying into programs, pedagogies, and practices aimed at helping disenfranchised groups but that are based on deficit theories that actually harm students while allowing the disenfranchising systems to go unexamined (Gorski, 2010).

On the journey, we make use of the guiding principles in several related ways. First, they serve as reference points for us to consider and crystalize our own beliefs about culture and diversity. Next, they help us examine and improve, when necessary, the core values of our organization, both in who we say we are—our espoused values—and what we actually do—our values in use (Argyris & Shon, 1995). Finally, the principles provide a foundation on which we can develop a coherent approach to educating all students in a manner that values culture and diversity as assets.

Table 8.4 displays nine Guiding Principles of Cultural Proficiency. As you read through the table, keep in mind the following definitions: First, culture is the set of practices and beliefs shared by members of a particular group that distinguishes that group from other groups (Terrell & Lindsey, 2009, p. 16). Second, the dominant culture in a school, organization, or society is the established traits (e.g., values, beliefs, rituals, and customs) that are the norm for that school, organization, or society as a whole (Marshall, 1998).

Table 8.4 The Guiding Principles of Cultural Proficiency

1.	Culture is a predominant force in people's and schools' lives.
2.	People are served in varying degrees by the dominant culture.
3.	People have group identities and individual identities.
4.	Diversity within cultures is vast and significant.
5.	Each cultural group has unique cultural needs.
6.	The best of both worlds enhances the capacity of all.
7.	The family, as defined by each culture, is the primary system of support in the education of children.
8.	School systems must recognize that through necessity marginalized populations have to be at least bicultural and that this status creates a unique set of issues to which the system must be equipped to respond.
9.	Inherent in cross-cultural interactions are dynamics that educators must acknowledge, adjust to, and accept.

Source: Lindsey, Kearney, Estrada, Terrell, and Lindsey (2015).

Reflection

In the space below, record reactions, examples, personal connections, or questions in response to reading table 8.4.

_____

_____

_____

_____

DIALOGIC ACTIVITY

1. Individually write and/or review the reflection for this section.

2. Use the saying something protocol (table 8.5) to help participants share information, listen to different perspectives, and increase understanding of the guiding principles.

THE CONTINUUM

The Cultural Proficiency Continuum helps us to better understand and navigate our environments. It provides us with descriptive language in the form of six unique and

Table 8.5 Saying Something Protocol

Step	Procedure
1.	Each participant pairs with another participant.
2.	Divide the reading (table 8.4) into thirds.
3.	Group members silently read/review the first third of the reading. (In this case, read/review the first three guiding principles.)
4.	When partners are ready, each takes turns (designate approximate time) saying something: a question, brief summary, key point, interesting idea, or personal connection.
5.	After the facilitator alerts the group, conversations stop and group members repeat Step 3 to 4 twice more. (In this case, for Guiding Principles 4 to 6 and then 7 to 9.)
6.	Facilitator guides dialogue (small or large group) in response to processing the guiding principles in pairs.
Tip:	On chart paper, write the following list of options: "a question," "a brief summary," "a key point," "an interesting idea," or "a personal connection" for participant reference during rounds.

Source: Adapted from Creating Classrooms for Authors (1988) by Harste, Short, & Burke.

Table 8.6 The Cultural Proficiency Continuum: Depicting Two Paradigms

Cultural Destructiveness Eliminate Differences	Cultural Incapacity Demean Differences	Cultural Reductionism Dismiss Differences	Cultural Precompetence Respond Inadequately to Differences	Cultural Competence Effectively Engage with and Respond to Differences	Cultural Proficiency Learn about Culture and How to Effectively Engage and Respond to Differences
Unhealthy Paradigm Shaped by the barriers • Focus is on "them" • Tolerate diversity • Orientation is blame • Mind-set is scarcity • Conversations limit possibility			Healthy Paradigm Shaped by the guiding principles • Focus is on "our practice" • Value diversity • Orientation is responsibility • Mind-set is abundance • Conversations open limitless possibilities		
Motivations Self-assertion, anger, craving, fear, anguish, apathy, guilt/shame, and depersonalization			Motivations Exploration, cooperation, power-within, mastery, generativity, higher service, world soul, and enlightenment		

Source: Adapted from Lindsey, Nuri-Robins, and Terrell (2009).

distinct points. Table 8.6 displays the points from left to right as well as within two paradigms: unhealthy (destructiveness, incapacity, and reductionism) and healthy (precompetence, competence, and proficiency). These six points describe a range of perceiving and responding to differences: from destructiveness to proficiency.

Table 8.6 also clearly depicts two different worldviews. The one on the left represents a worldview shaped by beliefs consistent with the Barriers to Cultural Proficiency. The one on the right represents a worldview shaped by beliefs consistent with the Guiding Principles of Cultural Proficiency. Behavior aligned with points in each paradigm is fueled by different motivations or energy states: negative (unhealthy) and positive (healthy). Also, the points on the unhealthy side are static while those on the healthy side are developmental and illustrate a progression of expressed consciousness. The unhealthy side does not reflect that type of progression: a goal of improving culturally destructive practice by making it culturally incapacitating doesn't make sense. Instead, cultural precompetence is the minimal improvement goal for practice falling along any point on the unhealthy side.

The continuum, in the words of former Ventura Unified School District superintendent Trudy Arriaga, "helps participants in actually 'seeing' the dominant discourse at their schools about the students they serve" (Arriaga & Lindsey, 2016, p. 28). Table 8.7 invites

Table 8.7 The Cultural Proficiency Continuum—Examples

Point	Description	Examples
Cultural Destructiveness	Eliminate differences: The elimination of groups and other people's cultures	• "I teach only the cream of the crop. I've been here for decades and don't teach 'those' kids. I've earned my keep." • "If we could get rid of those apartment and trailer park kids, our school would be good again." • Preventing a group of students from accessing the curriculum. • Refusing to teach students who don't respond well to the instruction, and insisting a specialist work with them.
Cultural Incapacity	Demean differences: Belief in the superiority of one's own culture and behavior that leads to disempowering another's culture	• "Here are my plums and those are my prunes. Over there are my pits." • "Why do you think 'those' kids are so slow? Their parents just don't care." • Institutionalizing low expectations through tracking practices. • "Those kids just don't learn how I teach."
Cultural Reductionism	Dismiss differences: Minimizing the importance of cultural differences, acting like they do not matter, or not recognizing that there are differences among and between cultures	• "Every child achieves to the best of their ability. They just need to take advantage of opportunities." • Ignoring diversity. "I don't see color in any of my kids. I treat them all the same. I'm not prejudiced." • Neglecting individual and group needs in favor of whole-group instruction. Teaching to one learning modality—the teacher's preferred style. • "I don't know how many black students I have in my class. I've never really looked at them that way."

(Continued)

Table 8.7 (Continued)

Point	Description	Examples
Cultural Precompetence	Respond inadequately to the dynamics of difference: Awareness of the limitations of one's skills or an organization's practices when interacting with other cultural groups	• Interventions and support groups for underserved students and staff. • Episodic events such as Hispanic Heritage Month, Black History Month, and International Night that honor students' diverse backgrounds. • Grouping students for instruction with limited effectiveness and intentionality. • Reading a book or attending a presentation about an ethnicity different from your own to learn about students, families, and colleagues.
Cultural Competence	Engage effectively with differences using standards: Using the five Essential Elements of Cultural Proficiency as the standards for individual behavior and organizational practices	• Creating a culture of high expectations where everyone shares a belief in the importance of learning and students hold themselves to high standards. • Shaping an inclusive environment that taps into the benefits of diversity to enrich learning and well-being for all. • Differentiating instruction to effectively support all learners. • "I notice the voices of our families who practice Islam are not present. We can't make a decision until we engage them in the process."
Cultural Proficiency	Esteem and learn from differences as a lifelong practice: Knowing how to learn about and from individual and organizational culture; interacting effectively in a variety of cultural environments; advocating for others	• Learning how to surface, examine, challenge, and change (if necessary) personal and organizational assumptions. • Working to understand how the classroom or school cultural norms serve people to varying degrees. • Learning to apply social justice principles to engage students in curriculum and instruction. • "I'm starting to seek conversations and learn about how people who self-identify as other than white may react to me because of my whiteness."

Source: Adapted with permission from CampbellJones, CampbellJones, and Lindsey (2010).

you to consider dominant discourse and common practices in your school or organization as you read about each of the six points on the Cultural Proficiency Continuum.

Those of us experienced with the Cultural Proficiency Framework may have noticed cultural reductionism (Nuri-Robins & Bundy, 2016) as an alternative to the original term *cultural blindness* (Cross, 1989; Lindsey et al., 1999). The primary intention behind this linguistic change within this book is to bring the Cultural Proficiency Framework more into alignment with its purpose. Although quite prevalent in diversity and social justice literature, terms such as *color blindness, color muteness,* and *cultural blindness* are ableist when viewed from a critical disability perspective. The episode in chapter 12 of this book illuminates this conflict.

Practitioners and social justice leaders have chosen to respond to this linguistic dilemma in various ways. (This book does not promote one correct way to respond.) Some people acknowledge the contradiction but continue to use the language in order to avoid the confusion of alternative terms (Michael, 2015, p. 18) or in order to reference the terms as used by academics to describe a specific and significant social phenomenon (Adams & Bell, 2016, p. 138). The author of this book acknowledges the risk of causing confusion by using alternative terms yet chooses to use cultural reductionism as an illustration, in and of itself, of Cultural Proficiency. Specifically, this illustrates engaging and learning about linguistic microaggressions and then adapting in order to address and improve a perceived unhealthy practice.

As you, the reader, navigate the dilemma involving language best suited for describing this point on the continuum, consider it an opportunity to initiate a critical conversation and decision-making process at the local level. After all, that type of conversation represents the utilitarian value, in general, of the continuum. It initiates critical and informed discussions about where we are and where we want to be with regard to diversity and social justice.

Reflection

The space below invites you to review table 8.7 and write examples familiar to you for each of the continuum points.

_____

_____

_____

_____

DIALOGIC ACTIVITY

1. Individually write and/or review the reflection from this section.

2. Use affinity mapping protocol (table 8.8) to help participants share information, listen to different perspectives, and increase understanding of the continuum.

Table 8.8 Affinity Mapping Protocol

Step	Procedure
1.	Group divides into smaller groups of four to six participants.
2.	Each participant silently writes examples of the various categories (one example per sticky note or index card) without writing the title of the category.
3.	In silence, participants put all sticky notes/index cards on the group's table.
4.	Continuing in silence, participants organize or group sticky notes/index cards into categories.
5.	Once participants have settled on categories, they discuss and name their categories, insights, and process.

(Continued)

Step	Procedure
6.	Each small group shares insights with the large group.
7.	Facilitator guides a discussion.
Tip:	Groups can use chart paper instead of table tops.

Source: Adapted from National School Reform Faculty, as revised and described by Ross Peterson-Veatch http://www.nsrfharmony.org/system/files/protocols/affinity_mapping_0.pdf

THE ESSENTIAL ELEMENTS

The Essential Elements of Cultural Proficiency function as our standards for cultural competence in personal and professional behavior as well as in organizational policies and practices. Our use of the essential elements to redress inequity and improve our K–12 education system, taken as a whole, will provide justice and fairness to our nation's children—too many of whom we have underserved. Our use of these standards will also provide students with the cross-cultural and global competence skills and dispositions that will foster social and economic prosperity for our students and our nation (U.S. Department of Education, 2013, p. 9).

The need for action that redresses inequities and supports diversity and inclusion is urgent (U.S. Department of Education, 2012, 2013; Wells, Fox, & Cordova-Cobo, 2016). However, the journey to this type of intentional moral action is through awareness. Meaningful and sustainable use of the essential elements to plan, implement, and measure actions is contingent on our values and beliefs.

As Lindsey and colleagues (2015, p. 45) caution, "blind adherence to these five standards will, most assuredly, lead to frustration." What they mean is: We can't fake it. We can't just add a program that happens to align with the standards. We can't just check off the box that we've adopted a culturally competent strategy or done a diversity activity. Instead, we need to change our minds about diversity, equity, and inclusion at the foundational level. Change begins within. It doesn't result from adding an external activity. But as we change our minds, we change our realities through our actions. Ultimately we change the educational experiences of our students for the better.

Effective use of the essential elements requires a worldview aligned with the right-hand side of the continuum, with beliefs and core values consistent with the guiding principles (Terrell & Lindsey, 2009). Therefore, when working with groups, facilitators should not start with the essential elements. Instead, they should use them with groups at the appropriate stage of the journey—the Action Phase. This phase happens after the Awareness Phase and after we have established a commitment to excellence with equity in education. Table 8.9 displays the five standards for cultural competence: the Essential Elements of Cultural Proficiency.

Table 8.9 The Essential Elements of Cultural Proficiency

Essential Elements	Conceptual Definitions
Assessing Cultural Knowledge	Identifying the differences between and among yourself and the people in your environment; being aware of what you know about your own culture, the cultures of others, how you react to differences between yourself and others, and what you need to do to be effective in cross-cultural situations
Valuing Diversity	Embracing differences as assets that contribute to the value of the environment; making the effort to be inclusive of people whose viewpoints and experiences are different from yours and will enrich conversations, decision making, and problem solving
Managing the Dynamics of Difference	Reframing differences so that diversity isn't the problem to be solved; viewing conflict as a natural and normal process that has cultural contexts that can be understood and can be supported in creative problem solving
Adapting to Diversity	Teaching and learning about differences and how to respond to them effectively; having the will to learn about others and the ability to use others' cultural experiences and backgrounds in educational settings
Institutionalizing Cultural Knowledge	Changing systems to ensure healthy and effective responses to diversity; making learning about cultural groups and their experiences and perspectives an integral part of your ongoing learning

Sources: Adapted with permission from

- Lindsey, Roberts, and CampbellJones (2013).
- Lindsey, Graham, Westphal, and Jew (2008).

Reflection

Please review table 8.9 and record examples of behavior, practice, or policy aligned with each of the essential elements.

_____

_____

_____

_____

DIALOGIC ACTIVITY

1. Individually write and/or review reflections from this chapter.

2. Use the jigsaw protocol (table 8.10)—using the five essential elements as the topics—to help participants efficiently share information, listen to different perspectives, and increase understanding of the essential elements.

Step	Procedure
1.	Large group divides into small groups that contain the same number of participants as there are topics. This is their home group. Within home groups, each participant is assigned one of the topics.
2.	In silence, each participant reads about and reflects on their assigned topic and records insights (summary, connections, examples, etc.).
3.	Participants reassemble into expert groups to discuss their assigned topics with other people assigned the same topic.
4.	Participants return to home groups. Each participant takes a turn sharing information about their assigned topic.
5.	Home groups discuss insights about the broader concept.
Tips:	• Provide each participant with additional readings about their assigned topics. • Participants can find additional online information about their assigned topics. • Consider designating a specific amount of sharing time for Step 4.

Table 8.10 Jigsaw Protocol

Source: Adapted from the Jigsaw strategy, developed by Elliott Aronson (Aronson, Blaney, Sikes, Stephan, & Snapp, 1975) as a strategy to counter the intergroup hostility observed in 1971 after school desegregation in Austin, Texas. Aronson attributed the hostility to competitive classroom environments. https://www.jigsaw.org/#history

THE CULTURAL PROFICIENCY FRAMEWORK

Central to a culturally proficient facilitator's knowledge base is an in-depth and experiential understanding of the Cultural Proficiency Framework. It's not enough to understand the why (the democratic purposes and goals of excellence with equity as well as the need for a process, supportive learning environment, etc.). To fully understand the framework is to understand the how (how to use Cultural Proficiency to reach excellence with equity in education) in addition to the why, as addressed in part I of this book. To address a critical component of the how, let's take a closer look at each of the framework's four tools.

When interacting together, the four tools form the Cultural Proficiency Framework. Table 8.11 displays a fresh iteration of the original framework (CampbellJones et al., 2010, p. 32; Lindsey et al., 2009). In order to recognize how actions spring from belief systems, read the framework from bottom to top. Conversely, reading the framework from top to bottom will help you see how we express values through our behaviors, practices, and policies.

This version of the framework builds on the content and format of its predecessors by delineating

- Two distinct paradigms and the goal of moving from left to right,
- Core values that represent the fundamental aspects of each set of principles,
- Principles that mirror the guiding principles and impede Cultural Proficiency,
- The invasive nature of the Barriers to Cultural Proficiency that commandeer every aspect of the unhealthy paradigm, and
- Types of actions that mirror the essential elements and represent typical ineffective cross-cultural behaviors, practices, and policies.

Table 8.11 Cultural Proficiency Framework: Two Paradigms

THE CULTURAL PROFICIENCY FRAMEWORK*						
Unhealthy Paradigm **Informed by the Barriers**				**Healthy Paradigm** **Informed by the Guiding Principles**		
The Barriers • Aberrations to culturally competent practice and policy • Reactive Behaviors		**ETHCAL TENSION**		**The Essential Elements** • Standards for culturally competent practice & policy • Proactive Behaviors		
– Resisting Change – Dismissing Systems of Oppression and Privilege – Benefiting from a Sense of Entitlement – Remaining Unaware of the Need to Adapt – Misusing or Abusing Power		**Differing Actions** ↑		– Assessing Culture – Valuing Diversity – Managing the Dynamics of Difference – Adapting to Diversity – Institutionalizing Cultural Knowledge		
(Unhealthy Worldview)		**The Cultural Proficiency Continuum**				**(Healthy Worldview)**
Cultural Destruction *Destroy:* Differences are wrong and should be eliminated	**Cultural Incapacity** *Demean:* Differences are demeaned and the norm is revered	**Cultural Reductionism** *Discount:* Differences don't exist or matter and should be dismissed or ignored	**Differing Worldviews** ↑	**Cultural Pre-competence** *Accommodate:* Differences deserve a positive response	**Cultural Competence** *Collaborate:* Differences should be valued, engaged with, adapted to, and institutionalized	**Cultural Proficiency** *Cocreate:* Difference is our way of being; we should advocate for and learn from differences
Impeding Principles			**Differing Beliefs** ↑	**Guiding Principles**		
– The system provides everyone a fair opportunity. – Systems of oppression and privilege do not exist. – Disproportionate outcomes are attributable to group differences, not to the system. – Change is a threat. – Others should adapt to our current conditions. – All benefits, special treatment, and advantages are deserved because they are earned and awarded exclusively according to merit. – People with more power are justified in using their power however they deem appropriate with people that have less power.			**Differing Core Values**	– Culture is a predominant force – People are served in varying degrees by the dominant culture. – People have group identities and individual identities. – Diversity within cultures is vast and significant. – Each cultural group has unique cultural needs. – The best of both worlds enhances the capacity of all. – The family, as defined by each culture, is the primary system of support in the education of children. – Marginalized populations have to be at least bicultural and that this status creates a unique set of issues to which the systems must be equipped to respond. – Inherent in cross-cultural interactions are dynamics that must be acknowledged, adjusted to, and accepted.		
uniformity, exclusion, status quo, disregard, inequality, tyranny, oppression, dominance, self-importance				diversity, inclusion, culture, consciousness, equality, democracy, justice, freedom, humility		

*Adapted from
- CampbellJones, CampbellJones, and Lindsey (2010).
- Lindsey, Nuri-Robins, and Terrell (2009).

In the framework, each paradigm illustrates a way of responding to differences. Assuming our goal of a thriving pluralistic democracy and educational system, the right side of the framework is described as healthy in that it is productive, views culture and differences as assets, and brings out the best in people. The other side is described as unhealthy because it has the opposite effects (Lindsey et al., 2009). The Barriers to Cultural Proficiency permeate the entire unhealthy paradigm. Think of the barriers as parasites that attack and poison the humanity in our actions, worldviews, beliefs, and values. The result is a sick and weakened organism or society.

Flowing from bottom-to-top, the progression through the framework is as follows.

- Core values elementally describe what we appreciate, desire, or seek to achieve.
- Beliefs incorporate core values and describe what we hold to be true.
- A set of beliefs form a worldview. A worldview also serves to validate our beliefs and values.
- Action manifests from our worldviews; we codify into practice and policy our assumptions about ourselves and the world around us.
- Action takes the form of behaviors, practices, and policies.

The Cultural Proficiency Framework clearly implies the goal of moving from left to right. In other words, a primary focus of facilitators of Cultural Proficiency (especially in the Awareness Phase of the journey) is to help groups experience a paradigm shift. This paradigm shift is the result of an individual or group choosing to cross the line that divides the framework in half—the important line that represents ethical tension.

RESOLVING ETHICAL TENSION

Ethical tension implies a struggle to decide what is right and to choose to act accordingly, even if it is uncomfortable, difficult, and a complete shift in values, beliefs, and behaviors. What is right becomes a moral imperative. However, what is right to one person may not be right to another. In the context of the Cultural Proficiency Framework, this means individuals will reside within whichever paradigm represents their truths. So when individuals come together to form a group, that group is certain to contain a range of truths— a range of beliefs regarding what is right. As such, the Awareness Phase of the journey requires a facilitator to assist the group as it resolves its ethical tension.

Resolving the tension necessitates that a group first develop clarity about its core values and beliefs, and in the process of developing that clarity, individuals and the group as a whole will face a fundamental choice. Lindsey and colleagues (2015) explain this choice as a choice to operate within one side of the framework or the other. As a way of being or a worldview, the unhealthy side of the framework involves the group choosing to perceive itself in one or more of these ways:

- Existing as victims of social forces
- Maintaining or adopting deficit-theory beliefs about marginalized communities
- Maintaining or adopting beliefs that they themselves are powerless to overcome or dismantle the systemic oppression affecting marginalized communities because the difficulty of doing so is beyond individual or group capacity and capabilities

The healthy side of the framework as a way of being involves the group perceiving itself in these ways.

- Existing as self-empowered agents of socially just and fair change
- Believing in the need to create conditions that facilitate self-empowerment of others
- Working to increase self- and collective-efficacy (the "yes, we can" mentality) with regard to responsibly and effectively educating all students within a pluralistic democracy

The role of a facilitator is to make it easier for the group to choose the healthy paradigm. The result of choosing the healthy paradigm is a group commitment to the goal of excellence with equity in education.

The Cultural Proficiency Framework is a basic toolkit. It provides groups with the conceptual tools they need in order to build their knowledge, navigate their journey, and increase their collective-efficacy. For facilitators, this framework serves as a mental model that they can use to plan for and respond to a group.

The ultimate goal is to make it easier for groups to align their behaviors, practices, and policies with standards for cultural competence. However, a group's effectiveness in its use of the essential elements depends on the extent to which its values align with those of the healthy paradigm (Terrell & Lindsey, 2009). Does the group value cultural differences and see them as assets rather than as liabilities? Does it esteem diversity as something that enriches rather than view it as an aberration that must be made conformable to the dominant culture? Answers to these types of questions must be "yes." This is why, early in the group's journey, the facilitator's job is to help a group address its values, beliefs, and worldview—in other words, to help the group resolve its ethical tension.

Consider this final thought regarding the process of resolving ethical tension and making the choice to deal with power in a way that allows us to reside on the healthy side of the framework. For those of us accustomed to systemic oppression, it means resisting the allure of tokenism and instead committing to self-determination by working with colleagues to become leaders in the development of fair and just practices and policies (Lindsey et al., 2013, p. 45). For those of us accustomed to systemic privilege or entitlement, that choice involves the possibility of giving up benefits and advantages that we may have taken for granted. To enrich your rumination about this dynamic, consider this quote from Frederick Douglass (1849/1991).

If there is no struggle, there is no progress. Those who profess to favor freedom, and yet depreciate agitation, are men who want crops without plowing up the ground. They want rain without thunder and lightning. They want the ocean without the awful roar of its many waters. This struggle may be a moral one; or it may be a physical one; or it may be both moral and physical; but it must be a struggle. Power concedes nothing without a demand. It never did and it never will.

Culturally proficient facilitators help individuals and groups through the struggle of resolving the ethical tension that arises when responding to the moral implications of excellence with equity in education.

Reflection

The space below invites you to reflect on this entire chapter. Please review this chapter on the Cultural Proficiency Framework. Below, record your thoughts, reactions, and questions.

_____

_____

_____

_____

Please return to the Cultural Proficiency Framework (table 8.11). What ideas reinforce your beliefs? What ideas are new to you and/or challenge your beliefs? What questions does this framework provoke?

_____

_____

_____

_____

If you were completely new to the Cultural Proficiency Framework, how has this chapter helped you? If you have had past experiences using the framework, describe how this chapter can enhance your use of it.

_____

_____

_____

_____

DIALOGIC ACTIVITY

1. Individually write and/or review reflections from this chapter.

2. Use the four A's text protocol (table 8.12)—to help participants engage in critical reflection in response to the text, share and listen to various critical perspectives, and increase understanding of Cultural Proficiency as a framework.

Table 8.12 Four A's Text Protocol

Step	Procedure
1.	Facilitator posts four questions, each involving a different "A": assumptions, agreements, arguments, and aspirations. • What assumptions of the author does the text imply? • What do you agree with in the text? • What do you want to argue with in the text? • What parts of the text do you aspire to?
2.	Participants read/review text and personal reflections, highlighting and writing responses to the questions posed by the facilitator.
3.	The large group divides into small groups of three to five participants.
4.	In rounds, participants share responses to one of the questions. When not sharing, participants listen without offering commentary or engaging in discussion.
5.	Continue rounds through each of the four A questions.
6.	Open a discussion framed around a larger question such as, "What does this mean to us as developing facilitators?"
Tips:	• Consider the option of opening a discussion between rounds.

Source: Adapted from National School Reform Faculty as originally developed by Judith Gray of Seattle, WA in 2005. Retrieved from: http://www.nsrfharmony.org/system/files/protocols/4_a_text_0.pdf

9 The Cultural Proficiency Journey (The Process)

We shall not cease from exploration, and the end of all our exploring will be to arrive where we started and know the place for the first time.

—T. S. Eliot (Four Quartets, 1943)

Discomfort is always a necessary part of the process of enlightenment.

—Pearl Cleage
(What Crazy Looks Like on an Ordinary Day, 1997)

Liberation is the path of transcendence. Manifestation is the path of immanence. Both lead to the same place: the divine.

—Anodea Judith (Eastern Body, Western Mind, 2004)

In the concept of a fall followed by an ascent, process takes on a shape and becomes something we can describe.

—Arthur M. Young (The Reflexive Universe, 1976)

GETTING CENTERED

These quotes represent themes in this chapter on Cultural Proficiency as process. As you read them from top to bottom, notice how you are reacting. What words or phrases are meaningful? Why? What represents your aspirations as a culturally proficient leader of professional learning?

_____

_____

_____

_____

AN INSIDE-OUT PROCESS

The previous chapter discussed Cultural Proficiency as content. This chapter explores Cultural Proficiency as process. The purpose of the chapter is to provide a foundation for facilitating groups through the process, which is an individual and collective journey of discovery and change. The journey is one of inward exploration into uncharted terrain: the inner world of unconscious assumptions and cultural conditioning. That is why the process has been referred to as an inside-out approach (Lindsey et al., 2009 p. 23).

However, the term *inside-out* is currently at risk of becoming hackneyed when it is repeatedly and thoughtlessly used to describe Cultural Proficiency without realizing and appreciating the depth and demands of the approach. The term *inside-out* represents the connection between inward reflection that results in outward behaviors (practices) that become nestled within organizational policy and procedure. Peter Senge, organizational learning thought-leader (1999) uses the term *profound change* to describe the results of this inside-out process. Profound change is the "organizational change that combines inner shifts in people's values, aspirations, and behaviors with the 'outer' shifts in processes, strategies, practices, and systems" (Senge, 1999, p. 15).

Cultural Proficiency is a process of developing awareness (inside) and commitment-plus-action (out) that gives us the inside-out approach. Because of the interior dimension, facilitating this process cannot simply be presenting information to an audience. The inside-out approach means, in effect, guiding and leading the group through a transformative process. You can't present a journey that a group will take; this concept is an axiom for facilitators. The group must make its own journey.

A facilitator is someone with experience of this transformation process who can help make the process easier for the group. The facilitator can assist individuals and groups navigate their inner space, discover who they are and who they want to be, find their own direction, and take action based on that awareness. Essentially, the function of facilitators of Cultural Proficiency is to lead by example, guiding people step by step through the transformative process into a new, better world where educators educate all children effectively in support of our diverse democracy. To do this, facilitators must be experienced and practiced with the inside-out process.

A FACILITATOR MAP FOR CULTURAL PROFICIENCY

General knowledge of theory is not enough. Specific application is necessary. What is needed is a good map. A facilitator needs a detailed map that provides guidance through inner excavations, moral turnarounds, and rocky climbs to higher grounds. In short, they need a map to support the educators who dare go beyond what's always been thought and done, and who have courage to press on to become their better selves. This map is a mental model that describes, among other things, the steps or stages through which the group will travel. It shows the landmarks of predictable dynamics on the journey, and it helps the facilitator assess the group's current location and plan the next step.

Figure 9.1 is a process mental model that provides a map for facilitators of Cultural Proficiency. The model is complex, thus the progression of the chapter examines it step by step through its layers.

- Collective-Efficacy
  - Four Levels
  - Arc of Process
  - Seven Stages
- Spiral Journey

Figure 9.1 Cultural Proficiency Facilitator Map

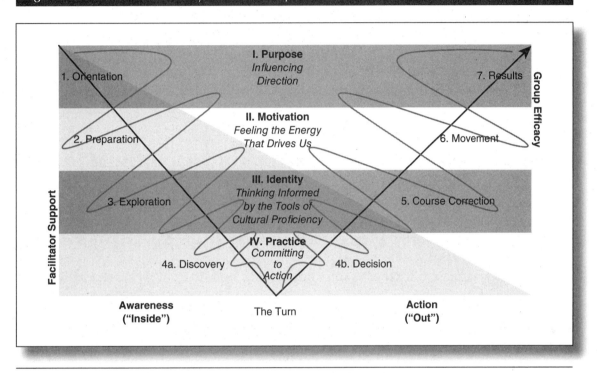

Source: Adapted from Arthur M. Young (1976). *The Reflexive Universe: Evolution of Consciousness.*

Reflection

As you look at figure 9.1, what do you notice? What predictions are you forming? What inferences are you drawing? What questions do you have? What reflects information discussed previously in this book? What is new? Please record your responses in the space below.

_____

_____

_____

_____

COLLECTIVE-EFFICACY

As discussed in chapter 6, culturally proficient facilitators aim—from the beginning—to work themselves out of their current job or role. In other words, when facilitators do their job well, over time the group should outgrow its need for them. Minimally, the group should need the facilitator to take on a different or less-involved role. Thus, facilitators give away their knowledge and skills to the group in order to help the group eventually facilitate itself. In other words, they help the group develop collective-efficacy.

According to Gibson (2003), *collective-efficacy* is a term that represents the group members' shared beliefs in the group's capabilities to mobilize the motivation, cognitive resources, and courses of action needed to succeed in achieving a specific goal. A facilitator's primary duty is to equip a group with the knowledge, attitudes, skills, aspirations, and behaviors necessary to increase its collective-efficacy and begin to facilitate its own journey.

The concept of collective-efficacy is derived from the concept of self-efficacy. Self-efficacy reflects an individual's beliefs in their own capabilities to engage in and successfully complete a course of action (Bandura, 1997). Because self-efficacy insufficiently explains group performance, the concept was extended and applied to group behaviors. The concept of collective-efficacy runs parallel on the group level to the concept of self-efficacy on the individual level (Katz-Navon & Erez, 2005).

However, collective-efficacy is not simply the sum total of the self-efficacy of each individual group member. Instead, it is a property of the group as a whole that emerges from the group engaging in its work. To group members, collective-efficacy reflects "what we think about us" (Mischel & Northcraft, 1997). The shift from the self-efficacy of individual group members to the group's collective-efficacy occurs in two steps (Chan, 1998):

- Group members shift their frames of reference from their individual capabilities to those of the team.
- The group brings the concept of collective-efficacy to the forefront of its consciousness through discussion, evaluation, and agreement.

The facilitator's trajectory in helping the group develop its collective-efficacy is a simple one: the higher the group's collective-efficacy, the less structure and support from the facilitator is necessary for group success. Early in a group's journey, facilitators provide the greatest amount of support. As they work with the group, facilitators model effective structures, strategies, and stances. They may even take a quick step out of the facilitator role and into the presenter role to explain to the group how and why they did what they did (what their process was).

As groups build collective-efficacy, facilitators gradually release more and more responsibility to the group, as represented in figure 9.2, the first layer of the facilitator map. Effective facilitators operate by the rule of providing the least amount of support for the most amount of success. Over time, the amount of necessary support decreases and dwindles as the group's collective-efficacy grows until the group no longer needs the relationship with the facilitator in the same way. This happens once the group believes it has the capacity to guide its own journey.

THEORY OF PROCESS

The next three layers of the map are based on Arthur Young's (1976) Theory of Process, which was later adapted by Drexler, Sibbet, and Forrester (1988) for purposes of group

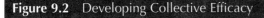

Figure 9.2 Developing Collective Efficacy

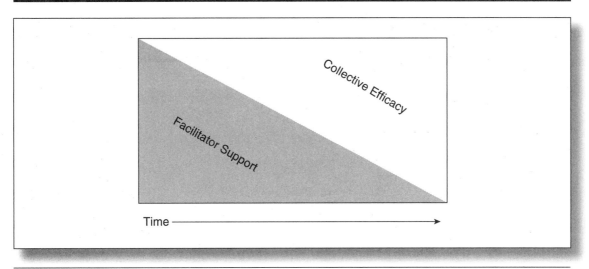

facilitation and team development. Young's model is brilliant and elegant. It is based on the facts of the development of all the kingdoms of nature. Through his theory, Young explains a universal evolution—or transformation—of consciousness. From his process theory emerges the next layers of the Cultural Proficiency facilitator map.

- Four Levels
- Arc of Process
- Seven Stages

Four Levels

As groups progress on the Cultural Proficiency journey, they move through four levels (figure 9.3). Each level represents a realm of group activity and reality at any particular moment. The top of the map (Level I) represents the most abstract activity, while the bottom (Level IV) represents the most concrete. Sibbet (2002, p. 10) describes group activity at the top of the map as "in the air" and activity at the bottom as "on the ground." Thus, in the air involves imagined and visionary activity, while on the ground involves operational and logistical activity. It should, though, be noted that groups (like the individuals in each group) are multidimensional; thus a group can and does operate on different levels simultaneously.

While operating within one of the four levels, a group benefits from a particular type of intervention from the facilitator that is different from interventions appropriate to the other three levels. Technically, *intervention* is a term for facilitator action. Intervention is anything a facilitator does or says that influences the group in a way that is different from what would happen if the facilitator were not present (Hunter, 2007, p. 78). However, the term *intervention* usually applies to facilitator actions intended to mediate group activity. As Garmston and Zimmerman (2013, p. 3) say, "To intervene means to take action to

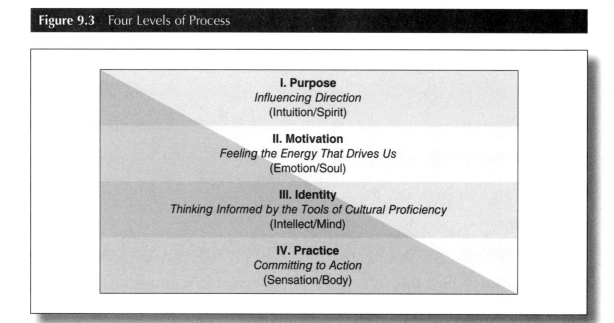

Figure 9.3 Four Levels of Process

I. Purpose
Influencing Direction
(Intuition/Spirit)

II. Motivation
Feeling the Energy That Drives Us
(Emotion/Soul)

III. Identity
Thinking Informed by the Tools of Cultural Proficiency
(Intellect/Mind)

IV. Practice
Committing to Action
(Sensation/Body)

Source: Adapted from *The Four Levels of Process* by Arthur M. Young. Unpublished essay http://arthuryoung.com/41evels.html

change what is happening or might happen in order to prevent counterproductive behaviors and increase group productivity and learning." A culturally proficient facilitator engages, adapts, and intervenes to help a group move forward on its journey. That requires an understanding of the four levels of group activity.

When a facilitator effectively intervenes with a group in sync with its level of operation, it may appear like magic to participants. It can even feel like a spiritual experience when facilitators connect with a group at its level of activity and help it gain insight regarding its core state of being. When this happens, these types of questions are commonplace among participants: "How did you do that?" "How did you know to ask that question?" "What just happened?" "What did you just do that brought us together so quickly?" "What did you notice that made you do that?" What may look like magic is actually high-level facilitator skills, particularly with the four levels.

Learning to effectively intervene is an ongoing process, and good facilitators are always learning. Chapter 10 (Facilitation and Cultural Proficiency) and chapter 14 (Adapting to Diversity) discuss facilitator interventions in greater detail. For now, let's take a closer look at the four levels of process as informed by Arthur M. Young's (1976) descriptions and David Sibbet's (2002) interpretations. Keep in mind that facilitators who are capable of intervening effectively are conversant with each level of group activity.

I. The Level of Purpose:
Focusing Attention and Influencing Direction

The purpose level is the firelike realm of potential, possibility, and being. For participants, activity at the purpose level includes focusing their attention to the group's purpose and to their own inner world by developing mindfulness and—later in the process—observing the influential effects of culturally competent and proficient action that ripple through an organization.

When a group is operating at this level, the facilitator's primary job is to help the group manage its attention. Facilitators act as visionaries, guiding groups from a future that has yet to emerge. They help groups become oriented to the inside-out journey and thus help them turn inward to become students of their own assumptions. Facilitators also help groups step back and mindfully observe the results of the journey. Level I is a dimension of the spirit where we function best with intuition. It is the realm of freedom of possibility.

II. The Level of Motivation: Feeling the Energy That Drives Us

The motivation level is the watery realm of emotion. For participants, activity includes visceral experiences, interacting with others, finding value, developing trust, practicing communication skills, and implementing culturally competent and proficient practices and policies.

When a group is operating on this level, the facilitator's primary job is to encourage participants to feel their inner urge—yearning, lacking, or desiring—for relationship and wholeness. This inner urge is not for a specific condition, idea, item, or object. (Forming and naming specific goals or objects of our desire happens at Level III.) Instead, facilitators help groups get in touch with the preformative gut feelings that actually are the energies that fuel their journey. It's by amplifying and directing this energy that a facilitator helps a group move forward toward change—the new, the future.

Facilitators provide support for processing emotions and developing capacity for rational thought and action. They help members develop trust within the group and process through emotions when implementing change. Level II is a dimension of the soul where we function best with emotion.

III. The Level of Identity: Thinking Informed by the Tools of Cultural Proficiency

The identity level is the airy realm of thinking, information, and mental models. For participants, activity takes place in the context of the Cultural Proficiency Framework and includes putting communication skills into practice: storytelling, exploring, and reflecting.

Facilitators help groups manage information from a variety of sources. They use the tools of Cultural Proficiency with groups with the goal of helping them resolve ethical tension and plan for continuous improvement. When a group is in the Awareness Phase, participants within the group shift modes of discourse into greater focus (convergent thinking and conversation) as it moves forward toward commitment. When a group is in the Action Phase, participants open up their modes of discourse (divergent thinking and conversation). Facilitators use a variety of strategies to leverage dialogue, draw out information, and cultivate strategic planning. They help members share, listen, and plan. Level III is the dimension of the mind where we function best with intellect.

IV. The Level of Practice: Committing to Action

The practice level is the earthy level of discovery and decision, choice and commitment. For participants, activity includes articulating insights, making connections to specific practices and policies, choosing to change, and committing to culturally competent and proficient action (behavior, practice, and policy).

Facilitators help groups become grounded and bring their thinking and conversations into focused points of decision and commitment. They help groups attend to operations and logistics. The facilitators also act as midwives who assist in the natural process of birthing insight. They don't create the insight nor do they control or force the birthing process. Instead, they guide, support, and assist—nurturing the content (insight) as it emerges from participants. In doing so, they engage participants' free will to embrace cocreation of a healthy future. Level IV is the dimension of the body where we operate best with sensation. It is the realm of most constraint, focus, and certainty (whereas Level I is the realm of most freedom, possibility and uncertainty).

Reflection

So far, what information about Cultural Proficiency as process resonates with you? What information gives language to your prior experiences? What relates to information discussed earlier in this book? What questions do you have?

_____

_____

_____

_____

Arc of Process

In explaining his theory, Arthur M. Young (1976) posits that a description of process must begin with its purposiveness—its goal. For Cultural Proficiency in education, the goal is excellence with equity. To reach that goal, we need the means, starting with direction.

The overall direction of the journey is forward, toward the goal. This directionality is represented by the left-to-right arrow in figure 9.4. Groups move through the four levels, descending from freedom (Level I) to constraint (Level IV) and then ascending back to freedom (Level I). This process is depicted as the V-shaped arrow that Young called the arc of process.

Level I (Purpose) represents a state of limitless possibility: a space where anything can happen and all things are possible, everything from contemplating possible outcomes for a seminar to creating truly inclusive and equitable schools for all students. Although the Cultural Proficiency journey never ends, each iteration of the journey starts and ends at this level.

After embarking, a group descends through the levels, decreasing in freedom and increasing in constraint until they reach Level IV (practice), the place of most constraint,

Figure 9.4 Arc of Process

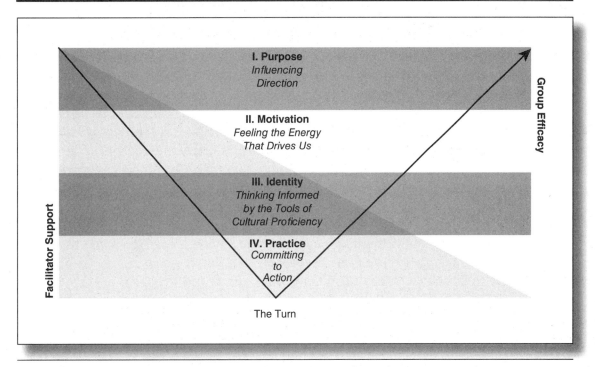

Source: Adapted from Arthur M. Young (1976). *The Reflexive Universe: Evolution of Consciousness.*

contraction, and clarity. This is the realm of resolution. Like a photographer who resolves an image by moving the lens to bring the aperture of a camera into focus, a facilitator helps a group make a resolution to take a certain course of action. This moment of clarity and choice brings a group to a singularity that mirrors that of Level I. This is what Young referred to as *the turn,* the point where group consciousness and activity shifts. On the Cultural Proficiency journey, the turn represents a group's commitment to intentional moral action in support of excellence with equity in education.

Although the group moves together on the journey, each individual participant makes the turn in their own unique way. At Level IV individuals who choose transformation begin to recognize and manifest a new kind of group-ness, based on redefined perceptions of hierarchy captured by the realization that every person in the hierarchy is as important as every other person. Each person is different in many ways, and each provides equal context for everyone else. It is critical that the individuals in a group express their differences within the group so they may progress and develop together as a group, beyond the turn.

A well-known scene from the science fiction movie *The Matrix* (1999) illustrates the essence of the turn. In it, Morpheus (Laurence Fishburne) presents Neo (Keanu Reeves) with a choice. Up until that point, Neo had progressed on his journey to the point of questioning the reality surrounding him. Morpheus explains to Neo that his reality is an illusion and not what he has believed it to be, that he is a computer programmer in a cosmopolitan city who moonlights as a hacker. Instead, Neo is simply experiencing a computer-generated virtual reality or simulated life. In reality, Neo and all human-kind have been taken captive by intelligent machines; the machines keep each person in a pod, senseless and dreaming the computer programs, while the machines continu-ously harvest the humans' bioelectricity to power themselves. Although humans in this so-called matrix believe they are free, they are actually subjugated by a system of complete control.

Neo is stunned by this revelation, but something in him suspects it is true. Morpheus then presents Neo with two pills, one in each hand. He says, "This is your last chance. After this there is no turning back. You take the blue pill—the story ends, you wake up in your bed and believe whatever you want to believe. You take the red pill—you stay in Wonderland, and I show you how deep the rabbit hole goes. Remember: All I'm offering is the truth. Nothing more." Neo must choose. He could return to mindless, suppressed ignorance, or he could embrace the painful reality, see the illusionary world as the oppres-sive system it really is, and dedicate his life to emancipation. But first he must liberate himself. He must change his mind. He must make a choice. Once Neo made the choice and chose the red pill, the choice was irrevocable.

Choice is the dynamic of the turn. Once individuals and groups have turned their focus inward, explored, and discovered new possibilities, they must choose. Often this is a choice between two perceived realities or paradigms. The first (the blue pill) is aligned with the Barriers to Cultural Proficiency, a worldview that—at best—reduces, minimizes, and ignores differences. The other (the red pill) is a reality aligned with the Guiding Principles of Cultural Proficiency, a worldview that esteems diverse cultures and recognizes that we can dismantle systemic barriers to equal access, opportunity, and achievement.

Making this commitment to Cultural Proficiency serves to resolve the ethical tension described in chapter 8. Like Morpheus in the movie, the facilitator plays a key role in accelerating the process and making it easier and more explicit. Although the group moves together on the journey, each individual participant makes the turn in their own unique way. Once a participant has made the commitment, there is no going back. When it comes to transformation, you cannot unsee what you see nor forget what you learn. The butterfly can't change back into a caterpillar. The ethical tension between the two world-views is resolved. Participants describe this step as letting go of a huge burden, of seeing their way clearly to becoming their better selves, and as experiencing the self-confidence that comes with being honest and authentic with themselves and others.

Phases of the Process

Chapter 4 uses light as a metaphor for consciousness and describes the phases of the journey as sitting in the darkness, emerging from darkness, and moving toward the light. Stated differently, those phases are the Awareness Phase, Commitment Phase, and Action Phase (figure 9.5). The descent that ends in The Turn is the side of the arc that represents the Awareness Phase (the inside of the inside-out process). This side represents the trans-formation from a group of disoriented individuals walking into the first day of a profes-sional learning seminar to a group unified in its commitment to change for excellence with equity in education. It is through this leg of the journey that individuals and groups have the opportunity to choose to change their minds.

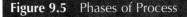

Figure 9.5 Phases of Process

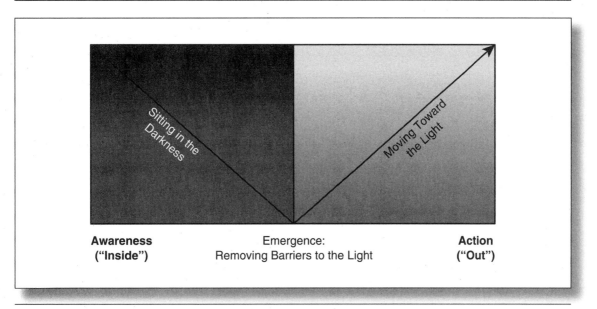

Awareness
("Inside")

Emergence:
Removing Barriers to the Light

Action
("Out")

Source: Adapted from Arthur M. Young (1976). *The Reflexive Universe: Evolution of Consciousness*

The turn happens at the place of most restraint within the process. It is here that the group sees the world differently; their perception is now aligned with the principles for healthy cross-cultural existence. After the turn, the upward path begins and freedom is regained as the group ascends back toward Level I. As the group progresses, it uses the tools of Cultural Proficiency to improve behaviors, practices, and policies. Individuals within the group work together in a concerted effort to turn their system into one where transformation can happen: a system where predictable disparities in opportunity, access, and achievement no longer exist; a system where every learner receives the benefits of diversity; a system where every educator effectively educates every child; a system where educators, students, and families all see themselves as learners emancipated from the vestiges of systemic oppression and privilege.

The ascent is the side of the arc that represents the Action Phase (the out of the inside-out process). It represents a dedicated and motivated group of individuals each of whom comprehensively fulfills their roles to make the necessary changes in practices and policies so that every child has access to a high-quality education. It is important to note that this action emerges from a shift in consciousness, not from external actions. As Anaïs Nin, American writer and diarist (1961, p. 124), wrote, "We don't see things as they are; we see them as we are." Simply put, seeing is not believing—believing is seeing. Culturally proficient facilitators work from this axiom and with this trajectory. Since we experience the world through our values and beliefs, it is on values and beliefs that a facilitator helps a group focus first. Where an idea originates is where the idea needs to be changed. Only after values, beliefs, and ideas shift to a healthy paradigm can the facilitator productively support the group in the taking of sustainable and transformative actions.

Reflection

How does the information about the Arc of Process and the phases of the journey enhance your understanding of Cultural Proficiency as process? From these sections, what information gives language to your prior experiences?

_____

_____

_____

_____

Seven Stages

One definition of process is "a series of actions or operations conducing to an end." The series on this facilitator map consists of seven steps or stages. The stages are sequential and additive—the process builds on itself. Each stage is associated with one of the four levels (figure 9.6). Furthermore, each of these seven stages contains seven substages with the same progression and powers. Thus, the process illustrated on the facilitator

Figure 9.6 Seven Stages of the Journey

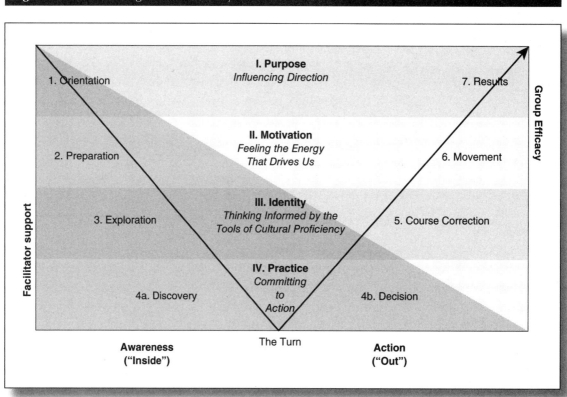

Source: Adapted from Arthur M. Young (1976). _The Reflexive Universe: Evolution of Consciousness._

map is actually a meta-process. The following is information about each of the stages of the Cultural Proficiency journey, based on Arthur M. Young's descriptions of seven kingdoms or stages.

1. Orientation

People who first enter into a conversation (workshop, seminar, meeting, etc.) about Cultural Proficiency usually bring with them all of their past experiences and associations with diversity, inclusion, equity, and social justice. Sometimes they bring only what they've heard about others' experience. Regardless, too often this baggage is negative. Some people may expect the leader (speaker, presenter, facilitator, etc.) to treat them with less than complete respect. At worst, participants expect blame and shame. At best, they expect to be told what they're doing wrong and what they should be doing differently. Especially when the event is mandated, some expect to be treated as vessels to be filled and to be fed information about cultures different from their own.

Thus at this early stage of Cultural Proficiency, it's critical that the facilitator attend to the moral purpose of the process to inspire a new and shared vision, helping participants focus inward to examine their own belief systems. Paradoxically, this may necessitate disorientation; the facilitator may need to shake things up to cause the group's existing frame of reference to be insufficient for a journey that involves critical reflection, dialogue, and changes in practice. Overall during this stage, the facilitator helps the group see the incredible potential and rewards of the journey: becoming their better selves and doing right by children. Leaving this stage, participant feedback often reflects the thought, "This is not what I expected."

2. Preparation

Once group members' orientation is directed inward, the group needs to prepare for the journey. First and foremost, group members must trust their fellow journeyers, for they cannot do it alone. Second, they must learn and unlearn communication techniques and become equipped with dialogic (speaking and listening) skills around sensitive issues. Essentially, they must become outfitted with appropriate and helpful tools for the journey.

During this preparation stage, facilitators attend to emotional dynamics of trust while building the group's capacity for productive conversations and future use of the tools of Cultural Proficiency. Helping participants learn and practice communication skills and interact with a number of other participants at this stage facilitates group bonds of trust. This is the groundwork that prepares the group for success in future stages of the journey by building its internal resources and getting in touch with the energy that will drive it toward change.

The nonnegotiable necessity of the preparation stage was dramatically highlighted when in 2015 the coffee-shop giant Starbucks initiated a bold new campaign called "Race Together," in which baristas were encouraged to talk about race relations with their customers. The campaign, although well-intentioned, was unsuccessful and short-lived. Even if the baristas had been prepared for this dialogue, that was no guarantee that the customers were. To succeed in such an endeavor, the baristas and the customers (the whole community) would have needed to be prepared and aligned. They weren't and the campaign ended abruptly.

3. Exploration

Prepared with the requisite skills and dispositions, groups then explore the perspectives and experiences of their various members. They use the tools of Cultural Proficiency to frame the essential conversations: conversations about diversity, equity, and social justice. This stage allows a group to progress in resolving the ethical tension between an unhealthy paradigm informed by barriers and a healthy paradigm informed by the guiding principles.

During this time, facilitators use the tools with groups and leverage dialogue. With skill and sensitivity, they draw out stories and information from the group. Based on what they know about the group, facilitators choose and use sources of information (articles, videos, guest speakers, etc.) that give the group just what it needs to catalyze constructive conversations. They choreograph relationships so that participants gain information different from their own; a variety of information is necessary because it helps shape a more spacious vision, one that is aligned with cultural competence and proficiency. In these ways, the facilitator helps the group form its identity.

4. Commitment to Intentional Moral Action (The Turn)

Stage 4 is twofold. The first component, discovery, takes place on the awareness side of the turn. The second component, decision, is on the action side of the turn. The primary focus of the facilitator at the turn stage is to help the group see the results of its exploration.

During discovery, content emerges from the process and the internal transformation takes form, much like a butterfly about to emerge from its chrysalis. As individuals within the group begin making the turn—each in their own unique way—they begin articulate insights, and the group forms as one entity (identity) in breakthrough understandings. The facilitator focuses on nurturing the content as it emerges and on assisting the group in (1) articulating new perspectives of how it sees itself and (2) letting go of unhealthy values, beliefs, and practices. It is here that a group makes the turn and is ready for action to spring from its awareness.

The turn represents commitment to intentional moral action: the decision to change and accept nothing less than high expectations, equity, and inclusion for every student. During the decision stage, a group becomes focused on the necessary decision and employs its free will to choose. As it begins its ascent and broadens its perspective (the action side of the turn), the group starts to recognize new horizons that were once beyond its range of vision. These are the horizons that provide the contexts for charting a new course on its journey with a path that is uniquely its own. When a group is in the turn phase, the facilitator catalyzes the focus, engages free will, exposes recognition of new horizons, and helps embrace the cocreation of a healthy, albeit still unknown, future.

5. Course Correction

With the recognition of new and exciting horizons, the group moves into a stage aligned with strategic planning, the course correction stage. Here the group again explicitly uses the tools of Cultural Proficiency. However, this time the tools are used for the external transformation of practices and policies. The facilitator makes this stage easier by supporting the group in its use of the tools. Facilitators help groups assess their current state, envision a desired state, build a roadmap, and develop strategies to redress inequities and ensure cultural competence. In short, the facilitator nurtures new growth in the course correction stage.

6. Movement

After charting a new course, the group can implement its plan with intentional moral action. Group members work in coordinated alignment to make changes in behaviors, practices, and policies. These changes are systematic improvements that move practice toward standards of cultural competence.

In the movement stage, the facilitator's role is to assist and support implementation through coaching and feedback. The support often takes the form of assisting with emotional reactions as group members work to make changes to the status quo and encounter resistance and kickback within their organizations. The facilitator provides feedback and helps the group stay focused on the broader ethical context as it encounters implementation challenges. In this stage, the substages are particularly apparent. Facilitators often must help individuals process emotions, think rationally, and reconfirm commitments. This is because the individuals implementing new practices or policies often must reexperience the ethical tension involved with doing with is right as they encounter the negative motivations and the manifestation of barriers within colleagues who have not yet embarked on the Cultural Proficiency journey and who see no problem with the status quo.

7. Results

Once a group implements its plan, it needs to step back and study its influence so it can move on to the next iteration of its process. The results stage means that the group shifts its focus from doing to learning. The learning involves harvesting and sharing results.

The facilitator helps the group realize its actions by studying results, leveraging improvements, and scaling and institutionalizing effective practices throughout the organization. During the results stage, the facilitator pays attention to the influence of the group's efforts by helping to share results through relationships throughout the organization.

They also nurture the spirit of the group by promoting celebrations and ceremonial events that promote renewal and help a group move on to its next endeavor in its Cultural Proficiency journey.

SPIRAL JOURNEY

The next layer on the facilitator map consists of spiral loops that serve to remind the facilitator of several concepts, including the vibrant nature of process. However, it is with this layer of the map that we depart from Arthur M. Young's precise geometric thinking. The loops do not represent the Theory of Process, which Young built as carefully as he built his invention of the Bell helicopter—the first aircraft capable of vertical flight. Therefore, the loops do not represent an attempt to alter his theory. Doing so would risk losing its representation of the natural world (which includes us) and the theory's ability to work in application to human conditions (since the process is built into us). After all,

Figure 9.7 Cultural Proficiency Facilitator Map

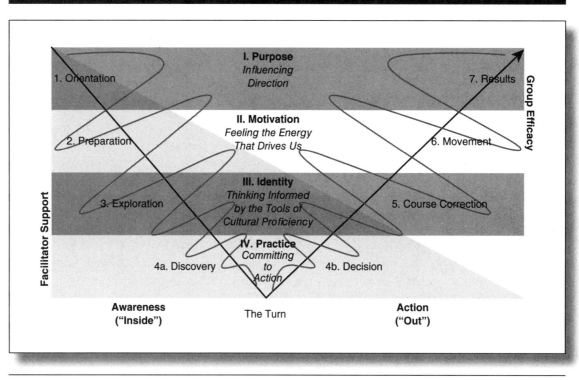

Source: Adapted from Arthur M. Young (1976). *The Reflexive Universe: Evolution of Consciousness.*

a helicopter might look better with its tail trimmed off, but doing so would destine it to unsafe flight, at best.

Instead of representing the Theory of Process, the loops simply serve to remind the facilitator of dynamics. The V-shaped arc of process may seem to imply an up-and-down linear progression, but group dynamics aren't that simple. The Cultural Proficiency journey does indeed have direction, but the process is better represented as a spiral journey than as a straight shot, as illustrated by figure 9.7.

During the earlier and later parts of the process, the loops in the spiral are relatively large. During the first and second loop, a group may pass through three of the four levels, only to spiral back. For instance, a group may quickly move through (1) orientation, (2) preparation, and (3) exploration only to circle back and address unresolved issues involving its purpose (Stage 1: orientation) and trust (Stage 2: preparation). Thus, the journey moves back and forth between the levels, and the facilitator assists by intervening in helpful ways that are appropriate to the various levels. As the group moves forward in a convergent manner, the intensity of the loops become more focused. The spiral gets tighter through the progression toward the turn. After the turn, the loops in the spiral again become increasingly large.

It should be noted that Arthur M. Young's theory does account for some of this. As explained earlier in this chapter, groups seem to move around from level to level at times. This occurrence is accounted for by the fact that each stage has seven substages that recapitulate the main stages over and over again.

Still the spiral journey on this facilitator map represents at least two concepts important to facilitators:

1. The convergent movement from uncertainty/abstract (possibility) to certainty/ concrete form (commitment) and divergent movement after the turn.

2. The circular and spiraling shape of dialogue. (For more information on dialogue, please see chapter 13: Managing the Dynamics of Difference.)

The first and last stages of the process happen in Level I, the place of infinite potential. The first stage (orientation) contains the pure potential of what could happen as the result of embarking on the Cultural Proficiency journey. The seventh stage (results) contains the infinite potential of what could happen as a result of a group's intentional moral action. As a group moves toward Level IV, it focuses its attention inward (the Awareness Phase) and experiences a dynamic within which the field of possibility collapses to a single commitment. The collapse follows this general sequence:

- Being aware of the possibility of exploration and discovery
- Developing skills and trust to explore
- Exploring a range of topics
- Discovering meaning within the exploration
- Committing to becoming our better selves

After the turn, the group experiences the inverse of this sequence. The group manifests its commitment in ways that expand the field of possibility. And after progressing to Stage 7, the field becomes infinite. The results of the group's intentional moral action will ripple out in ways that eventually elude its range of vision. Its influence will touch people that the group will never see. Group members may affect generations that they will never meet.

Because dialogue is essential to Cultural Proficiency, the spiral also represents its shape. Dialogue is a circular process of inquiry that is the most effective way known to "bring about deep motivational shift and the resulting behavioral change in a group or an organizational culture" (Zohar and Marshall, 2004, p. 118). The rules, structure, and dynamic of dialogue help groups surface and challenge deeply held values, assumptions, and beliefs. Dialogue is about equality, seeking to understand, sharing, listening, learning, and opening new possibilities. It is the engine (fueled by vulnerability and authentic engagement) that powers our vehicle (Cultural Proficiency Framework) that helps make the journey.

Reflect

Return to the Cultural Proficiency facilitator map (figure 9.1). What new understandings do you bring to it? In what ways does it reflect your own journey? What have you learned through exploring the layers of the map? How can it serve you in improving your practice as a culturally proficient facilitator? What questions do you still have?

_____

_____

_____

_____

DIALOGIC ACTIVITY

1. Individually write and/or review reflections from this chapter. Identify the section within the chapter you would most like to review and discuss in detail in a small group.

2. Use the focused review protocol (table 9.1) to help participants engage with each other in response to a selected section of text, share and listen to various critical perspectives, and increase understanding of Cultural Proficiency as process.

Table 9.1 Focused Review Protocol

Step	Procedure
1.	After individual participants have read a text, the large group divides into small groups of three to five participants.
2.	For a designated amount of time (e.g., three minutes), small-group participants take turns sharing which section they would like to discuss as a small group.
3.	Each small group makes a decision and identifies a section of text to discuss.
4.	In silence, group members review and mark the text with specific codes, such as /(checkmark) = I have prior knowledge of this. @ = I've experienced this firsthand. <3(heart) = This is meaningful to me at a deep level. ! = This surprised me. ? = I want to know more about this.
5.	Round-robin style, each participant shares a marked item, sharing one at a time while others listen.
6.	Participants discuss and explore items marked ! and ?.
Tips:	• Consider, time permitting, repeating process with a different section of text.

Source: Adapted from Focused Reading strategy, as presented by Robert Garmston and Bruce Wellman (2009). *The Adaptive School.* Norwood, MA: Christopher-Gordon Publishers, Inc.

PART III

What—Culturally Proficient Facilitation

Any facilitator of a group aspiring to goals related to diversity and inclusion, equity, cultural competence and/or proficiency, or social justice has a responsibility to work in a manner consistent with those goals. Otherwise they risk contradicting and betraying the core values of the work. Therefore, the Cultural Proficiency Framework is useful for facilitator reflection and improvement of practice. Their degree of Cultural Proficiency becomes a measure of their effectiveness.

Actually, this is true for all leaders of professional learning, and not just those serving groups explicitly focused on Cultural Proficiency or diversity, equity, and inclusion in general. Just as culturally proficient PK–12 educators aim to serve all students well, facilitators of professional learning communities (regardless of whether their focus is math, reading, or other) aim to provide inclusive and equitable service to every participant by facilitating in a culturally proficient manner. Furthermore, the primary ethical goal of any PK–12 educator—including curriculum or professional development specialists—should be excellence with equity in education.

To that end, the Cultural Proficiency Framework becomes pragmatic means. To assist facilitators with reflection and goal setting, two of its components are especially useful: the essential elements and the continuum. Used together, they form a rubric for culturally proficient facilitation (table 10.1). This rubric contains operational definitions for each of the five essential elements (that function as specific criteria for effective facilitation) as well as illustrative language for each of the continuum points (that function as gradients of various quality relative to the criteria). This rubric was inspired by the rubrics presented in *Culturally Proficient Inquiry* (Lindsey et al., 2008) and subsequent Cultural Proficiency texts (Lindsey et al., 2015; Stephens & Lindsey, 2011). It also serves as the foundation for part III of this book.

Part I focused on the why:

- Assuming we value excellence with equity in education, why do we need Cultural Proficiency and culturally proficient facilitators of the process?

Part II focused on the how:

- How can we use Cultural Proficiency as content (framework) and process (journey) to actualize excellence with equity in education?

Part III provides sensible, down-to-earth examples and illustrations of culturally proficient facilitation. Part III focuses on the what:

- What will facilitators do in order to work with groups in a culturally proficient manner?

Chapter 10 provides an overview of core facilitator abilities and skills and then applies the lens of Cultural Proficiency to them, culminating with the facilitation rubric. Chapters 11 to 15 each explores one of the five essential elements, which function as standards for culturally proficient facilitation. These chapters enable us to interact with the rubric, guided by a series of episodes. The book culminates by offering an opportunity for you to craft a professional learning plan for your next steps as a culturally proficient facilitator.

The use of vignettes, cases, or episodes as a method of presenting ideas is helpful as they illustrate concepts. These episodes also highlight illustrative examples of the types of activities, protocols, strategies, and moves culturally proficient facilitators might choose to employ. You will see them presented in **bold-faced** text. The resources section of this book provides annotations for these techniques.

These episodes are also limiting by their very nature. Within these part III episodes, the characters (facilitators) make impromptu decisions with varying degrees of success. However, even the most successful decisions are but one right answer among many possible right answers. Thus, this book continues to offer opportunities for reflection and dialogue to encourage critical thinking, exploration, and the discovery of more right answers.

Through the episodes, we return to the ongoing narrative and perspective of Jack McManus. Just over two years have passed since he began learning to facilitate with Barbara as his mentor. Much has happened since then. After one year of apprenticeship, facilitating became a full-time position for Jack instead of a role tacked on to his math curriculum specialist duties. He was named the coordinator of Professional Development for Excellence with Equity (PDEE)—a newly established, two-person team within the Department of Organizational Development in the Stocklin County Public School System. PDEE was the embodiment of the vision to have Cultural Proficiency be the district's "way of being," as Lillie Cohen had stated when she first invited Jack to begin his facilitator training. Fatima Akram joined the team as facilitator of PDEE. Barbara and Frank still had over a year left on their five-year contract, so the PDEE team continued to engage their services, albeit more for coaching nowadays than actually cofacilitating with them.

10 Facilitation and Cultural Proficiency

Most people do not listen with the intent to understand; they listen with the intent to reply.

—*Stephen R. Covey*
(The 7 Habits of Highly Effective People, *1989*)

Our culture made a virtue of living only as extroverts. We discouraged the inner journey, the quest for a center. So we lost our center and have to find it again.

—*Anaïs Nin*
(In Favor of the Sensitive Man and Other Essays, *1976*)

The kind of inquiry I am talking about derives from an attitude of interest and curiosity. It implies a desire to build a relationship that will lead to more open communication. It also implies that one makes oneself vulnerable and, thereby, arouses positive helping behavior in the other person.

—*Edgar H. Schein* (Humble Inquiry, *2013*)

Whoever travels without a guide needs two hundred years for a two-day journey.

—*Rumi (quoted in Fadiman & Frager, 1997)*

GETTING CENTERED

Consider the term *facilitator of Cultural Proficiency*. Now consider the term *culturally proficient facilitator*. How would you describe the similarity and difference between these two terms? Please use the space below to write your thoughts.

_____

_____

_____

_____

CORE FACILITATOR ABILITIES

Before plunging into part III of this book, let's review and build on basic information about facilitation mentioned in part I. Group facilitation is a set of values, skills, knowledge, principles, and practices that help a group move toward achieving its goals. A simple dictionary definition of the verb *facilitate* is "to help bring about," which means that the role of a facilitator is to make the group's process easier, smoother, and quicker than if the group were left to its own devices. The facilitation role requires three main responsibilities: attending to (1) the progress and well-being of the group, (2) the design and implementation of the professional learning events or meetings, and (3) the sustainability of the work within the school or organization.

To carry out these responsibilities, facilitators must possess three broad sets of abilities (Allen & Blythe, 2004). These abilities are supported by skill development and knowledge acquisition. Table 10.1 displays samples of skills and knowledge that support the three facilitator abilities. Within these three abilities, we will take a closer look at the vital skills of listening, mindfulness, and questioning.

Table 10.1 Three Facilitator Abilities

Abilities	Skills to Develop	Sample Knowledge
1. Ability to read the group	Listening, questioning, mindfulness, observation, and intuition skills	Energy, motivations, process, systems, self, others, groups, learning designs
2. Ability to respond to group needs	Questioning, listening, improvisation, interpersonal/human-relation, speaking, and mindfulness skills	Interventions, processes, protocols, strategies, activities, moves, systems, authentic engagement, self, others, groups
3. Ability to reflect, learn, and encourage reflection	Mindfulness, questioning, critical thinking, reflective practice, listening, and intrapersonal skills	Critical reflection, process, change, systems, self, others, groups

LISTENING

Listening is the key to healing and building strong relationships. It's fundamental to effective communication. It's the foundation of dialogue and is the primary skill of facilitation. Just because one can hear does not mean one can listen well. Hearing is a physical process that deals with receiving sounds. However, listening—as defined by the International Listening Association—is a cognitive "process that deals with receiving, constructing meaning, and responding to spoken and nonverbal messages" (Bentley & Bacon, 1996, p. 1). Without good listening, relationships break down or do not develop at all.

Listening is our most-often used mode of communication. Hunter (2007) goes as far as to describe communication as 80 percent listening and 20 percent speaking. Yet ironically, listening is the skill we least often develop well. Common claims related to a widespread lack of and need for listening skills (Carter, 2003; International Listening Association, 2016) include the following:

- We spend 80 percent of our waking time communicating. Of that, we spend 45 percent listening. Yet, when listening, 75 percent of the time we are distracted, preoccupied, or forgetful (Lindahi, 2003, p. 3).
- Less than 2 percent of us report having formal training on listening skills (Verderber, Sellnow, & Verderber, 2016, p. 38).
- Only about 8 percent of instructional time throughout a child's basic education is devoted to acquiring listening skills (Jalongo, 2008, p. 4).
- Even in required basic communication courses at the university level, less than 7 percent of the time is dedicated to learning how to listen (Neal, 2014, p. 38).
- Untrained listeners remember only about 25 percent of what was said, and most of what they remember is distorted or inaccurate (Wong, 2011, p. 289).

From the preponderance of available evidence, we can draw several broad conclusions: (1) Listening is extraordinarily important. (2) We are not very good at listening. (3) And as a society we have overlooked the importance of developing good listening skills. In fact, if you think back on your years of formal education, the majority of language arts teaching and learning was most likely focused on reading and writing and—to a lesser degree—speaking (U.S. Department of Labor, 1991). Unless you were a communications major in college, it's likely you had little to no formal education in listening skills, outside of periodic admonitions such as "Listen up," "One, two, three—eyes and ears on me," or even "Earth to John!"

Effective facilitators invest in the development of their own listening skills so they can model much-needed communication processes and foster healthy relationships with the groups they serve. Listening is a way of saying "You are important," "I see you without judgment," and "I am with you." It nurtures trust and helps people feel acknowledged, valued, appreciated, validated, respected, understood, and comfortable. These are all indicators of a healthy relationship. Furthermore, they are an indicator of a culturally proficient group, organization, community, or society.

If one area of competence holds the potential for shaping a socially fair, just, and inclusive organization or society, it is listening. It's the communication mode that heals, builds, and sustains community. As leaders of professional and organizational learning, we need to recognize that now is the time for us to elevate the importance of developing listening skills. For thousands of years, spiritual wisdom leaders have stressed the importance of listening. Since the 1950s researchers have made clear the impact of listening (or lack thereof) on relationships. For example,

- Poor listening skills on the part of a leader result in the withdrawal of staff members from conversations about problems that matter, feeding the growth of the problems until they become monsters that plague the workplace (Nichols & Stevens, 1957).
- Ineffective listening results in low morale, high absenteeism and turnover, lack of upward communication, and ineffective horizontal communication (Brownell, 2016).

- Forty-six percent of people who quit their jobs did so because they did not feel listened to and therefore felt unappreciated (Spencer, 2014).
- Listening to employees positively impacts their productivity (Papa & Glenn, 1988).
- The quality of listening correlates with the effectiveness of a leader (Bechler & Johnson, 1995; Johnson & Bechler, 1998).
- Formal education in listening and nonverbal communication significantly influences multicultural sensitivity and cross-cultural effectiveness (Timm & Schroeder, 2000).

As the final bulleted item suggests, listening skills deal with verbal and nonverbal communication. In fact, studies have shown that people construct the majority of meaning through nonverbal communication, with spoken words only accounting for 30–35 percent of the meaning (Birdwhistell, 1970). Albert Mehrabian's (1981) ground-breaking work showed this was particularly true when related to understanding another person's feelings and attitudes: 7 percent of meaning is from words that are spoken, 38 percent is from paralinguistic information (the tone or way the words are said), and 55 percent is from body language and facial expression.

It's fair to say that listening requires much from us. It requires us to be fully present in the moment: completely focused on the other person. It requires us to attend to the other person's spoken words, volume and tone of voice, and body language such as facial expressions and gestures. It requires us to put the brakes on our mind-wandering and set aside unproductive patterns of listening. In short, it requires us to develop mindfulness skills.

MINDFUL LISTENING

Mindfulness is the art of conscious living (Kabat-Zinn, 1994). It's about realizing the power of now through an awareness that helps us connect with ourselves as part of the greater whole. Here are two definitions:

- Bringing one's complete attention to the present experience on a moment-to-moment basis. (Marlatt & Kristeller, 1999, p. 68)
- Paying attention in a particular way: on purpose; in the present moment; and nonjudgmentally. (Kabat-Zinn, 1994, p. 4)

Facilitators can develop mindfulness (and help groups do the same) by practicing skills. Table 10.2 displays six mindfulness skills offered by Marsha M. Linehan (1993), originator of dialectical behavior therapy. The first three are the "what" skills of mindfulness. The second three are the "how" skills. A quick Internet search yields numerous exercises and suggestions for practicing these types of mindfulness skills.

When applying these skills to listening, it may make sense to equate mindfulness to the first stage of the listening process: attending. However, mindful listeners apply these skills to every moment and every stage in the listening process. Table 10.3 illustrates mindfulness as a listener might practice it within each of the three degrees of active listening. Mindfulness takes active listening practices to the next level by putting a listener in a unique position to determine when their own psychological barriers are affecting how they receive, process, and respond to a speaker's message.

Table 10.2 Mindfulness Skills

Skill	Type	Explanation
Observe	What	Step back and just notice how you are responding without getting caught up in the experience or trying to change your response. The goal is to become more aware of what is occurring within and around you. Engage all of your senses without words or control.
Describe	What	Put words to your experience, without interpretation. Just state the facts. Name your emotions and thoughts. Continue to step back and observe your thoughts and feelings, and—this time—classify them.
Participate	What	Throw yourself into the moment without self-consciousness. Respond intuitively and be present in the now. Observing and describing are tools to help you become one with your current experience.
Non-Judgmentally	How	Do not assign meaning (value) to the data; eliminate the interpretation of good or bad. Identify assumptions and conclusions but don't act on them or jump to them. Take a nonevaluative approach and focus on the consequences of behaviors or situations.
One-Mindfully	How	Do one thing at a time; do not multitask. Dedicate your full attention to the task at hand. Practice controlling your attention by identifying and letting go of distractions.
Effectively	How	Do what is needed for the current situation. Maintain focus on understanding the situation and skillfully take action with behavior driven by mastery. Keep your objectives and what works in mind.

Source: Adapted from Marsha M. Linehan (1993). *Cognitive-Behavioral Treatment of Borderline Personality Disorder.* New York, NY: Guilford Press.

Table 10.3 Mindfulness Within Active Listening

	Three Degrees of Active Listening		
Mindfully_____	Repeat	Paraphrase	Reflect
Attend	Removes distractions. Fully attends to receiving data: the subtleties of the speaker's words, body language, and energy.		
Interpret	Suspends self-orientation. Opens mind to the unknown/unexpected. Consciousness of one's own values, assumptions, and beliefs used to assign meaning to and draw inferences from the speaker's verbal and nonverbal data.		
Respond	Responds to the speaker in the most helpful manner. Has awareness of different possible responses and their implications.		
	Mirror data: Use speaker's exact words. Mimic body language. Pro: Can build trust and validate speaker's experiences and emotions.	Use words and phrase arrangements similar to those of speaker. Pro: Can clarify meaning and help speaker feel appreciated.	Process data and summarize it in your own words. Pro: Can support understanding and lead to bonding and deep connections.

(Continued)

Table 10.3 (Continued)

	Three Degrees of Active Listening		
Mindfully_____	Repeat	Paraphrase	Reflect
	Con: May seem like a crude attempt to listen if not done skillfully.	Con: May misinterpret words and damage trust if left unchecked.	Con: May change speaker's meaning and damage trust.
Remember	Selective and intentional in choosing to remember key words, basic ideas, and general impressions that will assist the group later in its process.		

Active listening is also empathetic listening. Thus, one of its goals is to understand another's emotions, which are expressions of our energy—the vibes entangled with verbal and nonverbal data that we give off. We can learn to listen to energy as it expresses itself. However, we do so with our intuition more than with our ears. Practicing mindfulness is the path to developing the intuitive capacities required to gauge energy by listening to its expressions.

Those highly skilled in this area realize that—as living beings—we are each a coalescence of energy in a shared field of consciousness. For facilitators, developing energy-listening

Table 10.4 The Art of Listening

1.	Listen to what is being said and what is not.
2.	Observe the language of the body.
3.	Notice *how* something is being expressed and what *words* are used.
4.	What you *feel* is as important as what you hear and see.
5.	Be willing to adapt and adjust to the moment.
6.	Notice how your body and words express your projections.
7.	Notice when you are asleep and why.
8.	Keep breathing. Allow space for humor, warmth, and grief.
9.	Compassion is one of the highest forms of being present.
10.	Acknowledge and utilize the wisdom that is in each person.
11.	Accept and validate the truthfulness of each person's perception.
12.	Notice where someone begins and ends.
13.	Notice what is in the middle of the room.
14.	Model the acceptance and openness to conflict, anger, and pain.
15.	Acknowledge the courage and intimacy of being vulnerable.
16.	Be kind to yourself and others.

Source: Lee Mun Wah (2004). *The Art of Mindful Facilitation*. Berkeley, CA: Stir Fry Seminars & Consulting. Used with permission.

skills support the ability to read a group. Subsequent chapters in part III provide more information on energy states to help facilitators read groups by extending mindfulness through listening.

Mindfulness is the energy of being awake in the here and now. Therefore, in its absence it makes sense that one could be "asleep" to the present moment, dreaming of another place and time and thing, even while being physically present in the appearance of a listener. The concept of active or awake listening is core to the work of mindful facilitation expert and master diversity trainer Lee Mun Wah (2004), who offers sixteen tips for facilitators who aspire to incorporate mindfulness within their listening practices and their ability to read a group (table 10.4, p. 168).

Reflection

What resonates with you in this section on listening? What experiences or emotions connect you to this section? What are you thinking about listening skills and your development as a facilitator? What can you commit to doing to improve in this area?

_____

_____

_____

_____

Review table 10.4. What reinforces your beliefs? What points do you want to remember? What questions do you have about the listening tips?

_____

_____

_____

_____

READING AND RESPONDING

The ability to respond to a group's needs is an extension of the ability to read the group. Effective responses meet the group where they are. In other words, the nature of a facilitator's response is based on the level on which the group is operating. But how does the facilitator notice the level when reading the group? How many levels are there? What facilitator responses are helpful at particular levels?

As described in chapter 9, the Cultural Proficiency process map delineates four different levels within which individuals and groups operate and through which they traverse on their journey. Movement from Levels I to IV means progressing from freedom to constraint. Phrased differently, it's moving from endless possibility to focused commitment. Also, activity at higher levels pumps energy into a group, whereas activity at lower levels tends to drain groups.

A facilitator can notice the level of operation when reading the group by exercising mindfulness with skills such as listening and observing. They read the group by attending to data such as

- Words and phrases spoken;
- Verbal tone, pitch, sound, and speed;
- Energy given off;
- Shifts in energy states;
- Body language, physical movement, and facial expressions; and
- Frequency, length, and quality of silence.

Table 10.5 Responding on Different Levels

Observe Data	Describe Level	Participate by Responding
• I sense _____. • My instinct _____. • What if _____? • Imagine _____. • Wouldn't it be awesome if _____? • (Generative energy state)	1. (Purpose) Aspirational Level	• Encourage inclusion, rituals, and artistic self-expression. • Encourage discussion of what is in the room but invisible or yet undiscussed. • Pose "what if" questions to inspire discussion of an emerging future. • Use questions that tap into intuition: What needs to be said? What just happened?
• I feel _____. • I fear that _____. • It's great! • We absolutely love when _____. • It's hard for me _____. • (Tears) • (Laughing) • (Tense silence)	2. (Motivation) Emotional Level	• Mirror and encourage mirroring: Repeat speaker's statements verbatim and mimic body language. • Encourage mindfulness. Pose questions to help them observe, describe, and participate with their emotional response. • Use questioning techniques (e.g., ORID) that help the speaker move through the levels (process emotions).
• I think _____. • I understand _____. • I believe _____. • It's my assumption _____. • (Gazing upwards) • (Cooperative energy state)	3. (Identity) Thinking Level	• Mirror: Repeat key words that express values, assumptions, or beliefs. • Use phrases such as "say more" to encourage the speaker to continue. • Paraphrase. • Use divergent questions and probe for deeper understanding. • Use critical questions (figure 14.1).
• When is break? • It's too hot _____. • We need to decide _____. • (Head resting in hands, eyes downcast) • (Self-assertion energy state)	4. (Practice) Commitment Level	• Encourage speaker to express needs. Affirm needs. Pose questions that solicit actions they would like to see happen. • Use direct and convergent questions as a group gets closer to commitment. • Provide responses to direct questions about operations. • In advance, forecast possible physical needs and plan to respond to them.

Note: ORID = Objective, Reflective, Interpretive, and Decisional.

Noticing a level of operation allows a facilitator to sync their response with that level, increasing the effectiveness of the response. Table 10.5 (p. 170) presents examples of data and responses at different levels.

QUESTIONING

Posing questions is a facilitator's bread and butter when it comes to responding to a group. It's the most distinctive feature of the facilitator, just as telling is the most distinctive feature of the presenter. Through questions, facilitators draw out stories and learnings that help a group along in its process. There is no doubt that a repertoire of questions is the most valuable tool in a facilitator's toolbox. However, like tools, different types of questions have different purposes. You wouldn't use a saw to do a hammer's job. Thus, effective use of questions is a core facilitation skill.

Effective questioning is all about the right type of questions at the right time, used with the intention of guiding the group through its process. Noticing and responding to a group's level of operation supports effectiveness. Additionally, there are some general techniques for wording and phrasing questions. Through deliberate practice, facilitators can convert these techniques (ability to perform a task) into skills (ability to perform the task authentically on game day).

1. **Pose open-ended (divergent) questions** (or statements) to draw out diverse and rich stories, experiences, and learnings. Sparingly use closed-ended questions and only in situations such as helping groups make decisions or checking for accuracy in paraphrases.
   (a) Open-ended: What was your experience like? Please share more. Why do you believe that to be so? Describe your emotional response.
   (b) Closed-ended: Was your experience_____? Can you share more? Do you believe that because_____? Was your emotional response_____?

2. **Use wording that maintains focus on participants.** Word and phrase questions so that intention and attention are on the group, not on the facilitator. It's not about you, so don't imply otherwise. If you as a facilitator are part of the question's wording, make sure it is clear that the purpose of the question is ultimately to serve the group. For instance, "It would help me suggest an activity if you could help me understand_____."
   (a) Group-focused: Why did you do that? Who taught you that truth?
   (b) Facilitator-focused: I'm just curious: Why did you do that? I need to know, who taught you that truth.

3. **Use positive presuppositions** to imply capacity, drive, and responsibility. The way a question is phrased can imply positive or negative qualities about the question's recipient. Negative presuppositions convey incapacity, apathy, and irresponsibility.
   (a) Positive presupposition: What conclusions have you drawn from your data? How do you go about creating a sense of belonging for every student? In what ways have you noticed your values affecting your students' experiences?
   (b) Negative presupposition: Have you looked at your data? Do you know what your students need to experience a sense of belonging? Have you thought about how your values impact your students?

4. **Use clear and concise language,** not murky verbiage. Use precise wording with clear intentions and language. Keep it succinct and make sure the question covers only one issue and does not contain multiple questions.
   (a) Clear and concise: What beliefs inform your actions?
   (b) Murky and wordy: When we think about these things, are you aware of the process and the beliefs or the values that you might have that show up in your behaviors?

5. **Sequence questions** to enhance the group's process. Draw from mental models to pose intentional questions that guide a group through process. Avoid arbitrary questions that result in seemingly purposeless question-answer sessions.
   (a) Sequenced: What beliefs inform your actions? Where or when did you learn this truth (belief)? What data might you not select because of your belief? How could you access the data that you cannot select?
   (b) Arbitrary: What beliefs inform your actions? So what do you think about that belief? Do you value it? Why do people act that way? What other actions and beliefs do you have? Why is it important for us to check our assumptions?

Sequenced questions are a good example of how expert facilitators have clear intentions with every aspect of their questioning practices. For instance, after reading the group and responding on its level, a facilitator might sequence questions with the purpose of helping the group process information of emotions within that particular level. Or, they might use sequenced questions to shift the group to a different level. Regardless, questions are always used to help the group with its journey, which means moving through the levels and stages of process. Thus, effective facilitators have a repertoire of questioning techniques that assist groups in moving through levels.

FOUR LEVELS OF QUESTIONING

One such technique is ORID (Stanfield, 2000). Standing for **O**bjective, **R**eflective, **I**nterpretive, and **D**ecisional, ORID is a method of focused conversation widely used by facilitators to employ dialogue as a process to leverage the wisdom of a group. The letters in the acronym represent four levels of inquiry, which parallel the four levels traversed during the Cultural Proficiency journey. ORID provides facilitators with a template or mental model from which they can draw when generating and posing questions that help a group move through each level of process and toward a commitment. ORID is particularly helpful when facilitators are helping a group debrief an experience or activity.

1. Objective. Questions at this level focus attention by drawing out relevant data from a field of possibility. Facilitators help participants share "just the facts." This ensures that groups explore their experiences and name the most relevant data for further exploration before (1) any of the data are analyzed, and/or before (2) the conversation follows a specific trail related to experiences relevant

to a participant or small group but not to the whole group. Sample objective-level questions include

(a) What resonated with you?

(b) To you, what words, phrases, or data stick out?

(c) What is sticking with you from that experience?

(d) Within this experience, what was most important to you?

2. Reflective. Questions at this level name and explore emotions, feelings, and connections to the data. Basically, these questions elicit participants' relationships with the data. The emotions these questions may draw out are—in and of themselves—important data. If acknowledged, validated, and explored they can strengthen future decisions. If ignored, future decisions will remain partially informed and of lesser quality.

(a) What's familiar about this?

(b) How did it feel to review the _____?

(c) What delighted you? What scared you?

(d) Step back and notice your emotional response to that important experience.

3. Interpretive. Questions at this level help the group discover deeper meanings. They do so by surfacing, exploring, and challenging systems of belief. The questions focus on helping individuals and groups examine values, assumptions, conclusions, and beliefs. The Ladder of Inference (depicted in figures 2.1 and 2.2) and critical questions for Level III (figure 14.1) are helpful mental models for sequencing Interpretive questions.

(a) What are you (we) learning from this?

(b) How might this affect our (your) work?

(c) What other data might we need to explore? Why?

(d) How does this challenge our beliefs?

4. Decisional. Questions at this level help groups make decisions that lead to actions. Good decisional questions pull insights gained through the previous levels into a group's process of making decisions and expressing commitments.

(a) What are our (your) next steps?

(b) What do you need from your team (group, organization, etc.)?

(c) What resources are we missing? How can we get them?

(d) What do we need to stop, start, or continue doing?

ORID serves as a mnemonic that—when applied by the facilitator—serves both the group and the facilitator. It helps the group to move from abstract to concrete and to experience the satisfaction of landing on something tangible. It helps the facilitators to stay focused on their purpose: helping the group along in its journey. For culturally proficient facilitators, this means helping the group with the inside portion of its inside-out process. With a quick glance through the lens of Cultural Proficiency, we would see a group moving toward the "D" in ORID as a group moving toward expressing its commitment to high expectations, inclusion, and equity in education.

Reflection

The space below invites you to record your reflections about these sections on responding and questioning. What information was familiar? What was intriguing? What was useful?

_____

_____

_____

_____

APPLYING THE LENS OF CULTURAL PROFICIENCY

A more thorough examination of culturally proficient facilitation starts with using the essential elements as standards for professional practice. Table 10.6 provides both operational and conceptual definitions for each of the five standards of cultural competence. The conceptual definitions represent general working definitions. The operational definitions specify how we would measure the effectiveness of facilitator practice in the context of cultural competence.

Table 10.6   The Essential Elements of Cultural Proficiency Applied to Facilitation

Essential Elements	Conceptual Definitions	Operational Definitions for Facilitation
Assessing Cultural Knowledge	Being aware of what you know about your own culture, the cultures of others, how you react to differences between yourself and others, and what you need to do to be effective in cross-cultural situations	Extent to which the facilitators lead and model learning about culture and what is necessary to facilitate Cultural Proficiency
Valuing Diversity	Making the effort to be inclusive of people whose viewpoints and experiences are different from yours and will enrich conversations, decision making, and problem solving	Extent to which facilitators embrace differences and focus on what is needed to shape a culture of excellence with equity
Managing the Dynamics of Difference	Viewing conflict as a natural and normal process that has cultural contexts that can be understood and supported in creative problem solving	Extent to which facilitators engender trust, foster brave space, and increase collective efficacy for inquiry, dialogue, conflict resolution, creative problem solving, and progressing toward excellence with equity
Adapting to Diversity	Having the will to learn about others and the ability to use others' cultural experiences and backgrounds in educational settings	Extent to which facilitators customize learning experiences and intervene to help groups

Essential Elements	Conceptual Definitions	Operational Definitions for Facilitation
Institutionalizing Cultural Knowledge	Making learning about cultural groups and their experiences and perspectives an integral part of your ongoing learning	Extent to which facilitators incorporate practices and policies that ensure culturally proficient professional learning and help organizations develop sustainability for Cultural Proficiency

Source: Adapted with permission from

- Lindsey, Roberts, and CampbellJones (2013).
- Lindsey, Graham, Westphal, and Jew (2008).

FACILITATION RUBRIC

These operational definitions of the five Essential Elements of Cultural Competence provide the foundation of the Facilitation Rubric (table 10.7). The rubric is—within this book—the most pragmatic tool for improving your facilitation practices through critical reflection, dialogue, and goal-setting. Use the following information as a guide to understanding the rubric and harnessing its power to help you become your better (facilitator) self.

- There are five key rows and seven columns.
- The first column provides an essential definition for each of the five standards of cultural competence
- Each of the five rows illustrates one of the standards by providing language that represents degrees of unhealthy and healthy facilitator practice.
- Each of the six subsequent columns (from left to right) represents one of the points on the Cultural Proficiency Continuum. The language in each of these columns' cells illustrates a unique way of perceiving difference.
- The first set of three points and illustrative language represent unhealthy practice. These points are informed by the Barriers to Cultural Proficiency as well as Andy Hargreaves's (2003) descriptions of performance-training sects. These points are somewhat evolving levels of negative practice yet episodic in nature. (Someone with destructive behaviors shouldn't aspire to be incapacitating.)
- The second set of three points and illustrative language represents healthy practice. These points are informed by the Guiding Principles of Cultural Proficiency as well as by the tenets of professional learning communities (Hargreaves, 2003; Learning Forward, 2011). These points are developmental in nature, representing emerging awareness; effective action; and future-focused planning, learning, and growth. Culturally proficient facilitators display behaviors represented in all three healthy columns.
- The language and format of the Cultural Proficiency column varies from the other five points. This is because of its unique, future, and process-oriented nature within the continuum.

(text continues on p. 181)

Table 10.7 Facilitation Rubric

	Training From a Divisive Past— Informed by the Barriers and Performance-Training		
	Cultural Destructiveness	**Cultural Incapacity**	**Cultural Reductionism**
Assessing Cultural Knowledge Extent to which the facilitators • lead and models learning about culture, and • understand what is necessary to facilitate Cultural Proficiency	Trainers • Maintain and operate from a fixed mind-set with generalizations and stereotypes about others • Blame those possessing historical or present-day distrust • Deliver rote training about cultural groups— including the participant group—as deficits and do not share personal information • Reject notion of building capacity; tell groups how they must purge their culture and adopt trainer's directives • Denounce process and maintain coercive stance of authoritative trainer • Wield negative motives such as fear, anger, guilt, or shame • Place the sole responsibility for success or failure on the participant group	Trainers • Transfer information to participants instead of developing capacity to assess culture • Dismiss the significance of understanding how historical distrust related to identity affects the group and the facilitators • Present ways to "fix" cultural groups— including the participant group—and misrepresent or hide information about one's own culture • Disregard tools; opt to present remedial actions that imply group's culture is wrong • Devalue process and maintain a stance of content-expert presenter • Act out of negative motives such as self-assertion or craving • Attribute problems to others: the difficult participant, the grumpy group, the overbearing facilitative partner, etc.	Trainers • Minimize importance learning about self and one's own culture, the group, and participants within the group • Disregard systemic issues of injustice, oppression, and privilege related to identity and dimensions of difference • Teach about cultural groups as monoliths, neglect reflection, and downplay the need to share personal information or assess one's own culture • Present oversimplified strategies or arbitrary content related to working in a diverse environment • Undervalue process and maintain the stance of a teacher • Ignore the motives that drive their behavior or those of the group • Depreciate the need to recognize when a group or individual is struggling to move forward
Valuing Diversity Extent to which facilitators embrace differences and focus on what is needed to shape a culture of excellence with equity	Trainers • Direct their energy toward blaming and shaming individuals from groups historically well-served (privileged) or underserved (oppressed) by the dominant culture • Delegitimize or disallow expression of diverse perspectives; amplify their own voice	Trainers • Focus attention on the achievement gap with implications that devalue the lives, experiences, or cultures of individuals from historically underserved groups; or belittle and blame teachers, schools, and communities • Mute participant voice through dismissal of diverse perspectives or intimidation	Trainers • Transfer information about cultural groups and diversity while neglecting knowledge of self and the need for equity due to vestiges of historical systems of oppression and privilege • Trivialize participant voice, failing to recognize the benefits of different perspectives

Facilitating From an Emerging Future—		
Informed by the Guiding Principles and Professional Learning		
Cultural Precompetence	**Cultural Competence**	**Cultural Proficiency**

Culturally Proficient Facilitators
 	
• Learn about the participant group
• Understand that distrust may exist due to history and cultural identities
• Model learning about diversity and cultural identity
• Teach Cultural Proficiency Framework to participants
• Espouse facilitation values
• Recognize and appreciate the need to attend to energy
• Appreciate difficult participants or groups as opportunities for growth
	And . . .
	
	• Develop self-awareness while learning about the culture of the group
	• Attend to relationship implications due to dimensions of their identity that may confer privilege
	• Demonstrate vulnerability when modeling learning about dimensions of one's own culture and one's response to differences
	• Use Cultural Proficiency Framework to learn along with participants
	• Align actions with espoused facilitation principles
	• Gauge energy states of self, groups, and individuals
	• Share responsibility for group's success with participants
		And . . .
		
		Seek and advocate for ongoing professional learning opportunities (coaching, communities of practice, etc.) to develop knowledge, skills, and abilities with regard to learning and modeling learning about
		
		• The culture of
		  ○ Self
		  ○ Others
		  ○ Groups/ learning communities
		  ○ Organizations
		• Facilitation
		  ○ Values and principles
		  ○ Strategies and moves
		  ○ Tools (protocols, activities, etc.)
		• Cultural Proficiency
		  ○ Purpose (goal)
		  ○ Content (framework)
		  ○ Process (journey)

Culturally Proficient Facilitators • Focus group attention on knowledge of self and others within a diverse environment and the need to close opportunity gaps • Elicit contributions from every participant and encourage diverse perspectives • Acknowledge the diversity of participants and affirm it as an asset during professional learning events	And . . . • Influence positive group energy focused on shaping school cultures of high expectations, inclusion, cultural competence, and equity • Amplify participant voice within the group by listening to, learning from, and leading with participants • Exercise and foster inclusion within professional learning environments	And . . . Seek and advocate for diverse forms of feedback from multiple perspectives and a variety of high-quality professional learning experiences in order to • Ensure excellence with equity in facilitation, learning, and environments • Develop and improve practices that help groups esteem and tap into the power of diversity • Learn how to work effectively for social justice

(Continued)

Table 10.7 (Continued)

	Training From a Divisive Past— Informed by the Barriers and Performance-Training		
	Cultural Destructiveness	**Cultural Incapacity**	**Cultural Reductionism**
	• Squelch the power of the group's, school's, or system's diversity through an exclusive training environment • Lecture about how the presenter is right and the group is wrong, disallowing participant interaction and involvement	• Marginalize participants through training environments that imply that diversity within the group is a problem to be fixed • Rely on stand-and-deliver presentation strategies that disengage participants and/or imply the presenter has the solution and the group is deficient	• Oversimplify, minimize, or ignore the diversity within the group while espousing a value for inclusive environments • Adopt one-size-fits-all strategies that restrict growth by not tapping into the power of the group's diversity
Managing the Dynamics of Difference Extent to which the facilitators engender trust, foster brave space, and increase collective efficacy for • inquiry • dialogue • conflict resolution • creative problem solving • progressing toward excellence with equity	Trainers • Shatter trust altogether • Enforce punitive ground rules that establish disproportionate power • Pressure participants into unstructured discussions about divisive topics • Rely on coercing participants to change • Use unhealthy activities and strategies that harm a group's state of being • Disdain positive energy in diversity trainings and instead trigger negative motivations such as anger, fear, anguish, guilt, and shame	Trainers • Provoke suspicion, doubt, and mistrust • Set down restrictive ground rules that negatively impact the group's engagement and allow power-over dynamics • Deliver content that initiates passive-aggressive behavior and counterproductive discussions • Speculate that impacting people and making them change is effective • Use activities and strategies that are obstructive to a group's healthy development • Discount the influence of their own negative energy states on group energy	Trainers • Fail to explicitly or implicitly address trust • Neglect ground rules or use them in a general manner that does not acknowledge power • Present content, valuing the product over the process • Operate from cursory, untested, and subconscious mental models of change • Use arbitrary activities that lack short- and long-term intention for a group • Disregard physical space, energy flow, or motivations when directing activities
Adapting to Diversity Extent to which the facilitators customize learning experiences and intervene to help groups	Trainers . . . • Expect groups to purge cultural norms and adapt to the agenda and expectations of the presenter	Trainers . . . • Disfavor input from the group during learning experiences, intending to assimilate the group into the presenters' worldview	Trainers . . . • Homogenize implementation of learning experiences regardless of group needs

Facilitating From an Emerging Future— Informed by the Guiding Principles and Professional Learning		
Cultural Precompetence	**Cultural Competence**	**Cultural Proficiency**
• Use a range of multimodal strategies and activities	• Infuse processes and content that reflect and draw out the diversity within the group	
Culturally Proficient Facilitators • Help the group learn about trust and historical distrust • Encourage risk-taking through working agreements and ground rules • Teach about processes such as dialogue and conflict resolution • Draw on effective change management mental models to help groups through the inside-out process • Incorporate group activities intended to help the group develop and grow • Attend to group energy when making decisions about strategies and physical space	And . . . • Demonstrate and nurture trust, vulnerability, and forgiveness • Cocreate and help group exercise responsibility for democratic norms of operation that foster brave space • Practice processes of inquiry, dialogue, conflict resolution, and creative problem solving with groups • Support groups in developing effective shared mental models to increase collective-efficacy for transformative change • Use group activities and strategies appropriate to the group's stage in its journey, articulating what, why, and how • Exercise principles of transformation that bring about positive energy states through their actions, processes, protocols, and structures	And . . . Seek, provide, and advocate for opportunities to learn about and develop principles, tools, and practices that help groups and individuals • Create a learning environment of brave space • Establish, extend, and restore trust • Develop as a self-directed and collaborative group • Use processes and strategies to progress through the different stages (awareness [inside], commitment, and action [out]) of their journey to excellence with equity
Culturally Proficient Facilitators • Craft learning experiences based on factors unique to the group • Respond and adapt the group's agenda based on the group's progression on its journey	And . . . • Customize agenda and activities based on the needs and culture of each group • Improvise and intervene in the face of uncertainty, drawing from intuition and revealing their thinking about intervention principles, techniques, and mental models	And . . . Seek, learn, and integrate innovative, effective, and culturally responsive ways of helping learning communities pursue excellence with equity by • customizing professional learning experiences

(Continued)

Table 10.7 (Continued)

| | Training From a Divisive Past— | | |
| | Informed by the Barriers and Performance-Training | | |
	Cultural Destructiveness	**Cultural Incapacity**	**Cultural Reductionism**
	• Prohibit differentiation to meet the needs of diverse groups • Refuse to shift stances, insisting the group adapt to the presenter • Act on unchecked or fallacious assumptions; blame and berate group for getting side-tracked • Wield anger, guilt, and shame to shift group energy to dysfunctional states	• Push the agenda of the presenters onto the group • Use stance of presenter to imply the group is deficient and in need of remediation • Intervene inappropriately in ways that harm group development, lacking knowledge and skills • Interrupt the group in ways that shift the group to lower energy states that impede, stop, or reverse their progress	• Adhere to the agenda regardless of the group's progression or lack thereof • Limit stance to that of presenters to give the group information • Ignore their assumptions about groups and discount the need to intervene on behalf of the group • Fall short of recognizing, acknowledging, or responding to energy—allowing group to get and remain stuck
Institutionalizing Cultural Knowledge Extent to which facilitators • Incorporate practices and policies that ensure culturally proficient professional learning • Help organizations develop sustainability for Cultural Proficiency	Trainers . . . • Assert own agenda of dividing people and/or gaining power over groups • Mandate trainings to punish individuals through approaches such as blame and shame for something that went wrong • Oppose practice that aligns with standards for professional learning	Trainers . . . • Belittle culture of the group through planning techniques framed by deficit thinking • Remediate through provision of one-and-done sensitivity trainings aimed at fixing people and/or providing the solution that "we" need to be more sensitive to "them" • Ignore research-based andragogy in favor of training methods proven to be ineffective for adult learning	Trainers . . . • Rely on generic planning practices that disregard cultural knowledge when preparing for trainings • Present an off-the-shelf diversity training program with no customization and offer train-the-trainer solutions opposed to building capacity and collective-efficacy • Oversimplify adult learning through use of basic training approaches

As you familiarize yourself with the rubric, consider experiences you have had as well as experiences you would like to have. As a facilitator, consider who you are as well as who you want to be.

Reflection

In what ways might the facilitation rubric help you and your cofacilitators as you work together to improve practice?

Facilitating From an Emerging Future— Informed by the Guiding Principles and Professional Learning		
Cultural Precompetence	**Cultural Competence**	**Cultural Proficiency**
• Ease group's journey by taking on stance of facilitator • Intervene effectively to refocus group or capture an opportunity for group learning • Recognize the need to help individuals and groups shift energy states to higher levels	• Shift stances (facilitator, collaborator, presenter) and facilitation styles to the bolster group's progression • Seek confirmation from groups on their assumptions and then strategically move between levels of intervention • Intervene with moves and strategies that apply principles of transformation to shift groups to higher motivations and move forward on their journey	• adapting agendas and processes • improvising and intervening
Culturally Proficient Facilitators • Gather information about groups within the planning processes • Provide service for groups in alignment with the organization's strategic plan and commitment to ongoing professional development for excellence with equity in education • Align work with research-based factors for effective professional development	And . . . • Plan and prepare using protocols that promote assessing culture, valuing diversity, managing the dynamics of difference, and adapting to diversity • Support an organization with a comprehensive system of Cultural Proficiency professional learning that includes multiple phases: awareness, action, and facilitator development • Align performance with standards for professional learning	And . . . Model and advocate for collaboration with organizations to ensure sustainability of professional and organizational development focused on excellence with equity by developing long-range plans that include multiyear professional development efforts aligned with standards for professional learning and Essential Elements of Cultural Competence • Account for phases of the change process • Develop the capacity and capabilities of individuals and organizations • Increase collective-efficacy

_____

_____

_____

_____

How has this chapter influenced your thinking of these two terms: *facilitator of Cultural Proficiency* and *culturally proficient facilitator*?

_____

_____

_____

_____

_____

DIALOGIC ACTIVITY

1. Individually review each page (five essential elements) of the facilitation rubric.

2. Use the adjectives and verbs protocol (table 10.8) to explore perspectives and develop understanding of the facilitation rubric, one Essential Element (criterion) at a time.

Step	Procedure
Table 10.8 Adjectives and Verbs Protocol	
Step	**Procedure**
1.	Focus on one criterion of the rubric.
2.	Read the operational definition of that criterion.
3.	Read each illustration of the criterion from left to right, across the rubric.
4.	Return to the first illustration. Circle or highlight verbs and adjectives. Do the same for each illustration across the rubric.
5.	In small groups, discuss: What do you notice as you study the verbs and adjectives from left to right? How are you reacting? What is familiar to you about the illustrations? In what ways is the language helpful for reflection and goal setting?
6.	Repeat Steps 1 to 5 for each remaining rubric criterion.
Tip:	• In Step 4, do the same for adverbs.

Source: Adapted from Stephens and Lindsey (2011).

11 Assessing Culture

The power is in you. The answer is in you. And you are the answer to all your searches: you are the goal. You are the answer. It's never on the outside.

—Eckhart Tolle (Facebook post, September 15, 2011)

When you know yourself, you are empowered. When you accept yourself, you are invincible.

—Tina Lifford (quoted in Humphries, 2016)

People who vibrate at the same frequency, vibrate toward each other. They call it—in science—sympathetic vibrations.

—Erykah Badu (quoted in Caroll, 2012)

Each group and each youngster is different. As a leader or coach, you get to know what they need.

—Mike Krzyzewski (Interview, 2008)

GETTING CENTERED

Imagine you are facilitating Cultural Proficiency for a group of thirty educators attending the first day of an awareness-level seminar. During the session, a self-described "average white guy" speaks his mind in front of the whole group, making these statements: "All this is nothing more than liberal nonsense. After all, the United States has had a black president, so what's the problem? I don't know why I'm here. What does any of this have to do with teaching anyway?"

Prior to the session, what types of cultural knowledge of the participant group would have helped you prepare to deal constructively with this situation?

_____

_____

_____

_____

EPISODE TEN: DON'T GUESS WHO'S COMING TO SEMINAR, JACK

Jack had become very accustomed to facilitating Day 1 of awareness-level seminars. He'd done it successfully dozens of times over the past three years, always cofacilitating with Barbara or Frank, or more recently with Fatima. In fact, when Jack and Fatima were cofacilitating together (as was more and more the case as Barbara and Frank receded into coaching roles), they had become so comfortable with the Day 1 agenda that they occasionally took shortcuts.

On this particular day, they'd taken a shortcut. It was a five-day seminar. There were thirty participants: three ten-person teams from three different schools. Standard planning would have included Jack and Fatima interviewing representatives from each school team to get a sense of their group. That information would have helped them tweak the agenda and—more importantly—would have prepared them to respond to each group specifically. But the day before this seminar, Jack and Fatima discovered that they'd neglected to schedule sufficient time for thorough preparation. As the demand for their services had increased, they occasionally allowed themselves to skip or skimp on planning and preparation. Because they were short on time, they decided to skip this stage.

To make matters worse, the day before the seminar Fatima went home sick. When she was still sick the next morning, Jack decided to continue with the seminar as the lone facilitator. After all, he could guide a group through the standard Day 1 agenda in his sleep. Surely doing it alone would be no big deal. Surely.

Reflection

What is familiar about this scenario? What is new to you or different from your experiences? What do you question? What information is important to you? Why?

_____

_____

_____

_____

Overall, everything ran smoothly through lunchtime. Jack saw no need for major adaptations: the group was progressing well through the standard Day 1 agenda. He did, however, notice some discord within one of the school teams.

It seemed to center on Scott, who had introduced himself to the group as a science teacher and an "average white guy." He was middle-aged and brawny with salt-and-pepper hair and a drooping mustache. His overall look was more casual than business, with tan khakis and a plain Oxford shirt—navy blue and unbuttoned at the top. Throughout the day Scott seemed tense and Jack picked up negative vibes. Scott seemed to assert himself often. Perhaps he was craving something—such as sympathy or support for his opinions—from his teammates. His body language indicated frustration: tapping his hand, shaking his leg, crossing his arms, rocking back in his chair, rolling his eyes. Jack overheard several of Scott's comments to his teammates.

- "Not everything is about race."
- "People just need to get over it."
- "You know, African people started slavery."

From Scott's body language, creased brow, turned-down mouth, and negative comments, Jack concluded that Scott was probably angry that he had to be here. Immediately after lunch break, Scott confirmed that conclusion.

Jack: Welcome back from lunch. We're going to take a close look at the Guiding Principles of Cultural Proficiency. Please turn to page 7 in your handouts.

Each of the three teams sat at a long table. One table stood straight ahead in back of the other two; one table was on the left and the other on the right, forming a semi-enclosed space. Jack stood in the opening of the enclosure. Scott sat at the table to the right in the chair closest to Jack. As everyone else flipped the pages of their handouts, Scott squirmed. He rubbed his nose and cleared his throat. He caught Jack's eye, raised his hand and started talking.

Scott: Hold on. I have something I want to get off my chest. Don't you think all of this is a little biased?

Jack: It sounds like you have a statement behind your question.

Scott: Well, yeah. We've been here for over three hours and everything I've seen tells me that you're pushing a political agenda. Haven't you heard of reverse racism?

Jack could feel his face begin to flush. He knew he was having an emotional reaction. He deliberately used a technique he had learned: Don't answer the question. Keep the person talking. Don't take the bait or get into a debate.

Reflection

What would you do if you were the facilitator? Why? How would you do it?

_____

_____

_____

_____

Jack: Say more.

Scott: This is all politically correct nonsense. It's racist against white people. It's a leftist agenda and all these materials here prove it.

Scott shoved the packet of handouts across the table. Jack watched them slide and drop off, plopping onto the floor about a yard from his feet. Jack felt his chest contract. His heart raced. He tried to remember techniques: Mirror Scott's words. Don't debate.

Don't take the bait. Help Scott process and then invite the rest of the group into the conversation.

Jack: You said, "All these materials prove it." Say more about the materials.

Scott lurched to his feet and stalked around the table to pick up his packet. He was now standing only a few feet away. Jack felt tight sensations in his stomach and noticed his hands had clenched.

Scott: Say more about the materials? Really? You know exactly what I'm talking about. Look at this: Day 2 handout is called "White Privilege." I'm not falling into your guilt trap. Is that why we're here? To make white people feel guilty? What's the use?

Scott held out both arms, with the handouts clutched in his right hand. His feet wide, he spun around and glared at the participants. He wore an air of purpose and expectation.

Scott: I mean, what does this have to do with teaching anyway? I don't even know why we're here.

Jack didn't even think; he just barked his response:

Jack: You don't know why we're here? Really? Ever heard of achievement or opportunity gaps? School to prison pipeline? Increasingly segregated and unequal schools? Social injustice and unrest? I guess you don't see anything wrong, do you? Well, I'm not okay with it. We're swept up in four hundred years of white supremacy in our country, and you can't even see it! How about that? That's why we're reading that article. That's why.

Reflection

What is familiar to you about this situation? Describe the energy.

_____

_____

_____

_____

Jack could hardly breathe. He hauled in a deep breath and blew it out. He looked around. The room was stunned. Most heads hung low, staring at the floor. Silence. Scott stumped back to his seat and threw himself down. He looked at his handouts and snorted.

Scott: Classic.

Jack: Well . . . I think we should take a break. Instead of our normal fifteen minutes, let's take twenty-five.

During the break, Jack took a short walk outside the building to decompress. He tried to breathe consciously, be present in the moment, and be aware of his body. These actions were Mindfulness Meditation stress-management techniques he'd learned during his apprenticeship. He knew he needed more help processing this incident, so he sent Barbara a text message: `Are you free later this afternoon for a coaching call? I need an hour. :( Really rough day—totally my fault. I think I blew it, big time.`

Barbara responded immediately and they scheduled a phone call for 7 p.m. Upon reentering the building, Jack spotted Scott, who was standing in front of the soda vending machine. Jack knew that less than five minutes remained in the break. He had to get back to the room, but he also couldn't act as if nothing happened. He had to deal with this situation as constructively as he could, so he took three deep breaths, straightened his shoulders, and approached Scott.

Jack: Scott, I'd like to talk to you about what just happened, if you're open to it. Break is almost over, so we'll have to be quick. But I think it would be worthwhile.

Scott: Okay, I guess.

Jack: The energy in there isn't positive right now. It's going to keep the group from creating a productive day if you and I don't work to change it. I'm feeling responsible for the group. I'm also disappointed that I responded to you so negatively. I took your comments as an attack, and that was counterproductive. I sincerely do value your honesty. Speaking our minds and struggling through the issues is why we're here. I apologize and ask for your help in making the rest of the day productive. I've said a lot here. What are you thinking?

Scott: Thanks. It's just that things like this always seem to blame white males. It's not fair and I'm tired of feeling like a target. Why should I sit here just to be blamed for society's problems? I mean . . . I became a teacher to help kids, and society.

Jack: So, you don't want to be here if you're going to be blamed for being white and for being male?

Scott: Darn right.

Jack: Good. I don't want that either. Part of my job is to shape a supportive environment. I'll do everything I can to keep things constructive. I'll intervene if not. Also, I'm not a fan of guilt. I'm even less of a fan of people who try to make people feel guilty. I can't believe that I exploded like that.

Scott: Yeah, you're kind of contradicting yourself.

Jack: I can do better, and that's what I'm choosing. I'm asking you to make a choice, too. Don't hold back your thoughts, but at the same time, I ask that you choose to give this process a chance. For a few hours, do you think you could leave your past experiences at the door? If you want to pick them back up afterward, that's fine.

Scott: I suppose so. I'll try.

Jack walked alongside Scott into the room and started the next activity. Jack struggled through the rest of the day. Nothing horrible happened, and Scott participated in conversations with his team. But the energy in the room wasn't particularly positive either. Jack knew his own energy wasn't good. He felt like a failure. He also felt tense energy in the room the entire time. He found himself wishing the day would end so he could talk things through with Barbara. That's just what he did later that evening.

Reflection

How did you react to Jack's exchange with Scott? How would you describe the way Jack handled the exchange? How would you have handled it?

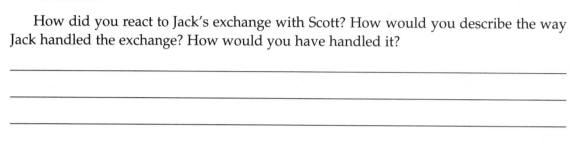

Later that evening, Jack's coaching phone session started with Barbara asking him to recount what had happened—just the facts—with no interpretations or assumptions. Jack recapped the events of the day. Then Barbara helped him stay in the air (exploring possibilities) before she posed questions that would eventually ground him in committing to action based on what he had learned. After Jack had given her the facts, she said, *this is what happened:*

Barbara: I have a few questions based on what you've told me. When you planned for this event, what did you learn about the participants from that school team?

Jack: Well . . . we didn't actually plan for this event as usual.

Barbara: So, how did you prepare yourself to respond to the group? I'm sure Scott's team leader had some sense of his disposition.

Jack: We never talked with her, or any of the other team leaders. We didn't do the interviews. Things got too busy at work.

Barbara: Things got too busy to prepare for this group?

Jack: We prepared, but not thoroughly. We prepared the standard Day 1 agenda.

Barbara: Tell me more about "we." You only mentioned you and Scott.

Jack: Fatima and me. We were supposed to cofacilitate. She got sick yesterday evening and was still sick today, on Day 1.

Barbara: What did you do to try to find a substitute facilitator for Fatima?

Jack: Um . . . I didn't try. I didn't think it was a big deal to do Day 1 by myself.

Barbara: Jack, I had today open. I could have cofacilitated. You also could have asked Julie, Tom, or even Frank.

Jack: I know, I know. I should have known better.

Barbara: You definitely do know better. Now tell me how you're feeling about all of this.

Jack: Down. The past few hours have been rough. I think I've been spiraling downward since the seminar ended. Now that I'm processing through this, I feel irresponsible and incompetent. Honestly, I'm wondering whether or not I'm really cut out for this work. Right now, I feel like hanging it up.

Barbara: Hey, Jack, come up for air. We've all been there: me, Frank, and anyone else who has ever attempted to facilitate Cultural Proficiency. I can tell you with complete honesty that you are most definitely cut out for this work. Scheduling this coaching session with me is another sign that you're a pro. So, let's surface your assumptions and learn from this situation. You believed it would be no big deal to facilitate by yourself and to cut corners in planning and preparation. What assumption was in play, behind your belief?

Jack: I assumed that facilitation is easy when you have experience with an agenda.

Barbara: Good. Now, why might that be a flawed assumption?

Jack: Because I might have experience with the activities on the agenda, but I don't have experience with this particular group.

Barbara: Why is that important?

Jack: Because the group is the content. It's all about them. The agenda just helps them along. Geez. I know this. I say it all the time. How am I so stupid?

Barbara: Let's not call ourselves nasty names, Jack. It's not productive. Remember—growth mind-set. You're not stupid; you did something stupid. Okay, let's make this a learning moment. What will you do differently in the future?

Jack: Always have a cofacilitator. Put the time and effort into knowing who's coming—preparation is a nonnegotiable priority. Remember that even if I've used a protocol hundreds of times, it's always a new experience because it's always a new group. Thanks, Barbara. This was helpful.

Reflection

Within this coaching session, what is important to you? What do you notice about Barbara's approach to helping Jack learn? How did she help him become a student of his assumptions?

_____

_____

_____

_____

Barbara: You're welcome, Jack. Two more things. First, you said that you were feeling like walking away from this work. I think you said you felt like hanging it up. That reminded me of a conversation we had way back. Do you remember?

Jack: Yes. Thanks for reminding me. I described what I interpreted as an example of how well-served I am by the dominant culture: that because of my whiteness, I could walk away from Cultural Proficiency work and my life wouldn't change. Actually, my life might seem easier if I were to stop my personal journey, stop acknowledging systems of oppression, and pretend that differences didn't matter. You responded that you, as a black woman, didn't have that option.

Barbara: That's right. And the second thing: consider journaling about your experience with Scott. I'd highly recommend that. You may discover things about yourself and how you respond to white men who get defensive in diversity-related conversations. Underneath your aggressive response to Scott, you might find motivations with regard to whiteness, race, or gender that—if processed—could lead you to deeper understandings of your sense of self.

Jack: Are you suggesting I have unresolved issues with race . . . or gender?

Barbara: I believe we all do. The journey is ongoing. It may help to consider how you might have responded if Scott were black. If he were Hispanic? Asian? Indigenous? What if Scott were a woman? What if you knew that he was gay? What barriers got in your way of culturally proficient facilitation with Scott the "average white guy," as he described himself? Reflecting on this experience is an opportunity to further develop your knowledge of self. It could only improve your effectiveness as a facilitator. Becoming a social justice ally is an ongoing process.

Jack: Wow . . . I'm going to have to step back and think about this. I also think I'm going to need a new Cultural Proficiency journal soon.

Barbara: I'm honored to be your colleague, Jack. Call me in a couple of days, after you reflect some more. We'll have a dialogue. Talk to you soon.

Reflection

Describe your reaction to Barbara's suggestions. What is interesting or important to you?

_____

_____

_____

_____

Using the healthy side of the rubric (table 11.1), analyze this episode in its entirety. What examples do you find of culturally precompetent, competent, and proficient practice? What recommendations do you have for maintaining or improving healthy practice?

_____

_____

_____

_____

Table 11.1 Assessing Cultural Knowledge—Healthy

	Facilitating From an Emerging Future—Informed by the Guiding Principles		
	Cultural Precompetence	**Cultural Competence**	**Cultural Proficiency**
Assessing Cultural Knowledge Extent to which the facilitators • lead and model learning about culture, and • understand what is necessary to facilitate Cultural Proficiency	Culturally proficient facilitators • Learn about the participant group • Understand distrust may exist due to history and cultural identities • Model learning about diversity and cultural identity • Teach Cultural Proficiency Framework to participants • Espouse facilitation values • Recognize and appreciate the need to attend to energy • Appreciate difficult participants or groups as opportunities for growth	And . . . • Develop self-awareness while learning about the culture of the group • Attend to relationship implications due to dimensions of their identity that may confer privilege • Demonstrate vulnerability when modeling learning about dimensions of one's own culture and one's response to differences • Use Cultural Proficiency Framework to learn with participants • Align actions with espoused facilitation principles • Gauge energy states of self, groups, and participants • Share responsibility for group's success with participants	And . . . Seek and advocate for ongoing professional learning opportunities (coaching, communities of practice, etc.) to develop knowledge, skills, and abilities with regard to learning and modeling learning about (1) The culture of • Self • Others • Groups/learning communities • Organizations (2) Facilitation • Values and principles • Strategies and moves • Tools (protocols, activities, etc.) (3) Cultural Proficiency • Purpose (goal) • Content (framework) • Process (journey)

Table 11.2 Assessing Cultural Knowledge—Unhealthy

	Training From a Divisive Past—Informed by the Barriers		
	Cultural Destructiveness	**Cultural Incapacity**	**Cultural Reductionism**
Assessing Cultural Knowledge Extent to which the facilitators • lead and model learning about culture, and • understand what is necessary to facilitate Cultural Proficiency	Trainers • Maintain and operate from a fixed mind-set with generalizations and stereotypes about others • Blame those possessing historical or present-day distrust • Deliver rote training about cultural groups—including the participant group—as deficits and do not share personal information	Trainers • Transfer information to participants instead of developing capacity to assess culture • Dismiss the significance of understanding how historical distrust related to identity affects the group and the facilitators • Present ways to "fix" cultural groups—including the participant group—and misrepresent or hide information about one's own culture	Trainers • Minimize importance learning about self and one's own culture, the group, and participants within the group • Disregard systemic issues of injustice, oppression, and privilege related to identity and dimensions of difference • Teach about cultural groups as monoliths, neglect reflection, and downplay the need share personal information or assess one's own culture

(Continued)

Table 11.2	(Continued)		
	Training From a Divisive Past—Informed by the Barriers		
	Cultural Destructiveness	**Cultural Incapacity**	**Cultural Reductionism**
	• Reject notion of building capacity; tell groups how they must purge their culture and adopt trainer's directives • Denounce process and maintain coercive stance of authoritative trainer • Wield negative motives such as fear, anger, guilt, or shame • Place the sole responsibility for success or failure on the participant group	• Disregard tools; opt to present remedial actions that imply group's culture is wrong • Devalue process and maintain a stance of content-expert presenter • Act out of negative motives such as self-assertion or craving • Attribute problems to others: the difficult participant, the grumpy group, the overbearing facilitative partner, etc.	• Present oversimplified strategies or arbitrary content related to working in a diverse environment • Undervalue process and maintain the stance of a teacher • Ignore the motives that drive their behavior or those of the group • Depreciate the need to recognize when a group or individual is struggling to move forward

Using the unhealthy rubric (table 11.2), continue to analyze the entire episode. What examples do you find of culturally destructive, incapacitating, or reductionistic facilitator practice? What recommendations do you have that would shift practice from unhealthy to healthy?

_____

_____

_____

_____

DIALOGIC ACTIVITY

1. Individually write and/or review reflections at the end of this episode.

2. Use think-pair-square-share protocol (table 11.3) to help participants share information, listen to different perspectives, and increase understanding of culturally proficient facilitation.

ASSESSING CULTURE

This chapter's episode ends with Barbara inviting Jack to reflect on his unhealthy response to Scott. Within that invitation, Barbara encourages Jack to continue on his own Cultural Proficiency journey by assessing culture. That begins with exercising the will and skill to look within and assess one's own culture, which at its core involves critical and honest reflection about one's own identity development. It's an ongoing process of

Table 11.3   Think-Pair-Square-Share Protocol

Step	Procedure
1.	Form groups of four individuals. Within each group, form pairs.
2.	Each participant spends time individually writing or reviewing reflections at the end of the text.
3.	Pairs discuss reflections.
4.	Within the group of four, each pair summarizes its discussion with the other pair.
5.	Each small group shares the content of its discussion with the large group.

Source: Adapted from Frank Lyman (1981). The Responsive Classroom Discussion: The Inclusion of All Students. *Mainstreaming Digest*. College Park: University of Maryland.

becoming more sophisticated in understanding the complex layers of one's identity: personal, social, or professional (McEwen, 2003). It involves developing a sense of self within the various dimensions of difference: race, class, culture, religion, age, and so on. The capacity to assess culture also extends outward to include the facilitator's willingness and ability to develop an understanding of participant groups as well as that of individual participants within the group.

If facilitators do not possess such will and skill, their unknown, unexplored, or under-developed knowledge of self can easily become a barrier to culturally proficient facilitation, which will end up impeding the group's journey. This barrier is illustrated in the episode through Jack's angry and unhelpful response to Scott (the incident uncovered for Jack his need to more thoroughly understand his own identity and response to difference), in addition to Jack's neglect to learn about the group ahead of time (which was a failure to assess the culture of the group). It's also apparent within professional development workshops and seminars around the world when presenters or facilitators attempt to lead groups through conversations about diversity, inclusion, and equity without working to develop a complex and sophisticated understanding of their own identities.

KNOWLEDGE OF SELF

The most important asset of a culturally proficient facilitator is self-knowledge. Understanding their own values, assumptions, and beliefs helps them to successfully navigate the ups and downs of their work by serving as their foundation for effective practice (Garmston & Wellman, 2009; Howard, 2015a; Terrell & Lindsey, 2009). Such knowledge doesn't magically happen in a single moment; a facilitator develops it through an ongoing and ever-growing process that involves experiences, reflection, and dialogue about their intersectionality—the interconnected nature of dimensions of their identity that form their sense of self (table 11.4)—as well as the manner in which they respond to individuals and groups that differ from them according to those same dimensions. Because Cultural Proficiency is a process of growth, effective facilitators also never fully arrive. Like the group, they are on the journey, although they probably possess more experience with the process.

Table 11.4 Lenses of Difference

Age	Gender	Race
Religion	Economics	Language
Disability	Culture	Accent
Values	Role/Position	Status
Appearance	Education Level	Body Size
Personality	Sexual Orientation	Politics
Learning Styles	Family Background	Other?

Source: Used with Permission from Howard (2015a).

UNDERSTANDING IDENTITY

In her book *Other People's Children: Cultural Conflict in the Classroom*, Lisa Delpit (1996, p. 46) captures the importance of attending to identity: "We do not really see through our eyes or hear through our ears, but through our beliefs." Our identity (sense of self) organizes our belief systems (values, beliefs, and meanings). These systems give rise to our capabilities—our strategies and mental maps—that in turn guide our behaviors. Thus, addressing the development of identity has a greater effect on sustainable change in behavior, practice, and policy than attending to the development of capabilities or behaviors (Garmston & Wellman, 2009; Lindsey et al., 2015). This is true for groups ("Who are we?") and individuals ("Who am I?"), including facilitators.

Table 11.5 My Journey From Cultural Precompetence to Cultural Proficiency

	Cultural Precompetence	Cultural Competence	Cultural Proficiency
Descriptors	**Learning**	**Doing**	**Achieving**
Refer to your areas of future growth . . . and list key words: 1. 2. 3. 4. 5. Refer to the leadership implications . . . and fill in the blanks: I want to learn more about _____ (e.g., cultural group[s]) because_____.	After considering the questions in the previous column, what do you want to learn?	Once you have learned, how will you use your new knowledge and skills?	What are the observable outcomes for • You, • Your participants, • Your participant groups, • Your colleagues, • Your organization, and • The community you serve.

Source: Adapted from Terrell and Lindsey (2009). Used with permission.

Like the individuals and the groups they serve, culturally proficient facilitators are also on the personal journey of cultural identity exploration. Although they have done the work of embarking on the journey and developing a solid understanding of themselves in the context of cross-cultural effectiveness, they also know that their process is ongoing. Therefore, they attend to the next steps in their own development.

Raymond Terrell and Randall Lindsey provide support for such development in *Culturally Proficient Leadership* (2009). In that book, the authors provide a step-by-step guide to assist those on the journey with their identity development and awareness. The book leads the reader through a process of understanding their areas of future growth and leadership implications regarding their Cultural Proficiency with each of these cultural groups: race, ethnicity, or national origin; language; gender; social class; sexual orientation; faith; and ableness. The process culminates with the development of a plan for taking next steps (table 11.5, p. 194). Such ongoing identity development is critical for facilitators to expand their skills, remain relevant, and increase the effectiveness of their practice.

IDENTITY DEVELOPMENT MODELS

Since the 1950s, psychologists and theorists have developed a number of identity development models to provide frameworks to support the understanding of how an individual forms an understanding of self. In general, such models include stages of unawareness; psychological discomfort and exploration; and resolution of personal, group, and societal factors that influence one's identity.

Multicultural theories of identity development emerged in the 1970s, when the field of psychology began placing more emphasis on sociocultural factors. These theories recognized that "race, ethnicity and culture are powerful variables in influencing how people think, make decisions, and define events" (Sue & Sue, 2003, p. 15). Currently, the literature includes a variety of models focused on the identity development of nondominant as well as dominant cultural groups in the United States. Up to this point in time, the conceptualization of identity models has been primarily limited to the level of specific cultural group (e.g., race, ethnicity, gender), with implied progressions of linear development. Thus, there is a need for more-complex models that address intersectionality by providing a framework for understanding identity as dynamic interplay of various markers of cultural difference (Bardhan and Orbe, 2012; Ferguson, 2016).

DOMINANT-GROUP IDENTITY DEVELOPMENT

Although the future holds much exciting new work in the area of identity theory, existing racial and cultural identity development models have much value to facilitators on the Cultural Proficiency journey. As described in chapter 6, the Aspiring Social Justice Ally Identity Model (Edwards, 2006) provides support for facilitators to better understand how they see themselves and want to see themselves in this work. Furthermore, other models and frameworks that support facilitators in assessing the development of their dominant-group identities (e.g., white, male, Christian, heterosexual, cisgender, able-bodied, able-minded, etc.) help them to better understand the nature of their privilege and oppression. Thus they better understand the development of their own cultural competence and pro-

Table 11.6 White Identity Orientations—Along the Cultural Proficiency Continuum

Identity Orientation	Fundamentalist White Identity			Integrationist White Identity			Transformationist White Identity		
Response	Cultural Destruction and Incapacity			Cultural Reductionism and Precompetence			Cultural Competence and Proficiency		
	Eliminate or Demean Differences			*Dismiss or Respond Inadequately to Differences*			*Effectively Engage and Learn How to Engage With and Respond to Differences*		
Thinking	Ignorance	Supremacy	Denial	Awareness	Curiosity	Dissonance	Questioning	Self-Reflective	Affirming
Feeling	Fear	Anger	Hostility	Defensive	Guilty	Missionary Zeal	Humility	Courage	Respect
Acting	Assimilation	Judgmental	Racist	Paternalistic	Color blind	Compliance	Advocacy	Antiracist	Shifting Power

Source: Adapted from Howard (2015a). *We Can't Lead Where We Won't Go: An Educator's Guide to Equity.* Thousand Oaks, CA: Corwin. Used with permission. Note: For more detail and discussion related to these White Identity Orientations, please see chapter 6 in Gary Howard's book *We Can't Teach What We Don't Know: White Teachers, Multiracial Schools,* 3rd Edition (2016), Teachers College Press

ficiency, regardless of their unique intersectionality of dimensions of difference (Howard, 2015a; Terrell & Lindsey, 2009; Worthington & Mohr, 2002). Since the goal of identity development is "to foster a more complex and sophisticated consciousness that is more stable and less likely to regress or recycle through earlier statuses" (Edwards, 2006, p. 53), culturally proficient facilitators continuously attend to their own identity development with a focus on understanding the dimensions that may confer power and unearned entitlements.

For example, in his book *We Can't Teach What We Don't Know: White Teachers, Multiracial Schools,* Gary Howard (2016) presents well-established theories of racial identity development (Carter, 1995; Cross, 1971; Helms, 1990; Tatum, 1992) and focuses on the need for white teachers (85 to 90 percent of the U.S. teaching population)—including himself—to develop a healthy racial identity as part of the process of undoing race-based inequities in schools. He then offers a White Identity Orientations Model (table 11.6) as a conceptual framework to fuel reflection, dialogue, and growth in understanding about the various ways people who are white may respond to race and their lived experiences in possession of whiteness. The broad goal of this type of work is to promote social justice by considering changes needed by groups best served by the dominant culture, according to the various dimensions of difference.

Reflection

From this section, what information is new to you that rings true? What information affirms your lived experience? How so? Conversely, what information do you question? Why?

_____

_____

_____

_____

KNOWLEDGE OF THE GROUP

Attending to one's own identity development is an inward manifestation of assessing culture. For facilitators, assessing culture also extends outward, beyond knowledge of self and into knowledge of the group. As Jack was reminded within this chapter's episode, culturally proficient facilitators put in the time and effort to know who's coming. They plan and prepare for professional learning events using questions such as those listed in table 11.7 to gather critical information about the groups they serve. This provides the context that informs subsequent stages of planning and preparation. (For more information on the planning process, please see chapter 15: Institutionalizing Cultural Knowledge.)

Table 11.7 Sample "Who's Coming?" Questions

1. What is the group's sense of itself (identity = "Who are we?")?
2. What is the group's understanding of why they are attending? Why this? Why now? Why this way?
3. What is the dominant culture (predominant shared values and beliefs) of the school?
4. What cultural identities and cultural groups are within the group?
5. What are the degrees to which participants are served by the dominant school culture?
6. What types of diversity exist within the group?
7. What are unique cultural needs of this group?
8. What relevant historical events dominate the group's memory?
9. What is the nature of trust within the group? Within the school?
10. What undiscussables related to culture and diversity exist within the school?
11. What prior Cultural Proficiency work has been done by the group? By individuals?
12. What were the intended and unintended outcomes of any past work?
13. What attitudes exist about the upcoming event?
14. Did participants have the choice whether to attend?
15. Who are the formal and informal leaders?
16. Who might be skeptical of Cultural Proficiency?
17. What degrees of self-efficacy or collective-efficacy exist with regard to the following?
    a. Dialogue
    b. Discussing undiscussables
    c. Conflict management
    d. Creative problem solving
    e. Self-directed teamwork
18. Where do individual preferences and styles fall on a spectrum between
    a. Task _____ Relationship
    b. Certainty _____ Ambiguity
    c. Detail _____ Big Picture
    d. Autonomy _____ Collaboration

Sources: Adapted from

- *Event Design* developed by Suzanne Bailey of Bailey and Associates, Vacaville, California.
- *Event Design Questions* developed by CampbellJones and Associates, West Friendship, Maryland.

ASSESSING ENERGY STATES

Once the professional learning event has started, culturally proficient facilitators continue to assess culture by gauging the energy states of self, the group, and individual participants. An energy state is a driving force or motivation. The behaviors and thinking of individuals and cultures are driven by these motivations. For instance, an argumentative workshop participant is likely driven by self-assertion, which is a negative motivation associated with winning/losing, pride, and competition. Furthermore, entire groups can possess a shared motivation ranging from extreme negative (e.g., apathy, guilt and shame, depersonalization) to extreme positive (e.g., higher service, world soul, enlightenment). It's a rule of thumb: whatever the motivation, the behavior will follow.

This concept is central to effective facilitation. Cultural Proficiency is fueled by positive group motivation. Groups must be motivated by positive energy. For example, productive dialogue is a requisite for Cultural Proficiency. Positive motivations fuel dialogue. If we were to put a label on the type of motivation that makes dialogue possible, we would say that dialogue is fueled by the positive motive of exploration.

On the other hand, negative motivations will result in group malaise and dysfunction (until and unless a facilitator effectively intervenes). Thus, skilled facilitators possess the ability to assess energy states as well as to intervene in a way that helps individuals and groups shift to positive motivations. Facilitators operate beneath the surface level of behaviors, and they must be keenly attuned to feelings and emotions, assumptions, and values. They do this by drawing on both intuition and trained observation. Tools such as the *Scale of Motivations* (Zohar & Marshall, 2004) help by providing language to describe various energy states.

Zohar and Marshall (2004) define energy states as motives, not consciously chosen, and offer sixteen such states on their scale of motivations. The scale (table 11.8) expands Abraham Maslow's (1943) pyramid of needs, separates half of the energy states into deficiency needs and the other half into higher needs, and places all of the states into a hierarchy of relative negative or positive power. The larger the number is on the scale, the stronger the energy state.

On the Cultural Proficiency journey a positive motive such as exploration (+1) is certainly more helpful than negative motive such as self-assertion (–1). However, a –1 motive is relatively better than a –4 motive (fear). Thus, a facilitator must work harder (drawing from much higher energy states) to have a positive influence on someone with –4 energy than on someone with –1 energy.

Take, for instance, the situation with Jack and Scott in this chapter's episode. Let's assume Scott's behavior was fueled by anger (–2). Just to counter and neutralize that negative energy, Jack's behavior would have had to have been driven by cooperation (+2). To have had a greater positive influence on Scott and the group, Jack's energy state would have needed to have been higher, such as power-within (+3) or mastery (+4). But Jack didn't have it in him at that point in time. So instead, Scott's energy pulled Jack down to self-assertive behavior (–1), at best.

Regardless of its relative intensity, shifting the energy of individuals and groups from negative to positive (and from positive to more positive) is a central responsibility of culturally proficient facilitators. But they can shift the energy only if they are first able to gauge it. (For more information on shifting energy states through facilitator interventions, please see chapter 14: Adapting to Diversity.)

Table 11.8 The Scale of Motivations

Energy State/Motive	Power	Description
Enlightenment	+8	Possessing the wisdom, clarity, and tranquillity resulting from liberating yourself from negative motivations by leaving this world and returning transformed—like Buddha
World Soul	+7	Serving like a conduit from a higher level who is connected with all living beings and called to be of service to the world yet out of the world of daily affairs—like monks or some artists
Higher Service	+6	Providing service of something beyond self—like values of justice, truth, goodness, etc.—by creating new ways for organizations to serve or people to relate to one another and the world around them
Generativity	+5	Identifying and enjoying work due to creativity driven by love or passion, excitement of creating anything—like creating new traditions or paradigms—that arouses interest, piques curiosity, and adds value to organizations and people's lives
Mastery	+4	Drawing from the work of past leaders of a craft or tradition and exercising that expertise rooted in the wider interpersonal values and skills of a profession, vocation, system of understanding, or body of work—like facilitation
Power-Within	+3	Achieving centeredness and peace and establishing integrity, trustworthiness, and responsibility by living in alignment; knowing what you love, appreciate, and value—such as vision or mission statements—and acting in accordance
Gregariousness and Cooperation	+2	Creating the glue that keeps communities together; seeking others to share activity and experiences; willing to see other's points of view
Exploration	+1	Looking, listening, and easily engaging with a sense of wonder and curiosity in order to gain new information and experiences
Self-Assertion	−1	Engaging in short-sighted and aggressive competition aimed at saving face, being right, winning, and gaining power over a person or group
Anger	−2	Blaming others for the feelings of annoyance, displeasure, or hostility; perceiving slights that trigger explosive reactions due to past experiences
Craving	−3	Yearning and acting from a sense of lacking wholeness, inner emptiness, or insatiable appetite that manifests as greed, jealousy, envy, pride, or resentment
Fear	−4	Protecting or defending with an anxiety and suspicion that is based on a perceived threat or danger
Anguish	−5	Possessing a sense of being lost, helpless, or without potential that results in an inability to make decisions; having no strategies because of inability to see any strategies
Apathy	−6	Having an overwhelming sense of no role to play in life that shows up as deep depression; showing little interest in anything, having very little energy, and often neglecting yourself and your affairs
Guilt and Shame	−7	Feeling condemned and unworthy because of past negative conduct—like violating trust—and creating and experiencing distance from authenticity and a deeper sense of connection; believing you're a bad person because of past negative conduct and perceiving that the world is worse because of your presence
Depersonalization	−8	Existing with an absence of humanity and an emptiness that appears as a coreless and heartless shell

Source: Adapted from Danah Zohar and Ian Marshall. (2004). *Spiritual Capital: Wealth We Can Live By*. San Francisco, CA: Berrett-Koehler Publishers, Inc.

Reflection

What about the scale of motivations do you find compelling? What do you find useful?

_____

_____

_____

_____

Using table 11.8 (p. 199), consider a professional group that comes to mind when reviewing the energy states. Describe the group and name the motive that seemed to drive it. What evidence existed that suggested this was the driving motive? How did the energy states affect behaviors? What needed to happen to influence the group to shift to higher (positive) energy states?

_____

_____

_____

_____

KNOWLEDGE OF COFACILITATION PARTNERSHIP

Just as a facilitator positively or negatively influences a group's energy state, a group or participant also influences that of the facilitator. This chapter's episode provides an example of how quickly and easily it can happen: Scott's negative energy state shifted Jack's into negative territory. This is a primary reason why facilitating Cultural Proficiency with a partner is a wise choice.

Table 11.9 Assessing Our Cofacilitation Partnership

Item		Low			High	
1. We have knowledge of each other's core values.	1	2	3	4	5
2. We have explicit shared values.	1	2	3	4	5
3. We understand our shared beliefs about facilitation.	1	2	3	4	5
4. We have knowledge of our own and each other's individual cultures and identities.	1	2	3	4	5
5. We have a shared partnership identity (i.e., who we are).	1	2	3	4	5
6. We gauge each other's sense of belonging within the partnership.	1	2	3	4	5

Item		Low		High	
7. We are equals. We both have voice. We listen to, learn from, and lead with each other.	1	2	3	4	5
8. We recognize, value, and leverage our differences.	1	2	3	4	5
9. We can describe the rationale for the "way we do things around here" within our facilitation.	1	2	3	4	5
10. We have healthy traditions and rituals.	1	2	3	4	5
11. We work to identify and address conflict.	1	2	3	4	5
12. We are able to gauge the energy of self and the other.	1	2	3	4	5
13. We adapt to each other's differences.	1	2	3	4	5
14. We seek feedback and collect data on how our partnership affects those we serve.	1	2	3	4	5
15. We make changes to our partnership to improve the quality of our facilitation.	1	2	3	4	5

Like any relationship, cofacilitation is a partnership—a living entity whose health benefits from attention and maintenance. Thus, assessing the culture of their partnership should be a routine practice for cofacilitators. Table 11.9 provides several items to assist with this type of check-up. The table serves as a tool for individual reflection and dialogue through which cofacilitators can develop the shared understanding needed to make effective changes to their partnership.

Reflection

From this chapter about assessing culture, what resonated with you? Why? With what ideas are you struggling? Why?

_____

_____

_____

_____

In what ways are you connecting with the ideas within the chapter? What kind of emotional reactions did you have to ideas presented this chapter? Which ideas? Which ideas illustrate prior experiences?

_____

_____

_____

_____

What information within this chapter do you find most useful? How will you use it effectively to serve groups as a culturally proficient facilitator?

_____

_____

_____

_____

DIALOGIC ACTIVITY

1. Individually write and/or review the three reflections at the end of this chapter.

2. Use helping trios protocol (table 11.10) to help participants share information, listen to different perspectives, and increase understanding of culturally proficient facilitation.

Table 11.10 Helping Trios Protocol

Step	Procedure
1.	Participants form triads. Letter off A–B–C.
2.	Person A selects, shares, and talks about their reflections without interruption. B and C listen (for a designated time period such as four minutes).
3.	B and C ask clarifying questions and A responds (half of the time period in Step 2).
4.	A, B, and C dialogue about A's reflections (same time period as Step 2).
5.	Repeat Steps 2 to 4 for B and then repeat again for C.
Tips:	• Display the time parameters for Steps 2 to 4 on chart paper. Consider projecting a timer if there are numerous trios.

Source: Adapted from CampbellJones, CampbellJones, and Lindsey (2010), p. 47.

12 Valuing Diversity

Certainly there are very real differences between us of race, age, and sex. But it is not those differences between us that are separating us. It is rather our refusal to recognize those differences, and to examine the distortions which result from our misnaming them and their effects upon human behavior and expectation.

—Audre Lorde (Sister Outsider, 1984)

Diversity is being invited to the party; inclusion is being asked to dance.

—Vernã Myers (Moving Diversity Forward, 2012)

Being oppressed means the absence of choices.

—bell hooks (Feminist Theory, 1984)

I'm for truth, no matter who tells it. I'm for justice, no matter who it is for or against. I'm a human being, first and foremost, and as such I'm for whoever and whatever benefits humanity as a whole.

—Malcolm X (Haley & X, 1964)

GETTING CENTERED

Review the quotes that represent themes in this chapter, then consider these questions from the perspective of a facilitator of professional learning and group process:

- Why is inclusion within a professional learning environment important?
- What techniques do/can you use to shape an inclusive environment?
- How can you ensure your techniques foster a sense of belonging for every participant?
- How can you ensure your techniques tap into the power of diversity?

Please use the space below to record your thoughts about the questions in the order they appear above.

_____

_____

_____

_____

EPISODE ELEVEN: JACK'S METAPHORIC BLIND SPOT TO ABLEISM

Early one Monday morning, Jack and Fatima sat at the table in Jack's cubicle. They were planning an event for a unique group whose journey they would facilitate in just over two weeks. This event was different from others because of the group's wide range of participants; it was the annual event when district, government, and community leaders gathered for an awareness-level seminar. The district had started this three-day event the previous year with the goal of fostering a shared commitment to excellence with equity throughout Stocklin County. Last year Frank cofacilitated with Jack. Since a seminar of this scope was a new experience for Fatima, she and Jack made sure to secure additional planning time. As always, they began by talking about the group before getting into goals, outcomes, or activities.

Fatima: So, what did you learn from last year's experience with this type of group?

Jack: That we should concentrate more than usual on creating an inclusive environment. There are a couple of reasons. First, participants are from various organizations and are likely not to know anyone else. Second, although we always have visible and invisible diversity within our seminar groups, we're usually working with educators. This group will have another layer of diversity—we'll only have a handful of district staff. Here, I printed a copy of our roster.

Jack pulled a document out of his laptop case and nudged it across the table. On it were people who had RSVP'd for the seminar: heads of local government agencies such as parks and recreation, leaders from faith-based organizations, heads of community organizations such as the domestic violence center, and representatives from the district's business partners. Fatima scanned the list.

Jack: It's quite a diverse group in many ways. You're so good at acknowledging and celebrating diversity, and I'm continuously impressed with how naturally you create welcoming and safe environments where all of our participants feel a sense of belonging. What ideas do you have for this group?

Fatima: My first reaction is that I want even more information about the participants than usual. How about sending each of them a brief online survey through e-mail? We can ask a few questions about how they self-identify and what they'd like to get out of the seminar. They can also tell us anything they think we should know about them to make this experience a positive investment of time.

Jack: Great idea! It will help us customize the plan. Equally important: it will convey a message that we respect and care about them as participants.

Fatima: I was also thinking that we should mix up the interaction and relationships as much as possible on Day 1. What about you? What ideas do you have?

Jack: I need to focus on inclusive language. I have a hard enough time catching myself using only male pronouns or slipping into gender-exclusive language. I'm going to need your help. And we need to monitor our use of education jargon. Last year at lunchtime, someone from the county government told me she and others were having a hard time understanding what we were talking about all morning. I'd been using educational jargon and acronyms that were meaningless to many people in the room. I don't want that to happen again.

Fatima: Yes. We'd marginalize most of the group with too much edu-speak.

Jack and Fatima continued to work through the planning process: assessing the group, crafting a goal and outcomes, planning activities, and moving toward a draft agenda for Day 1. They emailed the brief survey to every participant. A week later they met again to discuss the survey results, review the agenda, and revise as necessary. As facilitators, an inclusive environment was always critical, but for this seminar it seemed even more so.

Reflection

Within this section, what information is important to you? If you were one of the facilitators, what else might you plan to do to create an inclusive environment for this diverse group?

_____

_____

_____

_____

The next two weeks passed quickly and the seminar date arrived. On Day 1 Fatima and Jack arrived early to finish up last-minute preparations before participants arrived. The room was particularly wide, so they arranged the five round tables in a slight arc from one side to the other. This number of participants would require six chairs around each table. Fatima set up the projector and PowerPoint while Jack hung six large pieces of chart paper on the back wall, each labeled with one of the six points on the Cultural Proficiency Continuum. They placed small supply bins on each table, along with table tents displaying quotes related to the day and a Twitter hashtag with encouragement to participants to tweet their own quotes.

Outside the room they set up a sign-in station with handouts, nametags, and a sign-up sheet. Finally, they started their "Meet & Greet" music playlist, filled with uplifting songs with tempos of at least seventy-two beats per minute to stimulate participants' beta brainwaves and help them become in sync with upbeat energy. When they were finished, they looked around at their work and exchanged a smile. They were ready. Now they could dedicate 100 percent of their energy to greeting participants as they arrived and striking up conversations with them.

Individuals began to trickle in around fifteen minutes before start time. They signed in—laptops, briefcases, purses under arms, and coffees in hand. At 8:30 a.m. everyone was sitting and settled, with coats and jackets on the backs of their chairs. Jack and Fatima stood together in the front center of the room on opposite sides of a projector screen that reflected an image of slide containing the title of the seminar and their names. They issued a welcome and a promise that this workshop would be well worth participants' time. People smiled in response.

Jack beamed around the room. "Thank you for coming!" He paid attention to his voice intonation and held his palms up in a welcoming gesture. Fatima shared her and Jack's names, their job titles, and their roles as group facilitators.

Jack and Fatima then immediately conducted **Like Me** (Garmston & Wellman, 2009, p. 241), a short inclusion exercise designed to help people in new groups start to develop a sense of belonging. Then Jack reviewed the desired outcomes, working agreements, and the agenda. Doing this was part of Jack and Fatima's usual opening, their first agenda item. They moved on to the second item, **Introductory Grid** (Lindsey et al., 2009, p. 212), an activity in which participants explored diversity and commonalities within the group; the protocol ensured that everyone shared their perspectives. In addition, each participant introduced another participant to the group until every person had been introduced. Throughout the morning, participants interacted with one another within several configurations: pairs, triads, and groups of four. Most participants seemed eager to speak in front of the entire group at one point or another.

As the group started its fifteen-minute morning break and headed toward the refreshments buffet, Jack and Fatima gauged the energy in the room. It was positive; they sensed gregariousness and cooperation as they watched participants mingle and chat. The participants seemed quite comfortable sharing and voicing what was on their minds. This amiability would surely come in handy during the next activity.

Jack: Welcome back. We are going to move into an activity called **Exploring Behaviors Along the Continuum** (Lindsey et al., 2009, p. 281). This will help us build our capabilities by learning to use descriptive language that will help us have conversations as we journey together over these next three days.

Fatima: And this is how we're going to do that. Jack and I will expose you to the Cultural Proficiency Continuum. Each of its six points describes a unique way of valuing and responding to diversity: from cultural destructiveness to Cultural Proficiency. We'll explain each point individually, and we'll share examples for each point. Then, during forty-five seconds of silence, you will write examples—on sticky notes—of values, behaviors, practices, or policies within your organization having to do with that particular point. One example per sticky note. Take a moment and get a chunk of at least ten sticky notes from the bin in the center of your table.

Jack: Do you have any questions about our directions?

Jack paused and held the silence. Participants reached for their sticky notes. No one voiced a question or raised their hand.

Fatima: We'll start with cultural destructiveness, the first point on the unhealthy side of the continuum. It's all about purging differences: see the difference, eliminate it. Examples for cultural destructiveness include_____.

Fatima and Jack guided the group through the steps of the activity. Participants generated and wrote examples on sticky notes for each of the six Cultural Proficiency Continuum points: (1) cultural destructiveness, (2) incapacity, (3) blindness, (4) precompetence, (5) competence, and (6) proficiency. Then, as instructed, they left their seats and affixed each of the sticky notes onto the respective sheet of chart paper on the wall at the back of the room. This resulted in a large range of examples from diverse perspectives and experiences for each of the six points. Jack then invited the group to conduct a **Gallery Walk** (Fasse & Kolodner, 2000) in silence, spending about thirty seconds at each chart paper. After three minutes Fatima broke the silence.

Reflection

What squares with your beliefs within this section? What do you question? If you were one of the facilitators, what actions could you take next to help the group progress while valuing and tapping into the power of the group's diversity?

_____

_____

_____

_____

Fatima: You've had time to read examples across the points on the continuum. What observations have you been making? Stay objective and literal. When you're ready, pair with someone standing near you and swap observations.

Participants shared for several minutes before Fatima rang the chime to call the whole group back together. She elicited observations from participants and then posed this question:

Fatima: Think about how you reacted while you were writing your examples and when you were reading the sticky notes during the Gallery Walk. What kind of emotional responses were you experiencing?

A handful of participants shared a range of emotions that included sadness that the unhealthy examples were so easy to identify, shock from reading about behaviors that they themselves had enacted in the past, and excitement that they were actually having this discussion since such explorations didn't usually happen at work. Then a woman named Meirit Freidman spoke up. A petite middle-aged woman with short sandy hair, she had earlier self-identified as white and Jewish, and she had shared that she worked for the county government as the director of the Department of Disability Services.

Meirit: I'm frustrated. But probably not because of any reason you'd guess. It really bothers me that you use the term *cultural blindness* as a category on the unhealthy side of the continuum.

Fatima: Please, say more about what is frustrating you.

Meirit: It's the use of the words *blindness* and *blind.* I understand that it's intended as a metaphor, just like the phrase *colorblind.* Nevertheless, there are a couple of things that bother me. First, I find terms like this contribute to systemic ableism. The dominant culture appropriates terms from disability culture and then distorts their meaning to serve its own goals. Many people without sight choose to self-identify using the term *blind.* To them, the term is positive. It defines their social identity in a healthy way. My point is that using the word *blind* as you are doing is disrespectful to whole groups of people who physically do not have the ability to see. And I mean literally see, not metaphorically.

Fatima: You said there were a couple of things. Please say more.

Meirit: When you used *cultural blindness* as a term to describe unhealthy practices and policies, I had an intense emotional reaction—like, "Here we go again." Language matters. It's well established that it shapes the way we think. Your use of this term continues a history of oppression, stigmatization, and marginalization of people with disabilities. It's hypocrisy in an environment like this.

Fatima: Is it okay with the entire group if we stay here for a bit and process the information Meirit is bringing to us? It's a gift that we can unwrap together.

Fatima scanned the room and saw plenty of surprised faces, but lots of heads were nodding, including Jack's. She glanced back at Meirit, who also nodded.

Reflection

How are you reacting to information in this section? What do you find intriguing and why? What broader implications does this scenario contain in terms of facilitation and Cultural Proficiency?

_____

_____

_____

_____

If you were one of the facilitators, what would you do in this situation? Why? How?

_____

_____

_____

_____

Fatima: With the same partner you were with a few minutes ago, talk about what you heard Meirit say.

While participants turned and talked, Jack walked over to Fatima so they could collaborate.

Jack: Wow. I've never thought about it like that.

Fatima: Honestly, me neither. I know we need to stay here. It's going to eat up a good bit of time. But it's an opportunity to invest in trust and patience. And, we'll be able to help the group practice valuing, affirming, and using inquiry to understand each other's perspective. We can always return later to finish debriefing **Exploring Behaviors along the Continuum**.

Jack: Agreed. For now, let's use the **Fostering Mutual Understanding** (Kaner, 2014, p. 283) strategy. The one where we usually have a focus person volunteer. This time, we don't need a volunteer or a contrived topic; we'll use what's in the room.

Fatima: Good idea. Let's make sure Meirit is comfortable with staying in the spotlight.

Fatima walked over to Meirit and asked if she could interrupt her conversation with another participant. After a brief exchange, Fatima looked over at Jack and nodded. Jack rang the chime and waited for the group to quiet down.

Jack: We're going to take some time to learn more about Meirit's perspective. To accomplish this, we're going to use a basic method: asking questions. This will help us get comfortable—as a group—with inquiry. In other words, we will learn how to welcome questions and to not perceive them as criticism. Anyone can ask Merit a question such as "When you said_____, what did you mean?" or "Can you please say more about_____?" "Who'll start?"

Sterlind Banks and Rosario Martinez-Day raised their hands. Jack used the **Airplane Stacking** (Garmston & Wellman, 2009, p. 185) facilitator move by gesturing toward Rosario and then Sterlind, saying, "one" and then, "two."

Rosario: I've never heard the term _ableism_. I've figured out that it's discrimination against people with disabilities. But what do you mean "institutional ableism"?

Meirit: It's a form of systematic mistreatment of people based on a person's membership in an identity group. By "institutional ableism," I'm talking about our dominant culture not serving people with disabilities well. I'm also talking about microaggressions: brief and commonplace behaviors and practices that hurt people who self-identify as blind. I'm not talking about individual actions intended to harm. So, I'm not saying that the facilitators are intentionally doing something hurtful by using the term *cultural blindness* the way they're using it. I am, however, suggesting that they are perpetuating a system that favors so-called able-bodied and able-minded people by granting them power and superiority over people with disabilities.

Jack: Rosario, is that clear to you now?

Rosario: Not quite. I'm still struggling to understand.

Jack: That's fine. This is a process. First, tell Meirit what you believe she just said. Then, state what you still find to be unclear.

Rosario: Meirit, I think that you said that institutional ableism is a type of mistreatment that is systemic, not intentional mistreatment by individuals. It would help me if you described some examples.

Meirit: Of course. Since I've worked in the Department of Disability Services for a long time, I've seen lots. It may help to think of the widespread examples prior to when the Americans with Disabilities Act became law in 1990. For example, buildings—with rare exceptions—were inaccessible to wheelchairs, and elevators did not have Braille plates next to the buttons. Beyond that, there are tons of examples encoded in our everyday speech. The "Spread the Word to End the Word" campaign focused on helping us stop using the word *retarded* in ways that are hurtful and disrespectful to people with intellectual disabilities.

Rosario: That helps. I get it. Thank you.

Jack glanced over at Sterlind and nodded to signal it was his turn.

Sterlind: I understand the R-word example. But when you say using the word *blind* is disrespectful, what do you mean?

Meirit: I meant that I took issue with using the term *cultural blindness* to describe less-than-desirable behaviors, practices, and policies. I find that particular use of the term disrespectful. It devalues the lives of people with disabilities. I don't know how you self-identify, Sterlind, but try to imagine if your group identity was used—without your group's permission—as a category to describe bad things.

Sterlind: Oh, okay. I understand what you mean.

Jack scanned the room and held the silence. After a few seconds, he looked at Fatima.

Fatima: This question is for the whole group: What should we do next?

Sterlind: I think we should come up with a better term.

Rosario: I agree.

Jack looked around the room and saw nodding heads. The group was in agreement.

Reflection

The facilitators chose this strategy to promote understanding (not to resolve differences). Do you think this choice was a good use of time? Why or why not? What do you find intriguing? What would you do differently?

_____

_____

_____

_____

If you were one of the facilitators, what would you do next? Why? How?

_____

_____

_____

_____

Fatima: In a moment, you'll head back to your tables. Each table group will brainstorm ideas. Jack or I will give each table a piece of chart paper to record your ideas. You'll brainstorm terms that we may be able to use instead of the term _cultural blindness._

Jack: There are a few simple rules we use for brainstorming: (1) Accept all ideas. (2) Don't get sidetracked by discussions. (3) The more ideas the better. Questions?

Fatima signaled them to return to their tables. The groups began brainstorming. Meanwhile, Fatima and Jack got together to discuss what strategy they would use next in order to help the group make a decision about what term would replace the term _cultural blindness._

Reflection

What would you do next if you were one of the facilitators? What strategies could you use?

_____

_____

_____

_____

Using the healthy side of the rubric (table 12.1), analyze this episode in its entirety. What examples do you find of culturally precompetent, competent, and proficient

Table 12.1 Valuing Diversity—Healthy

	Facilitating From an Emerging Future—Informed by the Guiding Principles		
	Cultural Precompetence	**Cultural Competence**	**Cultural Proficiency**
Valuing Diversity Extent to which facilitators embrace differences and focus on what is needed to shape a culture of excellence with equity	Culturally proficient facilitators • Focus group attention on knowledge of self and others within a diverse environment and the need to close opportunity gaps. • Elicit contributions from every participant and encourage diverse perspectives. • Acknowledge the diversity of participants and affirm it as an asset during professional learning events. • Use a range of multimodal strategies and activities.	And . . . • Influence positive group energy focused on shaping school cultures of high expectations, inclusion, cultural competence, and equity. • Amplify participant voice within the group by listening to, learning from, and leading with participants. • Exercise and foster inclusion within professional learning environments. • Infuse processes and content that reflect and draw out the diversity within the group.	And . . . Seek and advocate for diverse forms of feedback from multiple perspectives and a variety of high-quality professional learning experiences in order to • Ensure excellence with equity in facilitation, learning, and environments. • Develop and improve practices that help groups esteem and tap into the power of diversity. • Learn how to work effectively for social justice.

practice? What recommendations do you have for maintaining or improving healthy practice?

_____

_____

_____

_____

Using the unhealthy side of rubric (table 12.2), analyze this episode in its entirety. What, if any, examples do you find of culturally destructive, incapacitating, or reductionistic facilitator practice? Does any of the rubric language trigger memories of past experiences for you? If so, describe them below.

_____

_____

_____

_____

	Training From a Divisive Past—Informed by the Barriers		
	Cultural Destructiveness	**Cultural Incapacity**	**Cultural Reductionism**
Valuing Diversity Extent to which facilitators embrace differences and focus on what is needed to shape a culture of excellence with equity	Trainers • Direct their energy toward blaming and shaming individuals from groups historically well-served (privileged) or underserved (oppressed) by the dominant culture. • Delegitimize or disallow expression of diverse perspectives; amplify their own voice. • Squelch the power of the group's, school's, or system's diversity through an exclusive training environment. • Lecture about how the presenter is right and the group is wrong, disallowing participant interaction and involvement.	Trainers • Focus attention on the achievement gap with implications that devalue the lives, experiences or cultures of individuals from historically underserved groups; or belittle and blame teachers, schools, and communities. • Mute participant voice through dismissal of diverse perspectives or intimidation. • Marginalize participants through training environments that imply that diversity within the group is a problem to be fixed. • Rely on stand-and-deliver presentation strategies that disengage participants and/or imply the presenter has the solution and the group is deficient.	Trainers • Transfer information about cultural groups and diversity while neglecting knowledge of self and the need for equity due to vestiges of historical systems of oppression and privilege. • Trivialize participant voice, failing to recognize the benefits of different perspectives. • Oversimplify, minimize, or ignore the diversity within the group while espousing a value for inclusive environments. • Adopt one-size-fits-all strategies that restrict growth by not tapping into the power of the group's diversity.

Table 12.2 Valuing Diversity—Unhealthy

DIALOGIC ACTIVITY

1. Individually write and/or review reflections at the end of this episode.

2. Use think-pair-square-share protocol (table 12.3) to help participants share information, listen to different perspectives, and increase understanding of culturally proficient facilitation.

Table 12.3 Think-Pair-Square-Share Protocol

Step	Procedure
1.	Form groups of four individuals. Within each group, form pairs.
2.	Each participant spends time individually writing or reviewing reflections at the end of the text.

(Continued)

Table 12.3 (Continued)

Step	Procedure
3.	Pairs discuss reflections.
4.	Within the group of four, each pair summarizes its discussion with the other pair.
5.	Each small group shares the content of its discussion with the large group.

Source: Adapted from Frank Lyman (1981). The Responsive Classroom Discussion: The Inclusion of All Students. *Mainstreaming Digest*. College Park: University of Maryland.

VALUING DIVERSITY

In the context of group facilitation, understanding what it means to value diversity first involves defining the nature of difference, variation, and divergence involved with helping a group journey toward excellence with equity. Culturally proficient facilitators recognize and appreciate various manifestations of diversity (table 12.4). They take action based on the belief that diversity is an asset.

Table 12.4 Diversity Within Group Facilitation

Manifestation	Implications for Facilitators
Moral purpose of schools in a pluralistic democracy	Help groups establish focus of developing the capacity and capabilities to ensure a healthy response to diversity: inclusion, high expectations, cultural competence, and equity in education.
Need for inclusion of individual participants with diverse and multidimensional cultural identities	Create a sense of belonging for all participants, paying attention to dimensions of diversity present in the room and society at large. Understand that systemic oppression—and its vestiges—exist and affect inclusion. Creating a sense of belong for some people requires vulnerability, cultural competence, and equity on behalf of the facilitator. A facilitator's choices of materials (articles, videos, etc.), language, actions, and energy all matter.
Participant voice within professional learning environments	Value differences between the facilitator and the group by creating an environment with conditions that enable participants to empower themselves.
Perspectives and thought from a variety of lived experiences	Shape an environment where differences in perspective, experience, and thought are prized, affirmed, and sought out by the group.
Styles and preferences of participants and groups	Anticipate, acknowledge, and balance predictable tensions that arise from different participant styles and preferences: task–relationship, certainty–ambiguity, detail–big picture, and autonomy–collaboration (Lipton & Wellman, 2011b).

INCLUSION

A fundamental responsibility of any facilitator is to exercise and nurture inclusion (Garmston & Wellman, 2009; Landreman, 2013, Sibbet, 2002). Inclusion is the belief that each individual, regardless of labels, should be a full member and experience an equal sense of belonging in community where differences are assets. Therefore, facilitators must relieve any participant doubts that may negatively affect their engagement. These are the doubts nestled within three questions posed by Stanford University professor Gregory Walton (Miller, 2015): Do I belong? Am I smart enough? Does this matter?

Certainly, like Fatima and Jack's use of **Like Me**, culturally proficient facilitators use introductory activities with the intent of fostering a sense of belonging within every participant. They also attend to diversity and inclusion long after such activities. In fact, they never stop. With every decision and action, they display an appreciation for the various dimensions of diversity within the immediate environment as well as the broader community and society.

This is no easy feat, as illustrated in this chapter's episode. Within that scene, a seminar participant named Meirit voiced a concern that the facilitators' use of the term cultural blindness contradicted their purpose of promoting inclusion and equity. Meirit's comments helped the facilitators increase their awareness of their own practice.

The entire situation also illustrates an important quality of culturally proficient facilitators—they never arrive. At best, they are in a perpetual state of becoming proficient. They understand they are not perfect. Thus, their Cultural Proficiency is not only reflected by the effectiveness of their practices, but is also reflected by the manner in which they respond when they fall short. In the episode, the facilitators respond in a manner that values diversity by amplifying participant voice.

PARTICIPANT VOICE

Within any typical professional development seminar or workshop, one of the most obvious dimensions of difference exists between the roles of facilitator and participant. This relationship is defined by the permission that groups freely give to facilitators to guide their journey. Culturally proficient facilitators use that permission to create conditions within which participants empower themselves. This means they share power with the group. The term *participant voice* represents this concept.

For our purposes, participant voice parallels Russell Quaglia's (2016) model of student voice—a three-tiered model for educators who value the diversity of roles within the learning process and aspire to share power and enable student agency. Similarly, culturally proficient facilitators do more than merely listen to participants. They amplify participant voice by listening to, learning from, and leading with participants (table 12.5) by creating learning environments with conditions that enable participants to empower themselves. In doing so, they display a high value for the role of participant and involve them as partners in making decisions about their professional learning experiences.

Table 12.5 Participant Voice for Inclusion and Equity

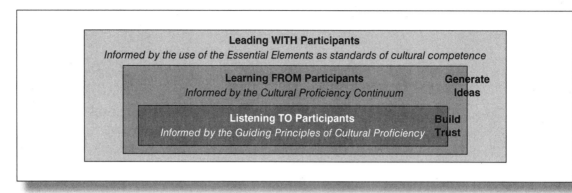

Sources: Adapted from

- Quaglia and Corso (2014).
- Lindsey, Nuri-Robins, and Terrell (2009).

One of the primary goals of a culturally proficient facilitator is to shape a culturally competent and proficient professional learning environment. To that end, they exercise and nurture inclusion across the dimensions of difference among participants by engaging participant voice through the lens of Cultural Proficiency. For instance, they recognize that the group may not be living its espoused values (e.g., norms of operation) and the group may be practicing degrees of exclusion and inequity. Furthermore, they remain aware that their own practices may be shaping a professional learning environment (culture and climate) that falls short of high expectations, inclusion, and equity. So, they create space for participant voice within their facilitation.

These culturally proficient facilitators start by using the guiding principles as the filter through which they listen to participants during group activity as well as informal and formal check-ins. During check-ins, they use questions aligned with the guiding principles (table 12.6). Then they use the language from the Cultural Proficiency Continuum to learn from participants, describing and developing an understanding of facilitator practices, group behaviors, and the current and desired conditions within the seminar. Finally,

Table 12.6 Sample Participant Voice Questions

To what extent is the current culture (the way we do things) and climate (the way it feels) within our seminar_____
<ul><li>Aligning with our norms of operation?</li><li>Creating inclusion? Promoting equity? Displaying high expectations?</li><li>Working for you? Working against you?</li><li>Displaying value for various dimensions of difference (race, gender, culture, religion, sexual orientation, etc.)?</li><li>Positively recognizing and displaying appreciation for the dimensions of your cultural identity?</li></ul>

the facilitators share decision-making power and lead with participants, using the essential elements as standards. By amplifying participant voice, facilitators can increase inclusivity, promote equity, and display a high value for the various roles within the professional learning environment.

Reflection

From this chapter about valuing diversity, what resonated with you? Why? With what ideas are you struggling? Why? Within professional learning environments, what other manifestations of diversity exist that are not explored in this chapter? What might be missing from table 12.4?

_____

_____

_____

_____

In what ways are you connecting with the ideas within the chapter? What kind of emotional reactions did you have to ideas presented this chapter? Which ideas? Which ideas illustrate prior experiences?

_____

_____

_____

_____

What information within this chapter do you find most useful? How will you use it effectively to serve groups as a culturally proficient facilitator?

_____

_____

_____

_____

DIALOGIC ACTIVITY

1. Individually write and/or review the three reflections at the end of this chapter.

2. Use helping trios protocol (table 12.7) to help participants share information, listen to different perspectives, and increase understanding of culturally proficient facilitation.

Table 12.7 Helping Trios Protocol

Step	Procedure
1.	Participants form triads. Letter off A–B–C.
2.	Person A selects, shares, and talks about their reflections without interruption. B and C listen (for a designated time period such as four minutes).
3.	B and C ask clarifying questions and A responds (half of the time period in Step 2).
4.	A, B, and C dialogue about A's reflections (same time period as Step 2).
5.	Repeat Steps 2 to 4 for B and then repeat again for C.
Tips:	• Display the time parameters for Steps 2 to 4 on chart paper. Consider projecting a timer if there are numerous trios.

Source: Adapted from CampbellJones, CampbellJones, and Lindsey (2010), p. 47.

13 Managing the Dynamics of Difference

Ron Chernow's writing had eliminated the distance between me and the dead white guy on the $10 bill.

—Lin-Manuel Miranda *(Speech, 2015b)*

I remain convinced that most human conflicts can be solved through genuine dialogue conducted with a spirit of openness and reconciliation.

—The Dalai Lama *(Speech, 2001)*

But you can't forgive without loving. I don't mean sentimentality; I don't mean mush. I mean having enough courage to stand up and say, "I forgive. I'm finished with it."

—Maya Angelou *(quoted in Andrews, 2013)*

Peace is sustainable only when there is social justice and democracy.

—Shirin Ebadi *(Boll, 2012)*

GETTING CENTERED

You are the facilitator of group of thirty educators in an awareness-level seminar. During a discussion, a participant offers comments that suggest she holds negative feelings toward a group of people. She and the participant group give you permission to help her explore.

- Why (for what group and individual purposes) would you help her explore?
- How might you structure this dialogue, involving both the participant and the group?
- What must you pay attention to, and in what ways must you be prepared to respond?
- Where would you begin to help the participant and group? Through questioning, where would you guide the group?

Use the space below to record your thoughts.

_____

_____

_____

_____

EPISODE TWELVE: JACK MANAGES THE DYNAMICS OF THE OFFICERS' CLUB

Jack and Barbara were cofacilitating a group of thirty educators (twenty-five teachers, two paraeducators, two assistant principals, and one principal) from various schools in the district. It was early in the second day of a three-day seminar, and participants were engaged in an activity called **The Diversity Lifeline** (Lindsey et al., 2009 p. 184). While participants held small group (triad) discussions, the facilitators decided that Jack would lead a whole-group debriefing (stepping back to reflect on, discuss, and learn from the experience). Debriefing experiences with this particular activity always provided a bountiful harvest. Jack rang a chime that signaled participants to wrap up conversations. He then invited individuals to share insights.

Jack: So what was this process like for you?

He scanned the room and paused, holding the silence with which he had become comfortable. There were five rectangular tables, each with six participants: two sitting on each side and one on each end of the table. This had made it easy to form two triads at each table.

Eden was the first to speak. She was in her early thirties. Her blonde hair haloed her face in clusters of natural curls, softening her sharp facial features, and fine freckles dotted her pale skin from cheek to cheek. Eden had identified as a white high-school teacher. To her right was Mimala, a woman in the same age group with black hair, ice-blue eyes, and a tawny complexion. Mimala had shared that she self-identifies as Native American—specifically as Lakota Sioux—and as a special education teacher and a military brat.

Eden: It helped me consider how much my upbringing affects me nowadays. I was raised military. Mimala and Howard were in my triad. That's when I found out that Mimala also grew up in the military. At first we celebrated that connection, but we quickly discovered that our experiences were quite different.

Mimala: When I was listening to Eden, at first I thought, "Me too, me too." until she talked about spending lots of time in the Officers' Club. I must have made a face because she stopped, looked at me, and said, "Yeah, I get that a lot. I don't know why." I wondered: What's coming up for me? What was it that Eden was seeing? We were just working through it when you signaled us to stop. Actually, I don't want to speak for Eden. I should say that I was working through it.

Reflection

Put yourself in the place of the facilitators. Before you consider what you would do, think about what you know so far. What information is important? What important information is not known yet? What opportunities do you see for the group to learn and develop?

_____

_____

_____

_____

If you were Jack, how would you respond to Mimala? Eden? The group?

_____

_____

_____

_____

Although Jack has opened up this discussion, both facilitators are always on. What would you be doing if you were Barbara?

_____

_____

_____

_____

Jack: You said you were "just working through it" when we called you back. Would you like to continue to work through it?

Mimala: Yes. But I don't want to slow down the group or your agenda.

Jack: You won't. All of you are the content today, in fact; it's your agenda. Remember, this is all about you. If you'd like to continue working through it, are you willing to work through it with the whole group? It would provide a learning opportunity for all of us. Or would you rather Barbara or I help you process privately?

Mimala: Here, definitely. I'd like that, as long as the group is fine with it.

Jack: Let's check. Group: Is everyone willing to stay here for a bit? Please nod or give a thumbs-up if it is okay with you.

Jack looked around and noted that everyone was signaling "yes." He had permission.

Barbara: Eden, this involved you, too. If we help Mimala process this, part of your conversation may be shared with the whole group. Are you okay with that?

Eden: Thanks for asking. Yes, I'm 100 percent okay with it! I'd like to be involved, too.

Barbara: Great. Thank you.

Based on Eden's and Mimala's initial comments, Jack inferred that their different military experiences most likely had to do with power and privilege. If he engaged them in a dialogic activity, he could help them deepen knowledge of others, themselves, and possibly the Barriers to Cultural Proficiency. Simultaneously, he could help the group build its efficacy with dialogue.

Jack stepped forward, which was the signal he and Barbara used to communicate when one of them wanted to take the lead. Right now he had a specific strategy in mind. He glanced over at Barbara. She nodded, signaling that she was okay with him continuing to take the lead.

Jack: We'll use a strategy called **Fishbowl** (Eitington, 1996, pp. 67–70). This particular strategy will help us observe a dialogue and learn about facilitative questioning and listening. Here's how we'll do it: Mimala, Eden, and I will sit together and have a discussion in the center of the room, and everyone else will silently observe. Observers will move their chairs to form a circle around ours. The three of us will be inside the circle like fish in a fishbowl. Observers will be outside the fishbowl. Howard, you were part of the original triad. Would you like to be in or out of the fishbowl?

Howard: Um, I'm out. I'll watch.

Reflection

The facilitators **Asked Permission** (Garmston & Wellman, 2009, p. 100) of individuals and the group. This is an example of a facilitator move (a quick, unscripted, and helpful facilitator action). Why might this move be important to the group?

_____

_____

_____

_____

During the earlier parts of the scene, what do you think Barbara might have been doing to work as an effective cofacilitator? Later, how did she display effective cofacilitation?

_____

_____

_____

_____

Jack: Eden, what was it you said after Mimala made a face?

Eden: Something like, "I get that response pretty often but I'm not quite sure why."

Jack: What was familiar about Mimala's response?

Eden: Well, it wasn't really the face that she made. It was the emotion behind it.

Jack: How would you describe that emotion?

Eden: Not sure. But it wasn't good. Mimala, what exactly did I say that bothered you?

Mimala: That you spent most of your childhood in the Officers' Club, swimming and so on. Immediately, I had a negative reaction. I knew you could see it. What's going on in my head is always visible. My face tells all.

Jack: What were you feeling when you made that face?

Mimala: Hmm. I was feeling . . . like . . ."UGH!"

Jack: Why "UGH"? What emotion does "UGH" represent?

Mimala: Well, I don't want to say disgust, but . . .

Mimala wrinkled her nose and face as she said the word *disgust*.

Jack: But . . . you did just say it. Shall we go with disgust?

Jack mirrored Mimala's scrunched face as he said the word.

Mimala: Ha! Yes. If I'm going to be honest, I'll say that disgust captures it. Sorry, Eden.

Eden: Don't apologize. It's okay. Why disgust?

Mimala: I don't know quite why I feel that way because I had male friends who were officers. But they were all enlisted men. They weren't officers who came straight from college. We called those officers "ring-knockers" because they flaunted their obnoxiously large college graduation rings. The stereotype is they got good positions because of their rings, not their competence. Eden, when you started talking about being a military brat, I was with you. But when you linked your childhood with the Officers' Club, that's all I needed to know. That wasn't *my* military.

Jack: You said, "That wasn't *my* military." What was *your* military?

Mimala: My military is enlisted people. Eden's people aren't *my* people.

Reflection

What do you notice about the facilitation approach? What is familiar to you about the approach thus far? What is new to you? What actions square with your values and beliefs about facilitation? What do you question?

_____

_____

_____

_____

So far the facilitator has used two different levels of inquiry (questioning). Review the questions posed. How would you describe the two categories of questions? Consider referring back to the four levels on the facilitator map in chapter 9.

_____

_____

_____

_____

Jack: I heard you say, "Eden's people aren't my people." Who are your people?

Mimala: My people definitely weren't the ring-knockers. I grew up military but in a poor neighborhood. And, no, it wasn't on a reservation. The military provided housing on base or a stipend. My parents chose the stipend, but they made some poor life choices. As a result, we had it rough. Our house was infested with cockroaches. Our furniture was from dump yards, and our doors were plywood. Snow and ice built up on the inside during winter. We had one wood-burning stove. I grew up on government cheese, oily canned peanut butter, powdered milk, and pasta. We got Angel Tree Christmas presents, and we collected soda pop cans out of trash cans for the recycling money. I've worked since I was seven, when I delivered two thousand guide papers every week. I got a paper route at ten. When I was thirteen, I was a motel maid. When I was sixteen, I moved up to the motel's front desk. I was a street kid with a foul mouth and a bad temper. I got into street fights and never saw myself graduating high school, let alone college. The officers I knew were similar in that they had to work hard to move up. They weren't the guys or gals who went from college to military. So, my people definitely weren't Eden's people.

Jack: So, you felt disgust?

Mimala: Yes. I'm sorry, Eden. It's nothing personal.

Eden: I know. I want to know more. I just don't know the right question to ask.

Jack: Let me ask you this, Mimala. When Eden talked about the Officers' Club, what else came up for you? What was familiar?

Mimala: Oh, lots. For instance, I felt the same way when I moved here to Stocklin County. The first time I drove around, I felt the same disgust. Every house had a manicured lawn and new car out front . . . everything looked so perfect. To me, it was some sort of Stepford Wives neighborhood. You know, _those_ kind of people.

Jack: What do you believe about "_those_ kind" of people?

Mimala: They're highly educated and have money and options. They've got the power . . . you know, they can get what they want.

Jack: Mimala, I heard you say "they're highly educated." I assume that since you're a teacher, you also have a college education?

Mimala: Yes, I got my master's degree from Johns Hopkins University.

Jack: So, you're also a highly educated person. . . .

Mimala paused and slowly smiled.

Mimala: Ahhh, yes . . . and now I have money and options, too. And a nice car . . .

Mimala paused. Jack held the silence.

Mimala: Those people with nice lawns . . . some of them could have also worked their ways up.

Reflection

Within this section of the episode, what facilitator actions interest you? What do you question?

_____

_____

_____

_____

What would you do next? Why? How?

_____

_____

_____

_____

Jack: Yes, they might have worked their ways up. Let's stay focused on you, though. I'm certain that if you reflect and explore what's going inside of you, you'll find how all this affects your teaching and your interaction with students.

Mimala's eyes popped open. Her mouth opened wide. No sound came out. She looked off toward the window, slowly inhaling. The room held the silence.

Jack: You just found something, didn't you?

Mimala: I sure did. I found it, immediately. And I'm sure it's all over my face . . . again.

Jack: Yes. It is. Earlier you said your face tells all. If the look on your face could actually speak—if it could tell us what you just realized—what would it say?

Mimala: It would say that I have a pretty serious bias against people whom I perceive as having money and options. People I believe have power. I'm kind of embarrassed.

I've always thought that I was the one without bias. It was everyone else who was all messed up. Okay, group. I know we said we wanted this to be brave space, but please remember that we agreed "what's shared here stays here."

Jack: Yes. You also agreed that "it's always your choice to share or not to share." It's your choice whether or not to share right now.

Mimala: I'm fine sharing. I can see it right now. The first school where I worked. Filled with mostly middle to upper-middle class kids. Mostly white and Asian. But the ones who fell through the cracks—those were my kids. They had disciplinary problems and were below grade level. I taught a bunch of senior kids, struggling to graduate in a junior class. It was filled with black and brown students. Nobody else wanted to teach them. I did. They were my first period class, and I was there for them—100 percent—always.

Jack: How do they relate to your ah-ha moment?

Mimala: Well, I taught other kids. I had other classes filled with the norm for that school: middle-class, mostly white. It wasn't like I ignored them, but . . .

Jack: You said, "It wasn't like I ignored them." What *was* it like?

Mimala: I guess I didn't give them my all. I helped them but probably waited for them to let me know they needed me. I know I treated them differently. I didn't realize I was carrying all of this into my professional life. Wow, that's hard.

Jack: What's hard for you right now?

Mimala: If I'm honest with myself, I have to think about the disgust I felt at those well-manicured yards, the yards of most of my students. I knew working there was a struggle for me, but I've never realized this. I didn't give those students what they deserved, and that's really hard to admit. I'm embarrassed. No wonder I transferred out of that school as quickly as I could.

Jack: How has this played out in the rest of your career?

Mimala: I've put myself in a special school for students with special needs. Disabilities. I've never felt the same personal struggle in that environment. To me, disabilities don't really have a socioeconomic status, you know? So I've always looked at every student in my school as needing me. I can hardly believe all of this.

Jack: What's hard to believe?

Mimala: It's hard to believe I could be carrying that into what I love—my teaching. I don't want to be someone who carries bias into her classroom. I'm here to help students. When I look at myself, I don't want to see that.

Jack: Thank you, Mimala. This is probably a good time to go outside of the fishbowl. We'll come back to you soon. For now, we'll hear from everyone around the circle. Mimala just said what she doesn't want to see when she looks at herself. Let's go around the circle. Everyone, tell Mimala what you see when you look at her. For instance: Mimala, when I look at you, I see bravery.

Each of the outside-circle participants took turns offering what they saw: someone who is changing the world, a survivor, an inspiration, someone who just did something I hope I can do, my role model, a leader, and so on. Barbara was the last to share.

Barbara: Mimala, when I look into your eyes, I see . . . a reflection of your better self.

Jack: Mimala, what was that like for you to hear each person share what they see?

Mimala: Affirming. Life-giving. Absolutely amazing. Thank you.

Barbara: Thank you for your vulnerability. This was healthy for all of us. Now, we'll debrief; we'll step back and learn from what just happened by examining, discussing, and reflecting on it. We'll look at the experience rather than being in the experience.

Reflection

Within this section of the episode, what intrigues you? What do you question?

_____

_____

_____

_____

What would you do to facilitate a group debriefing of this experience? Why? How?

_____

_____

_____

_____

Barbara: Our debriefing will start with a focus on the process. We'll look at what took place and how it happened. First, those of us who were observing from outside of the fishbowl will share our reflections.

This debriefing was an opportunity to help the group continue to build its collective-efficacy for inquiry, dialogue, and conflict resolution. Barbara proceeded to facilitate the observers' reflections and discussion. When appropriate, she intervened to redirect focus to the process (the how) of the dialogue whenever it shifted too far toward the content (the what) that emerged from the dialogue. These questions guided the discussion:

- What resonated with you?
- How did it feel observing the dialogue? What moved you?
- What can we learn from this? How can this help our group function more effectively?
- What will you now do differently as we continue our journey?

During the discussion, Jack walked outside the circle to get chart paper and markers. On the chart, he recorded what the group said was important. He planned to keep this chart, titled "Dialogue Tips," on display for group reference during the workshop. The tips included the following:

- Be vulnerable.
- Pause—be comfortable with silence.
- Listen for important words and phrases.
- Listen to body language.
- When posing questions, mirror verbal and body language.
- Paraphrase and be careful not to put words in people's mouths.
- Ask different types (levels) of questions.
- Help each other pay attention to self: slow down and put language to feelings.
- Meet each other where we are—not where we want each other to be.

The observers shared how this experience helped them learn approaches and techniques for dialogue that would help them have authentic conversations as they journeyed forward. Barbara then directed attention to Mimala and Eden.

Barbara: Mimala, what do you notice when you look back at this experience?

Mimala: The questions. They progressed so naturally and helped me to explore and discover something completely new to me.

Barbara: What did it feel like to explore and discover something new?

Mimala: Scary. Embarrassing. Horrifying to discover that I've treated kids unfairly because of my own bias. Ugh. But when I heard the affirmations, they lifted me right back up. I felt gratitude. It helped me remember core beliefs that I live by.

Barbara: Would you mind sharing one of those beliefs?

Mimala: Sure. One that came to mind was, "To whom much is given, much is expected."

Barbara: In light of this experience, how will that belief drive your action in the future?

Mimala: I've never considered myself privileged. It was always others who had privilege. What I'm discovering now is that I, too, have privilege in ways I've never considered. As a teacher, the culture grants me power. In that role, I have the ability to do and get what I want—at least in comparison to the students. I realize that I may have misused my power in some ways. It's because I didn't see it.

Barbara: And your belief? "To whom much is given, much is expected"?

Mimala: I'm realizing the magnitude of responsibility that accompanies the power I have been given in the role of teacher. I've been given much responsibility. I realize more clearly what that means, I have to do my part. I could stay feeling horrified. I could get stuck in guilt for not being my best self in the past. But what good would that do moving forward? No good at all.

Barbara: So, what will you do moving forward?

Mimala: I'll never take my role for granted. I'll remind myself that every student needs me. When my biases pop up, I'm going to recognize them and override them, or let them go, or deal with them in some way so I can have healthy relationships with all my students.

Barbara: Thank you. What about you, Eden? You've spent a lot of this time listening. What have you found worthwhile about this entire experience?

Eden: Tons. Just now, I was processing my privilege as Mimala was speaking. Earlier I was feeling shameful for my unawareness during my military experiences. But just a few minutes ago, Mimala helped me let go of that shame . . .

Barbara: Mimala is sitting right next to you. Instead of telling us about how she helped you, tell her. Tell her whatever you want to tell her.

Eden turned and looked directly at Mimala.

Eden: I have a couple of things. First, I'm sorry. For my ignorance. I realize that growing up as a child of an officer in the military, I never had to think about the experiences and perspectives of other military groups. I was in a bubble, served well by the dominant culture, with no motivation or need to look beyond that.

Mimala: I appreciate that. Thank you. It wasn't your fault, though. I want to apologize to you, too. For judging you negatively and lumping you in with all the other people throughout my life whom I've considered privileged and deserving of my harsh judgment. But it's a new day for me!

Eden: I love how you're choosing to shed your disgust, and you're also choosing not to get stuck in the past and in guilt. You're taking what you're learning and moving forward in a positive way. You inspire me. I'll never take for granted the responsibility I have as a teacher, either . . .

Eden's voice cracked. Her eyes suddenly overflowed with tears. Mimala reached over with both arms and hugged her. Eden hugged back. Barbara grabbed a tissue box out of their supply bin in the corner of the room and offered a tissue to each. She paused a few seconds.

Barbara: Is there anything else either of you would like to say about this experience?

Eden: I'm grateful to Mimala for her openness and to all of you for supporting our process. What else? Well, besides being conscious of the power given to me as a teacher . . . I also have to consider the unearned benefits I've received. I walk through the world as a white person. So, I know I have privilege. I have it whether I want it or not. What I want to think about is: What do I do with it?

Barbara: After we take a break, we'll explore that excellent question: Once we recognize the ways the dominant culture awards us unearned benefits, what do we do? What is our responsibility? We all have privilege and entitlement in various ways. Peggy McIntosh (Rothman, 2014) reminds us that "everybody has a combination of unearned advantage and unearned disadvantage in life." Whiteness is one variable—albeit a very important one because (1) historical vestiges of racism are strong in our modern society (Moore, 2007, p. 40), (2) the markers of race are so visible, and (3) racial classifications are currently immutable, in the sense that they are external to our subjective preferences (Crenshaw et al., 1995, p. 260). As a black woman, I can't wake up and say, "I think I'll have a white day today!" However, there are numerous other variables we all experience and some are more flexible and intersect with our racial classifications: class, language, national origin, body type, and so on.

Mimala: Barbara, hold on. What you just said . . . about privilege. That's helpful and rings true. Privilege is more layered and fluid than fixed. This is new insight for me. I just realized that I've been thinking about privilege and oppression as binary states: either you're one or the other. It's a bit more nuanced than that.

Barbara: Yes. McIntosh recommends that it's helpful for us to try to see ourselves in the context of multiple societal patterns of discrimination and oppression. In about twenty minutes, we'll get into the details of the Cultural Proficiency Framework to understand how we can use our power—including privilege—to redress inequities and create environments where power is shared.

Jack: Before we go to break, let's examine the questioning technique Barbara used during our debriefing session. It's a simple mnemonic—ORID—that we can use as a mental model for inquiry and dialogue.

Barbara wrote ORID (Stanfield, 2000) on the chart paper and explained each of the letters in the mnemonic: O = Objective (gathering facts and data), R = Reflective (eliciting emotions and reactions to the data), I = Interpretive (examine assumptions, values, and implications), and D = Decisional (develop options and determine priorities).

As they transitioned into a fifteen-minute break, Jack turned on their reflective break playlist, filled with songs having tempos between sixty and seventy-two beats per minute in order to nurture alpha brain waves and encourage reflection, learning, imagery production, and creativity.

Reflection

What was helpful to you within this section? With what, if anything, do you take issue or question? What are your thoughts with regard to Barbara's question: What is our responsibility? How does that question relate to you as a present or future facilitator?

_____

_____

_____

_____

Using the healthy side of the rubric (table 13.1), analyze this episode in its entirety. What examples do you find of culturally precompetent, competent, and proficient practice? What recommendations do you have for maintaining or improving healthy practice?

_____

_____

_____

_____

Using the unhealthy side of rubric (table 13.2), analyze this episode in its entirety. What, if any, examples do you find of culturally destructive, incapacitating, or reductionistic facilitator practice? Does any of the rubric language trigger memories of past experiences for you? If so, describe them below.

_____

_____

_____

_____

Table 13.1 Managing the Dynamics of Difference—Healthy

	Facilitating From an Emerging Future—Informed by the Guiding Principles		
	Cultural Precompetence	**Cultural Competence**	**Cultural Proficiency**
Managing the Dynamics of Difference Extent to which the facilitators engender trust, foster brave space, and increase collective efficacy for • inquiry • dialogue • conflict resolution • creative problem solving • progressing toward excellence with equity	Culturally proficient facilitators • Help group learn about trust and historical distrust • Encourage risk-taking through working agreements and ground rules • Teach about processes such as dialogue and conflict resolution • Draw on effective change management mental models to help groups through the inside-out process • Incorporate group activities intended to help the group develop and grow • Attend to group energy when making decisions about strategies and physical space	And . . . • Demonstrate and nurture trust, vulnerability, and forgiveness • Cocreate and help group exercise responsibility for democratic norms of operation that foster brave space • Practice processes of inquiry, dialogue, conflict resolution, and creative problem solving with groups • Support groups in developing effective shared mental models to increase collective-efficacy for transformative change • Use group activities and strategies appropriate to the group's stage in its journey, articulating what, why, and how • Exercise principles of transformation that bring about positive energy states through their actions, processes, protocols, and structures	And . . . Seek and provide opportunities to learn about and develop principles, tools, and practices that help groups and individuals • Create a learning environment of brave space • Establish, extend, and restore trust • Develop as a self-directed and collaborative group • Use processes and strategies to progress through the different stages (awareness [inside], commitment, and action [out]) of their journey to excellence with equity

Table 13.2 Managing the Dynamics of Difference—Unhealthy

	Training From a Divisive Past—Informed by the Barriers		
	Cultural Destructiveness	**Cultural Incapacity**	**Cultural Reductionism**
Managing the Dynamics of Difference Extent to which the facilitators engender trust, foster brave space, and increase collective efficacy for • inquiry • dialogue • conflict resolution • creative problem solving • progressing toward excellence with equity	Trainers • Shatter trust altogether • Enforce punitive ground rules that establish disproportionate power • Pressure participants into unstructured discussions about divisive topics • Rely on coercing participants to change • Use unhealthy activities and strategies that harm a group's state of being • Disdain positive energy in diversity trainings and instead trigger negative motivations such as anger, fear, anguish, guilt, and shame	Trainers • Provoke suspicion, doubt, and mistrust • Lay down restrictive ground rules that negatively impact the group's engagement and allow power-over dynamics • Deliver content that initiates passive-aggressive behavior and counterproductive discussions • Speculate that impacting people and making them change is effective • Use activities and strategies that obstruct a group's healthy development • Discount the influence of their own negative energy states on group energy	Trainers • Fail to explicitly or implicitly address trust • Neglect ground rules or use them in a general manner that does not acknowledge power • Present content, valuing the product over the process • Operate from cursory, untested, and subconscious mental models of change • Use arbitrary activities that lack short- and long-term intention for a group • Disregard physical space, energy flow, or motivations when directing activities

DIALOGIC ACTIVITY

1. Individually write and/or review reflections at the end of this episode.

2. Use think-pair-square-share protocol (table 13.3) to help participants share information, listen to different perspectives, and increase understanding of culturally proficient facilitation.

Table 13.3 Think-Pair-Square-Share Protocol

Step	Procedure
1.	Form groups of four individuals. Within each group, form pairs.
2.	Each participant spends time individually writing or reviewing reflections at the end of the text.
3.	Pairs discuss reflections.
4.	Within each group of four, each pair summarizes its discussion with the other pair.
5.	Each small group shares the content of its discussion with the large group.

Source: Adapted from Frank Lyman (1981). The Responsive Classroom Discussion: The Inclusion of All Students. *Mainstreaming Digest*. College Park: University of Maryland.

ACTUALIZING BRAVE SPACE

Within this episode, Mimala displayed the courage present in a brave space. At one point, she even referred to the group's aspiration for brave space—a professional learning environment that acknowledges and encourages the unavoidable risk, struggle, and discomfort that accompanies authentic engagement with Cultural Proficiency. Chapter 3 of this book discusses brave space as a concept. When it comes to operationalizing brave space, facilitators can start with a few simple steps.

Table 13.4 Courageous Learning Environment

FROM Safe Space	TO Brave Space
• Belief that learning requires comfort • Illusion of safety • Polite discussion • Guarded conversations • Acceptance of oppression and subordination • Unawareness of entitlement and privilege or inactivity in response to awareness	• Belief that learning requires disequilibrium • Reality of risk • Courageous conversation • Genuine dialogue • Self-determination • Personal responsibility

The first step in helping groups actualize brave space is simply introducing and using the term with groups. Facilitators then engage participants' critical lenses by helping them discuss the possible intentions behind the facilitators' use of the term as an alternative to the term *safe space* (table 13.4). Next, facilitators help groups establish their own ground rules, agreements, norms of operation that promote vulnerability—"our most accurate measure of courage" (Brown, 2012b). Furthermore, culturally proficient facilitators understand that helping groups shape their own agreements is more aligned with social justice work than is constructing these expectations for the group and imposing them from the outside (Freire, 1970; hooks, 1994).

TRUST AND MISTRUST

Cocreating and sharing brave space requires participants to extend trust to one another and to the process. For our purposes, trust is the belief in the reliability, truth, ability, or strength of someone or something. It's an essential component of a group's ability to journey together. Thus, early in the process facilitators help a group bond and develop trust. They foster brave space. They help a group normalize dialogue, and they model inquiry strategies. They construct, choose, and conduct activities that help participants get to know one another.

But even after employing such techniques, mistrust within the group can still remain below the surface. Sometimes it's due to unresolved personal conflicts. Often it involves power and its misuse or abuse by one group or individual against another, either currently or historically. Vestiges of systemic oppression and privilege show up as historical distrust. It's unresolved conflict on individual, group, and institutional levels. Culturally proficient facilitators are aware of and foresee these dynamics. They understand history and its role in shaping our current culture, which in turn influences our perceptions of one another and our behaviors with one another.

Facilitators are not above these dynamics themselves. Each facilitator possesses numerous dimensions of identity. Participants' beliefs about a facilitator's perceived social identities will influence the dynamics of difference between the group and facilitator. For instance, in the United States race and gender have been—and continue to be—two of the most visible markers of social group membership (Healey, 2010). Each also represents a system of oppression with its own particular history and implicit assumptions within society (Rothenberg, 2007). Through cultural socialization, people learn to recognize (so-called) race and gender by assigning meaning to physical appearance (Ferguson, 2016). Therefore, upon walking into a room, the first things participants will most likely notice, draw conclusions about, or question about a facilitator are their race and their gender.

Of course, this too is dynamic. The defining lines of race have changed over time, have varied from one geographic place to another, and continue to shift (Adelman, 2003). Every decade, the U.S. Census Bureau reviews and adapts race, ethnicity, and ancestry questions and makes changes to keep pace with our changing society. Even if the face of the United States is becoming increasingly racially ambiguous, it is a society with a legacy of racial stratification and preoccupation with racial measurement (Perez & Hirschman, 2009). For instance, those of us who do not do not fit neatly into boxes of racial categorization often hear the question, "What are you?" (Gaskins, 1999).

Likewise, as society is developing consciousness around gender fluidity, the immutability of gender is also changing. Increasingly, people are questioning assumptions of gender as binary. Still, even if people do not immediately categorize each other into boxes of race or gender, the outward manifestations of race and gender are still present. Phrased differently, even if someone wonders where another person falls on the gender continuum, the fact that they wonder in the first place means that gender is still something they notice and on which they assign value.

Returning to the context of professional learning communities: seminar and workshop participants bring with them perceptions of race and gender that include unconscious attitudes and behaviors. These are implicit assumptions and may be completely incompatible with the participants' conscious values. For example, even people who consider themselves enlightened and progressive in matters of race are still likely to have implicit preferences for whites. Yes, you read that correctly. Malcolm Gladwell illustrated this bias in his book *Blink* (2005), in which he described research from Harvard's Implicit Associations Test (IAT) that exposes the overwhelming implicit bias for whiteness that is present in our society, even among people of color. The culturally proficient facilitator is aware of the presence of this type of implicit assumptions and biases.

RESPONSIBILITY AND SELF-DETERMINATION

Given that historical distrust is likely below the surface, unchecked by participants at the start of any seminar, how can facilitators best use their power? First, culturally proficient facilitators recognize the power they possess. Like Mimala's realization of the power granted to her as a teacher, facilitators realize that they have power granted to them by the group. They understand the great responsibility that accompanies that power.

Second, facilitators use that power to develop and nurture trust with and within the group. One way they do so is by demonstrating vulnerability: they intentionally and authentically share personal lived experiences, and they explicitly connect those experiences to their own social identities and associated societal expectations. They put systems of privilege and oppression on the table, so to speak, and they acknowledge their participation in these systems: how they have colluded and how they have been hurt. This involves awareness and a willingness to publicly recognize both the systemic unearned benefits and the unjust penalties they've received.

On the privilege side of the coin, the facilitator's use of their power manifests as taking personal responsibility. This starts with an awareness of how they have directly benefited from the oppression of others. Facilitators recognize unearned power and resources systemically granted to them through dimensions of their identities (white, upper-middle class, heterosexual, cisgender, able-bodied, Christian, standard English–speaking, etc.) along with the very real outcomes of privilege and entitlement (Lindsey et al., 2013).

Then personal responsibility moves beyond awareness into action. Minimally, culturally proficient facilitators skillfully, publicly, and authentically acknowledge the nature of their unearned entitlements and conferred dominance in ways that can make life-, relationship-, and institution-altering differences (Kendall, 2013). It's what Gary Howard (2015a, p. 134) calls "the alchemy of privilege."

On the oppression side of the coin, the facilitator's use of power manifests as self-determination. This also starts with awareness: understanding the systemic nature of oppression. Then it involves the facilitator rejecting the notion that they are powerless to change the system (Lindsey et al., 2013). Facilitators commit themselves to sharing details of how legacies of oppression have personally impacted them.

However, in and of itself, sharing personal stories isn't what is most important. Of greatest importance to the well-being of the group is the manner in which the facilitator shares such stories and information. Ideally, they do so with confidence in a manner that is healthy, acting out of positive energy states such as exploration, collaboration, mastery, and generativity. In contrast, a facilitator could publicly share their experiences as a beneficiary of systemic privilege or targets of systemic oppression with a group in harmful ways. When this happens, the facilitator chooses to act from negative energy states such as anger, fear, craving, guilt, or shame. Doing so is unhealthy and can influence the group in ways that are counterproductive to its Cultural Proficiency journey (Howard, 2015; Lindsey et al., 2013; Zohar and Marshall, 2004).

FACILITATOR VULNERABILITY IN ACTION

So, when is it appropriate for a facilitator to share such personal information? After all, their job is to help the group with its journey; the overall group focus is not on the facilitator as it would be with a presenter. One answer is that a facilitator can share when the group requests such information. However, personal information that requires vulnerability may remain undiscussable unless the environment is one of high trust, especially when it is information that deals directly with privilege, entitlement, and oppression.

Many facilitators have found that a natural time to demonstrate vulnerability is when they are introducing an activity.

When introducing an activity, an effective and dependable facilitator move is to **Describe What, Why, and How** (Lipton and Wellman, 2011b, p. 45). The facilitator first names the activity. Then they describe the purpose and rationale behind the choice of activity, explaining its benefits in the context of the group's journey. Finally, the facilitator outlines the steps of the protocol or the general procedure. At this point, right before the activity begins, it's usually helpful for the facilitator to provide an example of the activity. Pausing for an example also provides a window of opportunity for the facilitator to share personal information and demonstrate vulnerability by being explicit about their own participation in systems of oppression and privilege. This vulnerability positively influences the energy of the group. A statement attributed to Malcolm X captures this premise of facilitation (Howard, 2015a, p. xv; Lipton and Wellman, 2011b, p.12): "You can't lead where you won't go."

What does the facilitation move of using the introduction of an activity as an opportunity to model vulnerability look like? Let's use the **My Culture** (Lindsey, 1996) exercise as an example. This activity invites participants to reflect on various aspects of their cultures, such as their names, culture identities, and values. Within that reflection, participants consider two frames: how they experience those aspects and how they believe others experience those aspects. After the facilitator introduces the activity using the **Describe What, Why, and How** method, they can easily and naturally follow up with some personal information. The facilitator can disclose a few details about how they experience certain aspects of their own culture. Then, when describing how they believe others experience those aspects, they can acknowledge systems of oppression and privilege and describe the general assumptions they believe people make about them based on their markers of race, gender, and so on.

As in my own case, perhaps your name and outward appearance lead others to make certain assumptions about you. For example, people often infer that my surname has Germanic origins and can assume that my cultural heritage is largely German, whereas in fact my heritage and national origin are predominantly Irish. My skin color—or other markers of race such as hair texture—coupled with my professional dress often activates assumptions within people that lead them to conclude that I had a white, suburban, middle-class upbringing, complete with all the benefits and advantages that the dominant culture gives people who look like me.

In reality, my upbringing was more complicated than that; a monolithic narrative about people classified as white does not tell my story. Other dimensions of my identity— social class, national origin, family, culture, and religion—all provide the nuanced details of my lived experience within my white and male classifications. Nevertheless, those two classifications confer unearned privileges. This is illustrated by the option I have to keep to myself the details of my invisible dimensions of difference that may run counter to common assumptions about whiteness and maleness. While keeping quiet allows me to be a beneficiary of assumptions, it also escalates my level of collusion with systems of oppression by making the choice not to interrupt, challenge, and do my part to dismantle those dominant assumptions.

People's assumptions may or may not be true. Regardless, assumptions affect perception and dynamics. Furthermore, we are not able to question and jettison unhealthy assumptions unless we first are able to see them. If we can't see them, they remain hidden in darkness. It is with this purpose—and only this purpose—in mind that a facilitator shares personal information: to help participants cocreate an environment that enables surfacing, recognizing, and bringing their assumptions into the light.

Facilitators should share information about themselves with positive energy and confidence rooted in the moral decision to responsibly use their privilege and/or power to initiate constructive conversations about the Barriers to Cultural Proficiency and to work for social justice. This kind of sharing models vulnerability and helps extend and build trust between the facilitator and the group, and within the group.

Reflection

From this section on trust, what information is new to you yet rings true? What information affirms your lived experiences? How so? What information do you question? Why?

_____

_____

_____

_____

ACTING FROM HIGHER ENERGY STATES

Intentional facilitator actions can help a group dissolve unhealthy energy states and create new states that nurture relational trust. Such facilitator actions demonstrate a type of intelligence with which facilitators access their deepest meanings, values, purposes, and highest motivations. Zohar and Marshall (2004) call this spiritual intelligence; they outline twelve qualities of a person possessing this type of intelligence (table 13.5). Through demonstrating these qualities, culturally proficient facilitators are able to engender trust and influence a group to access and act out of its higher motivations.

Table 13.5 Principles of Transformation: Qualities of Spiritual Intelligence

Principle of Transformation	Facilitator fosters trust through_____	Facilitator harms trust through_____
Self-Awareness	Knowing own beliefs, values, motivations, and purpose	Being at the mercy of emotion; being superficial and ego-bound
Spontaneity	Being responsive and living in the moment	Exercising rigidity, practicing too much control, lacking self-confidence, being insensitive
Vision and Value Led	Acting from principles, beliefs, and values	Being cynical, overly pragmatic, self-serving, or opportunistic

(Continued)

Table 13.5 (Continued)

Holism	Seeing connectedness and developing a deep sense of belonging	Being fragmented, lost in the details, or a short-term thinker
Compassion	Empathizing deeply and "feeling with" others	Being insensitive, cruel, indifferent, unresponsive, cynical
Celebrate Diversity	Valuing others and unfamiliar situations for their differences	Acting in myopic, dictatorial, intolerant, or exclusive ways
Field Independence	Standing against the crowd and maintaining convictions	Needing support of a group or tradition; being conventional or suggestible
Asking Why?	Working to understand and find meaning	Lacking curiosity, being fearful, being gullible
Ability to Reframe	Standing back to examine the wider context and bigger picture	Always putting out fires, seeing only the here and now, being overly focused, having paradigm paralysis
The Positive Use of Adversity	Learning from mistakes and seeing problems as opportunities	Being prone to self-pity, feeling victimized, placing the blame on others, or being unable to deal with failure
Humility	Having an accurate view of oneself as part of the whole	Acting in prideful, arrogant, domineering ways, or having a grandiose and belittling leadership style
Sense of Vocation	Giving back through servant leadership	Taking things and people for granted, wanting to just get by in life, being unmotivated to contribute, being jaded

Source: Adapted from Danah Zohar and Ian Marshall. (2004). *Spiritual Capital: Wealth We Can Live By.* San Francisco, CA: Berrett-Koehler Publishers, Inc.

Not only do culturally proficient facilitators exercise these principles through their behaviors, but they also apply them to the processes they use with groups. The process most essential for progress on the Cultural Proficiency journey is the process of dialogue (Lindsey et al., 2013). According to Zohar and Marshall (2004, p. 118), dialogue is "the most effective way known to bring about deep motivational shift and the resulting behavioral change in a group or an organizational culture." Dialogue can activate all twelve principles of transformation.

MINDFUL INQUIRY

When guiding Mimala through her reflective process, Jack demonstrated principles of transformation through his mindful inquiry. As a process, mindful inquiry applies the mindfulness skills (table 10.2) to the ORID process (Stanfield, 2000) outlined in chapter 10. Table 13.6 displays the levels of a mindful inquiry process with sample questions developed by mindful facilitation expert Lee Mun Wah (2004).

Table 13.6 Mindful Inquiry Process

Level	Purpose	Sample Questions
Objective	Identify past experience.	What happened? What I heard you say happened was_____. Is that accurate?
Reflective	Elicit attachments and associations with the experience.	(1) What angered you about what happened? (2) What hurt you about what happened? (3) What is familiar about what happened? Raise your hand if you relate to what _____ is talking about.
Interpretive	Explore belief systems and discover meaning.	How did what happened affect you? How does it affect you today? In what ways did it influence your values and beliefs?
Decisions	Pull insights into decision making.	What do you need from _____? To what can you commit from this moment forward?

Sources: Adapted from

- ORID by Brian R. Stanfield (2000). *The art of focused conversation: 100 ways to access group wisdom in the workplace.* Gabriola Island, BC, Canada: New Society.
- Mindful Inquiry by Lee Mun Wah (2004). *The Art of Mindful Facilitation.* Berkeley, CA: Stir Fry Seminars & Consulting.

CONSTRUCTIVE CONVERSATION

Fueled by vulnerability and the twelve principles of transformation, a group's conversation is the engine that propels the group forward on its journey toward excellence with equity in education. In *The Culturally Proficient School* (Lindsey et al., 2013, pp. 121–136), the authors provide a comprehensive treatment of conversation as a critical skill for leaders of Cultural Proficiency. Facilitators exercise that skill by shaping constructive

Table 13.7 Dialogue: Transformative Conversation

Dialogue Involves		Debate Involves	Principles of Transformation
Finding		Knowing	Asking why?
Questions		Answers	Asking why?, humility, reframing, self-awareness
Sharing	rather than	Winning or losing	Compassion
Equal		Unequal	Celebration of diversity, humility, compassion, self-awareness
Respect		Power	Humility, reframing, celebrating diversity
Listening		Proving a point	Self-awareness, spontaneity

Source: Adapted from Danah Zohar and Ian Marshall. (2004). *Spiritual Capital: Wealth We Can Live By.* San Francisco, CA: Berrett-Koehler Publishers, Inc.

(i.e., helpful) conversations. The best mode of conversation for the Cultural Proficiency journey (especially during the Awareness Phase) is dialogue. Dialogue is the one mode of conversation where the purpose is developing a collective understanding of a given topic (Senge, 1994).

Table 13.7 (p. 239) shows how dialogue differs from a fundamentally different mode of conversation: debate. It also illustrates how the principles of transformation become embedded in dialogue. Clearly, dialogue is a different paradigm than debate. However, debate is all too often the paradigm used for discussing issues such as racism, privilege, oppression, and entitlement; within the debate paradigm, perspectives become increasingly polarized (Lindsey et al., 2013, p. 133). Therefore, dialogue is the paradigm, process, and practice that can build trust, develop collective understanding, and bring about the energy states requisite for Cultural Proficiency.

Reflection

Review the Principles of Transformation in table 13.5. From your experience, what are some examples of effective facilitator or leadership behaviors that illustrate the principles?

_____

_____

_____

_____

From this chapter focused on managing the dynamics of difference within facilitation, what information is new to you yet rings true? What information affirms your experiences? In what ways? What information do you question? Why?

_____

_____

_____

_____

What information within this chapter do you find most useful? How will you use it effectively to serve groups as a culturally proficient facilitator?

_____

_____

_____

_____

DIALOGIC ACTIVITY

1. Individually write and/or review the three reflections at the end of this chapter.

2. Use helping trios protocol (table 13.8) to help participants share information, listen to different perspectives, and increase understanding of culturally proficient facilitation.

Table 13.8   Helping Trios Protocol

Step	Procedure
1.	Participants form triads. Letter off A–B–C.
2.	Person A selects, shares, and talks about their reflections without interruption. B and C listen (for a designated time period such as four minutes).
3.	B and C ask clarifying questions and A responds (half of the time period in Step 2).
4.	A, B, and C dialogue about A's reflections (same time period as Step 2).
5.	Repeat Steps 2 to 4 for B and then repeat again for C.
Tips:	• Display the time parameters for Steps 2 to 4 on chart paper. Consider projecting a timer if there are numerous trios.

Source: Adapted from CampbellJones, CampbellJones, and Lindsey (2010), p. 47.

14 Adapting to Diversity

A skilled facilitator must be able to manage unexpected group dynamics in a similar way to a jazz musician taking part in an improvised performance.

*—Alex Azarov
(Multi-Party Facilitation—Improvisation, 2009)*

Jazz is not just music, it's a way of life, it's a way of being, it's a way of thinking.

—Nina Simone (quoted in Taylor, 1977)

The more present we are as individuals and as organizations, the more choices we create. As awareness increases, we can engage with more possibilities. We are no longer held prisoner by habits, unexamined thoughts, or information we refuse to look at.

*—Margaret Wheatley and Myron
Kellner-Rogers (A Simpler Way, 1998)*

Every intention sets energy into motion, whether you are conscious of it or not.

—Gary Zukav (Seat of the Soul, 1989)

GETTING CENTERED

You are cofacilitating a school leadership retreat involving fifteen people. During a whole-group discussion, your cofacilitator intervenes on a thinking level by asking questions intended to help a particular participant examine beliefs and surface assumptions. During that process, the participant articulates values learned from a family member and begins to show emotion. You notice the emotional response and consider intervening on an emotional level.

- What should you consider when deciding to intervene?
- If you decide to intervene, how might you do it?

_____

_____

_____

_____

EPISODE THIRTEEN: JACK AND FATIMA INTERVENE FOR A FATHER'S SON'S STUDENTS

Jack and Fatima were facilitating a School Improvement Team (SIT) retreat for a high school interested in Cultural Proficiency. The SIT had fifteen members, and the retreat lasted two consecutive days with a follow-up day four weeks later. Because of the time frame of two days with one follow-up date, the agenda was customized and chock-full of activities.

During Day 1 the group progressed well overall, although both Jack and Fatima noticed something that would inform an adaptation of the Day 2 agenda. Most of the group's conversations had focused on "them" (students and families) as opposed to "our practices." As experienced facilitators, Jack and Fatima's assessment of the group was that—overall—the group believed that diversity was a problem to be fixed. Although the group had progressed well on Day 1, members were still focused on diversity as opposed to equity through their own response to diversity. So Fatima suggested replacing the Day 2 opening activity with an exercise called **My Culture** (Lindsey, 1996). This exercise would help group members see themselves as active participants in a diverse community (rather than see themselves as the norm outside the diversity). It would also be an opportunity to shift the energy of the group in the positive direction through strategically demonstrating **Self-Awareness** and **Humility** (Zohar & Marshall, 2004) as they introduced the activity. Jack agreed.

Participants started Day 2 by engaging in the My Culture activity. They sat in triads and shared stories about how they believed others experienced their names and cultural identities. Meanwhile, Jack and Fatima checked in with each other to make sure they were on the same page with their next steps for facilitation.

They agreed that the group was poised for a successful day. Since the Day 2 agenda was packed, they decided it would be best for the group to have a quick, whole-group debrief of My Culture before lunch. Fatima would lead with the debriefing exercise. They moved to opposite sides of the room. Fatima broke the silence with this **Foreshadowing** move (Garmston & Wellman, 2009, p. 218).

Fatima: In a few minutes, we're going to take our morning break. Before that, let's hear a reflection from three different people. How did your My Culture experience affect your perspective of yourself and others?

Torrence was the first to raise his hand and speak. He was a tall man with dark brown skin in his early forties with a tight, faded haircut. His beard was trimmed and had a precise shape-up. Like the other members of his team, Torrence donned school spirit wear to the retreat—a bright green polo with the school name embroidered in dark blue just below the left side of the collar. Earlier, he had self-identified as African American and a teacher of language arts.

Torrence: Well, folks, I have to say, this exercise helped me better understand myself and my values: why I do what I do. I had an "aha" moment during the discussion. I have a slogan on a banner in my classroom. I live by it and teach it to my students: "Hard work pays off." I'd never realized the extent to which I'd learned that value from my own dear mother . . . from her example. She was a single mom and ran herself ragged working several jobs so I could have opportunities. Although she died young, I'm grateful that she lived long enough for me to recognize that she was my hero and to tell her so. Because of her, my life motto has been "work hard and harder." But sometimes my colleagues and even my own kids have told me that I'm a hard taskmaster. I've been told on more than one occasion to slow down and smell the roses. But they don't know where I've come from. I have to admit that I wasn't fully tuned in either.

Fatima: Thank you, Torrence. You said, "I wasn't fully tuned in." How many of us in the group could have said those same words this morning?

Many participants' hands shot up in response to her **Diverging Attention** move.

Fatima: Look around, Torrence. You're not alone in your discovery.

Torrence scanned the room and gave a slow, nodding, pleased smile. The participants lowered their hands. One hand remained. His name was David and he wore the same shirt as Torrence. Somewhere in his late thirties, stocky and athletic with a shaved head and a goatee, David had previously disclosed that he was a high school teacher of English as a second language, and had self-identified with some seeming discomfort as being white, sharing that he had European ancestry. Fatima slightly nodded while looking at him.

David: Like Torrence, I have a banner with a classroom slogan: "Take Responsibility— Stand on Your Own Two Feet." I believe it's an important message for my students to learn and live. Many are new to this country. I was reflecting on how that slogan shapes my classroom environment. I haven't thought it through and discovered as much insight as Torrence expressed, though.

Jack immediately knew they should abandon their plan of breezing through a few reflections and then going to break. David had just expressed a belief about teaching and learning. His words were an entry point to help David and the group further develop the capabilities to explore the effectiveness of practices and policies. Jack had a vision: he and Fatima could continue to influence positive energy through an intervention of

Asking "Why?" (Zohar & Marshal, 2004) and the strategy of **Critical Inquiry** (Campbell Jones et al., 2010) that provided questions appropriate for groups operating on Level III— the level of thinking and developing identity.

Jack glanced at Fatima and stepped forward to **Signal** that he was ready to intervene. Fatima looked at him and slightly raised her fingers, showing her palm. Her **Signal** conveyed, "Thanks, but I've got this." He was certain that she'd seen the same entry point and had a similar vision of what they needed to do as facilitators.

Reflection

What key words did David use that Jack may have interpreted as an entry point? Referring to the facilitator map in chapter 9, at which of the four levels do you believe the group is currently operating? Why? What would facilitator intervention look like at that level?

_____

_____

_____

_____

What are you relating to in this episode? Describe possible benefits of adapting the plan. If you were Fatima, what would you do in this situation? Why? How would you do it?

_____

_____

_____

_____

Fatima: David, if it's okay with you and the group, we can modify our process and stay here for a few minutes. It will help you develop insight. Simultaneously, the entire group will become more efficacious with inquiry and dialogue.

David: Yes, definitely. I'd like that.

Fatima scanned the group, deliberately looking at each participant. They were either nodding or offering thumbs-up. Then she turned to David.

Fatima: Okay, David, when you described your slogan, you were actually sharing a principle that governs your actions. Using different words, how could you articulate that slogan as a belief?

David: Hmm. I believe that people need to be responsible in order to be successful.

Fatima: Why do you believe that to be so?

David: Because people who are responsible are able to get things done.

Fatima: Why?

David: Because they don't need help from anyone else.

Fatima: Do you believe that success means getting things done without help?

David paused before responding. He rubbed his nose. The room held the silence.

David: I think I do. At least, I think I value people who are able to do that.

Fatima: Ah. So, do you value independence?

David: Kind of. But even more so, what I really value is self-reliance.

Fatima: Who taught you that value?

David: My dad. No doubt about it. My dad. He's a jack-of-all-trades as well as a one-man-band. He's a mechanic, carpenter, welder, gardener, landscaper, electrician, plumber, writer, hunter, etc.

Fatima: So that value has served him well. How well has that value served you throughout your life?

David: Actually, not so much. I'm nothing like my dad. I can't fix my own car, build my own house, or even program my TV remote by myself. Not only that, I actually enjoy working with other people. Still . . . I wish I was more self-reliant. . . . I often feel like a failure. I've beaten myself up for decades because of that.

Jack heard emotion in David's words and noticed his voice cracking. He stepped forward. Fatima held the silence, glanced at Jack, and nodded. This nod indicated that she was willing to let Jack take the lead now.

Reflection

What do you notice about Fatima's questioning technique? What else within this section of the episode intrigues you? What do you find useful? What do you question?

_____

_____

_____

_____

If you were Jack, what would you do next? Why? How?

_____

_____

_____

_____

Fatima had intervened with David on the thinking level. But at this point, Jack thought it would be most helpful to intervene and follow up at a different level—the emotional level—and use the strategy of **Mirroring** (Kaner, 2014, p. 46). That would help ensure that David felt heard and emotionally connected to the group. It would foster trust, assuring David that the other participants were in it with him so he didn't feel alienated or pull back. Mirroring his statements would also answer the "O" in the **ORID** questioning progression: Objective—gather information.

Jack: We're going to pause for a moment and hear from the group. What did you hear David say? We're going to mirror back several of his statements. Share one thing that you heard David say, and do not add any interpretation. For example, "David, I heard you say that your dad was a one-man-band." Is that correct?

David: Yes, I said that.

Jack: Thank you. Who's next?

One at a time, participants mirrored statements such as these back to David.

- You said you value people who can get things done without help.
- I heard you say that you value self-reliance.
- After you said self-reliance served your dad well, you said it did not serve you well.

Jack had to intervene only once: when a participant named Troy shared a statement but followed it with his interpretations of what he meant by it. Jack skillfully interrupted Troy: "Hold on. For now, let's stick with David's words only." Young-Hee, the woman sitting to David's right, was the last to speak.

Young-Hee: I heard you say it is important for your students to learn and live your slogan. You then added that many were new to the country.

In order to bring the group slowly back on the ground, Jack moved through the other letters in the ORID: Reflect, Interpret, and Decide. He planned on **Converging Attention** on David for a period and then **Diverging Attention** out to the group.

Jack: David, what did it feel like to hear your statements mirrored back to you?

David: I felt heard. Hopeful. Definitely valued and affirmed. I do, however, also feel a little off balance—off kilter, so to say. I'm thinking about the value of self-reliance. Fatima's statement that it "served my dad well" stuck with me. I'm thinking about my students and wondering which of them are well-served by the value of self-reliance. Fatima, what do you think?

Fatima: If you want our opinion, then I can take off my facilitator hat for a moment and speak as a presenter.

David nodded and said, "Yes, I'm really curious." Through her words, Fatima had already signaled a **Role Change** or **Stance Clarification** (Garmston & Wellman, 2009, p. 271).

However, she did more to ensure that participants knew she was stepping out of her facilitator role. She walked to an area in the back right of the room—an **Anchored Space** (Lipton & Wellman, 2011b, p. 48) that she and Jack had already established as their presenter space. They stood and spoke from that space only when taking a presenter stance. Once there, Fatima spoke using a **Credible Voice** (Grinder, 2007): dropped chin, still head, narrow range of modulation, and dropped tone at the end of statements. Her voice commanded attention and communicated her confidence in her knowledge.

Fatima: Self-reliance is an individualistic value. Some cultures—like the dominant culture in the United States—are more individualistic, and some cultures are more collectivistic. Think about it as a spectrum. On one side is individualism where the individual prevails and tasks tend to matter more than relationships. On the other side is collectivism where the group prevails and personal relationships matter more than tasks [Hofstede, 1991]. From what you shared, I would say that you are shaping more of an individualistic dominant culture in your classroom. That is going to give an advantage to your students who already come from families and cultures that share values similar to those of your classroom culture.

Now that Fatima had presented her opinion as David had requested, Jack thought it was time to shift the group's attention back to inquiry. To help accomplish this, he decided to contrast Fatima's credible voice. In order to stimulate a response by creating psychological safety, he deliberately spoke with an **Approachable Voice**: slightly bobbing head, wider voice modulation, and tone that curled up at the end of his question (Grinder, 1993).

Jack: David, what do you assume about the value of self-reliance? To what extent might this value validate your students' cultures and foster a sense of belonging?

David: That's a great question. I can't comprehensively answer off the top of my head. I have students from over ten different countries in my class. I'm going to have to learn more about their families, countries, heritages, and values. Based on the diversity in my classroom, I think I'm going to have to adapt my classroom culture. That starts with my slogan. I want to shape an inclusive environment, so I need a slogan that will affirm them . . . and not my dad.

Jack: That's an excellent next step. Thank you, David. This is an ideal time for all of us to think about what our own next steps might be. We'll use the **Journal** strategy [Garmston & Wellman, 2009, p. 236] because it will help us organize and integrate our thoughts. In the back of your handouts, you'll find several blank sheets. Think about this experience that we've shared thanks to David. Take the next few minutes to write about how it has influenced your perspective and list behaviors you could take as a result.

Jack glanced over at Fatima, who had walked away from the presenter space. Jack touched his watch, their **Signal** that they should go to break soon. Fatima lifted her right hand and crossed her index and middle finger—the signal that she wanted to have participants to partner-up and discuss something in pairs. She then pointed to herself, indicating that she would explain the protocol. A few minutes later, she broke the silence using the same **Foreshadowing** move she had used to open the discussion that resulted in this learning opportunity.

Fatima: In a few minutes, we'll take our morning break. Before that, we'll have an opportunity to quickly swap ideas about behaviors. We'll do that by summarizing and sharing what you've written with a person sitting near you.

Reflection

Within this episode segment, what intrigued you? What was useful? What do you question?

_____

_____

_____

_____

Using the healthy side of the rubric (table 14.1), analyze this episode in its entirety. What examples do you find of culturally precompetent, competent, and proficient practice? What recommendations do you have for maintaining or improving healthy practice?

_____

_____

_____

_____

Table 14.1 Adapting to Diversity—Healthy

| | Facilitating From an Emerging Future—Informed by the Guiding Principles | | |
	Cultural Precompetence	Cultural Competence	Cultural Proficiency
Adapting to Diversity Extent to which the facilitators customize learning experiences and intervene to help groups	Culturally proficient facilitators • Craft learning experiences based on factors unique to the group • Respond and adapt the group's agenda based on the group's progression on its journey • Ease the group's journey by taking on the stance of facilitator	And . . . • Customize agendas and activities based on the needs and cultures of each group • Improvise and intervene in the face of uncertainty, drawing from intuition and revealing their thinking about intervention principles, techniques, and mental models • Shift stances (facilitator, collaborator, presenter) and facilitation styles to bolster the group's progression	And . . . Seek, learn, and integrate innovative, effective, and culturally responsive ways of helping learning communities pursue excellence with equity by • Customizing professional learning experiences

	Facilitating From an Emerging Future—Informed by the Guiding Principles		
	Cultural Precompetence	**Cultural Competence**	**Cultural Proficiency**
Adapting to Diversity	• Intervene effectively to refocus the group or capture an opportunity for group learning • Recognize the need to help individuals and groups shift energy states to higher levels	• Seek confirmation from groups on their assumptions and then strategically move between levels of intervention • Intervene with moves and strategies that apply principles of transformation to shift groups to higher motivations and move forward on their journeys	• Adapting agendas and processes • Improvising and intervening

Using the unhealthy side of the rubric (table 14.2), analyze this episode in its entirety. What, if any, examples do you find of culturally destructive, incapacitating, or reductionistic facilitator practice? Does any of the rubric language trigger memories of past experiences for you? If so, describe them below.

_____

_____

_____

_____

Table 14.2 Adapting to Diversity—Unhealthy

	Training From a Divisive Past—Informed by the Barriers		
	Cultural Destructiveness	**Cultural Incapacity**	**Cultural Reductionism**
Adapting to Diversity Extent to which the facilitators customize learning experiences and intervene to help groups	Trainers . . . • Expect groups to purge cultural norms and adapt to the agenda and expectations of the presenter • Prohibit differentiation to meet the needs of diverse groups • Refuse to shift stances, insisting the group adapt to the presenter • Act on unchecked or fallacious assumptions • Blame and berate the group for getting sidetracked • Wield anger, guilt, and shame to shift group energy to dysfunctional states	Trainers . . . • Disfavor input from the group during learning experiences, intending to assimilate the group into the presenters' worldview • Push the agenda of the presenters onto the group • Use stance of presenter to imply the group is deficient and in need of remediation • Intervene inappropriately in ways that harm group development, in ways that lack knowledge and skills • Interrupt the group in ways that shift the group to lower energy states that impede, stop, or reverse the group's progress	Trainers . . . • Homogenize implementation of learning experiences regardless of group needs • Adhere to the agenda regardless of the group's progression or lack thereof • Limit stance to that of a presenter to give the group information • Ignore their assumptions about groups and discount the need to intervene on behalf of the group • Fall short of recognizing, acknowledging, or responding to energy, thus allowing the group to get and remain stuck

DIALOGIC ACTIVITY

1. Individually write and/or review reflections at the end of this episode.

2. Use the think-pair-square-share protocol (table 14.3) to help participants share information, listen to different perspectives, and increase understanding of culturally proficient facilitation.

Step	Procedure
Table 14.3 Think-Pair-Square-Share Protocol	
Step	**Procedure**
1.	Form groups of four individuals. Within each group, form pairs.
2.	Each participant spends time individually writing or reviewing reflections at the end of the text.
3.	Pairs discuss reflections.
4.	Within each group of four, each pair summarizes its discussion with the other pair.
5.	Each small group shares the content of its discussion with the large group.

Source: Adapted from Frank Lyman (1981). The Responsive Classroom Discussion: The Inclusion of All Students. *Mainstreaming Digest*. College Park: University of Maryland.

ADAPTING TO DIVERSITY

Adapting to diversity is all about change. In the context of culturally proficient facilitation, groups change as they learn and grow, and so does the facilitator. In fact, a facilitator's ability to continuously engage and adapt is central to their effectiveness. As Robert Garmston (2008, p. 65) puts it, "Facilitation is planned improvisation." This planned improvisation is most visible through facilitator moves and interventions.

FACILITATOR MOVES

Facilitator moves are unscripted actions differentiated from other interventions due to their brief and subtle nature. Often, they are nonverbal. According to Garmston and Wellman (2009, p. 172), moves "increase or deflect group energy, direct attention, affect information flow, promote memory, communicate respect, and create psychological safety." While some moves are predictable and habitual—such as getting a group's **Attention First** (Garmston & Wellman, 2009, p. 189)—others are spontaneous and responsive to the group. A facilitator pulls these finely drawn actions from a repertoire of moves, or makes up moves on the spot.

This chapter's episode contained many facilitator moves. Several were clearly on-the-fly adaptations. For instance, upon David's request Fatima stepped out of her role and stated that she was taking a temporary stance as a presenter. She reinforced that through her use of space and choice of voice. She used the credible voice to increase her effectiveness in communicating information. Jack chose the approachable voice to pull the group back into a facilitation mind-set. Moves such as these are on-demand adaptations, micro-interventions that can make a major difference in helping a group increase its effectiveness.

FACILITATOR INTERVENTIONS

In general, facilitator interventions are actions taken to help a group increase its effectiveness (Schwarz, 2002). They are based on a facilitator's real-time observations and assessments of the group. Often, the rationale for intervening is to help group members identify and correct behaviors that are not consistent with the group's ground rules, working agreements, and collaborative norms. However, there are numerous other reasons for intervening on behalf of the group. In his book *The Skilled Facilitator*, Robert Schwarz (2002) outlines the general types of interventions listed within table 14.4.

Table 14.4 General Types of Interventions

Type	Purpose Beneficial to Group	Example
Exploring	Understand a situation, how a series of events unfolded, or how group members think or feel about something.	• "Say more about that." • "What do you want to accomplish?" • "How does that make you feel?"
Seeking Specifics	Support effective group process by using specific examples.	• "Who are they?" • "Can you give us an example of _____?"
Emphasizing Process	Understand the process underlying a group's problems and progress.	• "What happened, exactly, that helped you to feel connected?" • "What did you do then?"
Diagnosing	Analyze a situation by exploring interests; identifying causes, symptoms, and consequences of a problem; pointing out similarities and differences among members' comments; and exploring theories and hypotheses about situations.	• "Let's use the guiding principles to inform this conversation about school culture." • "What leads you to believe that _____?" • "Who taught you that?" • "So you believe _____?" • "So you value _____?"
Confronting and other feedback	Reflect on some aspect of behavior the facilitator considers dysfunctional.	• "One of the norms of collaboration is putting inquiry at the center. How well do you believe the group is doing with that today?"
Managing Group Process and Structure	Determine what topic will be discussed, when, by whom, how, and for how long, including setting agendas, switching topics, recognizing people to speak, reducing interruptions, and monitoring time.	• "How about if we use dot voting to prioritize your suggestions?" • "You decided to have twenty-five minutes for team discussions. That time has passed. Do you want to extend time or transition into our next segment?"

(Continued)

Table 14.4 (Continued)

Type	Purpose Beneficial to Group	Example
Making Content Suggestions	Receive suggestions from the facilitator (facilitator first receives the group's permission and later asks if the suggestions were helpful).	• "Based on your conversation, I have some resources I could suggest, such as _____."
Teaching Concepts and Methods	Learn from facilitator concepts and methods it can use (facilitator signals role change to presenter).	• "This technique is called mirroring and it can help to _____." • "_____ is a model that will help the group to _____."
Reframing	Change the meaning it ascribes to events in order to change responses and behaviors.	• Help a group give feedback by framing honest feedback as an expression of care instead of a hurtful act.

Source: Adapted from Schwarz (2002).

DECIDING TO INTERVENE

Interventions are intentional interruptions that change the course of group progress. Therefore, culturally proficient facilitators develop and exercise the mental agility required to make effective interventions. Like everything viewed through the lens of Cultural Proficiency, effective interventions begin with a facilitator's knowledge of self. Possessing knowledge of the following areas helps a facilitator declutter their perceptive space, stay calm under pressure, and keep the interests of the group ahead of their own.

1. Knowledge of intentions. Before intervening, the facilitator possesses clarity of purpose and understands why they are working with the group, attending to specific behaviors and other data, or about to pose a particular question to the group.

2. Knowledge of assumptions. The facilitator is skilled in identifying assumptions that inform the conclusions and assessments they make about groups, and they are willing to test those assumptions for accuracy with the group.

3. Knowledge of internal processes. Because unproductive listening patterns interfere with the effective facilitation, the facilitator is able to notice and set aside solution, inquisitive, and autobiographical listening and responding (Garmston, 2008, p. 65). A facilitator's interventions and questionings reflect the internal processes of listening, as illustrated in table 14.5.

To help facilitators decide to intervene, Schwarz (2002) uses several reflective questions that facilitators should ask themselves:

1. Are my observations accurate?

2. Am I the best person to intervene?

3. Is it important enough?

Table 14.5 Inquiry as Indicators of Listening Patterns

Pattern of Listening	Example
Inquisitive	"I'm curious. Did you_____?"
Autobiographical	"I had that experience, too. When it happened to me, I_____."
Solution	"I understand what you're saying, and here's what you need to do."
Facilitative	"You said _____. What belief are you expressing? Where did you learn that? What assumptions are in play?"

Source: Adapted from Robert J. Garmston (Winter, 2008). "Four Mental Aptitudes Help Facilitators Facing Challenges." *Journal of Staff Development.* 29 (1) 65–66. Retrieved from http://learningforward.org/docs/jsd-winter-2008/garmston291.pdf?sfvrsn=2

4. Do I have the group's permission?

5. Can the group learn from it?

6. Will it be quick or take time?

Reflection

Consider the three types of unproductive listening and the examples provided. Why might interventions or questions similar to the examples prove ineffective?

_____

_____

_____

_____

Consider Schwarz's six questions. What sources of information would you consider in responding to them? Consider that interventions are improvisational and that they happen on the fly.

_____

_____

_____

_____

LEVELS OF INTERVENTION

The facilitator can always decide to do nothing. This in and of itself is an intervention. It is not passive and is done with the intent of trusting the group to handle its own learning and progress. It is the intervention with the degree of most freedom for the group.

Table 14.6 Alignment of Four Levels of Intervention

Dimension	Process Level	Intervention	Inquiry	Listening
1—(Spirit)	Intuition	Present observations	Objective	Generative
2—(Soul)	Emotion	Describe feelings	Reflective	Empathetic
3—(Mind)	Thought	Ask and analyze	Interpretive	Factual
4—(Body)	Sensation	Direct the Process	Decisional	Downloading

Sources: Arthur M. Young (1976), (*Process* Theory) *The Reflexive Universe;* Joellen Killion (1998), *Journal of Staff Development* ORID; Brian Stanfield for the Institute of Cultural Affairs, *The Art of Focused Conversation;* Otto Scharmer (2009), *Theory U: Leading from the Future as it Emerges.*

If the facilitator decides to intervene by doing something, they need to do so in an effective manner. This involves deciding the level at which to intervene. Joellen Killion (1998) describes four levels of intervention that parallel other levels of process described throughout this book (table 14.6).

Each level of intervention increases in complexity and degree of constraint. The first level simply involves describing what is happening in the room, using factual and specific language. For example, "I'm noticing that you have spent the past fifteen minutes taking turns sharing testimony about your experiences within the current culture of the school system." The intervention ends after sharing that observation. This is a form of **Mirroring** that helps a group see its own actions. It is up to the group to decide what it will do with that information. One possibility is that the group could ask the facilitator for assistance.

The second level of intervention involves describing feelings. If the facilitator is describing their feelings, they are doing it with the intent of helping the group understand the effects of its behaviors. When doing this, the facilitator must be sure not to project their own feelings onto the group. The intervention can also involve posing an inquiry into how group members are feeling. For example, "After Tamara shared her belief that not everyone in this room believes that the Black Lives Matter movement is constructive, the energy in the room changed. What words describe the emotions you are experiencing right now?"

Mirroring can also come in handy when intervening at the second level. Jack used it effectively in the previous episode by having group members reflect back to David his exact words and phrases. The intent was to help the group support David on an emotional level by letting him know that they were right there with him. Jack purposefully did not ask for **Paraphrasing** (Kaner, 2014, p. 44) because that would have guided the energy to the head (level of thought) instead of the heart (level of emotion). Paraphrasing would have involved interpretation and the group members inserting themselves into David's experience. Mirroring kept the focus on David, which Jack decided was the best intervention based on his observations of emotions surfacing for David.

If the second level represents the heart, then the third level represents the head. It involves asking questions and analysis. The facilitator checks their assumptions with the

Figure 14.1 Critical Questions for the Level Three: Thought

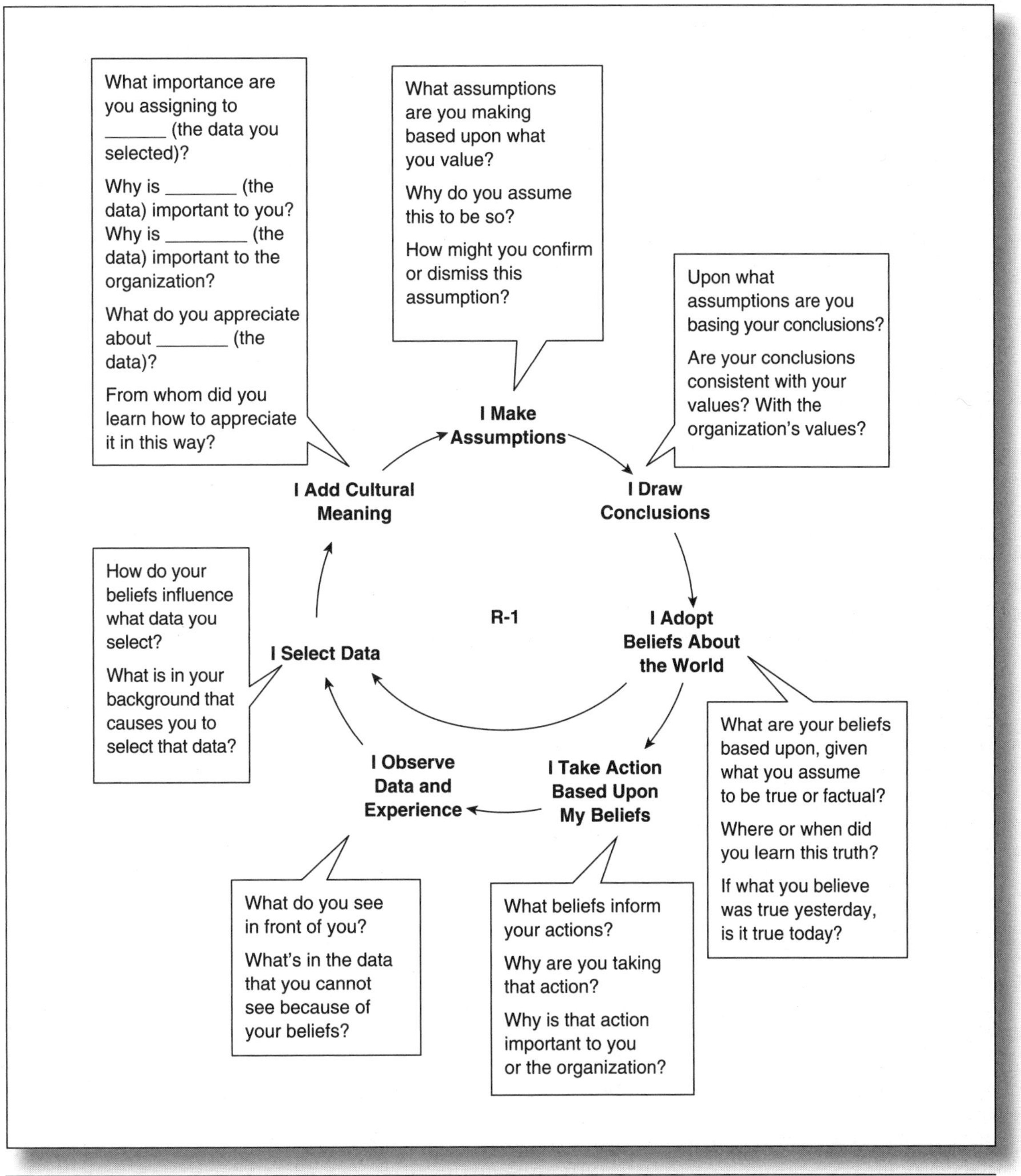

What importance are you assigning to _____ (the data you selected)?

Why is _____ (the data) important to you? Why is _____ (the data) important to the organization?

What do you appreciate about _____ (the data)?

From whom did you learn how to appreciate it in this way?

What assumptions are you making based upon what you value?

Why do you assume this to be so?

How might you confirm or dismiss this assumption?

Upon what assumptions are you basing your conclusions?

Are your conclusions consistent with your values? With the organization's values?

I Make Assumptions

I Add Cultural Meaning

I Draw Conclusions

How do your beliefs influence what data you select?

What is in your background that causes you to select that data?

R-1

I Select Data

I Adopt Beliefs About the World

What are your beliefs based upon, given what you assume to be true or factual?

Where or when did you learn this truth?

If what you believe was true yesterday, is it true today?

I Observe Data and Experience

I Take Action Based Upon My Beliefs

What do you see in front of you?

What's in the data that you cannot see because of your beliefs?

What beliefs inform your actions?

Why are you taking that action?

Why is that action important to you or the organization?

Source: Adapted with permission from CampbellJones, CampbellJones, and Lindsey (2010).

group, and asks the group for help with the content or process. For example, "What just happened? You seem hesitant to talk after that comment." Since this is the level of thought, the facilitator can also intervene in ways that help group members reflect, interpret, and analyze. When intervening at this level, the use of the Cultural Proficiency

Framework is particularly helpful. For example, "On the screen are the six points on the Cultural Proficiency Continuum. Remember these? I'm showing them right now to help you analyze how you have been interacting during our first hour together today. Where are you falling on the continuum this morning?"

The fourth level involves the facilitator directing the group with a strategy or process to use. It is the most constraining level because the facilitator does not extend trust to the group in making its own decisions or handling its own problems. Still, this level is especially effective when a group has lower collective-efficacy and is therefore in need of a higher degree of structure.

INTERVENING ON THE LEVEL OF THOUGHT

Level III is that of thought. When intervening at this level, it helps to draw from mental models such as the Ladder of Inference (depicted in figures 2.1 and 2.2) that help a facilitator understand the subjective thought processes that result in observable behavior.

In this chapter's episode, Fatima intervened with David on the level of thought. She noticed that he was expressing a deeply held belief through his classroom slogan. With the permission of David and the group, Fatima helped him explore through dialogic inquiry. She used critical questions aligned with the Ladder of Inference to help David develop an awareness of his bias and a willingness to examine it to better serve his students and their families. Along the way, Fatima built up the group's collective-efficacy to do the same.

In *The Cultural Proficiency Journey*, CampbellJones and colleagues (2010, p. 40) introduce examples of critical reflection questions based on the Ladder of Inference. Figure 14.1 presents these questions as a facilitator might phrase them during a **Critical Inquiry**.

Reflection

Within this segment, what intrigued you? What was useful? What do you question?

_____

_____

_____

_____

INFLUENCING ENERGY THROUGH TRANSFORMATIVE INTERVENTION

Through interventions, facilitators influence group energy. As described in chapter 11, groups and individuals possess energy states, or motives that are not consciously chosen. However, Zohar and Marshall (2004) assert that individuals and groups do consciously choose principles of transformation through free will. By consciously assessing group energy and intervening with intentionality, facilitators can use principles of transformation to pump new positive energy into a group's field of consciousness. This provides the opportunity for a group to choose to engage with a principle of transformation offered by a facilitator and, subsequently, shift its energy to higher states that help it progress on its Cultural Proficiency journey.

Table 14.7 lists energy states, starting with the most powerful negative motives and moving to those with less intensity, and then moving from less powerful positive motives to those with the most positive intensity. Next to each energy state is a principle of

Table 14.7 Shifting Energy Through Principles of Transformation

Energy State	Strategy and Principle for Shifting	Implications for Intervention (Helpful Group Processes)	Beware of Distortions
−6 Apathy	**Sense of Vocation** Give back through servant leadership	• Gratitude • Reflection • Passing on to others something given to you	• Fanatic • Guilty for not doing enough
−5 Anguish	**Celebrate Diversity** Value others and unfamiliar situations for their differences	• Dialogue with diverse participants • Attempting to take another's perspective and to live it • Involvement within different cultures • Developing awareness of and security in own culture	• Tokenistic • Superficial • Not claiming any point of view
−4 Fear	**The Positive Use of Adversity** Learn from mistakes: see problems as opportunities	• Developing resilience through cultivating a deep sense of self, awareness of fundamental values, and sense of an inner compass • Reflection and meditation	• Loss of vulnerability (stiff upper lip) • Recklessness: belief of being untouchable
−3 Craving	**Vision and Value Led** Act from principles, beliefs, and values	• Articulation of highest aspirations • Generation of possibilities • Examination of gaps between values/goals and actions	• Out-of-touch fanatic • Dreamer
−2 Anger	**Holism** See connectedness and develop a deep sense of belonging	• Looking for themes that emerge and unify • Looking at wider context • Following lines of causality back from or forward to an event/situation	• Lost in the big picture • Insensitive to importance of details
−1 Self-assertion	**Humility** Have an accurate view of oneself as part of the whole	• Gratitude • Reflecting on inner strengths that decrease the need for ego strokes • Being open to suggestions	• Submissiveness • Self-doubt • Low self-esteem • Indecisiveness
+1 Exploration	**Spontaneity** Be responsive and live in the here and now	• Awareness: self, others, situations, and possibilities • Exposure to unfamiliar experiences	• Impulsive or acts on a whim

(Continued)

Table 14.7 (Continued)

Energy State	Strategy and Principle for Shifting	Implications for Intervention (Helpful Group Processes)	Beware of Distortions
+2 Cooperation	**Self-awareness** Know own beliefs, values, motivations, and purpose	• Reflection and dialogue • Comfort in silence • Confidence in stepping out of comfort zone to examine self	• Self-interested or self-absorbed
+3 Power-Within	**Field Independence** Stand against the crowd and maintain convictions	• Meditation • Reflection about deep values and what it takes to live them • Checking self for integrity	• Stubborn/fanatical • Obstinate • Closed to criticism • Closed to diversity
+4 Mastery	**Ability to Reframe** Stand back to examine the wider context and bigger picture	• Surfacing and testing assumptions against other points of view • Contextualizing problems or issues with conceptual models and frameworks • Brainstorming with diverse people • Dialogue groups	• Flashy without substance • Impractical • Needlessly challenges assumptions
+5 Generativity	**Asking "Why?"** Work to understand and find meaning	• Encouraging questions from self and others • Openness to challenge • Looking for deeper truths or possibilities beneath answers or explanations • Attending to anomalies	• Undermining through clever questions • Afraid to take action due to seeing many alternatives
+6 Higher Service	**Compassion** Empathize deeply and "feel with"	• Honesty about own shortcomings • Awareness of the consequences of actions and feelings • Imagining what it feels like to have actions and feelings aimed at you	• Sentimental • Pitying • Bossy and interfering

Source: Adapted from: Danah Zohar and Ian Marshall (2004). *Spiritual Capital: Wealth We Can Live By.* San Francisco, CA: Berrett-Koehler Publishers, Inc.

transformation that represents a process of change. Each principle correlates with an energy state, implying that a group's engagement with the principle can help the group dissolve that energy state and create new and better states. Thus, each principle provides facilitators strategies for influencing energy in a positive manner.

Zohar and Marshall (2004) explain that aligning principles with individual energy states implies only one of the two ways that shift occurs: one-to-one shift. For instance, when influenced by holism, a group motivated by anger (–2) can shift anywhere between a –1 (self-assertion) to a +2 (cooperation). The latter shift of –2 to its opposite positive quality of +2 intimates a quantum leap.

The second way shift occurs is more general and holistic, where alignment of transformation principles is not necessary. Each principle is a fractal that contains all the other principles. When shift occurs in this type of way, it is as if the group has opened itself to the entire phenomenon of transformational principles.

Reflection

Review table 14.7. What examples of the intervention implications have you experienced? In what ways can you use the information within this table?

_____

_____

_____

_____

From this chapter focused on adapting to diversity, what information is new to you, yet rings true? What affirms your experiences? How so? What information do you question? Why?

_____

_____

_____

_____

What information within this chapter do you find most useful as a facilitator?

_____

_____

_____

_____

DIALOGIC ACTIVITY

1. Individually write and/or review the three reflections at the end of this chapter.

2. Use the helping trios protocol (table 14.8) to help participants share information, listen to different perspectives, and increase understanding of culturally proficient facilitation.

Table 14.8 Helping Trios Protocol

Step	Procedure
1.	Participants form triads. Letter off A–B–C.
2.	Person A selects, shares, and talks about their reflections without interruption. B and C listen (for a designated time period such as four minutes).

(Continued)

Table 14.8 (Continued)

Step	Procedure
3.	B and C ask clarifying questions and A responds (half of the time period in Step 2).
4.	A, B, and C dialogue about A's reflections (same time period as Step 2).
5.	Repeat Steps 2 to 4 for B and then repeat again for C.
Tips:	• Display the time parameters for Steps 2 to 4 on chart paper. Consider projecting a timer if there are numerous trios.

Source: Adapted from CampbellJones, CampbellJones, and Lindsey (2010), p. 47.

15 Institutionalizing Cultural Knowledge

We are looking ahead, as is one of the first mandates given us as chiefs, to make sure and to make every decision that we make relate to the welfare and well-being of the seventh generation to come.

—*Oren Lyons* (An Iroquois Perspective, 1980)

Culture does not change because we desire to change it. Culture changes when the organization is transformed; the culture reflects the realities of people working together every day.

—*Frances Hesselbein*
(The Key to Cultural Transformation, 1999)

The Tipping Point is the moment of critical mass, the threshold, the boiling point.

—*Malcolm Gladwell* (The Tipping Point, 2000)

Sustainable change, after all, depends not upon compliance with external mandates or blind adherence to regulation, but rather upon the pursuit of the greater good.

—*Douglas B. Reeves*
(Leading Change in Your School, 2009)

GETTING CENTERED

You are in the role of a professional development specialist with expertise in Cultural Proficiency. A school administrator contacts you, praises your reputation, expresses a need for their school to engage with Cultural Proficiency, and requests a workshop from you.

- Within this request, what should you consider? What are some implications?
- What dilemmas emerge from requests such as this?
- How do you frame a response to this request? Why?

Use the space below to record your thoughts.

_____

_____

_____

_____

EPISODE FOURTEEN: JACK HELPS CHANGE THE PLAN FOR SUSTAINABLE CHANGE

To: Jack McManus Thursday, January 14 9:04 a.m.
From: Benito Miranda

Subject:Upcoming Staff Meeting Request

Jack: Your team's good work is creating a buzz at our county-wide administrator meetings. My new principal, Candace Albert, has asked me to contact you so we can bring Cultural Proficiency to West Stocklin Middle School. I've worked here for two years. It's time.

Our February monthly staff meeting is five weeks from tomorrow. I think that staff meeting is our opportunity to make an impact and do the training. All staff have the time reserved to meet together. (Plus, it's Black History Month.) The meeting will be forty-five minutes. Candace and I won't be there because of a district-wide training on new assessments. Our eighth-grade team leader will start the meeting with administrative updates. Then there will be a few committee updates. Finally, we'd like to have a presentation from you or someone on your team. There will be about fifteen minutes for your part. I know that's not much time. We might be able to extend it to twenty or twenty-five minutes. Let me know if you can do this. Thank you.
Benito Miranda
Assistant Principal
West Stocklin Middle School

Jack read the e-mail, paused, and looked out the window. A couple years ago, he would have jumped at this invitation. Not now. He'd learned a thing or two. Staff meetings after a long school day were a poor context for his work. Attendees were more concerned about fighting rush-hour traffic to get home than embarking on the reflective journey of Cultural Proficiency. Plus, twenty-five minutes—the maximum length of time Benito said was available at this particular staff meeting—was barely enough time to generate interest.

If Jack accepted an invitation to a staff meeting, he would do so with a clear purpose: he'd wear the hat of a presenter, conduct a quick and compelling activity, and then inform the audience of either (1) the school's long-range commitment to Cultural Proficiency or (2) the various Cultural Proficiency professional learning opportunities available. With that in mind, Jack composed his response to Benito.

```
Dear Benito: It's great to read about your interest in helping
West Stocklin begin its Cultural Proficiency journey. Thank you
for your commitment to all our students in Stocklin County! I'd
like to meet with you and Candace to develop a long-range plan
for Cultural Proficiency. For now, let's hold off on a staff
meeting presentation until we have a comprehensive plan. Over the
years, I've seen how a staff meeting can be used to generate
interest. But in order for it to be effective, I believe it has
to be connected to a larger, ongoing plan. I can meet before or
after school any day next week. Please let me know what works
best for both of you. Thank you!—Jack
```

Benito promptly responded, and they agreed to meet in Candace's office the following Monday from 4:00 to 5:00 p.m. at West Stocklin Middle School. Jack set aside some time later that day to prepare for that meeting.

Reflection

What can you relate to within this segment of the episode? What key words do you notice within the e-mails? If you were Jack, how would you go about preparing for the meeting?

_____

_____

_____

_____

Jack arrived at West Stocklin Middle School at 3:50 Monday afternoon. He signed in at the front office, got a visitor's badge, and took a seat to wait for Candace. He'd brought documents that illustrated a comprehensive approach to Cultural Proficiency in professional development. He was prepared to advocate and present a plan, yet he knew that the most effective approach was to work in collaboration with Candace and Benito—the principal and assistant principal—to help them author the plan, and thus to own it.

Candace emerged from her office and walked directly to Jack. She looked to be in her early fifties and African American. Her chestnut, chin-length hair framed her russet, reddish-brown skin. She looked composed, dressed in a bright white jacket and black pencil skirt. She extended her arm in a handshake. Jack stood up and shook her hand.

Candace: You must be Jack. Good to meet you. Let's head into my office. You've been on my short list of people I've wanted to meet as I've been adjusting to life here as a principal in Stocklin. It's quite different from what I was used to in Florida.

They walked into Candace's office and sat down at a round table in the corner of the room. There was one empty chair for Benito.

Jack: Well, I'm flattered. Why am I on your short list?

Candace: Diversity and inclusion are priorities to me. Equity is my passion. I've been here for almost five months, and it wasn't until recently that I realized that your office is available to support schools. During our January principals' meeting, I heard more about Cultural Proficiency in Stocklin County. We were in small groups sharing success stories from the first half of the year.

Just as Jack was about to respond, Benito strode in and extended his hand to Jack, delivering a firm handshake with direct eye contact and a slight nod of the head. Like Jack, Benito was most likely in his mid-thirties. He was a brisk, compact man. His jet-black hair was cut in a flat-top style, which—reinforced by his fit physique—reminded Jack of the military. But Benito also had professional style: his purple cufflinks and necktie against his light-blue dress shirt complimented his tan complexion and added pizzazz and personality his tailored outfit. Candance handled the formal introduction.

Candace: Benito Miranda, this is Jack McManus. I was just sharing with him how I've heard several principals talking about professional development that mentioned the work of his team.

Jack: That's great to hear. Yes, we support schools and offices that commit to Cultural Proficiency. We help with ongoing, long-range, and comprehensive professional development focused on excellence with equity.

Benito: Perfect. That's what we want. I was thinking the staff meeting would be perfect.

Jack: I have a few questions that can help us start planning.

He pulled a notebook and pencil out of his laptop bag.

Jack: First, why Cultural Proficiency? Why now?

Candace: I've spent the first half of the year assessing our school's culture. I'm not noticing much intentional action to promote inclusion and equity. At a deeper level, I don't think there's a widespread commitment. I believe our expectations for every student can be higher. Our data reflect what I'm noticing. Like I said, I heard another principal—I think his name was Troy—talk about the growing commitment at his school and the improved practices he was seeing. He attributed this to the learning coming out of professional development efforts.

Jack: Good. So, why Cultural Proficiency in this way? Why the February staff meeting?

Benito: I've been here a little longer than Candace. Over my two years, I definitely see the need for focused training. We'll have the whole staff together at the meeting in February. They'd all get the same training.

Jack: Do you believe that all staff should engage in the same professional learning?

Benito: There's no time to waste. Practices need to change around here. So, yes.

Candace: Your question has me thinking, Jack. I agree, there's no time to waste. I also believe everyone should be expected to work on achieving equity and inclusion. However, I don't believe that we should have everyone do the same thing.

Jack: Why do you believe that to be so?

Candace: First, it contradicts the basic ideas of inclusion and equity. Equity in particular. Second, during my twelve years as a Florida administrator, my district mandated sensitivity training, which was basically a diversity awareness program. Everyone had to do it. Pretty disastrous! It set us back years. Most participants complained that they felt talked down to. I enjoyed most of the trainings, but—then again—I believed they were a good idea in the first place. Still, at times I did feel minimized because the whole endeavor implied that I had to be taught how to be sensitive . . . that I wasn't bringing anything to the table. After a year of bimonthly workshops for every staff member, I noticed that people were for the most part going through the motions. They'd endure the event and then criticize the trainings in the parking lot afterwards. There was never any direct follow-up after the events. For many people, the trainings became a running joke.

Benito: Wow, that's a good perspective for me. We don't want that to happen here. I've been an assistant principal for ten years in three school districts. My experiences with diversity-related professional development involved presentations where I've learned instructional strategies to teach diverse learners. I've never attended anything like a sensitivity training. So, I trust your perspective, Candace.

Candace: Thanks, Benito. If we include Cultural Proficiency on our staff meeting agenda, I'm thinking that it should be you and I expressing our commitment as the principal and assistant principal. The staff needs to know that we are leading this work. Later, we can frame Jack's team as a resource that helps us with our work.

Benito: I can see how that would help our staff view this as something that we own, not as a directive imposed from outside.

Jack: Exactly. I believe it's critical early in the process that a school's leadership articulate its vision for Cultural Proficiency. They need to communicate its values—in both words and actions—with the entire school. Meanwhile, I recommend assembling a motivated core group of staff members for in-depth professional learning focused on developing awareness and commitment to high expectations, diversity and inclusion, and equity and access.

Benito: Okay. This is all definitely very different for me. But it's starting to feel right.

Reflection

What do you notice about Jack's influence with the school administrators? Describe his intent and technique. If you were in his place, what would you do next? Why? How?

_____

_____

_____

_____

Candace: Jack, I'm assuming that your approach is different from my experiences. Obviously, your office is getting results, according to what I heard at the principals' meeting. It would help Benito and me if you shared more about how your office supports schools.

Jack proceeded to explain Stocklin County's Cultural Proficiency professional development program. He described the inside-out approach, and how Cultural Proficiency was the journey to excellence with equity. He described the need for reflection, dialogue,

Figure 15.1   Developing Collective Efficacy for Cultural Proficiency

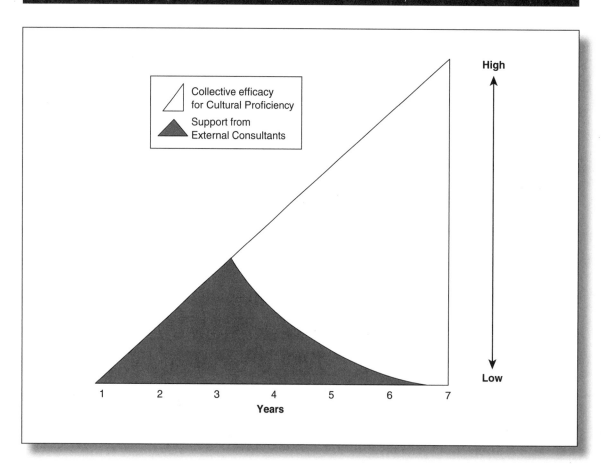

and a facilitator. He explained the three seminar levels (awareness, action, and facilitator development) and how they worked together for organizational sustainability. Last, he described schools that had developed capacity and collective-efficacy through three to seven years of focused effort. To illustrate these concepts, Jack pulled out a couple of documents and gave copies to both Candace and Benito. He first directed their attention to the document titled "Developing Collective Efficacy for Cultural Proficiency" (figure 15.1).

Jack: This graphic illustrates the general level of support we can provide you over the course of a seven-year plan. The goal is sustainability. We do that by building leadership capacity for Cultural Proficiency and simultaneously developing West Stocklin's collective-efficacy. What questions does this graphic provoke?

Candace: If I'm reading this correctly, your office provides the external consultants, and the support you provide increases until year three and then tapers off. Yet our collective-efficacy continues to grow after year three. Please say more about that.

Jack: Sure. During the third year, we would start developing internal consultants, the in-house facilitators and Cultural Proficiency champions at West Stocklin. They would start assuming some of the responsibilities for guiding the school's ongoing journey. After they're functioning confidently, our office would continue to support them and ensure their success. All of this fosters the "we can do this" belief that we refer to as collective-efficacy.

Candace: Ah, I see. Jack, this seems like a huge investment of resources.

Jack: It is. There's no question about it. My team has limits to the number of schools we can comprehensively serve every year. Thus, we support schools based on a number of factors, one of which is readiness and level of commitment. For us to commit to supporting you after initiation, we would need to work together to craft a seven-year plan, complete with accountability and measures of success.

Candace: Well, I have equity and inclusion running through my veins. There is nothing more important. And your program is different from anything I've ever encountered. It's consistent, logical, and aligned. Even the way you roll it out is inside-out.

Jack: I know what you mean. We don't even refer to it as *rolling out.* That term doesn't mesh with inside-out work. When initiatives get rolled out, it seems like some people may get rolled over! Rolling out is really presenting people with information rather than leading them through a transformative process that results in the kind of lasting change that will get us to inclusion and equity.

Candace: What do you know! I've never thought about it like that!

Jack: Instead, we think of this as emergent work. Our job is to guide people through a process of finding and bringing out their best selves. In the context of education, that also means collectively moving toward excellence with equity in practice and policy. Benito, you've been quiet. What are you thinking?

Benito: I'm just soaking all this in. It's almost like you're speaking another language. I have to say that I don't quite get it. That's okay. It feels right. And I trust Candace. She has the best moral compass of any of the five principals I've worked for in my career. If she's in, I'm in. I'm just not accustomed to being in a position where I don't have expertise. I'll need help with that.

Jack: Benito, I know exactly what you mean. Your comments remind me of some of my own, back when I started my Cultural Proficiency journey. I'll be here for you every step of the way. So will Fatima, whom you'll meet soon. I know for sure that you can do this. It'll feel awkward at first because Cultural Proficiency is a different approach. How are you feeling now?

Benito: Excited but also a little confused and unsure. It might just be fear of the unknown.

Jack: I get it. I'm here to help divest fear. What would help at this point?

Benito: To know details about the types of support you'd provide.

Jack: Yes, of course. Let's take a look at the document titled "Building Leadership Capacity for Cultural Proficiency" (table 15.1).

Table 15.1   Building Leadership Capacity for Cultural Proficiency

Year	External Support: Professional Development for Excellence with Equity (PDEE) Office	Internal Supports: West Stocklin Middle
1	• Awareness Seminar–Cohort A (10 people), 5 days	Administration
2	• Awareness Seminar–Cohort B (10 people), 5 days • Action Seminar–Cohort A (4 of 10 people), 5 days	Administration Cohort A
3	• Awareness Seminar–Cohort C (10 people), 5 days • Action Seminar–Cohort B (4 of 10 people), 5 days • Facilitation Seminar–Cohort A (2 of 4 people), 5 days	Administration Cohort A Cohort B
4	• Action Seminar–Cohort C (4 of 10 people), 5 days • Facilitation Seminar–Cohort B (2 of 4 people), 5 days • District Cultural Proficiency Network (2 people total)	Administration Cohort A Cohort B Cohort C District-wide network
5	• Facilitation Seminar–Cohort B (2 of 4 people), 5 days • District Cultural Proficiency Network (4 people total)	Administration Cohort A Cohort B Cohort C District-wide network
6 & 7	• District Cultural Proficiency Network (6 people total)	Administration Cohort A Cohort B Cohort C District-wide network

Reflection

Within this section of the episode, what is useful to you? What intrigues you? What questions does this section provoke?

_____

_____

_____

_____

Benito: If I'm reading this correctly, we won't ever get our whole staff trained! We have about sixty staff members. In seven years we'd have only thirty people through awareness training. That doesn't make sense to me. We'll never get there.

Jack: Borrowing from Malcolm Gladwell, we believe that we need to reach a tipping point of at least 10 percent of the staff passionate about inclusion and equity. That percentage comes from social dynamic theories about the concept of critical mass. Ten percent is the threshold where the work becomes self-sustaining.

Benito: By year six, we'd have 10 percent of staff in the district's Cultural Proficiency network.

Jack: Yes. And you'll have far more than that committed to the work. Those six people—the 10 percent—will be the champions who continue to ignite passion for Cultural Proficiency at West Stocklin.

Jack responded to a few more questions about the document and the trio discussed details behind the seminars, examples of other schools' journeys, and accountability and measures of success. Candace and Benito expressed interest in moving forward as soon as possible, but they had a few more questions.

Candace: I love this focus on building sustainability. Still, time is a nagging concern. It will take years! Our students can't wait. In 1776 our country proclaimed that "all men are created equal." I can't start something that requires us to ask our historically underserved families to wait any longer. How would you respond to that?

Jack: My response is both/and. This long-term plan is foundational to your school improvement plan (SIP), but it's not your only improvement strategy. It's the core professional development component of your SIP, but it's not your only coordinated professional learning effort. You'll build in other related learning opportunities, such as some of those strategy presentations you mentioned, Benito. In isolation, I don't believe strategy presentations would get us to where we need to be, but as part of a comprehensive plan with awareness at its core, they would definitely help. Once your staff moves into the Action Phase of Cultural Proficiency, they'll be learning from each other in many ways other than structured seminars. You'll have the momentum to go fast.

Candace: Yes, this makes sense. The long-range Cultural Proficiency plan is the foundation on which we can build.

Jack: Precisely. And, you'll be doing work aligned with Cultural Proficiency outside of professional development. Your SIP goals for areas such as curriculum and instruction, family and community outreach, and school environment would also focus on high expectations, inclusion, and equity.

Candace: Jack . . . I love it. I don't want to wait until next year to start. Is it possible that we start our first cohort this year?

Jack: Yes. Fatima and I can't accommodate another school team in any of our Awareness Seminars immediately, but we have a few open dates in March. We could schedule a multiple-day retreat and customize it squarely to your group's needs. Also, we could work with about fifteen staff and community members, which is more than the usual ten people on seminar teams. How about if we start by scheduling the retreat for three days? We'll assess the group's progress along the way and decide whether to schedule two additional days.

Candace: Let's do it. March is only six weeks away. What do we need to do next?

Jack: Let's pick a date to do our planning. Between now and then, assemble your team. They don't need to be positional leaders. Consider who has influence and who already shows interest in the goal of this work. Also, make the team a cross-section of your school. Include people in a variety of positions.

Benito: Don't we need to have our long-range plan done before you'll work with us?

Jack: We'll work on it along the way and finalize it once we've finished the retreat. That way, you'll be able to get a feel for Cultural Proficiency. If it doesn't work for you, you can and should back out of the long-term commitment. It will only be successful at your school if you're 100 percent behind the approach.

Candace: Sounds great. Thank you, Jack. I'll e-mail you dates when Benito and I are available to plan. Should I have the list of people attending finalized before then?

Jack: Yes. Knowing who's coming is the most critical part to planning a successful event.

Reflection

Within this episode section, what is useful to you? What intrigues you? What do you question?

_____

_____

_____

_____

Imagine you are in Jack's role. How could you best prepare for the planning meeting?

_____

_____

_____

_____

Candace, Benito, and Jack agreed to meet in two weeks to plan. Before that date Jack briefed Fatima, secured space for the retreat, and gathered planning materials. Since Fatima would cofacilitate, she attended the planning meeting. They arrived in Candace's office along with Benito and proceeded with introductions. Candace handed each person a document.

Figure 15.2 Culturally Proficient Event Design

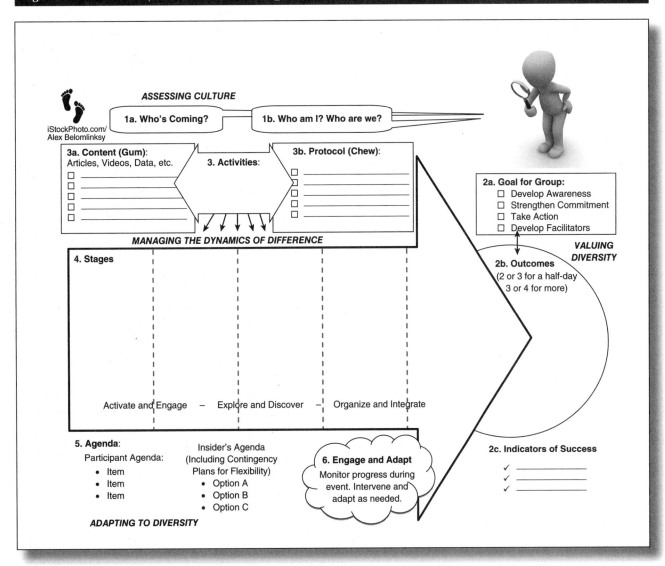

Source: Adapted from *Event Design,* created by Suzanne Bailey of Bailey and Associates, Vacaville, California.

Candace: Here are the names in our group. How should we proceed with our planning?

Jack: This list is a good start. The first thing we have to do is learn about the group.

Jack pulled some papers out of his laptop bag and handed one to each person. It was a graphic display of how he and Fatima approached planning (figure 15.2, p. 273).

Jack: We'll follow a planning protocol to customize the event. The steps are on this document. Take a look and then we'll discuss our approach to planning.

Jack: So, we'll spend the hour we have together today understanding who's coming.

Benito: I assumed that we would plan the retreat agenda today.

Jack: Actually, Benito, the agenda is our last step. For a three-day event, Fatima and I spend about a day planning and preparing. We spend about one-third of that time assessing culture: gaining knowledge of who's coming and then reflecting on who we are relative to the group. It's similar to detective work.

Benito: Do you really need to spend that much time just learning about the group?

Jack: In short . . . yes! Trust me on this for right now. Every group is unique. We don't want to plan an event for any group other than the group that will actually be there. If you flip over the paper, you'll see the questions that will guide our discussion today.

Benito, Candace, and Fatima turned over their pages to examine the "Sample Who's Coming? Questions" (table 11.7). As they asked and answered questions, they began the first step of designing a successful Cultural Proficiency event.

Reflection

Within this episode segment, what intrigued you? What was useful? What do you question?

_____

_____

_____

_____

Using the healthy side of the rubric (table 15.2), analyze this episode in its entirety. What examples do you find of culturally precompetent, competent, and proficient practice? What recommendations do you have for maintaining or improving healthy practice?

_____

_____

_____

_____

Table 15.2 Institutionalizing Cultural Knowledge—Healthy

	Facilitating From an Emerging Future—Informed by the Guiding Principles		
	Cultural Precompetence	**Cultural Competence**	**Cultural Proficiency**
Institutionalize Cultural Knowledge Extent to which facilitators Incorporate practices and policies that ensure culturally proficient professional learning Help organizations develop sustainability for Cultural Proficiency	Culturally proficient facilitators • Gather information about groups within the planning processes. • Provide service for groups in alignment with the organization's strategic plan and commitment to ongoing professional development for excellence with equity in education. • Align work with research-based factors for effective professional development.	And . . . • Plan and prepare using protocols that promote assessing culture, valuing diversity, managing the dynamics of difference, and adapting to diversity. • Support an organization with a comprehensive system of Cultural Proficiency professional learning that includes multiple phases: awareness, action, and facilitator development. • Align performance with standards for professional learning.	And . . . Model and advocate for collaboration with organizations to ensure sustainability of professional and organizational development focused on excellence with equity by developing long-range plans that • Include multiyear professional development efforts aligned with standards for professional learning and Essential Elements of Cultural Competence; • Account for phases of the change process; • Develop the capacity and capabilities of individuals and the organization; and • Increase collective efficacy.

Table 15.3 Institutionalizing Cultural Knowledge—Unhealthy

	Training From a Divisive Past—Informed by the Barriers		
	Cultural Destructiveness	**Cultural Incapacity**	**Cultural Reductionism**
Institutionalize Cultural Knowledge Extent to which facilitators Incorporate practices and policies that ensure culturally proficient professional learning Help organizations develop sustainability for Cultural Proficiency	Trainers . . . • Assert own agenda of dividing people and/ or gaining power over groups. • Mandate trainings to punish individuals through approaches such as blame and shame for something that went wrong. • Oppose practice that aligns with standards for professional learning.	Trainers . . . • Belittle culture of the group through planning techniques framed by deficit thinking. • Remediate through provision of one-and-done sensitivity trainings aimed at fixing people and/or providing the solution that "we" need to be more sensitive to "them." • Ignore research-based andragogy in favor of training methods proven to be ineffective for adult learning.	Trainers . . . • Rely on generic planning practices that disregard cultural knowledge when preparing for trainings. • Present an off-the-shelf diversity training program with no customization and offer train-the-trainer solutions opposed to building capacity and collective-efficacy. • Oversimplify adult learning through use of basic training approaches.

Using the unhealthy side of the rubric (table 15.3), analyze this episode in its entirety. What, if any, examples do you find of culturally destructive, incapacitating, or reductionistic facilitator practice? Does any of the rubric language trigger memories of past experiences for you? If so, describe them below.

_____

_____

_____

_____

DIALOGIC ACTIVITY

1. Individually write and/or review reflections at the end of this episode.

2. Use the think-pair-square-share protocol (table 15.4) to help participants share information, listen to different perspectives, and increase understanding of culturally proficient facilitation.

Table 15.4 Think-Pair-Square-Share Protocol

Step	Procedure
1.	Form groups of four individuals. Within each group, form pairs.
2.	Each participant spends time individually writing or reviewing reflections at the end of the text.
3.	Pairs discuss reflections.
4.	Within each group of four, each pair summarizes its discussion with the other pair.
5.	Each small group shares the content of its discussion with the large group.

Source: Adapted from Frank Lyman (1981). The Responsive Classroom Discussion: The Inclusion of All Students. *Mainstreaming Digest*. College Park: University of Maryland.

CULTURALLY PROFICIENT EVENT DESIGN

Culturally proficient facilitators plan and prepare for professional learning events using the Essential Elements of Cultural Competence as standards. Figure 15.2 is a graphic display of a helpful planning protocol based on the Event Design created by Suzanne Bailey of Bailey and Associates (Garmston & Wellman, 1992, p. 13). It represents the steps within a culturally proficient facilitator's thinking when planning and preparing for a group.

The first step involves assessing culture. First, facilitators gather information about groups using questions such as those listed in table 11.7. This provides the context that informs subsequent stages. Before leaving this stage, facilitators look within and consider their most critical asset: themselves (Garmston & Wellman, 2009). They consider

Table 15.5 Group Goals for Cultural Proficiency Events

Goal of Process Phase	Examples
Awareness	• Build a professional community of learners. • Use the Tools of Cultural Proficiency to develop consciousness of personal and organizational responses to differences. • Increase knowledge of self: values, assumptions, beliefs, attitudes, and biases. • Develop understanding of the need for excellence with equity. • Learn and practice communication skills fundamental to cultural competence and proficiency.
Commitment	• Dedicate oneself to ensuring excellence with equity in education. • Increase knowledge of cross-cultural effectiveness.
Action	• Apply the Tools of Cultural Proficiency to plan for equitable and inclusive change. • Transform practices and policies. • Learn to implement and institutionalize change within the organization. • Nurture consciousness of personal and organizational response to differences.
Sustainability (Facilitator Development)	• Deepen knowledge of the need for excellence with equity in education. • Develop knowledge of group facilitation. • Learn and practice facilitation skills foundational to guiding Cultural Proficiency for groups. • Apply the Cultural Proficiency Framework to group facilitation.

self-knowledge, including their own cultural identities, histories, values, beliefs, and perspectives. Furthermore, they consider their cognitive styles, emotional states, strengths, and limitations. Most of all, they consider what all of this means relative to their knowledge of the group.

The second step involves valuing diversity within the process of determining the group's goal(s) and crafting outcomes for its professional learning event. Above all, facilitators ensure that event goals and outcomes support excellence with equity. They set a broad goal based on their assessment of whatever journey phase is next for the group: awareness, commitment, action, or sustainability (facilitator development). Table 15.5 offers descriptors for each type of goal.

Table 15.6 Relational and Task Outcomes

Category	Types of Outcomes
Relational Outcomes that support group development	• Knowledge of self, others, effective groups: Understanding one's own personal and organizational culture: values, assumptions, beliefs, and practices in the context of excellence with equity • Skills: Listening for understanding, verbal and nonverbal tools, assessment, and feedback • Dispositions: Valuing cognitive conflict, investing in mutual professional learning, taking responsibility

(Continued)

Table 15.6 (Continued)

Category	Types of Outcomes
Task Outcomes that support successful group work	• Results: Products, performance, decisions • Actions: Implementation, transferring, desisting • Technical knowledge: Declarative, procedural, conditional

Source: Adapted from Lipton, Laura and Wellman, Bruce (2011b). *Leading Groups: Effective Strategies for Building Professional Community*. Sherman, CT: MiraVia.

After identifying the overall goal, culturally proficient facilitators consider the nature of the group's ethical tension, represented in the Cultural Proficiency Framework (table 8.11) and the specific stages within the Facilitator Map (figure 9.1). They consider relational as well as task outcomes, detailed within table 15.6. Finally, exercising pragmatism, they craft two or three outcomes for a half-day event and no more than four outcomes for an event lasting a full day or more (Hollins & Govan, 2015).

With outcomes in mind, facilitators develop indicators of success. These are specific knowledge, skills, abilities, attitudes, or behaviors of the group indicative of the outcome. In harmony, well-crafted outcomes and indicators reflect the acronym SMART: Specific, Measurable, Attainable, Relevant, and Tactically sound (Garmston & Wellman, 2009, p. 82). Table 15.7 illustrates the interrelatedness of goals, outcomes, and indicators of success. The indicator is related to the outcome is related to the goal is related to who's coming.

The third step of the Cultural Proficiency Event Design involves managing the dynamics of difference in choosing and/or creating activities that are (1) intended to help the group grow and (2) are appropriate to the group's phase and stage in its journey. Activities must fit the group. For instance, a group with lower collective-efficacy would benefit from a protocol with a high degree of structure. Additionally, activity selection should take into account group size and composition, as well as length of time that the group will stay together (Lipton and Wellman, 2011a).

Table 15.7 Sample Interrelated Goal, Outcome, and Indicators

	The group will . . .
Goal	Develop awareness.
Outcome	Build capacity to foster trust.
Indicators	Display ability to engage in dialogue. Display skills for effective listening and questioning. Display an attitude of transparency and vulnerability within conversations.

Table 15.8 Sample: Creating an Activity

Steps	Sample components of an activity
Determine Purpose	Task: To use Cultural Proficiency Framework to draw out personal stories. Relational: To improve capabilities for listening and speaking across differences.
Choose Content	Guiding Principles of Cultural Proficiency
Choose Protocol	Constructivist Listening Dyads
Give Activity a Name	Swapping Culture Stories
Outline Activity Steps	1. Review agreements for constructivist listening dyads protocol: I agree to listen to and think about you for a fixed period of time in exchange for you doing the same for me. I keep in my mind that my listening is for your benefit so I do not ask questions for my information. 2. Participants sit in pairs. 3. Participants independently read two of the Guiding Principles of Cultural Proficiency. 4. Each person is given equal time to talk and share a personal story related to one of the guiding principles. (Everyone deserves to be listened to.) 5. The listener does not interpret, paraphrase, analyze, give advice, or break in with a personal story. (People can solve their own problems.) 6. Participants maintain confidentiality. (People need to know they can be completely authentic.) 7. The speaker does not criticize or complain about listeners or about mutual colleagues during their time to talk. (A person cannot listen well when they are feeling attacked or defensive.) 8. Repeat protocol for the next two guiding principles.

Source: Protocol adapted from *The Constructivist Listening Dyad,* School Reform Initiative, retrieved from: http://schoolreforminitiative.org/doc/dyad.pdf

Cultural Proficiency: A Manual for School Leaders (Lindsey et al., 2009) contains a multitude of high-quality activities that are suitable for facilitators to use with a group at various stages in their journey. Facilitators can also adapt these exercises and create their own activities, attending to content ("gum") and protocol ("chewing"). Table 15.8 provides a template for creating activities.

The metaphor of gum and chewing (Doyle & Strauss, 1976) represents the planning dilemma of balancing content (what information will be shared and in what form: article, video, etc.) with process (how the group will interact with the content to learn together and progress on its journey). To frame process, facilitators use protocols, which draw boundaries around conversations, inform the type of thinking the group will do, and provide psychological safety (Garmston and von Frank, 2012, p. 182).

The question that informs a culturally proficient facilitator's thinking during this step is, "What group activity will nurture the thought process that will generate the real content that will help the group move forward?" This question is different from the question that informs a presenter's thinking: "What is the content?"

Table 15.9 Types of Activity (Information Processing): Collaborative Learning Cycle

Type of Activity	Why	When
Activate and Engage	• Set the tone. • Establish or increase relevancy. • Surface experiences and expectations.	Early in a segment or event
Explore and Discover	• Support collective understanding. • Analyze information. • Explore multiple perspectives.	Middle of a segment or event
Organize and Integrate	• Generate theories of causation. • Generate theories of action. • Transition from awareness to action.	End of a segment event

Source: Adapted from Lipton, Laura and Wellman, Bruce (2004). *Got Data? Now What?* Bloomington, Indiana: Solution Tree Press.

The fourth step of the Cultural Proficiency event design extends the need to manage the dynamics of difference to the task of staging the event. During this step, it's helpful to arrange group activities into accumulative segments or phases within the event. Laura Lipton and Bruce Wellman's *Got Data?* (2004) offers a model for structuring both the overall event and the segments within the event. The model contains three phases—or, in other words—three different sequential types of group activity. Therefore, the collaborative learning cycle provides structure to manage the different segments (phases) of the event as well as the activities within the segments. We can think of each segment within a Cultural Proficiency event as an iteration of the collaborative learning cycle (table 15.9).

Additionally, the staging of the event includes planning an opening and a closing as bookends to the event. Openings typically include focusing energy and attention; clarifying roles; presenting the agenda, outcomes, and working agreements; developing inclusion (sense of belonging); and activating relevant knowledge (Garmston & Wellman, 2009). Closings typically include conveying an inspirational message or experience; soliciting participant feedback, assessment, or evaluations; articulating expectations for next steps; and affirming the work completed throughout the event (Hollins & Govan, 2015).

The fifth step in this design process involves adapting to diversity by customizing the agenda in both the public (participant) and the private (insider's) forms. Furthermore, culturally proficient facilitators prepare in advance to adapt to diversity once the event has started. Such preparations involve techniques such as keeping the public agenda broad, simple, and logical; including event start and end times on the agenda but omitting specific times for breaks and lunch to preserve flexibility; and preparing contingency plans and alternative activities with the requisite materials.

The sixth step in figure 15.2 takes place after planning and preparation: it happens once the event has started. It captures the mantra of Cultural Proficiency: Engage and adapt. Remember that the agenda belongs to the group, which means that a successful facilitator monitors the group, intervenes when helpful, and works with the group to adjust the agenda on the fly if the need arises in order to best serve the group's needs for growth and progression on its journey.

Reflection

Regarding the process of designing Cultural Proficiency events, what intrigued you? What was useful? What do you question?

_____

_____

_____

_____

STANDARDS FOR PROFESSIONAL LEARNING

Cultural Proficiency events hold incredible potential to transform lives. The likelihood of realizing that potential depends on the quality of the individual and collective professional learning that the event encourages and supports. Therefore, facilitators concerned with quality make use of standards for professional learning when designing their events.

In 2011 Learning Forward (an international association focused solely on increasing educator effectiveness through professional learning and school improvement) released its third iteration of *Standards for Professional Learning*. The standards are designed to engage educators as partners to increase and ensure the effectiveness of professional learning. When used well, the standards help educators "increase equity of access to high-quality education for every student, not just for those lucky enough to attend schools in more advantaged communities" (Learning Forward, 2011). Applied to Cultural Proficiency, these seven standards outline the characteristics of professional learning that lead to the educator growth and school improvement required of excellence with equity in education.

- Learning Communities: Conduct learning within communities committed to continuous improvement, collective responsibility, and goal alignment.
- Resources: Prioritize, monitor, and coordinate resources for educator learning.
- Learning Designs: Integrate theories, research, and models of human learning to achieve its intended outcomes.
- Outcomes: Align outcomes with educator performance and student curriculum standards.
- Leadership: Engage skillful leaders who develop capacity, advocate, and create support systems for professional learning.
- Data: Use a variety of sources and types of student, educator, and system data to plan, assess, and evaluate professional learning.
- Implementation: Apply research on change and sustain support for implementation of professional learning for long-term change.

With the release of the *Standards for Professional Learning*, Learning Forward (2011) shifted its language away from professional "development" to professional "learning." Joellen Killion (Kentucky Department of Education, 2013), senior adviser to Learning Forward, explains that this represents a shift in focus: away from the events and episodes and toward the process of learning and growth that occurs through those events. In other words, the shift helps us focus on the outcomes of professional development events: learning and growth.

RESEARCH ON PROFESSIONAL DEVELOPMENT

When we are focusing on professional development programs and events, how do we know that what we are planning is likely to ultimately make a positive difference for students? John Hattie (2009) offers implications from an impressive meta-analysis (Timperley, Wilson, Barrar, & Fung, 2007) that incorporated seventy-two research studies that assessed the effects of professional development on student outcomes. The authors discovered seven themes about what works best in professional development. Effective professional development

1. Occurs over a long period of time (three to seven years);

2. Involves external experts, which increases likelihood of success compared with efforts initiated and implemented solely by within-school staff;

3. Engages educators in the learning process;

4. Challenges existing beliefs, prevailing discourse, and assumptions;

5. Supports communication about education between educators in a professional community of practice;

6. Has school leaders who support opportunities to learn (when they have relevant expertise) and who provide opportunities to process learning in the community; and

7. Is not contingent on funding, release time, or voluntary or compulsory status.

Reflection

What squares with your beliefs about professional learning standards and research on professional development? What points do you want to remember? What do you question?

_____

_____

_____

_____

PLANNING FOR LONG-TERM CHANGE

Ultimately, a facilitator makes Cultural Proficiency easier for an organization by helping that organization plan for sustainability: developing collective-efficacy, becoming self-sufficient,

Figure 15.3 Overlapping Phases of Change for Cultural Proficiency

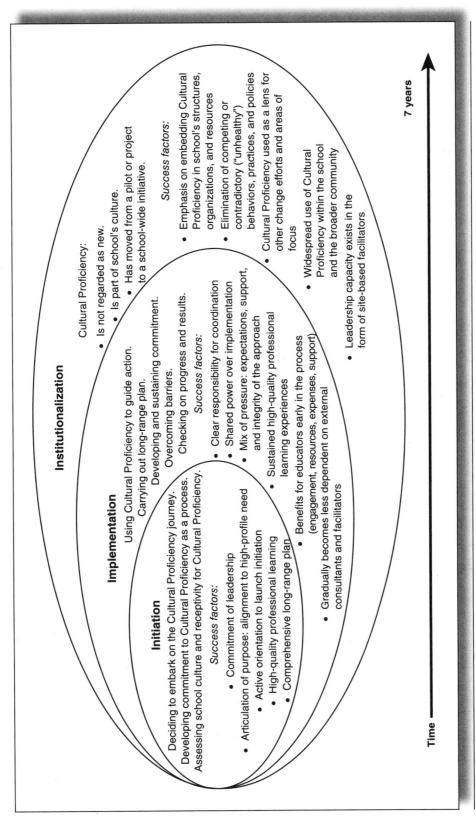

Initiation

Deciding to embark on the Cultural Proficiency journey.
Developing commitment to Cultural Proficiency as a process.
Assessing school culture and receptivity for Cultural Proficiency.

Success factors:

- Commitment of leadership
- Articulation of purpose: alignment to high-profile need
- Active orientation to launch initiation
- High-quality professional learning
- Comprehensive long-range plan

Implementation

Using Cultural Proficiency to guide action.
Carrying out long-range plan.
Developing and sustaining commitment.
Overcoming barriers.
Checking on progress and results.

Success factors:

- Clear responsibility for coordination
- Shared power over implementation
- Mix of pressure: expectations, support, and integrity of the approach
- Sustained high-quality professional learning experiences
- Benefits for educators early in the process (engagement, resources, expenses, support)
- Gradually becomes less dependent on external consultants and facilitators

Institutionalization

Cultural Proficiency:

- Is not regarded as new.
- Is part of school's culture.
- Has moved from a pilot or project to a school-wide initiative.

Success factors:

- Emphasis on embedding Cultural Proficiency in school's structures, organizations, and resources
- Elimination of competing or contradictory ("unhealthy") behaviors, practices, and policies
- Cultural Proficiency used as a lens for other change efforts and areas of focus
- Widespread use of Cultural Proficiency within the school and the broader community
- Leadership capacity exists in the form of site-based facilitators

Time   7 years

Source: Adapted from Miles, M. B., Ekholm, M., & Vanderberghe, R. (1987). *Lasting school improvement: Exploring the process of institutionalization* (ISIP Vol. 5). Leuven/Amersfoort: Acco.

Table 15.10 Eight Basic Lessons of the New Paradigm of Change

Lessons From Michael Fullan		Implications for Cultural Proficiency
Lesson 1	You can't mandate what matters. (The more complex the change, the less we can force it.)	
Lesson 2	Change is a journey, not a blueprint. (Change is nonlinear, loaded with uncertainty and excitement.)	
Lesson 3	Problems are our friends. (Problems are inevitable and we can't learn without them.)	
Lesson 4	Vision and strategic planning come later. (Premature visions and planning without understanding undermine the change process.)	
Lesson 5	Individualism and collectivism must have equal power. (There are no one-sided solutions to isolation and group-think.)	
Lesson 6	Neither centralization nor decentralization works. (Top-down and bottom-up strategies are both necessary.)	
Lesson 7	Connection with the wider environment is critical for success. (The best organizations learn externally as well as internally.)	
Lesson 8	Every person is a change agent. (Change is too important to leave to outside experts; educators must continuously work to develop mastery and personal mind-set.)	

Source: Adapted from Fullan (1993).

and institutionalizing Cultural Proficiency as its way of being. To do this involves both understanding the change process as well as possessing skill in how to use the predictable phases of the change process to their advantage through strategic long-range planning.

Matthew Miles (Miles, Ekholm, & Vanderberge, 1987) described the change process as a series of three overlapping phases: initiation, implementation, and institutionalization. Figure 15.3 (p. 283) illustrates this process applied to an organization embarking on its Cultural Proficiency journey and working toward institutionalization: sustained change for excellence with equity.

In his work on change management, Michael Fullan (2006) describes the implementation dip—a temporary decline in confidence and performance—as groups on the journey struggle through changes in beliefs and behaviors. This dip is predictable. Facilitators benefit from taking this predictability into account when helping organizations plan for institutionalization of Cultural Proficiency. The dip will likely happen when the group is progressing beyond awareness and into action. It is also likely to happen shortly after transitioning from initiation into early implementation.

During the dip the work feels hard. It takes sustained and deliberate effort to redress inequities and to transform practices and policies that support high expectations and inclusion. At times, this may feel like swimming upstream against the current, in organizations where the Barriers to Cultural Proficiency are deeply entrenched in tradition. People may experience negative motivators and feel confused, anxious, fearful, cautious, overwhelmed, or unskilled. This is the time to call on the experts. Drawing on insight gleaned from the discussion of the scale of motivations in previous chapters, organizations experiencing the implementation dip benefit—possibly more than at any other time in the change process—from the influence of facilitators and leaders with positive motivations/energy states such as mastery, generativity, and higher service. Additionally, groups may need new skills and technical knowledge in order to move through the Action Phase of the journey. Culturally proficient facilitators don't leave any of this to chance. They help organizations prepare for success through multiyear plans that take into account the phases of the change process, and they dedicate resources accordingly.

In summary, institutionalizing Cultural Proficiency requires an ability to deal with complexity. Traditional mind-sets with rational assumptions and mechanistic approaches regarding school improvement will not work with multidimensional and pervasive change processes (Hopkins, 2001) such as Cultural Proficiency. To help us plan for what will work, Michael Fullan (1993, p. 21–22) offers "eight basic lessons of the new paradigm of change" (table 15.10, p. 285). These lessons resonate with implications suggested throughout this book regarding effectively facilitating (making easier) sustainable Cultural Proficiency for organizations. Furthermore, what resonates with the general work of Cultural Proficiency is that these lessons be viewed systemically because of the paradoxical nature of viewing each lesson in isolation from the others.

Reflection

Consider Michael Fullan's eight change lessons relative to your insights gleaned about Cultural Proficiency from this chapter and the book as a whole. Write implications for your work with Cultural Proficiency in table 15.10. Use the space below to synthesize the implications and capture your significant insights about Cultural Proficiency that you do not want to forget.

From this chapter focused on Institutionalizing Cultural Knowledge within facilitation, what information is new to you, yet rings true? What information affirms your experiences? In what ways? What information do you question? Why?

_____

_____

_____

_____

What information within this chapter do you find most useful? How will you use it effectively to serve groups as a culturally proficient facilitator?

_____

_____

_____

_____

DIALOGIC ACTIVITY

1. Individually write and/or review the three reflections at the end of this chapter.

2. Use the helping trios protocol (table 15.11) to help participants share information, listen to different perspectives, and increase understanding of culturally proficient facilitation.

Table 15.11   Helping Trios Protocol

Step	Procedure
1.	Participants form triads. Letter off A–B–C.
2.	Person A selects, shares, and talks about their reflections without interruption. B and C listen. (For a designated time period such as four minutes)
3.	B and C ask clarifying questions and A responds (half of the time period in Step 2).
4.	A, B, and C dialogue about A's reflections (same time period as Step 2.)
5.	Repeat Steps 2 to 4 for B and then repeat again for C.
Tips:	Display the time parameters for Steps 2 to 4 on chart paper. Consider projecting a timer if there are numerous trios.

Source: Adapted from CampbellJones, CampbellJones, and Lindsey (2010), p. 47.

16 Your Professional Learning Plan for Culturally Proficient Facilitation

Knowing others is intelligence. Knowing yourself is true wisdom. Mastering others is strength. Mastering yourself is true power.

—Lao Tzu (Lao Tzu & Mitchell [tr.], 1988)

We need to forget what we think we are, so that we can really become what we are.

—Paulo Coelho (The Zahir, 2005)

The flight attendant demonstrates how to put on the oxygen mask. . . . We are instructed to put on our own mask before helping someone else. . . . This philosophy applies to all caring activities. If we don't do a good job of taking care of our own needs, we will have difficulty keeping up with the needs of others.

—Patricia A. Jennings (Mindfulness for Teachers, 2015)

Planning is the only way to keep yourself on track. Plan your moments to be joyous. Plan your days to be filled with peace. Plan your life to be an experience of growth. When you know where you are going, the universe will clear a path for you.

—Iyanla Vanzant (Acts of Faith, 1993)

GETTING CENTERED

Review these quotes that represent themes in this final chapter, within which you will craft a plan for the next steps in your growth as a culturally proficient facilitator. Within the quotations, what words or ideas resonate with you? Why? What are your initial thoughts regarding the next steps you can take to continue your growth?

_____

_____

_____

_____

EPISODE FIFTEEN: NEXT STEPS FOR JACK AND STOCKLIN COUNTY

Five years had passed since Lillie Cohen and the leadership of Stocklin County's school district had decided it was in the best interests of all their students to bring in Barbara Campbell and Frank Eastman as consultants to help the school system make Cultural Proficiency its way of being. Barbara and Frank's contract was about to end, but the work they had started remained strong, inspired, and sustainable.

From the beginning, Frank and Barbara had helped Lillie and the district leaders create a realistic and long-range plan to transform their entire school system into a model of a learning organization that truly valued high expectations, inclusion, and equity. These were the positive results that followed when a well-designed, well-implemented Cultural Proficiency initiative became the norm within an organization. The context and climate of Stocklin County Public School System had become one within which educators and students empowered themselves.

Over the course of five years, the district had identified variables that served as mediating factors for excellence with equity. It measured these factors (measures of success) on an ongoing basis to gauge the effects of Cultural Proficiency within the system. Sure enough, each of these measures of success had improved: student and teacher engagement, well-being, school environment, work environment, teacher–student relationships, teacher cultural competence, and professional capital. Curricula and school and classroom environments were now more inclusive and equitable in form.

Barbara and Frank began their relationship with Stocklin with the explicit expectation that they were working to ensure lasting change. They had worked with the district to invest in the development of people within the school system whom they believed would make solid in-house facilitators of Cultural Proficiency. They first invited Jack McManus, through Lillie Cohen, to start training under their mentorship, which included cofacilitating seminars with them for a basic period of two years. Along the way, three other persons were invited to be mentored: Fatima Akram, Julie Cho, and Tom Joy. When this facilitator development effort had successfully gotten under way, Jack had been invited to lead the newly created Professional Development for Excellence with Equity (PDEE) within the Department of Organizational Development. Fatima soon followed as a second full-time facilitator. As demand for their services had grown, Julie had joined the team in another board-approved facilitator position. Tom had continued to work as a culturally proficient professional development facilitator in his position as coordinator of the Department of Fine Arts, and he sometimes joined one of the PDEE team members to cofacilitate seminars.

At times, the learning curve had been steep for the new facilitators, but Barbara and Frank had been devoted and conscientious mentors, fully aware of the difficulties of switching from the presenting/teaching role to that of a facilitator. They had mentored, they had observed, and they had given feedback and praise.

After three years, the Stocklin in-house team of Cultural Proficiency facilitators was pretty much self-sufficient. More and more, Barbara and Frank were stepping into the background. Since Barbara lived nearby, she was the most active: giving consultation to district leaders and providing coaching services for the PDEE team as its members developed into efficacious facilitators. During the final year of the contract, the external consultants were mostly cheering from the sidelines.

At that point in time—with a week remaining on the external consultants' contract—Lillie Cohen called for an early Saturday morning meeting with Barbara, Frank, Jack, Fatima, Tom, and Julie in her office to put the final touches on a report and presentation to the Stocklin County Board of Education. Lillie would lead the presentation to the board, showcasing facts and figures from the past five years that showed increases in the mediating factors for excellence with equity and would demonstrate how the district's focus on Cultural Proficiency was improving schools for all students. Within the presentation, Lillie also planned to incorporate several students and teachers who had particularly relevant stories to tell about their experiences since Cultural Proficiency had been introduced into their schools.

The report was almost complete, except for the final part—the next steps for Cultural Proficiency in Stocklin. The presentation to the board was the following week (three days away), and the only time everyone was available was Saturday morning. This caused a dilemma for Jack. He could attend but he'd probably have to bring his two young children, Eileen and Fionnuala. His ex-wife would be away that weekend, and babysitters in his neighborhood were notoriously difficult to get on Saturdays, especially on such short notice.

He went to Lillie's office to share his situation with her in person. Lillie put her hand on his forearm. "Don't worry about it, Jack. Bring the girls. They're how old—eight and eleven now?—old enough to sit quietly. Even more important, I think they'd enjoy seeing what Daddy does at work." Jack breathed a sigh of relief.

That Saturday morning, Jack had Eileen and Fionnuala settled comfortably on folding chairs at the back of Lillie's office. Each girl was supplied with (quiet) snacks and an electronic tablet loaded with educational apps. "Can we ask questions?" asked wide-eyed Eileen, the older girl, who was taking great interest in her intramural government debating team.

"Yeah, Daddy, there might be some stuff we need to know, like what you really do at work," added Fionnuala.

Jack rubbed their heads and said, "Yes, you can both ask a question at the end, but only after I give you the signal. Until then, just listen to what's being said so that you can come up with a really good question. Okay?"

"Okay, Daddy," they said in unison. "You can count on us."

People were sitting around the large table and Lillie started the meeting. She asked each person to share two things: first, something that they'd had to let go to be present this morning and, second, a hope for the future of Cultural Proficiency in Stocklin. As each person shared, Jack realized that all of them hadn't been together in the same room since that very first five-day seminar, when he'd been a reluctant participant. He felt the warm comfort of family.

The group worked for an hour, nailing down concrete next steps for Stocklin. These steps included strengthening school-improvement efforts by applying the Cultural Proficiency Framework to the concept of student voice, which had become a district-wide initiative aimed at sharing power with students and fostering learner-centered schools and classroom. Also included was an investment in the district's Cultural Proficiency Network of school-based champions. Lillie planned to propose to the school board that a stipend be institutionalized at every school to support comprehensive culturally proficient leadership for professional learning at every school site. The investment would also involve the development of resources to support high-quality professional learning.

The group brainstormed a list of sample resources to share with the board. At the top of the list was the creation of a professional learning planning guide to support every educator (including facilitators) in planning the next steps in their personal Cultural Proficiency journey. The guide would include self-assessment, 360-degree feedback tools, inventories, templates, and guidance.

It had been a productive morning. The time had gone quickly. Jack glanced over at his girls, who were involved with their tablets. As the group came to a point of agreement that their work was done for the day, Lillie invited questions.

"Thank you, everyone. I'm sincerely honored to know and work with each of you. The past five years have been the highlight of my career, and I'm looking forward to all that is in store for Stocklin County's students moving forward. Before we leave today, what lingering questions do we have about our Cultural Proficiency presentation?"

Eileen's face looked up quickly from the screen of her tablet. She threw her hand in the air and said, "Ooh, ooh."

Jack looked over at Lillie and with slight embarrassment said, "Sorry."

"I think it's wonderful," said Lillie. She looked at Eileen and invited her question.

Eileen stood up and smiled. "What exactly is Cultural Proficiency anyway? I really don't understand what it means."

Jack felt a little surprised at her question. Over the years, he'd tried to explain his work to his children. Fionnuala was only four when he'd started facilitating Cultural Proficiency. During circle time at her preschool, she'd shared, "My Daddy leads circle time for other teachers." As they grew, he'd tried to increase the level of complexity and nuance when he explained his work to them. It was always a challenge. Still, he figured they'd gotten the gist of it, especially Eileen who was the older of the two.

The room was silent, and all of Jack's colleagues were smiling and looking at him. He thought he'd give it one more shot.

So he began: "Imagine a big boat. We all live on that boat. There's no 'them.' There's no 'those other people; we don't like them.' There's only 'us.' We might look different from each other, but we're all really the same because we're all in the same boat. Cultural Proficiency is a set of tools to help us live together happily on that boat and to become our better selves. These tools help us act in ways that are good for every single person. These tools help us run our schools so that everyone is treated fairly, has exactly what they need to learn, and has every opportunity to succeed. Cultural Proficiency helps us not do things that benefit some people but are unfair to other people in the boat. Does that make sense?"

Eileen smiled. "Well . . . Daddy, why in the world would we all live on a boat? I mean, everyone? That would have to be a really big boat. I mean really big. And you're talking about fitting schools in that boat, too?"

The room erupted with laughter. Eileen beamed. She was enjoying this.

Fionnuala waved her hand frantically. She jumped to her feet, knocking over her chair with a clatter.

"I know what you mean, Daddy. You're saying that Cultural Proficiency helps us treat each other the way each of us wants to be treated," she announced loudly.

"Yes, yes, that's it. That's good!" Jack answered.

"And that's not all," chimed in Eileen. "You're saying that Cultural Proficiency helps all of us students be a family at school, where no one gets hurt and everyone is happy and successful."

"You've got it! Both of you." said Jack, realizing his daughters were teaching him a valuable lesson in simplicity, which showed him his own next steps. He had to get better at explaining and doing this work in simpler and more accessible terms, cutting through the jargon, abstract language, and edu-speak.

"Yes!" Fionnuala cried out, pumping the air with her little fist. "That's so cool, Daddy! So, do you still do circle time with teachers?"

Jack's work family roared with laughter, alongside his children. Jack smiled and wondered if this was his best day ever.

YOUR PROFESSIONAL LEARNING PLAN

In this episode, Jack and company discussed next steps for Stocklin County. Jack also discovered some personal next steps. Now that your experience with this book is coming to a close, it's time for you to explore and plan your own next steps. What follows is material to guide you in developing a personal professional development plan for your own Cultural Proficiency journey.

STEP 1: NEEDS ANALYSIS

A. Self-Assessing

The first step in developing your professional learning plan is to analyze needs that emerge from data. The Culturally Proficient facilitator self-assessment (figure 16.1) is designed to assist you in generating data that can be used for such a purpose.

Figure 16.1 Culturally Proficient Facilitator Self-Assessment

This inventory provides a means for self-assessment. It examines the extent to which the Essential Elements of Cultural Proficiency align with your perceived facilitator capabilities. Mark each item with a number between 1 and 5. Marking the number one (1) would indicate that you believe your current capabilities are low for that item. Marking the number five (5) would indicate a belief of high capabilities for that item.

(Continued)

Figure 16.1 (Continued)

1	2	3	4	5

strongly disagree   strongly agree

I believe I display the ability to_____

_____1. Learn about a participant group's culture, the culture of its individuals, and the broader organizational culture in order to prepare for professional learning events.

_____2. Focus group attention and energy on developing knowledge of self within a diverse environment in order to shape a culture of excellence with equity.

_____3. Demonstrate worthiness, vulnerability, and authenticity with groups to help participants cocreate a brave space.

_____4. Customize and adapt agendas and activities based on the needs and culture of each participant group.

_____5. Use planning protocols aligned with standards of cultural competence to ensure I am prepared to lead professional learning events in a culturally proficient manner.

_____6. Learn about my response to cultures different from my own, my own cultural identity and its intersecting dimensions of difference, and how my culture affects trust and relationships with participants and groups.

_____7. Amplify participant voice for inclusion and equity within professional learning events.

_____8. Model processes of mindful inquiry, dialogue, conflict resolution, and creative problem solving with groups.

_____9. Effectively improvise and intervene on behalf of the group, and reveal my thinking about intervention principles, techniques, and mental models to the group.

_____10. Support schools or organizations with a comprehensive, multifaceted system of culturally proficient professional learning.

_____11. Use the Cultural Proficiency Framework with groups at a deep level.

_____12. Esteem diversity of participants and continuously foster inclusion.

_____13. Draw on change models to support group transformation.

_____14. Shift stances and facilitation styles to bolster the group's progression on its journey.

_____15. Align my work with standards for professional learning and research on professional development.

_____16. Demonstrate values and principles of effective group facilitation in my practice.

_____17. Employ materials, strategies, processes, and content that value differences.

_____18. Consider a group's stage in its journey when selecting activities and strategies.

_____19. Effectively intervene at the appropriate level of group activity.

_____20. Strategically plan in collaboration with a school or organization for ongoing professional development to support its commitment to inclusion and equity.

_____21. Recognize and gauge different types of energy states or motivations.

_____22. Learn how to be effective in support and advocacy for social justice issues.

_____23. Exercise principles of transformation within actions, processes, and protocols to bring about positive energy states for groups and individual participants.

_____24. Apply principles of transformation when intervening with moves and strategies in order to shift groups to higher energy states.

_____25. Develop long-range (three to seven years) plans for organizations to develop collective-efficacy and become self-sufficient with Cultural Proficiency.

B. Scoring Your Self-Assessment

For each item, write your number (1–5) in the appropriate cell (figure 16.2). Add the cells in each column and write the total at the bottom.

Figure 16.2 Scoring Tool—Culturally Proficient Facilitator Self-Assessment

Assessing Cultural Knowledge	Valuing Diversity	Managing the Dynamics of Difference	Adapting to Diversity	Institutionalizing Cultural Knowledge
_____ 1.	_____ 2.	_____ 3.	_____ 4.	_____ 5.
_____ 6.	_____ 7.	_____ 8.	_____ 9.	_____ 10.
_____ 11.	_____ 12.	_____ 13.	_____ 14.	_____ 15.
_____ 16.	_____ 17.	_____ 18.	_____ 19.	_____ 20.
_____ 21.	_____ 22.	_____ 23.	_____ 24.	_____ 25.
_____ TOTAL	_____ TOTAL	_____ TOTAL	_____ TOTAL	_____ TOTAL

C. Interpreting Your Scores

For each Essential Element, your score can range from 5 to 25. Each score represents the extent to which you believe you are currently able to meet that standard (i.e., the Essential Element) as a culturally proficient facilitator. A score between 20 to 25 indicates perceived consistency between your professional practice and the standard. A score between 5 to 10 indicates perceived inconsistency between your professional practice and the standard (table 16.1). The lower the score, the greater the opportunity for growth into culturally proficient facilitator practices.

D. Collecting Additional Data

The results of your self-assessment may suffice as a needs assessment that helps you move forward with developing your professional learning plan. However, you might desire additional data. If so, consider using the Culturally Proficient facilitator self-assessment as a multisource assessment to provide you with 360-degree feedback about your facilitator practice and effectiveness.

Table 16.1 Standards for Culturally Proficient Facilitation

Total Score	Items	Essential Element	As a facilitator, I believe I am able to_____
	1.___6.___11.___16. ___21.___	Assessing Cultural Knowledge	Lead and model learning about culture and what is necessary to facilitate Cultural Proficiency for groups.
	2.___7.___12.___17. ___22.___	Valuing Diversity	Embrace differences and focus on what is needed to shape a culture of excellence with equity.
	3.___8.___13.___18. ___23.___	Managing the Dynamics of Difference	Engender trust, foster brave space, and increase a group's collective efficacy for inquiry, dialogue, conflict resolution, creative problem solving, and progressing toward excellence with equity.
	4.___9.___14.___19. ___24.___	Adapting to Diversity	Customize professional learning events/experiences and intervene to help groups move forward in their journeys.
	5.___10.___15.___20. ___25.___	Institutionalizing Cultural Knowledge	Incorporate practices and protocols that ensure culturally proficient professional learning and help organizations develop sustainability.

A 360-degree feedback process includes supplementing your self-assessment data with information solicited through the inventory (figure 16.1) from people in a variety of roles: participants, peers (colleagues), direct reports, and supervisors. 360-degree feedback is valuable for developmental purposes such as professional learning. It can leverage diversity by providing data from a variety of perspectives. If you plan to solicit 360-degree feedback through this inventory or any other means, consider these common tips:

1. Solicit feedback on relevant behaviors that providers were positioned to assess.

2. Advise feedback providers that their honest feedback will help you improve.

3. Use a representative sample (various perspectives) of quality providers.

4. Consider requesting additional qualitative feedback through open questions that solicit written comments.

5. Consider working with a coach to assist you with processing the feedback.

6. Use results to develop your professional learning plan.

E. Reflection

Review your score for each Essential Element. What do you notice? If discrepancies exist, what potential causes might have contributed to them? What conclusions are you drawing about the way you perceive yourself as a culturally proficient facilitator? On which Essential Element will you focus the next step in your own professional learning? Why?

_____

_____

_____

_____

STEP 2: DEVELOP YOUR PLAN

Once you have assessed your abilities, analyzed your needs, and identified an Essential Element on which to focus, you are ready to develop the rest of your professional learning plan. Figure 16.3 offers a template for crafting one. As you construct your plan and record its details, consult the chapter within this book that illustrates your identified Essential Element. Its concepts, details, references, and citations will inform your thinking.

Figure 16.3 My Facilitator Professional Learning Plan

Plan Elements	Details of My Plan
Needs Assessment Based on my analysis, my next step in developing as a culturally proficient facilitator will be focused on this Essential Element.	
My Goal The broad outcome of my professional learning. How my learning will affect my future participants and groups. (Use SMART language—Specific, Measurable, Attainable, Results-based, and Time-bound.) **Indicators of Success** How I will know I have taken action, demonstrated progress, and achieved my goal.	
Objectives Specific changes that need to occur to meet my goal. How my knowledge, attitudes, skills, aspirations, and behaviors (KASAB) will change to benefit participants and groups. **Measures of Success** How I will collect data or evidence to demonstrate indicators of success for my goal.	

(Continued)

Figure 16.3 (Continued)

Strategic Actions What I will do to accomplish the changes necessary to achieve my goal. **Evaluation Plan** My plan for measuring the success of my professional learning. (Use indicators of success and measures of success to guide data collection to determine if the goals and objectives were achieved, if strategic actions were appropriate, and what improvements can be made in subsequent professional learning plans.)	
Timeline When I will complete my actions and achieve my objectives and goals. **Resources (Inputs) Needed** Staff, technology, funding, materials, and time I need to accomplish my objectives and goals.	

Source: Adapted from Learning Forward (2013, December). "Develop a Professional Learning Plan." *Journal of Staff Development. 34*(6), 52–59.

Reflection

The development of a professional learning plan helps you start the next leg of your journey. How are you reacting to what lies ahead of you? The space below invites you to record your thoughts, reactions, and feelings.

_____

_____

_____

_____

FINAL THOUGHTS: WE NEED US

By engaging with this book to its very end and crafting a plan to support your own development as a culturally proficient facilitator, you are choosing a trajectory of becoming your better self in order to make it easier for our colleagues and our schools become their better selves in service of all our students. This is exactly what our society needs if we are to heal the lingering wounds of colonialism, oppression, racism, and cultural destructiveness, and so to choose to become the best we can be. We need you and ten thousand more like you. We need us, and we have no time to waste. The future of democracy is depending on us. Indeed, we are the ones we've been waiting for.

While our student population continues to become increasingly diverse, our schools are becoming increasingly separate and unequal. In 2016, the U.S. Government Accountability Office (GOA) released a report that highlighted data proving the nation's schools had become significantly more racially and socioeconomically segregated and isolated over the fifteen years prior to the report. This is unacceptable when measured against principles of democracy. As U.S. representative John Conyers (2016) said in response to the report, "There simply can be no excuse for allowing educational apartheid in the 21st century."

There is some good news, though. For our African American and Hispanic students, graduation rates are the highest and dropout rates are the lowest ever (U.S. Government Accountability Office, 2016). Still, that's not enough. Secretary of Education John King captured this sentiment in a U.S. Department of Education (2016) press release on the sixty-second anniversary of *Brown v. Board of Education:* "Six decades after Brown v. Board, we have failed to close opportunity and achievement gaps for our African-American and Latino students at every level of education. And in far too many schools, we continue to offer them less—less access to the best teachers and the most challenging courses; less access to the services and supports that affluent students often take for granted; and less access to what it takes to succeed academically."

As we look back at over two decades of heavy-handed accountability, top-down mandates, and narrow measures of success provided almost entirely from standardized tests, we must also recognize that the resultant Neo-Plessyism and so-called twenty-first-century educational apartheid is hurting all of our students, including white students of economic means. In addition to exacerbating gaps in expectations, opportunities, and access, demographically isolated (e.g., racially and socioeconomically isolated) schools and classrooms prevent every student from accessing the learning outcomes resulting from inclusion and diversity. These are the same outcomes needed to support the health and vitality of an inclusive democracy (Bowman, 2010; Crisp & Turner, 2011; Engberg, 2007; Gurin et al., 2002; Haas, 1999; Ruggs & Hebl, 2012). If we continue this trajectory, we will continue to make ourselves and our society sick and weak, headed toward our own social and spiritual demise.

The good news is that we don't have to continue this trajectory. We can choose a different course—the course that you have chosen and continue to choose. This book holds potential for transforming us and transforming schools. Without us, though, the book is worthless. But with the knowledge contained in this book and others that responsibly support our intentionality in addressing equity and inclusion, we can choose to change ourselves and change our schools. We can transform our schools from unhealthy spaces filled with negative energy such as the fear of failure, the craving for grades and test scores, and the guilt and anger that accompanies vestiges of systemic oppression and privilege. Like caterpillars, we can initiate this process by entering the darkness of our chrysalis and sitting with this work for as long as it takes. When it's time to emerge, we'll spread our wings and soar in a new and different form: a healthy butterfly, vital, beautiful, and fueled by the positive energy of cooperation, exploration, and creativity.

To make that type of change, we need an inside-out process—a transformative journey. Fortunately, such a journey exists. It's Cultural Proficiency, and this book contributes to the work by providing us a map for it. Coupled with the tools within the framework, we have the essentials for making the journey easier.

For perhaps it's not the goal of excellence with equity that has been elusive for so many schools and districts. Perhaps what has been so hard to find is an effective means of reaching that goal. And perhaps you are finding it within yourself—with the help of this book—as you continue to work on becoming your better self.

Appendix

The following tables contain information about the facilitative activities, protocols, strategies, and moves referenced in the chapters of this book. By no means does this annotated collection represent the repertoire of a culturally proficient facilitator. Instead, it provides a foundation on which facilitators can build and develop their craft in a manner that is authentic to them. It also supports leading culturally proficient professional learning for the groups facilitators serve.

ACTIVITIES

Activity Name	Ch. and Page	Source for More Information	Notes
My Journey	3, p. 40	CampbellJones & Associates (2004), Workshop materials, www.campbelljones.org	Orientation stage. Activating and Engaging activity. Participants reflect on and share their own assumptions about the professional learning event. Encourages vulnerability and authentic engagement.
Like Me	12, p. 206	Robert Garmston & Bruce Wellman (2009), *The Adaptive School,* p. 241	Orientation stage. Inclusion activity. Participants identify with personal and professional categories (e.g., "Please stand if . . . you are a classroom teacher/you drove over 10 miles to get here.") Helps quickly develop a sense of belonging and focus mental energy on the learning space.
Introductory Grid	12, p. 206	Randall B. Lindsey, Kikanza Nuri-Robins, & Raymond D. Terrell (2009), *Cultural Proficiency: A Manual for School Leaders,* p. 212	Preparation stage. Activating and Engaging activity. Participants record and share personal information according to categories (e.g., city of birth, favorite food, family value.) Helps develop relationships, build trust, and identify similarities and differences within the group.
Exploring Behaviors Along the Continuum	12, p. 206	Randall B. Lindsey, Kikanza Nuri-Robins, & Raymond D. Terrell (2009), *Cultural Proficiency: A Manual for School Leaders,* p. 281	Exploration stage. Exploring and Discovering activity. Participants generate and record examples of behaviors for each of the six points on the Cultural Proficiency Continuum. Helps build collective-efficacy with use of the tools and reinforce the relationship of behaviors that range from unhealthy to healthy.

(Continued)

(Continued)

Activity Name	Ch. and Page	Source for More Information	Notes
My Culture	13, p. 236 14, p. 244	Randall B. Lindsey (1996), *My Culture: USAF Youth At Risk Training Program*	Exploration stage. Activating and Engaging activity. Participants reflect on and share how they experience aspects of their own cultures and how they believe others perceive and hold expectations related to those same aspects (e.g., name, cultural identity, values learned from family.) Helps reinforce the importance of recognizing that culture is a predominant force in everyone's life, surfacing and challenging assumptions, and developing authentic relationships.
The Diversity Lifeline	13, p. 220	Randall B. Lindsey, Kikanza Nuri-Robins, & Raymond D. Terrell (2009), *Cultural Proficiency: A Manual for School Leaders,* p. 184	Exploration stage. Activating and Engaging activity. Participants analyze and share significant life events that have influenced their perceptions of diversity. Helps support understanding of the guiding principles in that diversity is a dynamic that has been, is, and will always be present in their lives.
Your Professional Learning Plan	16, p. 291		Course Correction stage. Organizing and Integrating activity. Participants use the essential elements to determine their next steps (movement) in their own professional learning and development as a culturally proficient facilitator.

PROTOCOLS

Protocol	Ch. and Page	Source	Notes
First Turn/Last Turn	1, p. 44	Robert Garmston & Bruce Wellman (2009), *The Adaptive School,* p. 212	Highly structured protocol for organizing dialogue. Most effective for groups with low-to-moderate collective-efficacy for dialogue. Participants take turns listening and responding to content and each other. One participant shares and each of the other participants has an opportunity to comment on what was shared before sharing in response to content. After all participants have had a turn, the group begins a dialogue about ideas presented.
Round-Robin Responding	2, p. 37	Laura Lipton & Bruce Wellman (2011a), *Groups at Work: Strategies and Structures for Professional Learning,* p. 89	Highly structured protocol that establishes a sequence for sharing in order to include all perspectives. Most effective for groups with low collective-efficacy for dialogue. A participant starts the sharing process, and the remaining members of the group share their responses one at a time (e.g., clockwise around a circle). Emphasizes listening.
Helping Trios	11, p. 202 12, p. 218 13, p. 241 14, p. 261 15, p. 286	Franklin CampbellJones, Brenda CampbellJones, & Randall B. Lindsey (2010), *The Cultural Proficiency Journey: Moving Beyond Ethical Barriers toward Profound School Change,* p. 47	Highly structured protocol that scaffolds feedback from multiple perspectives in order to provide ample opportunity for reflection and increased understanding. Most effective for groups with low to moderate collective-efficacy for dialogue. In trios, participants each identify as the letter A, B, or C. In subsequent rounds, each participant takes a turn sharing information while the other two participants pose clarifying questions and dialogue about the ideas shared by the first participant.

Protocol	Ch. and Page	Source	Notes
Three Step Interview	4, p. 72	Laura Lipton & Bruce Wellman (2011a), *Groups at Work: Strategies and Structures for Professional Learning*, p. 52	Structured protocol for organizing an exchange of information on any topic. Most effective for groups with low to moderate collective-efficacy for dialogue. Establishes a foundation of shared information and offers an exchange of information that illuminates thinking. Participants initially engage in a paired exchange and later join another pair for sharing and discussion.
Data-Influenced Dialogue	5, p. 75	Nancy Love (2002), *Using Data/Getting Results*	Structured protocol for developing shared meaning of data. Effective for groups with any degree of collective-efficacy for dialogue. Establishes equal voices of participants and assists them in suspending judgment in order to build awareness and understanding of each other's viewpoints, beliefs, and assumptions about data.
World Café	5, p. 88	Juanita Brown & David Issacs (1995), www.theworldcafe.com	Structured protocol for promoting a large group dialogue and exchange of ideas among a number of people. Most effective for groups with a moderate to high collective-efficacy for dialogue. Maximizes the exchange of ideas through different relationships in the learning space, providing participants ample opportunity to develop understanding. Participants move through several twenty-minute rounds of discussion, each round with different people and/or at a different table. The protocol ends with the entire group harvesting insights gleaned through the process.
Save the Last Word for Me	6, p. 102	Patricia Averette, adapted by National School Reform Faculty, http://www.nsrfharmony.org	Highly structured protocol for building on one another's thinking. Most effective for groups with low to moderate collective-efficacy for dialogue. Participants assume roles (e.g., timekeeper, facilitator). Each participant has an opportunity to share and listen to other participants' reactions to what they share before having the last word. Participants may open a dialogue after all turns.
Four Levels of Text	7, p. 120	Adapted from Southern Maine Partnership & Camilla Greene's *Rule of 3 Protocol* (2003), www.schoolreforminitiative.org	Highly structured protocol to explore perspectives, deepen understanding in response to text, and discover implications for practice. Most effective for groups with low to moderate collective-efficacy for dialogue. In small groups, each participant shares (1) a meaningful passage of text, (2) emotional response, (3) interpretation, and (4) implications for practice. After a participant shares, the rest of the group has an opportunity to respond to what was shared.
Idea-to-Example Mixer	8, p. 127	John Krownapple (2016), based on Frank Lyman's *ThinkTrix* (1987)	Structured protocol for generating examples and tapping into the experiences within the group. Most effective for groups with moderate collective-efficacy for dialogue. Small groups rotate from station to station, building on the existing list by generating additional examples for the idea/topic at each station. The lists of generated examples serve as foundation for discussion after entire rotation.
Say Something	8, p. 130	Jerome Harste, Kathy Short, & Carolyn Burke (1988), *Creating Classrooms for Authors*	Structured protocol for paired discussion in response to a text. Effective for groups with low to moderate collective-efficacy for dialogue. Participants pair up and individually read to a designated stopping point. When each reaches that

(Continued)

(Continued)

Protocol	Ch. and Page	Source	Notes
			point, they stop and each "says something" (e.g., summary, new idea, question, point of dissonance). Facilitators can tighten or loosen the degree of structure through the amount of provided time and the suggested categories.
Affinity Mapping	8, p. 133	Ross Peterson-Veatch (2006), National School Reform Faculty, http://www.nsrfharmony.org/system/files/protocols/affinity_mapping_0.pdf	Highly structured protocol for deepening a conversation about a specific topic. Effective for groups with any degree of collective-efficacy for dialogue. Process begins with individuals generating examples or defining elements of a topic or question, one idea per sticky note. Participants proceed in silence, first sharing all examples and then organizing them in natural categories. Participants then discuss names for each category. Groups share out and open a discussion.
Jigsaw	8, p. 136	Aronson, Blaney, Sikes, Stephan, & Snapp (1975), www.jigsaw.org/#history	Highly structured protocol for sharing and discussing a large amount of text or ideas in small groups. Most effective for groups with moderate collective-efficacy for dialogue. In small (home) groups, each participant assumes responsibility for a portion of text. Individuals read their portions and then meet with a temporary expert group of people from other small groups who read the same portion. Individuals return to home groups and report out. Small groups open up a discussion about the text or topic as a whole.
Four "A's" Text	8, p. 141	Judith Gray (2005), National School Reform Faculty, http://www.nsrfharmony.org/system/files/protocols/4_a_text_0.pdf	Structured protocol for deep exploration of content (e.g., text, video, speaker). Most effective for groups with moderate to high collective-efficacy for dialogue. While experiencing content, individuals identify assumptions, agreements, arguments, and aspirations. In small groups, individuals share one of these at a time as a foundation for discussion.
Focused Review	9, p. 160	Adapted from *Focused Reading* strategy, as presented by Robert Garmston & Bruce Wellman (2009), *The Adaptive School*, p. 215	Structured protocol for deep exploration of a text. Most effective for groups with moderate to high collective-efficacy for dialogue. After reading, small groups decide which portion of the text they would like to discuss in depth. Individuals return to the text and mark it with specific codes. Participants then take turns sharing a marked item, establishing a foundation for discussion.
Adjectives and Verbs	10, p. 182	Diana Stephens & Randall B. Lindsey (2011), *Culturally Proficient Collaboration: The Use and Misuse of School Counselors*	Structured protocol for developing understanding of a rubric and exploring perspectives in response to the rubric. Effective for groups with any degree of collective-efficacy for dialogue. Participants individually read a rubric and highlight verbs and adjectives. In small groups, they share insights and personal experiences connected to illustrative language in the rubric.
ORID	10, p. 172 13, pp. 230 & 239	R. Brian Stanfield (2000), *The Art of Focused Conversation*	Protocol for structuring focused conversation. Most effective for groups with high collective-efficacy for dialogue. Participants facilitate their own small-group discussion, progressing through levels of questioning (ORID: O = objective, R = reflective, I = interpretive, D = decisional) to bring their conversation into greater focus and ultimately to a point of decision, commitment, and/or action.

Protocol	Ch. and Page	Source	Notes
Think-Pair-Square-Share	11, p. 193 12, p. 214 13, p. 232 14, p. 252 15, p. 276	Adapted from Frank Lyman (1981), *The Responsive Classroom Discussion: The Inclusion of All Students*	Structured protocol for maximizing engagement, sharing information, listening to different perspectives, and developing shared understanding. Effective for groups with any degree of collective-efficacy for dialogue. Participant action follows the steps delineated in the title of the protocol: reflection, discussion with a partner, discussion in quads, and whole group sharing and discussion.
Culturally Proficient Event Design	15, p. 273	Adapted from *Event Design,* created by Suzanne Bailey of Bailey & Associates, Vacaville, California (in Garmston & Wellman, [2005])	Highly structured protocol for planning a professional learning event in a culturally competent manner. Most effective for facilitators with low to moderate collective-efficacy for planning for and facilitating Cultural Proficiency. Facilitators plan and prepare in a series of steps that align with the Essential Elements of Cultural Proficiency, beginning with Assessing Culture.

STRATEGIES

Strategy	Ch. and Page	Source	Notes
Synectics	6, p. 97	George Prince (1968), *The Operational Mechanism of Synectics*	Use metaphorical thinking to focus energy, include all voices, and promote conversation about a topic or concept. Most effective at the beginning or end of an activity, session, or event. Can support Activating and Engaging or Organizing and Integrating. Participants connect the topic at hand to a different and apparently irrelevant element (e.g., Cultural Proficiency is like an apple because ____.)
Gallery Walk	12, p. 207	Barbara Fasse & Janet Kolodner (2000), *Evaluating Classroom Practices Using Qualitative Research Methods*	Use physical movement to promote active engagement. Most effective when group energy is low and/or a group can benefit from movement or a physical change in perspective. Participants walk around the room to stations. They can work in pairs or small groups to share ideas and respond to content or questions.
Fostering Mutual Understanding	12, p. 209	Sam Kaner (2014), *Facilitator's Guide to Participatory Decision-Making,* p. 283	Use strategic questioning and listening skills to promote shared understanding within a group and normalize inquiry. Most effective for a group when there is divergent knowledge, experience, or perspectives within a group and the group has the opportunity to develop a shared understanding and learn to welcome questioning. After receiving a response to an inquiry, a participant states what they believe the speaker said and then states what they still find to be unclear.
Fishbowl	13, p. 222	Julius Eitington (1996), *The Winning Trainer: Winning Ways to Involve People in Learning,* pp. 67–70	Focus a group on learning how to work more productively together. Most effective for a group that can increase its collective-efficacy by observing a model of a process or practice. A small group of participants volunteers to model a process or practice (inner circle). The rest of the group forms a circle around the small group (outer circle). The outer circle watches the small group (in the fishbowl).

(Continued)

(Continued)

Strategy	Ch. and Page	Source	Notes
Actualizing Brave Space	13, p. 233	Brian Arao & Kristi Clemens (2013), *From Safe Spaces to Brave Spaces: A New Way to Frame Dialogue*	Shape an environment that encourages the unavoidable risk, struggle, and discomfort that accompanies authentic engagement with Cultural Proficiency. Use the term *brave space* with groups and have them discuss the intention behind use of the term as an alternative to *safe space*. Support participants in developing and agreeing on norms of operation or working agreements.
Mindful Inquiry	13, p. 238	Lee Mun Wah (2004), *The Art of Mindful Facilitation,* pp. 7–16	Use mindfulness skills and strategic questions to help individuals and groups process reactions. Most effective when individuals within a group are sharing personal and sensitive stories. After an individual or group reacts, the facilitator poses questions that move through these levels of inquiry: Observational, reflective (past/present), and action.
ORID	10, p. 172 13, pp. 230 & 239 14, p. 248	R. Brian Stanfield (2000), *The Art of Focused Conversation*	Use strategic questions based on four levels of inquiry to guide a group through action/decisions without jumping to conclusions before exploring perspectives. Most effective when facilitating a debriefing of an activity or when participants have an emotional response to an experience.
Mirroring	14, pp. 248 & 256	Sam Kaner (2014), *Facilitator's Guide to Participatory Decision-Making,* p. 46	Use a speaker's exact words to build trust or establish/reinforce neutrality. Most effective when a participant is having an emotional reaction to an experience or when a facilitator feels the need to ensure neutrality. Repeat (or have other participants repeat) a participant's words verbatim. This is an alternative to paraphrasing, which can be experienced as a veiled criticism or interpretation.
Journaling	14, p. 249	Robert Garmston & Bruce Wellman (2009), *The Adaptive School,* p. 236	Use quiet time for independent writing to stimulate thinking prior to processing information and discovering meaning. Most effective in enabling participants to work through their own thinking or to level the playing field when a variety of roles or styles are present. Give a reason for a prompt, provide prompt and clarify, set a time limit, and provide an environment conducive to quiet reflection and writing.
Paraphrasing	14, p. 256	Sam Kaner (2014), *Facilitator's Guide to Participatory Decision-Making,* p. 44	Use active listening to demonstrate that a participant's thoughts were heard and to check for understanding. Most effective when a participant speaker's statements are confusing, verbose, or convoluted. Summarize or otherwise interpret the speaker's statement(s) in a nonjudgmental manner and check for accuracy.
Critical Inquiry	14, pp. 246 & 258	Franklin CampbellJones, Brenda CampbellJones, & Randall B. Lindsey (2010), *The Cultural Proficiency Journey: Moving Beyond Ethical Barriers toward Profound School Change,* p. 40	Use strategic questions based on the levels of Chris Argyris's Ladder of Inference to help a participant or group explore their own belief systems and uncover deeply held values and assumptions. Most effective when a group is operating on the analytical level of thought. After a speaker shares a statement, identify what Ladder of Inference rung was expressed (e.g., "You said that you believe hard work pays off"). Then pose a question to help the participant move up or down the ladder (e.g., "What taught you that?").

Strategy	Ch. and Page	Source	Notes
Sense of Vocation	14, p. 259	Danah Zohar & Ian Marshall (2004), *Spiritual Capital*, pp. 105–106	Give back to the group through servant leadership in order to influence groups with very negative energy states. Demonstrate gratitude and reflection. To participants, pass on knowledge and skills that were passed on to you.
Celebrate Diversity	14, p. 259	Danah Zohar & Ian Marshall (2004), *Spiritual Capital*, pp. 94–96	Value other people in the room as well as unfamiliar situations for their differences (not in spite of them) in order to influence groups with very negative energy states. Demonstrate awareness of and security in your own cultural identity. Engage in genuine dialogue, show curiosity about others, attempt to take on another's perspective, and interact outside of your own culture.
Positive Use of Adversity	14, p. 259	Danah Zohar & Ian Marshall (2004), *Spiritual Capital*, pp. 102–103	Demonstrate learning from mistakes and seeing problems as opportunities in order to positively influence groups with negative energy states. Develop resilience by cultivating a deep sense of self.
Vision and Value Led	14, p. 259	Danah Zohar & Ian Marshall (2004), *Spiritual Capital*, pp. 87–89	Act from socially just principles, beliefs, and values in order to positively influence groups with negative energy states. Articulate your highest aspirations, generate possibilities, and examine gaps between values/goals and actions.
Holism	14, p. 259	Danah Zohar & Ian Marshall (2004), *Spiritual Capital*, pp. 89–91	See and articulate connectedness between and among people and ideas to positively influence groups with slightly negative energy states. Demonstrate ability to see unifying themes to emerge from group discussions, a wider context, and lines of causality that trace back from or forward to an event/situation.
Humility	14, pp. 244 & 259	Danah Zohar & Ian Marshall (2004), *Spiritual Capital*, pp. 104–105	Have an accurate view of oneself as part of the whole (not above the group, prideful, arrogant, or domineering) in order to positively influence groups with slightly negative energy states. Demonstrate openness to suggestions and eliminate the need for ego strokes.
Spontaneity	14, p. 259	Danah Zohar & Ian Marshall (2004), *Spiritual Capital*, pp. 85–87	Be responsive and live in the here and now in order to positively influence groups, including those with relatively positive energy states. Display awareness of the current situation and of possibilities. Adapt on the fly with options better suited for the group.
Self-awareness	14, pp. 244 & 260	Danah Zohar & Ian Marshall (2004), *Spiritual Capital*, pp. 83–84	Demonstrate that you understand yourself in order to positively influence groups, including those with relatively positive energy states. Display comfort in silence and confidence in stepping out of your comfort zone to examine your own beliefs, assumptions, and values.
Field Independence	14, p. 260	Danah Zohar & Ian Marshall (2004), *Spiritual Capital*, pp. 96–97	Stand against the crowd and maintain your convictions in order to positively influence groups, including those with positive energy states. Demonstrate reflection about deep values and what it takes to live them. Check yourself for integrity.

(Continued)

(Continued)

Strategy	Ch. and Page	Source	Notes
Reframe	14, p. 260	Danah Zohar & Ian Marshall (2004), *Spiritual Capital*, pp. 100–102	Stand back and examine the wider context and bigger order to positively influence groups, including those with positive energy states. Surface and test assumptions against other points of view, contextualize problems or issues with mental models and frameworks, or brainstorm possibilities with the group.
Ask "Why?"	14, pp. 246 & 260	Danah Zohar & Ian Marshall (2004), *Spiritual Capital*, pp. 98–100	Work to understand participants in order to positively influence groups, including those with very positive energy states. Encourage questioning, remain open to challenge, look for deeper truths or possibilities beneath responses, and help the group pay attention to anomalies and uncomfortable situations.
Compassion	14, p. 260	Danah Zohar & Ian Marshall (2004), *Spiritual Capital*, pp. 92–94	Empathize deeply in order to positively influence groups, including those with very positive energy states. Display honesty about your own shortcomings and awareness of the consequences of actions and feelings.

MOVES

Strategy	Ch. and Page	Source	Notes
Airplane Stacking	12, p. 209	Robert Garmston & Bruce Wellman (2009), *The Adaptive School*, p. 185	Use the metaphor of the facilitator as an airport control tower directing the landing order of airplanes in order to help people take turns when several people want to talk at once. When multiple hands are raised, assign numbers. Allow participants to share in order without facilitator commentary. Record any questions for later.
Ask Permission	13, p. 222	Robert Garmston & Bruce Wellman (2009), *The Adaptive School*, p. 100	Reinforce the role of facilitator by asking for and receiving permission from individuals and the group before helping the group explore something in greater depth than expected. Remember that groups allow themselves to be facilitated and that they will resist, subvert, or sabotage a facilitator's efforts if have not given the facilitator permission to lead.
Describe What, Why, and How	13, p. 236	Laura Lipton & Bruce Wellman (2011b), *Leading Groups: Effective Strategies for Building Professional Community*, p. 45	Display transparency about the thinking behind event design choices. When introducing an activity or protocol, begin by stating its name (the what) and then explain its intended outcome and its benefit to the group (the why) in the context of the group's overall purpose. Finally, explain the directions, steps, and procedures involved. It helps to have the steps displayed for participant reference. Most effective when stated using a credible voice.
Foreshadow	14, pp. 244 & 250	Robert Garmston & Bruce Wellman (2009), *The Adaptive School*, p. 218	Help groups use anticipation as an advance organizer by naming a topic or activity that will occur later in the event—after a break, for example. Facilitators can build additional suspense by withholding information such as topic but suggesting the impact on the group (e.g., "After the break, be prepared to have your mind blown. We will hear an inspirational story from a student.")

Strategy	Ch. and Page	Source	Notes
Diverge Attention	14, pp. 245 & 248	Based on Lee Mun Wah's mindful facilitation techniques, www.stirfryseminars.com	Foster inclusion, engagement, and emotional support for an individual by directing attention from an individual to the whole group (e.g., "Tameka just shared a personal and painful recollection of being excluded. How many of us have experienced similar pain?") or from an idea to divergent ideas. Be sure to return to original participant to check in.
Converge Attention	14, p. 248	Based on Lee Mun Wah's mindful facilitation techniques, www.stirfryseminars.com	Help the group learn how to engage in inquiry and dialogue by focusing attention on a participant or idea. Get individual's and group's permission while stating the benefits of converging attention (e.g., "David, if it's also okay with the group, can we keep our focus here with you and process your comments for the next few minutes? This is a great opportunity for the group to learn how to explore belief systems through dialogue and inquiry").
Signal	14, pp. 246 & 249	Prabu Naidu & Janice Lua (2011), *SPOT on Facilitation,*	Use nonverbal gestures to communicate with a cofacilitator without distracting the group. Using agreed-on coded signals allows for cofacilitators to communicate with their own language when working with a group (e.g., pinching an earlobe signals the cofacilitator to talk louder.)
Mirror	14, pp. 248 & 256	Sam Kaner (2014), *Facilitator's Guide to Participatory Decision-Making,* p. 46	Relate to individuals or groups on their levels of operation, or help a group see itself so it can make informed decisions by reflecting words, body language, actions, energy, emotions, and/or activity back to an individual or groups. For instance, replicate a speaker's intonation and body language when mirroring words, or tell a group how you see them from your perspective (e.g., "I heard several gasps and see several wide-eyed looks").
Role Change or Stance Clarification	14, p. 248	Laura Lipton & Bruce Wellman (2011b), *Leading Groups: Effective Strategies for Building Professional Community,* p. 48	Clarify expectations of the facilitator's role by explaining role and services (e.g., "Among my responsibilities as a facilitator is intervening when group actions are interfering with its progression through the stages in this process"). If the group's progress necessitates a change in stance from facilitator to presenter or collaborator, explain the temporary change in stance by explaining the role and services (e.g., "For now, I'll be wearing a presenter's hat which means____").
Anchor Space	14, p. 249	Laura Lipton & Bruce Wellman (2011b), *Leading Groups: Effective Strategies for Building Professional Community,* p. 46	Use location to hold memory by dedicating different spaces in the room for different purposes. For instance, consistently use the same spot in the room for giving directions and a different spot for eliciting comments and facilitating discussions. Reserve yet another spot in the room for taking on the temporary stance of presenter of information. If bad news is delivered from an area of that room, avoid using that space.
Use Credible Voice	14, p. 249	Michael Grinder (1993), *ENVOY: Your Personal Guide to Classroom Management*	Communicate with clarity and promote trust by choosing to use a credible voice when focusing attention, explaining directions, or presenting information. Using a credible voice involves speaking with a narrow range of modulation and flat tones that drop at the end of a statement. Move your head very little while speaking and drop your chin at the end of statements.

(Continued)

(Continued)

Strategy	Ch. and Page	Source	Notes
Use Approachable Voice	14, p. 249	Michael Grinder (1993), *ENVOY: Your Personal Guide to Classroom Management*	Create social and psychological safety, invite thinking, and increase engagement by choosing to use an approachable voice when seeking information, encouraging responses, or communicating acceptance of all ideas. Using an approachable voice involves speaking with wider range of modulation (than with a credible voice) with a rising pitch at the end of a statement. Move your head, maintain eye contact, smile, and lean toward the group.
Get Attention First	14, p. 252	Robert Garmston & Bruce Wellman (2009), *The Adaptive School*, p. 189	Use nonverbal and verbal communication to get group attention before delivering directions or other information. Use a frozen gesture (e.g., hand in the air) and an auditory cue (e.g., ring a chime, "Look here, please."). Use credible voice if speaking. When group is attentive, become unfrozen, break eye contact, breathe, and move to another anchored space. Break silence with an approachable voice.

References

Adams, M., & Bell, L. A., with Goodman, D. J. & Joshi, K. Y. (2016). *Teaching for diversity and social justice* (3rd ed.). New York, NY: Routledge.

Adelman, L. (Producer). (2003). *Race: The power of an illusion* [Motion picture]. United States: California Newsreel.

Allen, D., & Blythe, T. (2004). *The facilitator's book of questions: Tools for looking together at student and teacher work.* New York, NY: Teacher's College Press.

Ambandos, A. (Director), & Michaels, J. (Actor). (2012). *Jillian Michaels: Ripped in 30.* [DVD]. United States: Gaiam America.

Andrews, N. (2013, May). Oprah talks to Maya Angelou. *Oprah Magazine.* http://www.oprahmag.co.za/live-your-best-life/giving-back/oprah-talks-to-maya-angelou-part-2

Angelou, M. (1978). *And still I rise.* New York, NY: Random House Publishing Group.

Arao, B., & Clemens, K. (2013). From safe spaces to brave spaces: A new way to frame dialogue. In L. M. Landreman (Ed.), *The art of effective facilitation: Reflections from social justice educators* (135–150). Sterling, VA: Stylus.

Arena, M. J. (2009). Understanding large group intervention process: A complexity theory perspective. *Organizational Development Journal, 27*(1), 49–64.

Argyris, C. (1990). *Overcoming organizational defenses: Facilitating organizational learning.* Needham, MA: Allyn & Bacon.

Argyris, C., & Schon, D. A. (1995). *Organizational learning II: Theory, method, and practice.* Boston, MA: Addison-Wesley.

Aronson, E., Blaney, N., Sikes, J., Stephan, C., & Snapp, M. (1975, February). Busing and racial tension: The jigsaw route to learning and liking. *Psychology Today,* pp. 8, 43–50.

Arriaga, T. T., & Lindsey, R. B. (2016). *Opening doors: An implementation template for Cultural Proficiency.* Thousand Oaks, CA: Corwin.

Averette, P. (2014). Save the last word for me protocol. *School Reform Initiative.* http://www.nsrfharmony.org/system/files/protocols/save_last_word_0.pdf

Azarov, A. (2009, November). Multi-party facilitation—improvisation: How to "do the jazz" in multi-party facilitations. http://www.mediate.com/articles/how_to_do_the_jazz.cfm

Babauta, L. (2011, June 3). The illusion of control. [Web log post]. *Zen Habits.* http://zenhabits.net/control/

Bailey, S. Event design. In Garmston, R. J., & Wellman, B. M. (2005). *How to make presentations that teach and transform.* Arlington, VA: Association for Supervision and Curriculum Development.

Baldwin, J. (1985). *The price of the ticket: Collected nonfiction, 1948–1985.* New York, NY: St. Martin's Press.

Bandura, A. (1997). Self-efficacy and health behaviour. In A. Baum, S. Newman, J. Wienman, R. West, & C. McManus (Eds.), *Cambridge handbook of psychology, health and medicine* (pp. 160–162). Cambridge: Cambridge University Press.

Bardhan, N., & Orbe, M. P. (2012). *Identity research and communication: Intercultural reflections and future directions.* Lanham, MD: Lexington Books.

Barker, J. (1992). *The future edge: Discovering the new paradigms of success.* New York, NY: William Morrow.

Barnhardt, C. L., & Reyes, K. A. (2016, March 2). Embracing student activism [Web log post]. *Higher Education Today.* https://higheredtoday.org/2016/03/02/embracing-student-activism/

Baum, L. F. (1910). *The wizard of Oz.* Chicago: George M. Hill.

Bechler, C., & Johnson, S. D. (1995). Leadership and listening: A study of member perception. *Small Group Research, 26*(1), 77–85.

Bentley, S., & Bacon, S. E. (1996). The all new, state-of-the-art ILA definition of listening: Now that we have it, what do we do with it? *Listening Post,* 1–5.

Bentley, T. J. (2000). *Facilitation.* Stroud, UK: Space Between Publishing.

Birdwhistell, R. L. (1970). *Kinesics and context.* Philadelphia: University of Pennsylvania Press.

Blanchard, K. & Stoner, J. L. (2011). *Full steam ahead! Unleash the power of vision in your work and your life* (2nd ed.). San Francisco, CA: Berrett-Koehler.

Blankstein, A. M., & Noguera, P. (2015). *Excellence through equity: Five principles of courageous leadership to guide achievement for every student.* Thousand Oaks, CA: Corwin.

Boll, C. L. (2016, Summer). The Dalai Lama: Common ground for peace. *Syracuse University Magazine, 33*(2). http://sumagazine.syr.edu/2012fall-winter/features/dalailama.html

Boser, U. (2014, May). *Teacher diversity revisited: A new state-by-state analysis.* Washington, DC: Center for American Progress. https://cdn.americanprogress.org/wp-content/uploads/2014/05/TeacherDiversity.pdf

Bowman, N. A. (2010, March). College diversity experiences and cognitive development: A meta-analysis. *Review of Educational Research, 80*(1), 4–33.

Breathnach, S. B. (2008). *Simple abundance: A daybook of comfort and joy.* New York, NY: Grand Central Publishing.

Bridges, W. (2009). *Managing transitions: making the most of change* (3rd ed.). Cambridge, MA: Da Capo.

Brown, B. (2010). *The gifts of imperfection: Let go of who you think you're supposed to be and embrace who you are.* Center City, MN: Hazelden.

Brown, B. (2012a). *Daring greatly: How the courage to be vulnerable transforms the way we live, love, parent, and lead.* New York, NY: Gotham Books.

Brown, B. (2012b). Listening to shame. TED talk. https://www.ted.com/talks/brene_brown_listening_to_shame?language=en

Brown, B. (2012c, May 5). *Keynote speech.* [Speech]. Mom 2.0 Summit, Miami, FL.

Brown, B. (2015). *Rising strong: The reckoning, the rumble, the revolution.* New York, NY: Random House

Brown, J., & Isaacs, D. (1995). *The World Café: Shaping our futures through conversations that matter* (1st ed.). San Francisco, CA: Berrett-Koehler

Brown, R. M. (1984). *Unexpected news: Reading the Bible with third world eyes.* Louisville, KY: Westminster John Knox Press.

Brownell, J. (2016). *Listening: Attitudes, principles, and skills* (5th ed.). New York, NY: Routledge.

Burnes, B. (2004). Emergent change and planned change—Competitors or allies?: The case of WYZ Construction. *International Journal of Operations & Production Management, 24*(9), 886–902.

CampbellJones, B. (2002). Against the stream: White men who act in ways to eradicate racism and white privilege/entitlement in the United States of America. Unpublished doctoral dissertation, Claremont Graduate University, Los Angeles.

CampbellJones, B. (2014). *Conversations that matter.* [Keynote speech]. Beverly Hills, CA, June 29, 2014.

CampbellJones & Associates. (2005). Cultural proficiency seminar. [Workshop]. Ellicott City, MD, April 6, 2005.

CampbellJones & Associates. (2008). Cultural proficiency seminar. [Workshop]. Columbia, MD, November 5, 2008.

CampbellJones & Associates. (2013). Cultural proficiency seminar [Workshop]. Elkridge, MD, October 2, 2013.

CampbellJones, F., CampbellJones, B., & Lindsey, R. B. (2010). *The Cultural Proficiency journey: Moving beyond ethical barriers toward profound school change.* Thousand Oaks, CA: Corwin.

Caroll, D. (2012, February 8). Erykah Badu: Analog girl in a digital world. [Interview]. http://www.nzherald.co.nz/entertainment/news/article.cfm?c_id=1501119&objectid=10784000

Carter, C. (2003). *The power of listening.* Office of Human Resources, Employee Development Center. http://www.authorstream.com/Presentation/kfshrco-1000546-the-power-of-listening/

Carter, R. T. (1995). *The influence of race and racial identity in psychotherapy: Towards an inclusive model.* Hoboken, NJ: John Wiley & Sons.

Center on Education Policy. (2015). Answering the question that matters most: Has student achievement increased since no child left behind? http://eric.ed.gov/?id=ED520272

Chan, D. (1998). Functional relations among constructs in the same content domain at different levels of analysis: A typology of composition models. *Journal of Applied Psychology, 83*(2), 234–246.

Chism, M. (2015). *No drama leadership: How enlightened leaders transform culture in the workplace.* Brookline, MA: Bibliomotion.

Chödrön, P. (2005). *When things fall apart: Heart advice for difficult times.* Boston, MA: Shambhala.

Chopra, D. (2012). *Spiritual solutions: Answers to life's greatest challenges.* New York, NY: Harmony Books.

Cleage, P. (1997). *What crazy looks like on an ordinary day.* New York, NY: Avon Books.

Coelho, P. (2005). *The Zahir: A novel of obsession.* New York, NY: HarperCollins.

Conyers, J. (2016, May 17). Conyers, Scott unveil new GAO Report on segregation in public schools. [Press release] https://conyers.house.gov/media-center/press-releases/conyers-scott-unveil-new-gao-report-segregation-public-schools

Costa, A. L., & Garmston, R. J. (2016). *Cognitive coaching: Developing self-directed learners and leaders* (3rd ed.). Norwood, MA: Christopher-Gordon.

Covey, S. R. (1989). *The 7 habits of highly effective people.* New York, NY: Free Press.

Crenshaw, K., Gotanda, N., Peller, G., & Thomas, K. (1995). *Critical race theory: The key writings that formed the movement.* New York, NY: The New Press.

Crisp, R. J., & Turner, R. N. (2011). Cognitive adaptation to the experience of social and cultural diversity. *Psychological Bulletin, 137*(2), 242–266.

Cross, T. L. (1989, May 5). *Cultural issues and responses: Defining cultural competence in child welfare.* https://www.dshs.wa.gov/ca/appendix-cultural-legal-articles/cultural-issues-and-responses-defining-cultural-competence-child-welfare

Cross, T. L., Bazron, B. J., Dennis, K.W., & Isaacs, M. R. (1989). *Toward a culturally competent system of care:* Vol. 1. Washington, DC: Georgetown University Child Development Program, Child and Adolescent Service System Program.

Cross, W. E., Jr. (1971). The Negro to Black conversion experience. *Black World, 20*(9), 13–27.

The Dalai Lama. (2001). *The Dalai Lama to the European Parliament.* [Speech]. October 14, 2001, Strasbourg, France. http://www.dalailama.com/messages/tibet/strasbourg-speech-2001

Delpit, Lisa. (1996). *Other people's children: Cultural conflict in the classroom.* New York, NY: New Press.

Deming, W. E. (2000). *Out of the crisis* (reprint ed.). Cambridge, MA: MIT Press.

DiAngelo, R. (2011). White fragility. *International Journal of Critical Pedagogy, 3*(3), 54–70.

Dickens, P. M. (2012). Facilitating emergence: Complex, adaptive systems theory and the shape of change. Paper 114, *Dissertations & Theses,* Antioch University. http://aura.antioch.edu/etds/114

Douglass, F. [1849] (1991) Letter to an abolitionist associate. In K. Bobo, J. Kendall, & S. Max (Eds.), *Organizing for social change: A mandate for activity in the 1990s.* Washington, DC: Seven Locks Press.

Doyle, M., & Strauss, D. (1976). *How to make meetings work.* New York, NY: Penguin Putnam.

Drexler, A. B., Sibbet, D., & Forrester, R. (1988). The team performance model. In W. B. Reddy (Ed.), *Team building: Blueprints for productivity and satisfaction.* Alexandria, VA: NTL Institute for Applied Behavioral Science.

Dweck, C. S. (2006). *Mindset: The new psychology of success.* New York, NY: Random House.

Dyer, W. (2007). Change your thoughts—change your life: Living the wisdom of the Tao. Carlsbad, CA: Hay House.

Dyson, E. M. (2001). *I may not get there with you: The true Martin Luther King, Jr.* New York, NY: Simon & Schuster.

Edwards, K. E. (2006). Aspiring social justice ally identity development: A conceptual model. *NASPA Journal 43*(4): 39–60.

Eels, R. J. (2011). Meta-analysis of the relationship between collective teacher efficacy and student achievement. [Doctoral dissertation.] http://ecommons.luc.edu/luc_diss/133

Eitington, J. E. (1996). The winning trainer: Winning ways to involve people in learning. Houston, TX: Gulf.

Elementary and Secondary Education Act (ESEA) of 1965, 20 U.S.C. § 2701 et seq. (1965).

Eliott, T. S. (1943). *Four quartets.* New York, NY: Caedmon.

Ellison, R. (1952). *Invisible man.* New York, NY: Vintage Books.

Engberg, M. E. (2007). Educating the workforce for the 21st century: A cross-disciplinary analysis of the impact of the undergraduate experience on students' development of a pluralistic orientation. *Research in Higher Education, 48*(3), 283–317.

Ericsson, K.A., Krampe, R.Th., & Tesch-Romer, C. (1993). The role of deliberate practice in the acquisition of expert performance. *Psychological Review, 100,* 393–394.

Every Student Succeeds Act (ESSA) of 2015, Pub. L. 114–95 (2015).

Fadiman, J., & Frager, R. (1997). *Essential Sufism.* San Francisco, CA: HarperCollins.

Fasse, B., & Kolodner, J. (2000). Evaluating classroom practices using qualitative research methods: Defining and refining the process. In B. Fishman & S. O'Connor-Divelbiss (Eds.), *Proceedings of the Fourth International Conference of the Learning Sciences* (pp. 193–198). Mahwah, NJ: Erlbaum.

Ferguson, R. F. (2007). *Toward excellence with equity: An emerging vision for closing the achievement gap.* Cambridge, MA: Harvard Education Press.

Ferguson, R. F. (2015, Jan. 26). Getting to excellence with equity: Ferguson talks about opportunity, achievement, and raising the bar for all students. https://www.gse.harvard.edu/news/uk/15/01/getting-excellence-equity

Ferguson, S. J. (2016). *Race, gender, sexuality, and social class: Dimensions of inequality and identity* (2nd ed.). Thousand Oaks, CA: Sage.

Freire, P. (1970). *Pedagogy of the oppressed.* New York, NY: Seabury.

Freire, P. (1985). *The politics of education: Culture, power, and liberation.* Westport, CT: Bergin & Garvey.

Fullan, M. (1993). *Change forces: Probing the depths of educational reform.* Philadelphia, PA: Falmer Press.

Fullan, M. (2006). Turnaround leadership. San Francisco, CA: Jossey-Bass.

Fullan, M. (2014). *The principal: Three keys to maximizing impact.* San Francisco, CA: Jossey-Bass.

Garmston, R. J. (2008, Winter). Four mental aptitudes help facilitators facing challenges. *Journal of Staff Development 29*(1), 65–66. http://learningforward.org/docs/jsd-winter-2008/garmston291.pdf?sfvrsn=2

Garmston, R. J., & von Frank, V. (2012). *Unlocking group potential to improve schools.* Thousand Oaks, CA: Corwin.

Garmston, R. J., & Wellman, B. M. (1992). *How to make presentations that teach and transform.* Alexandria, VA: Association for Supervision and Curriculum Development.

Garmston, R. J., & Wellman, B. M. (2009). *The adaptive school: A sourcebook for developing collaborative groups*. Norwood, MA: Christopher-Gordon.

Garmston, R. J., & Zimmerman, D. P. (2013). *Lemons to lemonade: Resolving problems in meetings, workshops, and PLCs*. Thousand Oaks, CA: Corwin.

Gaskins, P. F. (1999). *What are you? Voices of multiracial young people*. New York, NY: Henry Holt.

Gibson, C. B. (2003). The efficacy advantage: Factors related to the formation of group efficacy. *Journal of Applied Social Psychology, 33*, 2153–2186.

Gino, F., Kouchaki, M., & Galinsky, A. D. (2015). The moral virtue of authenticity: How inauthenticity produces feelings of immorality and impurity. *Psychological Science, 26*(7), 983–996.

Gladwell, M. (2000). *The tipping point: How little things can make a big difference*. Boston, MA: Little, Brown.

Gladwell, M. (2005). *Blink: The power of thinking without thinking*. New York: Little, Brown.

Gladwell, M. (2008). *Outliers*. New York, NY: Little, Brown.

Goodell, J. (1994, June 16). Steve Jobs in 1994: The Rolling Stone interview. *Rolling Stone*. http://www.rollingstone.com/culture/news/steve-jobs-in-1994-the-rolling-stone-interview-20110117

Gorski, P. (2010). Unlearning deficit ideology and the scornful gaze: Thoughts on authenticating the class discourse in education. Retrieved from http://www.edchange.org/publications/deficit-ideology-scornful-ga

Grantmakers for Effective Organizations. (2004). *Funding effectiveness: Lessons in building nonprofit capacity* (1st ed.). San Francisco, CA: Jossey-Bass.

Gray, J. (2005). Four "A's Text Protocol. *National School Reform Faculty*. http://www.nsrfharmony.org/system/files/protocols/4_a_text_0.pdf

Greene, C. (2003, November 20). Rule of 3 Protocol. *School Reform Initiative*. http://www.tcpress.com/pdfs/9780807755457_protocols.pdf

Grinder, M. (1993). *ENVOY: Your personal guide to classroom management*. Melbourne: Hawker Brownlow.

Grinder, M. (2007). *The elusive obvious*. Battle Ground, WA: Michael Grinder & Associates.

Gurin, P., Dey, E. L., Hurtado, S., & Gurin, G. (2002). Diversity and higher education: Theory and impact on educational outcomes. *Harvard Educational Review, 72*(3), 330–366.

Haas, M. (1999, March 22). Research shows diverse environment has educational benefits. The University Record, University of Michigan. http://www.ur.umich.edu/9899/Mar22_99/10.htm

Haley, A. & X, M. (1964). *The autobiography of Malcolm X*. New York, NY: Random House Publishing Group.

Hargreaves, A. (2003). *Teaching in the knowledge society: Education in the age of insecurity*. New York, NY: Teachers College.

Hargrove, R. (2008). *Masterful coaching* (3rd ed.). San Francisco, CA: Jossey-Bass.

Harste, J., & Short, K. with Burke, C. (1988). *Creating classrooms for authors*. Portsmouth, NH: Heineman.

Harvey, J. B. (1974). The Abilene Paradox: The management of agreement. *Organizational Dynamics 3*, 63–80.

Hattie, J. (2009). *Visible learning: A synthesis of over 800 meta-analyses relating to achievement*. New York, NY: Routledge.

Hattie, J. (2011). *Visible learning for teachers: Maximizing impact on learning*. New York, NY: Routledge.

Hattie, J. (2015). The applicability of visible learning to higher education. *Scholarship of Teaching and Learning in Psychology, 1*(1), 79–91.

Healey, J. F. (2010). *Diversity and society: Race, ethnicity, and gender*. Thousand Oaks, CA: Sage.

Helms, J. E. (1990) (Ed.). *Black and White racial identity: Theory, research and practice*. Westport, CT: Greenwood.

Hesselbein, F. (1999, Spring). The key to cultural transformation. *Leader to Leader*, (12), 1–7.

Hilliard, A. (1991). Do we have the will to educate all children? *Educational Leadership, 40*(1), 31–36.

Hoffnung, A. (1970). *For the love of Torah: Laymen explore the Bible.* New York, NY: Jonathan David.

Hofstede, G. (1991). *Cultures and organizations: Software of the mind.* Maidenhead, UK: McGraw-Hill.

Holley, L. C., & Steiner, S. (2005). Safe space: Student perspectives on classroom environment. *Journal of Social Work Education, 41*(1), 49–64.

Hollins, C., & Govan, I. (2015). *Diversity, equity, and inclusion: Strategies for facilitating conversations on race.* Lanham, MD: Rowman & Littlefield.

hooks, b. (1984). *Feminist theory: From margin to center.* Cambridge, MA: South End Press.

hooks, b. (1989). *Talking back: Thinking feminist, thinking black.* Boston, MA: South End Press.

hooks, b. (1994). Teaching to transgress: Education as the practice of freedom. New York, NY: Routledge.

hooks, b. (2001). All about love: New visions. New York, NY: HarperCollins.

Hopkins, D. (2001). *School improvement for real.* New York, NY: RoutledgeFalmer.

Howard, G. (2015a). *We can't lead where we won't go: An educator's guide to equity.* Thousand Oaks, CA: Corwin.

Howard, G. (2015b). Deep equity. [Workshop]. Westlake Village, CA, January 9, 2015.

Howard, G. (2016). *We can't teach what we don't know: White teachers, multiracial schools* (3rd ed.). New York, NY: Teacher's College Press.

Hughes, Paul. Twitter post. May 15, 2016, 12:14 a.m. https://twitter.com/10mthinking/status/731744428252102656

Humphries, E. (2016). *I am my own superhero: Awaken your inner superhero by igniting your natural born superpowers.* Bloomington, IN: AuthorHouse.

Hunter, D. (2007). *The art of facilitation: The essentials for leading great meetings and creating group synergy.* San Francisco: Jossey-Bass.

Institute of Cultural Affairs. (2016). *Cautions: Misconceptions about facilitation.* http://www.icab.be/top/top_3.html

International Listening Association. (2016). *Facts about listening.* www.listen.org/FactsAbout Listening

Jalongo, M. R. (2008). Learning to listen, listening to learn. Washington, DC: National Association for the Education of Young Children.

Jennings, P. A. (2015). *Mindfulness for teachers: Simple skills for peace and productivity in the classroom.* New York, NY: W.W. Norton & Company.

Johnson, L. B. (1964). *Remarks upon signing the Civil Rights Bill.* [Speech]. Washington, DC, July 2, 1964. http://millercenter.org/president/speeches/speech-3525

Johnson, S. D., & Bechler, C. (1998). Examining the relationship between listening effectiveness and leadership emergence: Perceptions, behaviors, and recall. *Small Group Research, 29*(4), 452–471.

Jones, D. (1996). *Everyday creativity.* Minneapolis, MN: Star Thrower.

Judith, A. (2004). *Eastern body, Western mind: Psychology and the chakra system as a path to the self.* New York, NY: Random House.

Jung, C. G. (1967). *Alchemical studies,* vol. 13. Princeton, NJ: Princeton University Press.

Kabat-Zinn, J. (1994). *Wherever you go, there you are: Mindfulness meditation in everyday life.* New York, NY: Hyperion.

Kaner, S. (2014). *Facilitator's guide to participatory decision-making.* San Francisco, CA: Jossey-Bass.

Katz-Navon, T., & Erez, M. (2005). When collective- and self-efficacy affect team performance: The role of task interdependence. *Small Group Research, 36*(4), 437–465. Thousand Oaks, CA: Sage.

Keller, H. (1920). *Out of the dark: Essays, letters, and addresses on physical and social vision.* New York, NY: Doubleday, Page & Company.

Kendall, F. E. (2013). *Understanding white privilege: Creating pathways to authentic relationships across race* (2nd ed.). New York, NY: Routledge.

Kennedy, J. F. (1963). *The Civil Rights address.* [Speech]. Washington, DC, June 11, 1963. http://www.americanrhetoric.com/speeches/jfkcivilrights.htm

Kennedy, K., Molen, G., & Spielberg, S. (1993). *Jurassic Park*. [Motion picture]. United States: Amblin Entertainment.

Kentucky Department of Education. (2013, May 22). Professional development v. professional learning. *KDE Media Portal*. http://mediaportal.education.ky.gov/educator-effectiveness/2013/05/professional-development-vs-professional-learning/

Killion, J. (1998, Winter). Knowing when and how much to steer the ship. *Journal of Staff Development, 20*(1), 59–60.

King, M. L. (1963, August). Letter from Birmingham Jail. *Atlantic Monthly, 212*(2), 78–88.

Krzyzewski, M. (2008, August 26). *The Mike Krzyzewski interview*. [Interview]. http://www.achievement.org/autodoc/page/krz0int-3

Kurtz, G. & Lucas, G. (1977). *Star Wars*. [Motion picture.] United States: Lucasfilm.

Ladson-Billings, G. (2006, October). From the achievement gap to the education debt: Understanding achievement in U.S. schools. *Educational Researcher,* (35), 3–12.

LaDuke, W. (2008). *Launching a green economy for brown people: Building a good future for our communities and coming generations*. Callaway, MN: Honor the Earth. http://www.honorearth.org/launching_a_green_economy_for_brown_people

Landreman, L. M. (2013). *The art of effective facilitation: Reflections from social justice educators*. Sterling, VA: Stylus.

Lao Tzu, & Mitchell, S [tr.]. (1988). *Tao Te Ching: A new English version*. New York, NY: Harper & Row.

Learning Forward. (2011). *Standards for professional learning*. Oxford, OH: Author. http://learningforward.org/standards-for-professional-learning

Learning Forward. (2013, December). Develop a professional learning plan. *Journal of Staff Development, 34*(6), 52–59.

L'Engle, M. (1980). *A ring of endless light: The Austin family chronicles*. New York, NY: Macmillan.

Leonardo, Z., & Porter, R. K. (2010). Pedagogy of fear: Toward a Fanonian theory of "safety" in race dialogue. *Race Ethnicity and Education, 13*(2), 139–157.

Light, J. (2014, May 22). *These eight charts show why racial equality is a myth in America*. http://billmoyers.com/2014/05/22/these-eight-charts-show-why-racial-equality-is-a-myth-in-america/

Lindahi, K. (2003). *Practicing the sacred art of listening: A guide to enrich your relationships and kindle your spiritual life*. Woodstock, VT: Skylight Paths.

Lindsey, D. B., Kearney, K. M., Estrada, D., Terrell, R. D., and Lindsey, R. B. (2015). *A culturally proficient response to the common core: Ensuring equity through professional learning*. Thousand Oaks, CA: Corwin.

Lindsey, R. B. (1996). *My culture*. Hayward, CA: California School Leadership Academy.

Lindsey, R. B. (2011). *The best of Corwin*. Thousand Oaks, CA: Corwin.

Lindsey, R. B., Graham, S. M., Chris Westphal Jr., R., & Jew, C. L. (2008). *Culturally proficient inquiry: A lens for identifying and examining educational gaps*. Thousand Oaks, CA: Corwin.

Lindsey, R. B., Nuri-Robins, K. J., & Terrell, R. D. (1999). *Cultural proficiency: A manual for school leaders* (1st ed.). Thousand Oaks, CA: Corwin.

Lindsey, R. B., Nuri-Robins, K. J., & Terrell, R. D. (2001). *Cultural proficiency: A manual for school leaders* (2nd ed.). Thousand Oaks, CA: Corwin.

Lindsey, R. B., Nuri-Robins, K. J., & Terrell, R. D. (2009). *Cultural proficiency: A manual for school leaders* (3rd ed.). Thousand Oaks, CA: Corwin.

Lindsey, R. B., Roberts, L. M., & CampbellJones, F. (2013). *The culturally proficient school: An implementation guide for school leaders*. Thousand Oaks, CA: Corwin

Linehan, M. M. (1993). *Cognitive-behavioral treatment of borderline personality disorder*. New York, NY: Guilford Press.

Lipton, L., & Wellman, B. (2004). *Got data? Now what?* Bloomington, IN: Solution Tree Press.

Lipton, L., & Wellman, B. (2011a). *Groups at work: strategies and structures for professional learning*. Sherman, CT: MiraVia.

Lipton, L., & Wellman, B. (2011b). *Leading groups: Effective strategies for building professional community.* Sherman, CT: MiraVia.

Lorde, A. (1984) *Sister outsider: Essays and speeches.* New York, NY: Random House.

Lorenz, E. (1972, December 29). "Predictability: Does the Flap of a Butterfly's Wings in Brazil Set a Tornado in Texas?" [Speech]. 139th Meeting of the American Association for the Advancement of the Sciences, Washington, DC. http://eaps4.mit.edu/research/Lorenz/Butterfly_1972.pdf

Love, N. (2002). *Using data/getting results:* A practical guide for school improvement in mathematics and science. Norwood, MA: Christopher-Gordon.

Lyman, F. (1981). The responsive classroom discussion: The inclusion of all students. *Mainstreaming Digest.* College Park: University of Maryland.

Lyman, F. T. Jr., (1987) The think-trix: A classroom tool for thinking in response to reading. In *Reading issues and practices: Yearbook of the state of Maryland international reading association council.* Vol. 4, 15–18. Westminster, MD: State of Maryland International Reading Association.

Lyons, O. (1980). An Iroquois perspective. In C. Vecsey & R. W. Venables (Eds.), *American Indian environments: Ecological issues in Native American history* (pp. 171–174). Syracuse, NY: Syracuse University Press.

Macklemore, & Lewis, R. (2012). Ten thousand hours [song]. *The Heist.* Seattle, WA: Macklemore LLC.

Mandela, Nelson (1995). *Long walk to freedom.* New York, NY: Little, Brown and Company.

Marlatt, G. A., & Kristeller, J. L. (1999). Mindfulness and meditation. In W. R. Miller (Ed.), *Integrating spirituality into treatment* (pp. 67–84). Washington, DC: American Psychological Association.

Marshall, G. (Ed.) (1998). *The Oxford dictionary of sociology* (2nd ed.). Oxford: Oxford University Press.

Maslow, A. H. (1943). A theory of human motivation. *Psychological Review, 50,* 370–396. http://psychclassics.yorku.ca/Maslow/motivation.htm

McEntyre, M. C. (2004, March/April). What to do in the darkness. *Weavings: A Journal of the Christian Spiritual Life, 19*(2), 27.

McEwen, M. (2003). New perspectives on identity development. In S. R. Komives & D. Woodard, Jr. (Eds.), *Student services: A handbook for the profession* (4th ed., pp. 188–217). San Francisco, CA: Jossey-Bass.

McLeod, M. (1998, January 1). There's no place to go but up: Maya Angelou in conversation with bell hooks, moderated by Melvin McLeod. *Lion's Roar: Buddhist Wisdom for Our Time.* http://www.lionsroar.com/theres-no-place-to-go-but-up/

Mehrabian, A. (1981). *Silent messages: Implicit communication of emotions and attitudes.* Belmont, CA: Wadsworth.

Mezirow, J. (2000). Learning to think like an adult. In J. Mezirow & Associates (Eds.), *Learning as transformation: critical perspectives on a theory in progress* (pp. 3–34). San Francisco, CA: Jossey-Bass.

Michael, A. (2015). *Raising race questions: Whiteness and inquiry in education.* New York, NY: Teachers College Press.

Miles, M. B., Ekholm, M., & Vanderberghe, R. (1987). *Lasting school improvement: Exploring the process of institutionalization* (ISIP Vol. 5). Leuven/Amersfoort: Acco.

Miller, B. (2015, February 24). *Student success symposium: Researchers discuss how sense of belonging boosts student success rate.* http://www.udel.edu/udaily/2015/feb/student-success-022415.html

Miranda, L. (2015a, April 17). *Charlie Rose.* [Television Program].

Miranda, L. (2015b, May 20). *Broadway League's 2015 spring road conference.* [Speech]. May 20, 2015, Denver, CO. http://www.denvercenter.org/blog-posts/news-center/2015/05/20/lin-manuel-miranda-on-the-power-of-theatre-to-eliminate-distance

Mischel, L. J., & Northcraft, G. B. (1997). "I think we can, I think we can . . .": The role of efficacy beliefs in group and team effectiveness. *Advances in Group Processes, 14*, 177–197.

Moore, R. M., III. (2007). *They always said I would marry a white girl: Coming to grips with race in America.* Lanham, MD: Hamilton Books.

Morgan, G. (2006). *Images of organization* (2nd ed.). London, UK: Sage.

Mun Wah, L. (2004). *The art of mindful facilitation.* Berkeley, CA: Stir Fry Seminars & Consulting.

Myers, V. (2012). *Moving diversity forward: How to go from well-meaning to well-doing.* Chicago, IL: American Bar Association.

Naidu, P., & Lua, J. (2011). *SPOT on facilitation: Engaging people, empowering teams, exceeding goals.* Singapore: Candid Creation.

National Commission on Excellence in Education. (1983). *A nation at risk: The imperative for educational reform: a report to the nation and the secretary of the United States Department of Education.* Washington, DC: The Commission.

National Education Association (NEA). (2015 February 1). Effects of NCLB test-driven accountability on students. https://www.nea.org/assets/docs/One-Pager_Testing_Effects_Students.pdf

Neal, K. L. (2014). Six communication skills for records and information managers. New York, NY: Chandos Publishing.

Nichols, R. G. & Stevens, L. A. (1957, September). Listening to people. *Harvard Business Review, 35*(5), 85–92.

Nin, A. (1961). Seduction of the minotaur. Chicago, IL: Swallow Press.

Nin, A. (1976). *In favor of the sensitive man and other essays.* New York, NY: Harcourt Brace.

Nuri-Robins, K., & Bundy, L. (2016). *Fish out of water: Mentoring, managing, and self-monitoring people who don't fit in.* Thousand Oaks, CA: Corwin.

Nuri-Robins, K. J., Lindsey, D. B., Lindsey, R. B., & Terrell, R. D. (2001). *Culturally proficient instruction: A guide for people who teach.* Thousand Oaks, CA: Corwin.

Obama, B. (2016, May 7). *Howard University commencement address.* [Speech]. Washington, DC. https://www.c-span.org/video/?409107–1/president-obama-delivers-commencement-address-howard-university

Papa, M., & Glenn, E. (1988, Fall). Listening ability and performance with new technology. *Journal of Business Communication, 25*(4), 5–15.

Perez, A. D., & Hirschman, C. (2009). The changing racial and ethnic composition of the US population: Emerging American identities. *Population and Development Review, 35*, 1–51. doi: 10.1111/j.1728–4457.2009.00260.x

Peterson-Veatch, R. (2006). *Affinity mapping.* http://www.nsrfharmony.org/system/files/protocols/affinity_mapping_0.pdf

Powell, M. & Kantor, J. (2008, June 18). After attacks, Michelle Obama looks for a new introduction. *New York Times.* http://www.nytimes.com/2008/06/18/us/politics/18michelle.html?_r=0

Prince, G. (1968). The operational mechanism of synectics. *Journal of Creative Behavior, 2*, 1–13.

Proust, M., Clark C. [tr], & Collier, P. [tr]. (2003). *In search of lost time: The prisoner and the fugitive.* London, UK: Penguin Books.

Quaglia, R. (2016). *Principal voice: Listen, learn, lead.* Corwin Press.

Quaglia, R. J., & Corso, M. J. (2014). *Student voice: The instrument of change.* Thousand Oaks, CA: Corwin.

Redfield, J. (1993). *The Celestine prophecy: An adventure.* New York, NY: Grand Central Publishing.

Reeves, D. (2009). *Leading change in your school: How to conquer myths, build commitment, and get results.* Arlington, VA: ASCD.

Robinson, L. (2016, March). Questlove and Lin-Manuel Miranda give details of the Hamilton mixtape. *Vanity Fair.* http://www.vanityfair.com/culture/2016/03/questlove-lin-manuel-miranda-the-hamilton-mixtape

Rothenberg, P. S. (2007). *Race, class, and gender in the United States* (7th ed.). New York, NY: Worth.

Rothman, J. (2014, May 12). The origins of "privilege." *New Yorker.* http://www.newyorker.com/books/page-turner/the-origins-of-privilege

Ruggs, E., & Hebl, M. (2012) Diversity, inclusion, and cultural awareness for classroom and outreach education. In B. Bogue & E. Cady (Eds.), *Apply Research to Practice (ARP) resources.* https://www.engr.psu.edu/awe/ARPAbstracts/DiversityInclusion/ARP_DiversityInclusionCulturalAwareness_Overview.pdf

Scharmer, C. O. (2009). *Theory U: Leading from the future as it emerges.* San Francisco, CA: Berrett-Koehler.

Schein, E. H. (2010). *Organizational culture and leadership* (4th ed.). San Francisco, CA: Jossey-Bass.

Schein, E. H. (2013). *Humble inquiry: The gentle art of asking instead of telling.* San Francisco, CA: Berrett-Koehler.

Schwarz, R. (2002). *The skilled facilitator: A comprehensive resource for consultants, facilitators, managers, trainers, and coaches.* San Francisco, CA: Jossey-Bass.

Senge, P. M. (1994). *The fifth discipline fieldbook: Strategies and tools for building a learning organization.* New York: Crown Business.

Senge, P. M. (1999). *The dance of change: The challenges of sustaining momentum in learning organizations.* New York, NY: Currency/Doubleday.

Sibbet, D. (2002). *Principles of facilitation: The purpose and potential of leading group process.* San Francisco, CA: The Grove Consultants International.

Silver, J., Wachowski, L., & Wachowski, L. (1999). *The Matrix.* [Motion Picture]. United States: Village Roadshow Pictures.

Sinek, S. (2009). *Start with the why: How great leaders inspire everyone to take action.* New York, NY: Portfolio, Penguin Group.

Singleton, G., & Linton, C. (2006). *Courageous conversations about race: A field guide for achieving equity in schools.* Thousand Oaks, CA: Corwin.

Smith, R., King, D., Sidhu, R., & Skelsey, D. (2015). *The effective change manager's handbook: Essential guidance to change management body of knowledge.* Philadelphia, PA: Kogan Page.

Sparks, D. (2002). Conversations about race need to be fearless. *Journal of Staff Development, 23*(4), 60–64.

Spencer, D. (2014). *Live well between your ears: 110 ways to think like a psychologist, why it makes a difference, and the research to back it up.* Victoria, BC: Friesen Press.

Stanfield, B. R. (2000). *The art of focused conversation: 100 ways to access group wisdom in the workplace.* Gabriola Island, BC: New Society.

Starhawk (2005, Fall). Toward an activist spirituality. *Reclaiming Quarterly.* http://starhawk.org/pdfs/Toward%20an%20Activist%20Sprituality.pdf

Stephens, D., & Lindsey, R. B. (2011). *Culturally proficient collaboration: The use and misuse of school counselors.* Thousand Oaks, CA: Corwin.

Sue, D. W., & Sue, D. (2003). *Counseling the culturally diverse: Theory and practice* (4th ed.). Hoboken, NJ: Wiley.

Tatum, B. D. (1992) Talking about race, learning about racism: the application of racial identity development theory in the classroom. *Harvard Educational Review, 62*(1), 1–25.

Taylor, A. (1977). *Notes and tones: Musician-to-musician interviews.* New York, NY: Da Capo Press.

Tecumseh. (1810). *Address to general William Henry Harrison.* [Speech]. Vincennes, Indian Territory. http://www.americanrhetoric.com/speeches/nativeamericans/chieftecumseh.htm

Terrell, R. D., & Lindsey, R. B. (2009). *Culturally proficient leadership: The personal journey begins within.* Thousand Oaks, CA: Corwin.

Thomas, N. (Producer), & Nolan, C. (Director). (2010). *Inception.* [Motion picture]. United States: Legendary Pictures.

Timm, S., & Schroeder, B. L. (2000). Listening/nonverbal communication training. *International Journal of Listening, 14,* 109–128.

Timperley, H., Wilson, A., Barrar, H., & Fung, I. Y. Y. (2007). *Teacher professional learning and development: Best evidence synthesis iteration.* Wellington, New Zealand: Ministry of Education.

Tolle, E. (2011, September 15). *Facebook page.* Accessed August 4, 2016. https://www.facebook.com/Eckharttolle

U.S. Department of Education. (2012). *Helping to ensure equal access to education: Report to the president and secretary of education, Under Section 203(b)(1) of the Department of Education Organization Act, FY 2009–2012.* Washington, DC: Office for Civil Rights.

U.S. Department of Education. (2013). *For each and every child—A strategy for education equity and excellence.* Washington, DC: Author.

U.S. Department of Education. (2015). *Every Student Succeeds Act (ESSA).* Washington, DC: Author. http://www.ed.gov/essa

U.S. Department of Education. (2016, May 17). *U.S. Secretary of Education John B. King Jr. Statement on the Anniversary of Brown v. Board of Education.* Press Release. Washington, DC: Author. http://www.ed.gov/news/press-releases/us-secretary-education-john-b-king-jr-statement-anniversary-brown-v-board-education

U.S. Department of Labor. (1991, June). *What work requires of schools: A SCANS report for America.* Secretary's Commission on Achieving Necessary Skills. Washington, DC: Author. https://wdr.doleta.gov/SCANS/whatwork/whatwork.pdf

U.S. Government Accountability Office (GAO). (2016, April 21). *K–12 education: Better use of information could help agencies identify disparities and address racial discrimination.* Washington, DC: Author. http://www.gao.gov/products/GAO-16–345

Vanzant, I. (1993). *Acts of faith: Daily meditations for people of color.* New York, NY: Simon & Schuster.

Verderber, K. S., Sellnow, D. D., Verderber, R. F. (2016). *Speak3: Public speaking.* Boston, MA: Wadsworth.

Victor, B. (1998). *The lady: Aung San Suu Kyi: Nobel laureate and Burma's prison.* New York, New York: Faber and Faber.

Voltaire (1759/2000). *Candide and related texts.* Translated by David Wootton (French). Indianapolis, IN: Hackett.

Waldrop, M. (1992). *Complexity: The emerging science on the edge of order and chaos.* New York, NY: Touchstone.

Washington Post Magazine. (1978, April 9). A caged bird she's not. *Washington Post Magazine, p. 5.* https://www.washingtonpost.com/archive/lifestyle/magazine/1978/04/09/a-caged-bird-shes-not/bdab2d39–2047–4c81–877f-53c75885641f/

Wells, A. S., Fox, L. & Cordova-Cobo, D. (2016, February 9). *How racially diverse schools and classrooms can benefit all students.* Washington, DC: The Century Foundation. https://tcf.org/content/report/how-racially-diverse-schools-and-classrooms-can-benefit-all-students/

West, C. (2009). Cornell west's catastrophic love. [Interview]. November 3, 2009. http://bigthink.com/videos/cornel-wests-catastrophic-love

Wheatley, M. J. (1999). *Leadership and the new science: Discovering order in a chaotic world.* San Francisco: Berrett-Koehler.

Wheatley, M. J. (2001). *Disturb me, please!* Provo, UT: Berkana Institute. http://www.margaretwheatley.com/articles/pleasedisturb.html

Wheatley, M. J. (2006). *Leadership and the new science: Discovering order in a chaotic world.* San Francisco, CA: Berrett-Koehler.

Wheatley, M. J. (2007). *The unplanned organization: Learning from nature's emergent creativity.* Writings. http://www.margaretwheatley.com/articles/unplannedorganization.html

Wheatley, M. J. (2008). *Turning to one another.* San Francisco, CA: Barrett-Koehler.

Wheatley, M. J., & Kellner-Rogers, M. (1996, July/August). *The irresistible future of organizing. Writings.* http://www.margaretwheatley.com/articles/irresistiblefuture.html

Wheatley, M. J., & Kellner-Rogers, M. (1998). *A simpler way.* San Francisco, CA: Berrett-Koehler.

White House. (2002 January 8). *President G. W. Bush signs landmark No Child Left Behind Education Bill.* Washington, DC: Author. https://georgewbush-whitehouse.archives.gov/news/releases/2002/01/20020108–1.html

White House. (2015, December 10). *White House report: The Every Student Succeeds Act.* Washington, DC: Author. https://www.whitehouse.gov/the-press-office/2015/12/10/white-house-report-every-student-succeeds-act

Williamson, M. (1992). *A return to love: Reflections on the principles of "a course in miracles."* New York, NY: HarperCollins.

Wise, T. (2004, July 23). *No such place as safe: The trouble with white anti-racism.* http://www.timwise.org/2004/07/no-such-place-as-safe-the-trouble-with-white-anti-racism/

Wolvin, A. D., & Coakley, C. G. (1991). A survey of the status of listening training in some Fortune 500 companies. *Communication Education* (April).

Wong, A. (2015, May 21). The Renaissance of student activism. *The Atlantic.* http://www.theatlantic.com/education/archive/2015/05/the-renaissance-of-student-activism/393749/

Wong, L. (2011). *Essential study skills* (7th ed.). Boston, MA: Wadsworth.

Worthington, R. L., & Mohr, J. J. (2002). Theorizing heterosexual identity development. *The Counseling Psychologist, 30,* 491–495.

Young, A. M. (1976). *The reflexive universe: Evolution of consciousness.* New York, NY: Delacorte Press.

Young, A. M. (n.d.) *The four levels of process.* Anodos Foundation. http://www.arthuryoung.com/4levels.html

Zimmerman, B. (2010) *The Sage handbook of complexity and management.* Thousand Oaks, CA: Sage.

Zohar, D., & Marshall, I. (2004). *Spiritual capital: Wealth we can live by.* San Francisco, CA: Berrett-Koehler.

Zukav, G. (1989). *Seat of the soul.* New York, NY: Simon & Schuster.

Index

on reflection on metaphors of darkness and
    light, 66
resistance to cultural proficiency education,
    10–13
seeing with new eyes, 59–61
vulnerability dilemma and, 44–45, 53
See also Reflections
Tecumseh, Shawnee Chief, 9
Tension, ethical, 138–140
Terrell, Raymond D., 2, 15, 124, 134, 138, 195
Theory of Process, 146–157, 158
Think-pair-square-share protocol, 193 (table), 213–
    214 (table), 232 (table), 252 (table), 276 (table)
Three-step interview protocol, 72 (table)
Tipping Point, The, 263
Title IX, 16
Tolle, Eckhart, 183
Tools of cultural proficiency, 124–125
"Towards an Activist Spirituality," 73
Transformationist white identity, 196 (table)
Transformative conversation, 239
Transformative intervention, influencing energy
    through, 258–261
Transformative learning environments,
    50–52, 50 (table), 70–71
    qualities of spiritual intelligence and,
        237–238 (table)
Transformative process, 59, 71–72
Triple-loop learning, 70, 71 (figure)
Trust and mistrust, 233–234
Turning to One Another, 58, 73
Tutu, Desmond, 57
21st century skills, 12

United Farm Workers, 89

Valuing of diversity
    ableism and, 204–205
    as essential element, 135 (table), 174 (table),
        177 (table)
    getting centered for, 203–204
    healthy, 212 (table)
    inclusion and, 215
    participant voice and, 215–217

reflections on, 205–212
unhealthy, 213 (table)
Vanzant, Iyanla, 287
Victims of oppression in aspiring ally development,
    101 (table)
Victor, B., 123
View of justice in aspiring ally development,
    101 (table)
Vision and value led transformation, 237 (table)
Vocation, sense of, 238 (table)
Voice
    approachable, 249
    credible, 249
    participant, 215–217
Vulnerability
    dilemma, 44–45, 53
    managing dynamics of difference and facilitator,
        235–237
    removing armor through worthiness and,
        49–50 (table)
    shields as barriers to, 49 (table)
    skill incompetence and avoiding, 52
    social context and, 46–47

Washington Post Magazine, 27
Wellman, Bruce, 95, 252, 280
West, Cornell, 89
What Crazy Looks Like on an Ordinary Day, 143
Wheatley, Margaret, 58, 73, 80, 81, 84,
    85, 243
When Things Fall Apart, 57
White identity orientations, 195–196, 196 (table)
Wholehearted facilitation, 50–52
Williamson, Marianne, 27
Wise, Tim, 39
World Soul motivation, 199 (table)
Worthiness, 50–52, 50 (table)

Young, Arthur M., 143, 147, 148, 150, 158

Zahir, The, 287
Zimmerman, D. P., 147–148
Zohar, D., 36, 198, 237, 238
Zukav, Gary, 243